FRENCH THOUGHT IN THE EIGHTEENTH CENTURY

French Thought
in the Eighteenth Century

ROUSSEAU · VOLTAIRE · DIDEROT

presented by

Romain Rolland, André Maurois
and Edouard Herriot

with an Introduction by
Geoffrey Brereton

DAVID McKAY COMPANY, INC.
NEW YORK

First published 1953

80841

DEC 13 '56

All rights reserved

B
1911
F87

53-11348
11-30-56

MADE AND PRINTED IN GREAT BRITAIN BY
MORRISON AND GIBB LIMITED, LONDON AND EDINBURGH

CONTENTS

FRENCH THOUGHT IN THE EIGHTEENTH CENTURY

the basis of a great colonial empire. Her financial position grew
worse while succeeding ministers grappled helplessly with an evil
too deep-seated for them, and finally foundered
in an economic crisis. The well-intentioned Louis XVI and his
advisers prov   keep the State
solvent, or even functioning, the States-General was summoned
in May, 1789. From that moment the Revolution proved
inevitable.

INTRODUCTION

by GEOFFREY BRERETON

I

IN THE GENERAL HISTORY OF THOUGHT AND TASTE, THE
eighteenth century belongs particularly to France, as other
ages have belonged to Athens, Rome, or Italy. For the first
time since the Renaissance (and no doubt the last) it was possible
to say of one country that she set the tone for the civilized world.
Whatever was done in France had repercussions for the rest of
Europe, extending in the last quarter of the century to the newly
constituted United States of America. The predominant response
was admiration, accompanied by that most flattering of compliments—imitation. But even when the response was grudging or
hostile, notice had to be taken. French culture was creating a
climate which no local barriers could hope to shut out.

This intellectual ascendancy was achieved in a period of some
political uncertainty. The national zenith had been reached earlier,
when in the 'Great Century' the France of Louis XIV had built
herself up into the foremost European power. It was then that
ministers from Richelieu to Colbert had consolidated the State
internally and externally, that thinkers and theologians such as
Descartes, Pascal, Bossuet, and Malebranche had attacked trans-
cendental problems in the belief that solutions could be found
within the framework of their own confident civilization, and
that writers like Corneille, Molière, and Racine had set a seal of
literary excellence on an age inevitably called 'classic.'

In contrast, the eighteenth century appears at first sight to
show a decline. It opened sombrely with the failing years of a
great reign, with defeat in war and a general impoverishment of
the population. It continued under the surface glitter of Louis
XV's reign, during which the corruption of the Court revealed
the weakness of autocratic government by an incompetent auto-
crat. The rising power of England and Prussia involved France in
new, though not disastrous, set-backs. She lost, almost by default,
her possessions in India and America which could have formed

the basis of a great colonial empire. Her financial position grew worse while succeeding ministers grappled helplessly with an evil too deep-seated for a quick cure. The régime finally foundered in an economic crisis. The well-intentioned Louis XVI and his advisers proving powerless to raise the money to keep the State solvent, or even functioning, the States-General was summoned in May, 1789. From that moment the Revolution proved inevitable.

Yet only a political historian with his attention narrowly focused on the peak-greatness of the seventeenth century could describe the seventy-five years between the death of Louis XIV and the Revolution as a period of decadence. For one thing, if less formidable than in the past, France never ceased to rank among the great powers. She still had vast material and moral reserves, as the wars of the Revolution and her new triumphs under Napoleon were soon to show. But above all, she evolved during the Age of Enlightenment (which it would be more appropriate to rename the Age of Fertile Doubt) an outlook in keeping with new conditions which ensured her survival. This outlook, which is broadly that of liberal democracy, was valid not only for France at a particular moment as the political philosophy of the Great Century had been. It could be applied to other countries and later periods. If as a spiritual export it proved highly inflammable, that was in large part due to the skill of French thinkers as refiners even more than as creators. In fact, the better analogy is that of the re-export. Much of the raw material came from non-French sources. England in particular furnished Montesquieu and Voltaire with examples of religious tolerance and political equilibrium which they could not have found nearer home. The experimental philosophies of Bacon and Locke, the materialism of Hobbes and the revolution in physical science accomplished by Newton stimulated French thinkers to conclusions which they might never have reached unprompted.

It would be misleading, however, to speak of models, since the reworked material had a vitality and an originality of its own. When it returned to England at the end of the century, Englishmen as diverse as Burke and Blake regarded it not merely as a horror, but as a Gallic horror. By recombining and reformulating older ideas and, even more, by speculating beyond the point at which those ideas had originally stopped, French thought forged a dynamic new weapon. Its most spectacular function was, of course, political. Contemporaries, impressed by the drama of the Revolution, believed that the whole intellectual effort of the century had been directed to just that result. They were mistaken, as an analysis of the immediate economic causes of the Revolution easily shows. A single administrator of genius and influence might still have averted the breakdown, or at least postponed it for many years. Again, the so-called 'forerunners' of the Revolution were not themselves revolutionaries. They did not contemplate political action leading to the destruction of the régime. Some believed that the reforms they desired could be carried out within the existing order; others visualized a new order, but placed it in an unspecified future. They were, in the language of the time, 'philosophers' and not politicians. Indeed, the democratic conception of a politician as an ordinary citizen endowed with thought, speech, and a mandate and hence capable of influencing policy could hardly have existed in the autocratic state which they knew. Opinion and action were divorced—dangerously, as it turned out.

Yet in two important ways the thought of the eighteenth century was inseparable from the political conditions of the age. It was first the realization, present in a few minds before 1700 and endemic after 1750, that all was not well with the State and society which led Frenchmen to re-examine their institutions. Secondly, although the Revolution was not engineered by the thinkers, once it had broken out it adopted their principles with enthusiasm. With all their mistakes and excesses, the revolution-makers of the seventeen-nineties were conscious of ideals far surpassing their immediate problems. Because such men as Voltaire and Rousseau had existed, the cry of the First Republic was not merely for an economic new deal coupled with a demand for the liquidation of the privileged classes. It was for *liberty, equality, fraternity*—one of the noblest slogans under which any revolution has been brought about. If it was too Utopian, it was at least to remain on record as a reminder of democracy's ultimate objective.

II

The astonishing change in outlook which the eighteenth century effected can be measured by a quotation from La

Bruyère—by no means a backward-looking writer—who almost exactly a hundred years before the Revolution had observed: 'Everything has been said and we arrive too late at the end of seven thousand years during which thinking men have been in existence.[1] Where manners and customs are concerned, the best has already been skimmed. We must simply aim at thinking and speaking rightly without trying to convert others to our point of view. That is too great an undertaking.'

Rarely has a man of talent, sensitive to the weariness that was beginning to settle on his own age, proved so thoroughly out of tune with the next generation. Five years after he wrote, Voltaire was born. Fifty years later it is unlikely that the most conservative Frenchman would have agreed with any point in La Bruyère's paragraph. For the eighteenth century everything had emphatically *not* been said. Manners and customs were being examined in a new light—no longer as set subjects for the moralist's aphorisms but as surface symptoms of deeper causes. As for the self-denying clause—no proselytizing—the attempt to convince and convert runs through all the writing of the eighteenth century. Without a public to persuade or an opponent to refute its best minds would have been rudderless.

La Bruyère's feeling of impotence is explained by another of his remarks: 'For a Frenchman and a Christian, the field for satire is limited. The big subjects are forbidden him.'

The 'big subjects' were the Church, the Throne, and the Aristocracy; in other words: authority, spiritual and temporal.

Frenchmen in the seventeenth century had, on the whole, desired authority, had united in creating it, and were proud of it when it worked well. Few seriously held that it was infallible, but so long as it was effective there was no general desire to challenge it. When flaws began to appear and France became manifestly less prosperous and triumphant than she should have been, the small dissentient minority which had always existed began to acquire importance. From the time of Richelieu on, an undercurrent of doubt had been represented by the *libertins*, or free-thinkers. These formed no homogeneous group and put forward no developed philosophy. A typical *libertin* was a great lord who felt himself above common morality and wished to

[1] La Bruyère was following a dating of the Creation current among theologians of his time.

have some intellectual justification for his conduct. He might invoke the writings of Gassendi, from which a materialistic doctrine of enjoyment could be deduced, though Gassendi himself always remained a Catholic. The true *libertin* rarely preached in print. He kept his opinions for a small circle of like-minded people. His significance was that he represented a rationalistic tendency, however amateurish, on the highest levels of society. This tendency, at first clandestine, became open at the death of Louis XIV and was taken almost for granted in the *salons* of the next reign.

At a more strictly philosophical level, the ancestor of eighteenth-century rationalism was Descartes. His *Discours de la méthode* (1637) had laid down the means, as he conceived them, of reaching true conclusions. It was a method, essentially geometric, by which the human mind could arrive at a knowledge of the great realities, among which Descartes unquestioningly placed the existence of God. In his hands, Cartesianism remained broadly within the bounds of orthodox Catholic doctrine. But his method could also be used destructively. His appeal to the reasoning power of the individual, controlled by careful checks and tests, was in fact an invitation to critical spirits to limit belief rather than to extend it. A hundred years after its formulation, Cartesianism had become a powerful weapon for the atheist and the deist.

The eighteenth century revered Reason, which it invested with a special prestige. For Descartes's age it had meant little more than a 'reasonable' view (in the last analysis, a balanced view) of the relationship of man to God, of the individual to society. It had entailed the concepts of hierarchy and of harmony. But for the eighteenth century it was a rational process which anyone could handle to detect the errors in dogmatic beliefs. This made it an instrument. But, beyond that, it was gradually exalted until it became a principle by which far-reaching truths, hitherto obscured by 'superstition' and 'passion,' could be revealed—and so was in itself a source of light and a guide to right conduct.

The Age of Reason, a title which the century practically conferred on itself, is a misnomer if it suggests only the habit of rationalistic speculation. The difference between the pure Cartesian and the eighteenth-century *philosophe* was that the latter was ready to base his theories on the data which science could offer. A great revival in the sciences produced not only naturalists such as Réaumur and Buffon or chemists like Lavoisier, but wide circles of interested laymen. The gentleman who made an amateur's collection of specimens or the hostess who embellished her *salon* with a microscope and a bowl of tadpoles might only be flirting with science as their ancestors had only flirted with atheism, but such fashionable recognition was a tribute to a new force which would be ready in time to invade every domain of thought. 'General laws,' wrote Buffon, 'being simply the product of facts, only deserve the name of laws when they agree with all the facts.' The eighteenth century, therefore, was already aware of what was later to be called the scientific method. It should not be accused of constructing hypotheses on pure reason, but only of sometimes believing that it possessed 'all the facts' when it had only part of them, and those not always unimpeachable. Since speculation still outran knowledge, theories were often outlined which later research showed to be erroneous; but in compensation the very absence of detailed evidence sometimes encouraged bold generalizations which represented a leap forward in human thought and have stood the test of time.

III

After Reason, the second master-concept of the century was Nature, a word capable of several interpretations. In the first sense, 'natural' was equivalent to 'reasonable.' It was not 'natural' that an aristocratic weakling who, in Figaro's phrase, had merely taken the trouble to get born, should wield power over men with superior qualities; or that a financier should enrich himself from land he could never have cultivated while the tillers themselves (the technicians) went hungry; or that a monastic religion should condemn men and women to sterility. In Voltaire's view, these were obvious abuses sanctioned by bigotry and stupidity; for him, whose invocations of Nature were generally perfunctory, Reason, leading to the enlightenment of mankind through education, could supply a sufficient corrective. For Rousseau, a fundamentalist, they were inherent in civilization itself. The wrong turning had been taken at the moment when mankind had deviated from Nature and had begun to own property, to develop more than the basic minimum needs, to form communities which eventually led to the concentration of power in the hands of a tyrant. It was then that he had forfeited his 'natural rights' and had lost the 'innocence and equality' which had been his under the natural order.

It was in vain that Rousseau protested, when attacked by critics who included Voltaire, that he had no thought of a wholesale retrogression to the original innocence, that the time had long passed when such a return would have been possible. He did not withdraw his picture of the 'state of nature' which has become of such capital importance to the idealist, whether he is at heart a reformer, a revolutionary or an anarchist. It is, any of these might plead, only a postulate, a symbol, or an aspiration. But it is more than that, and Rousseau had the courage of his own logic in supposing that it was more. The moment an argument is based on 'natural rights,' it must, if pursued far enough, infer the existence of a 'natural state' in which those rights have been operative. Otherwise the argument falls into the absurdity of invoking a 'Nature' which has never existed. Where, then, is that state to be placed? In the childhood of the individual, before society corrupts him—but this is a fragile innocence which can only be preserved by the most patient and calculated efforts of others (see *Emile*). Also, historically, in primitive times which Rousseau conceived as a pastoral age in which man's simple needs could be easily satisfied, in which there was no competition because there was no scarcity. Finally, though no doubt in less perfection, in those primitive societies which were still to be found in the world and which the imagination, fed by the meagre accounts of travellers, pictured as happy—and so virtuous. The conviction that the native communities of America and the South Seas must be morally superior to the European because they had remained nearer to nature gave rise to the idea of the Noble Savage, one of the most cherished illusions of the eighteenth century. It was arrived at by wishful reasoning more than by observation and the modern anthropologist can easily laugh it back into thin air. Yet it does considerable credit to the minds which conceived it. There was perhaps more humanity and humility in them than in the seventeenth-century mind which tended to dismiss as barbarous any who did not share its culture, or in the nineteenth century which associated its earthly hopes with the railway-station and the well-equipped bathroom.

Nature, for Rousseau, also meant 'myself.' When his instinct prompted him to perform certain acts, when his feelings told him that certain things were good or bad, he ascribed this to the voice of the natural man within him. 'Follow your heart, it is never wrong,' might sum up this part of his creed and teaching. In the Romantic Movement of which he was one of the great precursors, it led to the glorification of the individual personality. Though the eighteenth century was not yet ready to draw that extreme conclusion, it follows inevitably once Nature is admitted into the domain of emotion, and emotion is linked with morality.

This Nature is a long way removed from that of the scientist, which also, as we have seen, played its part in eighteenth-century thought. Here 'the natural order' stood for the physical universe which Newton and his successors were revealing by a series of exact observations. Its laws seemed neither moral nor immoral, but merely absolute. Here the materialist could find his strongest justification, and often ´ d so in order to refute the divine laws taught by the theologians, the possibility of miracles, and so on. But he was still in opposition, still waging a guerilla war against a church still in possession of much of the intellectual field. Scientific materialism, equipped with a philosophy and—in Positivism—with something which even claimed to be a religion, had to wait another hundred years for its full development. The eighteenth century knew it chiefly as a spasmodic and destructive force. As handled by Diderot, however, it yielded some very interesting anticipations. Among them was the remark, irreconcilable with Rousseau's theories and equally opposed to classical dogma, that 'Nothing that exists can be against or outside Nature.'

Such were the dominating conceptions of the century. It is evident that Cartesian rationalism, an embryonic materialism founded on experimental science, and an idealism rooted ultimately in the human heart are divergent guides. At some point they must contradict each other and part company. The first signs of such a split appeared in the controversies which arose between Rousseau and the Encyclopædists, though these were as much wars of personalities as of ideas. But the great achievement of the age was, not to have evolved one universal system (though system-making by individuals was in the air) but to have raised questions of fundamental importance which until then had been hushed-up, to suggest lines of enquiry—in short to convert what might have been the complacent decadence of French classicism into one of the most fertile periods of human thought.

IV

More surprising than divergences of intellectual approach was the fact that principles so vital to humanity's understanding of itself—and in some instances so austere—should have been debated by one of the most deliciously artificial societies in history. In the fine arts, and in the art of living itself, the eighteenth century stands for a delicately hedonistic refinement. An elegance, never fussy though sometimes flowery, distinguishes the paintings, the furniture and interior decoration, the clothes and manners of the Louis Quinze period. Later, an enchantingly silly young queen like Marie-Antoinette could play at back-to-nature in her 'village' at the Trianon, so turning Rousseau's puritanical simplicity into fashionable pastoral. Grace, lightness, frivolity, futility were bound up into exquisite bouquets, labelled *Paris* as in later times (though the commercial motive was not yet in evidence) and eagerly bid for by the rest of the civilized world. From the Philistine wastes of the nineteenth and twentieth centuries possibly over-sensitive men have looked back with nostalgia to this last great period when art was judged by 'taste' and not by its social implications or its moral content.

It would be a profound mistake to suppose that this aspect of the eighteenth century had nothing to do with its intellectual aspect. It is an over-simplification to regard the aristocratic culture as a lacquered shell under which, independently, the true spirit of the age was evolving in quite a different sense. There were, of course, extremes of frivolity and profundity which did not meet, but on the whole this was a unified culture.

The marriage of intellect and society is best typified by the *salons*, where various hostesses gathered round them men of letters, artists, or scientists and encouraged them to talk of their particular interests. The *salons* differed considerably in character, according to the personalities of the hostesses and the habitués they attracted. But one or two generalizations can be made. One is that specialists coming together in a social setting are obliged to be less technical than when they remain among themselves. They must express their knowledge in language which the intelligent layman understands, and which allows him to join in the discussion. This condition made for clarity of style which carried over into the written language. It encouraged lightness and even wit, which is not always associated with the expression of serious ideas. Urbane and perfectly intelligible, French was perfected as a means of communication between mind and mind not only within France but throughout Europe. Its acceptance as a universal language of culture, replacing Latin in most fields, stems from the use made of it by the eighteenth-century writers. By 1784 Rivarol could write, in a work crowned by the Academy of Berlin, 'Whatever is not clear is not French,' and be generally considered to have defined the most important quality of his native tongue.

Certain sacrifices of depth and subtlety were entailed. The mathematician or the scientist cannot stop to explain himself at every step to the uninitiated—though it is perhaps a gain when he is obliged to sum up his findings in general terms. The greatest names in eighteenth-century speculative philosophy belong to Germans and Scandinavians, not to Frenchmen. But where the Frenchman excelled was in making the connection between philosophy proper and actual problems, in asking 'How?' and 'To what good?', and so contributing on the highest plane to an improvement in the art of living. By keeping in view a public of the *salon* type, he gained in immediate influence what he may have missed on the more remote peaks of thought. For through such a public he could permeate the whole of a society still concentrated in a small number of inter-related groups.

A conception of 'philosophy' grew up which was peculiar to the age. The word *philosophe* was used in a sense broadly equivalent to the modern 'intellectual.' It embraced the great general thinkers, Voltaire, Rousseau, and Diderot, but also men who were predominantly mathematicians, as d'Alembert, sociologists like Helvétius, or psychologists like Condillac—and even the economists Quesnay, Condorcet, and Turgot. In short, knowledge was not yet departmentalized and the 'philosophic spirit' ran through any examination of the physical world, of man as a biological and moral entity, and of his organization in societies.

The most effective grouping of 'philosophic' thought is

found in the *Encyclopédie*. This monumental work began to appear in 1751 under Diderot's editorship. It occupied some twenty years of his life and was his greatest single achievement. Its fortunes are described in detail in M. Herriot's introduction to his writings. In general, it need only be said that the *Encyclopédie* presents the factual knowledge of the age side by side with its most controversial doctrines. It was at the same time a compendium of information and an engine of propaganda. Its contributors ranged from Rousseau (who wrote, however, only on music) to the economists of the physiocrat school; from broad-minded priests like the abbé Morellet to Voltaire on one wing and the atheist d'Holbach on another.

Its publication was chiefly due to the heroic efforts of Diderot and one or two faithful assistants. But the *salons* may also be said to have played a part in producing it. Three of the most famous, those of Mme Geoffrin, Mme du Deffand, and Mlle de Lespinasse served as congenial meeting-places for the chief Encyclopædists. Mme Geoffrin even subscribed funds to help the work forward. Helvétius and d'Holbach, contributors of articles themselves, were also wealthy men who opened their houses to Diderot and his friends. Helvétius was one of the *fermiers-généraux*, or tax-farmers, who occupied in the financial hierarchy of the time a position comparable to that of the Wall Street magnate to-day. Altogether, if the thinkers enlightened and sometimes entertained society, an influential section of society responded readily. Without its moral and material support, an enterprise such as the *Encyclopédie* might have foundered at the half-way stage.

In other fields, aristocrats and even sovereigns paid homage to the intellectual. Mme du Châtelet, Mme de Pompadour, and Frederick of Prussia all showed in their varying ways their admiration for Voltaire. Diderot was invited to the court of Catherine of Russia, who came to his aid in the most tactful way possible by buying his library and leaving him the use of it for the rest of his life, together with a salary as her 'librarian.' Rousseau, a wild bird whose behaviour in captivity could be disconcerting, enjoyed the hospitality both of the wealthy middle class and of the aristocracy.

One important feature of the eighteenth-century temperament was common to the writers and to society. This was their sensibility. It ranges from the generous compassion felt by a

Montesquieu or a Voltaire for the victims of injustice to the expansive pity—sometimes self-pity—of a Rousseau in his more romantic moods. Towards 1750 a great increase in open sentimentality becomes apparent in French literature. It is sometimes attributed to English influence and connected with the moralizing novels of Richardson which the abbé Prévost translated and imitated. But it would be idle to look for a precise source or to interpret the vogue of Richardson as more than a symptom of a general re-awakening of feeling. The French novel, the drama and painting became increasingly receptive to pathos, and although in its origins this was a bourgeois tendency opposed to the more reserved culture of the aristocrat, the distinction rapidly disappeared. The tribulations of Clarissa, of Manon Lescaut, or of Julie appealed equally to the emotions of the great lady and of the merchant's wife. If there was a difference, it was in the subtlety of the analysis rather than in the nature of the emotional response.

This revival of sentiment, with its insistence on 'virtue,' was partly a reaction against the cynicism of the Court, where the pursuit of love had long been regarded as an ingenious and merciless game in which one party was bound to be the loser. In literature, it spelt a revolt against the stiffness of the now dwindling classical tradition. It can also be associated with a decrease in the religious faith which had formerly satisfied emotional needs when human relationships failed. The causes are complex, but the fact is certain. The appeal from heart to heart which in Voltaire's younger days would have seemed in bad taste, was an entirely natural gesture for Rousseau and Diderot, and one which suited them temperamentally.

V

These three men tower above their contemporaries, yet represent in their different ways all the main characteristics of the age. Voltaire was born nearly twenty years before the other two, in the last decade of the Great Century. He still has some of the steel of that age in his composition, sharpened to a razor-fineness. Before Rousseau or Diderot had published anything he had suffered social persecution and was celebrated as a dramatist, poet, and historian. Arriving earlier, he may be said to have had the harder task. He had to work upon a public opinion not yet fully receptive to ideas of change and this circumstance moulded his style and method for the rest of his life. His technique is markedly one of *attack*. He makes formidable use of the rational argument, conducted with all the wit and *brio* of the born polemist—that is, sometimes irrationally. He proceeds by irony rather than by preaching or open indignation. He parries hostility with laughter, complacency with a demonstration of self-evident truths which leaves his adversaries with no immediate alternative but to agree or lose their tempers. It is notorious that he evolved no comprehensive system, and the description of his work as 'a chaos of clear ideas' is on the whole a fair one. His function was to be the cutting edge which laid open society to a deeper probing by other minds. But from that to describing him as a purely destructive thinker is too big a step. He believed—passionately—in the power of knowledge and reason to improve mankind, if not to perfect it. He pondered over fundamental problems such as free will and the working of an intelligent principle in the universe. If he himself arrived only at provisional and utilitarian conclusions, he intended to open a path along which others could continue. That path was humanitarian rationalism. His advice to humanity would have been to cut its losses and be human. Though that advice may be rejected on several grounds, it cannot fairly be called negative.

Diderot, as a writer, is more difficult to define. Pointing out that until relatively recent times the French themselves hardly recognized his greatness, M. Herriot well describes him as 'a universal essayist.' He was a gifted editor and publicist, the first great scientific journalist, an art and dramatic critic and a writer of tales and plays. If all this work had been carried out in a polemical spirit, it might well have been comparable with Voltaire's. But it was exploratory rather than controversial—at least in intention. In the widest sense of the word, it was scientific, and provides the most comprehensive example of eighteenth-century 'philosophy.'

Diderot cannot be credited, any more than Voltaire, with a body of positive doctrine. His mind was a workshop of ideas some of which have appeared to the twentieth century as more fertile than those of Voltaire and more modern than those of Rousseau. He reached far beyond the science of his time in foreshadowing the theories of evolution and transformism. Marxists, writing off the rest of eighteenth-century political thought as bourgeois idealism, have hailed Diderot as a pioneer of dialectical materialism. His theory of naturalism in the theatre became the accepted doctrine of the late nineteenth century, though it is under a cloud to-day. As an art critic attracted by the moral and popular aspect of painting he would be in direct opposition to the modern æsthetic tradition of the West, but might very easily find favour in Eastern Europe. His work presents, and should continue to present, an ever-fresh interest of discovery for thinkers committed to various systems to which they believe Diderot can be attached as a forerunner. But at some point these attempts to capture or circumscribe Diderot break down. He cannot be truly separated from his eighteenth-century context, but remains in it as the supreme personification of the open mind backed by a tireless zeal for study and experiment.

Rousseau was a year older than Diderot and died a few weeks after Voltaire. It is tempting to single him out as the representative of the positive facet of eighteenth-century thought. While this does less than justice to the other two writers, it is true that Voltaire and Diderot are fragmentary and sometimes inconsistent, whereas only Rousseau attempted to work out a system. This system is not scientific; it is rational only superficially. Its basis, as we have seen, is in the emotions of its author, who 'feels' that mankind, beginning with himself, is naturally good and that salvation therefore consists in keeping as close as possible to the natural man. In Rousseau all the visionary elements of the Age of Enlightenment (a vision is not necessarily an illusion) come together to suggest a new hope for humanity founded on the strongest intimations of the unconscious. His standing is therefore that of a prophet more than of a philosopher. His teachings, beginning as rational demonstrations in accordance with contemporary practice, acquire a religious tinge as he grows older. Though he still speaks of reason, he has become, in fact, an *illuminé*. His Genevan birth, his upbringing, and his unstable, vagabond life contributed powerfully to that result. The man who, both during his lifetime and after, was to win the most passionate response from French society, had almost of necessity to be formed outside it.

The relationship of the three men in their own lifetime is

worth recalling briefly. Voltaire always stood a little outside the group of the Encyclopædists, which was formed when he had already acquired a great reputation. During the years when it was most active, he was living either in Berlin or on his properties near Geneva, coming rarely to Paris. He was closely linked, however, with d'Alembert and Diderot by correspondence. He never ceased to consider their cause his own, and whenever they were attacked his biting pen was at their service. Rousseau, arriving in Paris as an unknown young man, saw little of Voltaire, but struck up a close friendship with Diderot. This lasted for some fifteen years, by the end of which both men had tasted success. As the author of the first two *Discourses*, Rousseau was generally considered to belong to the 'philosophic' movement. In 1758 came the public signs of a rift. In his *Letter to d'Alembert on the Theatre*, Rousseau attacked an article by d'Alembert in the *Encyclopédie* which advocated the establishment of a theatre in Geneva. Certainly a principle was at stake—the question of the morality of the drama, which for Rousseau was an instrument of corruption. But there were also personal undertones, for d'Alembert's article had been inspired by Voltaire. Voltaire had been irritated by the disapproval shown by the puritanical authorities at Geneva of the theatrical performances which he gave at his house, and the article was meant as an oblique counter-attack.

This had been preceded by a more deeply personal quarrel which set Rousseau against his hostess, Mme d'Epinay, and her friends Diderot and Grimm. The two sides parted company, the honest Diderot believing that Rousseau had deserted the *Encyclopédie* at a critical moment in its existence, while Rousseau, congenitally suspicious and susceptible, was convinced that his closest friends had betrayed his trust. He went on to imagine a real conspiracy against him and that the Encyclopædists were pursuing him with relentless hatred. The breach was never healed. As for Voltaire, who had been less directly involved, he continued to write against Rousseau from motives partly of principle, but partly, it must be admitted, through literary jealousy. He was a mercurial and pugnacious spirit, with a dozen causes always on his hands, of which eleven were likely to be just. Rousseau had only one—himself and his doctrine. The lightest criticism of either affected him like a mortal attack.

These petty quarrels need only be recorded because they are reflected in each man's writings, particularly in Rousseau's. But by now it is two hundred years too late to take sides. At this distance of time the genius of the three writers appears as complementary, not as opposed. Their personalities may well seem so also.

They are significant not only as historical figures, preoccupied with the conditions and problems of their own time. They made a lasting and important contribution to human thought. What ideas did they launch which had not been current before? Or rather, if the true pedigree of an idea is too complex a thing to trace, what ideas did they formulate in such a way that the educated man could no longer ignore them? Judged by that standard, the chief legacies of the eighteenth century to the nineteenth and twentieth were these :

The concept of freedom. Nearly all the thinkers of the age stressed *liberty* as their most valued possession. In a general sense, they meant freedom of judgment and of conscience, with or without a religious reference. In the political sense, man was 'born free' and was not the chattel of a ruler (*The Social Contract*). The idea of a natural right to freedom, acquired at birth, carried with it the condemnation of all forms of oppression, including slavery. The emancipation of coloured slaves was advocated throughout the century, though not yet put into practice.

The concept of equality. Equality of rights in the political order and equality before the law followed from the concept of political freedom. In general, the eighteenth century put forward the proposition that all men are equal, but did not fully explore its implications.

The principle of tolerance. In the face of powerful opposition, political and religious toleration were steadfastly preached from the time of Montesquieu on. Various arguments were invoked— pragmatic, rational and humane—but the general principle was unquestioned. Persecution could not be countenanced, particularly when it involved physical cruelty.

The principle of pacifism. Both Voltaire and Rousseau were revolted by the barbarity of war, and said so in no uncertain terms. Their protest was new, since previously war had been generally regarded as an inevitable evil. They did not, however, put forward a specific doctrine of pacifism, but treated it as part of a larger question. War, they considered, was one of several abuses which would disappear with the spread of enlightenment, or the better organization of society.

The idea of progress. The eighteenth century was not unique in believing in progress, but such a belief can take several forms. The seventeenth century had held it in a somewhat complacent way. By looking back, it saw history as a leading-up to its own peak of achievement. The outlook of the nineteenth century was similar. The world had grown better than it used to be: it need only continue on the same lines to be better still. In contrast, the eighteenth-century view of progress was entirely forward-looking. It was not claimed that any perfection had been reached, but that humanity had the necessary qualities, if wisely used, to advance towards it. If a doctrine of progress is not to degenerate into the naïve optimism which Voltaire satirized in *Candide*, the eighteenth-century version seems the only possible choice.

JEAN-JACQUES
ROUSSEAU

JEAN-JACQUES ROUSSEAU was born at Geneva, the son of a watchmaker, on 28th June 1712. He was apprenticed to a notary, then to an engraver, from whom he ran away supposedly because of ill-treatment. He wandered about for several years, taking a variety of posts, and eventually entered the household of Madame de Warens at Annecy, where he settled down to a comfortable existence as her "domestic lover." He went to Paris in 1741 with a new system of musical notation, failed to obtain pupils and accepted the post of secretary to the Ambassador at Venice. He returned to Paris in 1745, where he made the acquaintance of Diderot and the Encyclopædists. In 1749, his *Discours sur les arts et les sciences* won him the prize offered by the Academy of Dijon, and brought him immediate fame. In 1756 he took up residence in the "Hermitage" at Montmorency, where he wrote *La Nouvelle Héloïse* (1761). *Le Contrat social* and *Emile* followed in 1762, and were almost immediately condemned by the French and Genevan Governments. After numerous forced moves he went to England in 1766, was lionized, then quarrelled with his host, David Hume, and fled to France in 1767. He finished the *Confessions*, begun in England, though he was by now half-insane, suffering from a persecution mania. Rousseau died at Ermenonville on 2nd July 1778.

JEAN-JACQUES ROUSSEAU

by ROMAIN ROLLAND

THE LIFE AND WORK OF JEAN-JACQUES ROUSSEAU OFFER IN literary history the case, perhaps unique, of a man of genius, upon whom genius descended not only unsolicited, but against his will.

He was born a little bourgeois of Geneva, timid, without will power, characterless, early delivered to all the risks of an adventurous life, dreamy, loafing, well enough endowed, but indolent, fickle, lazy, forgetful, at the mercy of every wind, with no spirit of application, no care for the morrow, and aspiring to nothing but the tranquillity of a mediocre and indolent existence—without any great needs beyond a sensual taste for romantic and erotic musings. Until his thirty-seventh year, nothing appears to have disturbed him. But suddenly, without warning, he was infused with genius, and like St. Paul, he was struck down by a thunderbolt of which I will speak; he was illuminated, and the pen—that fiery weapon—was placed in his hand. He found himself thrown into the arena where the most illustrious champions of the human spirit were in combat before the eyes of an assembled world. And from the first stroke, he surpassed them all. With surprise and not without fear, he heard his own voice, which he scarcely recognized, filling the amphitheatre with accents as powerful as those from a tribune of antiquity, attacking the most respected idols and shaking society to its very foundations.

He might well be terrified and swear that he would write no more. He was caught in the torrent which he himself had unleashed. He was the Republican who rose like an oak tree, high above the existing monarchical order. And this passionate being always retained an inflexible, an unbelievable lucidity. He, who to that time had been a vagabond and dreamer, a sentimental and weakly anarchist, made of himself the most enlightened and firm of law-makers.

All these powers within himself outdistanced him, and he

aspired to rid himself of them. It is as though a formidable and temporary gift were bestowed upon him, an order from on high imposing a mission upon him and raising him above himself for twelve exalted years, twelve years of genius—after which he sank back again into the life of vegetation and dreaming for which he had always longed. But unbalanced by the enormity of the effort he had been called upon to make, and by the stormy repercussions of his flaming words, he fell into a sort of tragic delirium in which his sorrow was lulled by the beauty of his song.

He was born, on 28th June 1712, in that amazing 'town and republic of Geneva,' home of the reformed evangelical religion, whose very existence was a paradox, surrounded and penetrated as it was by the great monarchical and Catholic States.

Jean-Jacques was proud of his origin, and all his life remained deeply marked by it. He signed himself: 'Jean-Jacques Rousseau, citizen of Geneva,' and he claimed his rights as the 'citizen of a free State and member of the sovereign people.' He dedicated 'to the Republic of Geneva' his Discours sur l'origine de l'inégalité. Jealously he watched over the defence of 'his fatherland,' despite the ingratitude it showed towards him and the persecutions of which he was the object. He never faltered in his praise of that city of working people and its republican customs. He always expressed for it a passionate love and sorrow at living away from it. 'Jean-Jacques, love your country!' his father said to him when he was a child. 'You are a Genevan; one day you shall see other peoples; never will you see the like of your own.' He never forgot this advice. 'Each time that he studied the question of government, he was always happy to find in his investigations new reasons to love that of his own country.' In his criticism of all governments, 'he set apart one alone and proposed it as an example.' It was that of Geneva.

He made no less staunch profession of Protestantism, although circumstances had led him in his youth to be converted to Catholicism. But in 1754 he solemnly re-entered the reformed Protestant church, in the full effulgence of his dawning glory, and he was bold enough to proclaim: 'I am a confessor of the Protestant faith in Paris.' And whatever were the storms that he raised among the pastors of Geneva and Neuchâtel by his broad interpretation of Christianity, his tolerance and humanity, he attested that he had always 'followed as nearly as he could the doctrine of the Gospel . . . I have loved it, I have adopted it, spread and interpreted it, I am attached to it with all the zeal of my heart. All my writings are imbued with the same love for the Gospel and the same veneration for Jesus Christ. Nothing can be compared to the Gospel. This book must be preserved as the rule of the Master, and my books only as the commentaries of a pupil.' At the time of his greatest triumphs in Paris, among the aristocracy of the court and the Encyclopædist philosophers, the enemies of God, he usually read the Bible in the evening; and he read it over from one end to the other five or six times successively in the seclusion of his long nights of sleeplessness. He called himself, with some exaggeration, 'the only man in France who believes in God.'

The Republic and God—this twofold love, this twofold faith —he had sucked at the breast of Geneva; and it was this that had gone into his blood. It was this which distinguished him in Paris from all the French writers of his time.

Nevertheless, we should add that even in proudly maintaining his Genevan independence, he always showed a preference for France. He tried in vain to stifle this; he admitted that he had always felt such a partiality for France that 'his heart beat with joy at its slightest success, and its reverses afflicted him as though they had befallen himself.'

His family was, moreover, of French origin. He was a descendant of Protestant refugees expelled from France. His mother, beautiful and intelligent, Suzanne Bernard, died in giving him birth. On the paternal side, his forebears had been artisan watchmakers, robust and intelligent. His father, Isaac Rousseau, was kind but careless, violent, restless, a vagabond and adventurer, an inveterate reader. He inculcated this taste in his son and transmitted to him his roving disposition. The father and child, who was then six or seven years old, would surfeit themselves with the reading of novels, often passing the whole night in this way. 'Sometimes the father, hearing in the morning the sound of the awakening swallows, would say shamefacedly: "Let us go to bed; I am more of a child than you. . . ."'

But Jean-Jacques's best teacher, his Mentor, who went with him from the cradle to the grave, was Plutarch. 'When I was six, Plutarch fell into my hands; I knew him by heart. I had read every novel; they had made me shed torrents of tears before the age when the heart is interested in novels. From this there was formed in me a taste for the heroic and romantic which has increased since, and which *ended by disgusting me with everything except that which fitted in with my fantasies.'*

The motherless child, abandoned by his father at the age of ten, ill fitted to life, found refuge from life in his dreams. A precocious *ennui du monde*, which is the precursor of romanticism, caused him to seek solitude in nature. He *'found himself more able to deal with the fanciful beings with which he surrounded himself, than with those he saw in the world.'* This *'society entirely supported by his imagination'* almost made him lose his way in life, and caused the dissolution of his will power. It is well that during his childhood and the opening of his adolescent life he had to do with good people. The memories of those years, in the first books of his *Confessions*, have a charming grace and abandon. Anyone who is not familiar with them, does not know the real Jean-Jacques. Usually he is only seen in the conventional picture created by his great books—argumentative, rhetorical, moralizing. It is to do him an injustice. His was a cheerful nature—loving, fascinating, light, volatile, forgetful, quick to follow every enthusiasm, incapable of resisting his inclinations, extremely weak and knowing it, but fundamentally sane, without malice or impurity. It is remarkable to note the incredible physical innocence which he kept in his wandering youth, without any guide to watch over him. This cygnet's path led across the most dubious places, even vicious and polluted, without tarnishing even one of his plumes.

He attracted people strangely, but he also disappointed them, by the unimaginable waywardness, giddiness, lack of consideration, lack of judgment, lack of memory, complete forgetfulness with which he let fall to-morrow persons and things with whom he had seemed most taken to-day. He followed nothing up, interrupted everything that he began. Where was he educated? At the age of twenty he knew nothing. Those who examined him, even the best disposed, came to the conclusion that he had no future, that the best he could do would be to become a little country *curé*. None of this worried him in the least.

The meeting with a woman decided his life. In 1728 at Annecy, he saw Madame de Warens, and he was smitten. Fifty years later in the last pages that came from his pen, he cries out with the same grateful love to his good *'maman'*: for the motherless child always sought maternity in love; and in Madame de Warens he found this.

After brief attempts to live away from her, in obedience to the young *maman*, who wished him to find a career for himself —but without any desire to succeed—the little vagabond who had travelled on foot the roads between Annecy and Turin, over the Alps, then to Lyons, to Lausanne and Neuchâtel, and from there, always on foot, always dreaming, always loitering, to Paris—again returned to his *maman* who had now removed to Chambéry. And she, at last discouraged but charmed, took her young lover into her home. She was, like himself, tender and sensual, careless and visionary, kind, easy to excess, but strangely indifferent even to those who most loved her, forgetting them as soon as they left her; she never knew what she had meant to Jean-Jacques; or, if she did know, she did not care. But those three years—the three delightful summers that they lived together in the cheerful house at Charmettes, near Chambéry (1738–1740) —were for Jean-Jacques a dream of Paradise. At the same time that he tasted '*happiness pure and complete*,' he pursued his literary education—vagabond like his early life and in keeping with what his character always was—reading, without any plan, Montaigne, La Bruyère, Bayle, Bossuet, Voltaire. It was the latter—his future enemy—whose *Lettres philosophiques*, by Rousseau's own admission, '*most attracted him to study*,' and first stimulated him to write. '*The taste*,' he says, '*which I formed for this reading inspired me with a desire to learn to write elegantly and to try to imitate the beautiful colouring of the author who so delighted me.*'

Nevertheless, in summing up, one may say that his education always remained incomplete and most inferior to that of the great Encyclopædists: he did not have any great knowledge of the classics with the exception of Plutarch, Tacitus, Seneca, a little of Plato and perhaps Virgil. But he was sufficiently a genius to divine by intuition and to bring to life what he imbibed in the quotations used by great readers such as Montaigne or Bossuet, and in his Swiss compatriot Muralt for English literature.

Besides, his greatest teacher was not any book. His master was nature. He loved her passionately from his childhood; and this passion is not expressed in his writings by cumbrous descriptions; nature imbued his whole being, she expressed herself by certain sober and arresting traits. She plunged him into ecstasies which were accentuated in his later days and which made him strangely akin to the great mystics of the Orient.

In 1741, bitterly deceived by Madame de Warens, his place beside her usurped during his absence from their nest, he expatriated himself and went to Paris. He was thirty years old, and his only resources were fifteen silver louis, the manuscript of a little comedy, and a new system of musical notation from which he expected fame and fortune. He always considered himself more of a musician than a writer; and even after his first successes with the pen, he persisted—humorously—in his infatuation with the spirit of music, although he was never more than a passable harmonist, with little invention and even less training.

He began by losing his time and his money, loafing in cafés and in salons. But this was not useless to him; it was in this way he came to know Fontenelle, Marivaux, Condillac and especially Diderot, who became his friend. He was also well liked by the ladies, who procured for this young Genevan vagabond, without qualifications—by a chance which was really scandalous (it was not surprising in those times!)—the post of secretary to the French embassy in Venice (May 1743). Having quarrelled with the ambassador, he quitted this place in 1744. In Paris he refound Diderot and the support of the powerful *fermiers-généraux* (tax-farmers); he presented on the stage some little musical plays and adaptations of Voltaire and Rameau. He went to live (1754) [1] with a young hotel maid, Thérèse Le Vasseur, who remained his companion until death parted them. He was later to have several children by her; alas, all deposited by him one after the other at the foundling home. He gave himself all sorts of unworthy reasons for the act, reasons which never really satisfied him and which left him to the end pursued by regret and remorse.

At thirty-seven, he still found himself among the crowd of aimless scribblers who gathered up crumbs from the table of the Midases of finance and their consorts; and there was nothing to indicate his destiny when, in the summer of 1749, he was felled by the thunderbolt of which I have spoken. Of this experience he could never speak without trembling.

He went one day to see Diderot, imprisoned for an infringement of the press laws in the dungeon of Vincennes. The heat was excessive. He had two leagues to go on foot, along an unshaded road. As he walked along, and in order to moderate his

---

[1] After twenty-five years of living together, he ended by marrying her.

steps, he turned the leaves of an issue of a literary review. His glance fell upon an announcement by the Academy of Dijon offering a prize for the best discussion of the following question: '*Has the progress of science and art contributed to the corruption or to the improvement of morals?*' He was suddenly '*pierced by a thousand rays of light; a multitude of living ideas*' assailed him; he was suffocated, inebriated; he fell beneath a tree near the avenue, and here he passed a half-hour in a delirium of thought, from which he emerged with the front of his jacket soaked with tears. '*At that instant,*' he wrote, '*I lived in another world, and I became another man.*' It was not only the answer to the question of the Academy which came to him, but in its train, as if the sluice-gates were opened, a torrent of '*great truths*' which would form the basic matter of his entire future work. The shock had revealed to him his true being.

He was exceptionally pleased to perceive the social unease which was brewing at this period. He did not belong to the French and Parisian circles, to the rule of absolute monarchy, tempered by a loosening of morals and an ironic attitude toward life, in which the most independent writers, the Encyclopædists, managed to adapt themselves, profiting by the very abuses which they combated. He had passed his first thirty years in a happy and sleepy atmosphere as a little Swiss tramp, which life had made him, into a truant schoolboy, regardless of social restraints and laws. He was thus all the more sensitive to the moral and almost physical repression of the artificial world of letters and court-life in Paris. At first, frightened and stifled, he had repressed his feelings of suffering, revolt, and disgust. But these feelings were accumulating. And now they had exploded! With one stroke, he uncovered the social evil—the corruption and iniquity of society. And the tremendous response to his first cry revealed a mission hitherto unsuspected by him.

For his success had surpassed by far not only his own expectations, but the rather mediocre value which he himself—rightly—attributed to his first work. Far more, public opinion seizing upon it gave it a revolutionary meaning which Rousseau denied stubbornly, but without success. In him was seen the destroyer of a civilization who claimed that all its conquests amounted to naught. His only claim was to save himself, and with him his little country of Geneva, by removing them from the contagion of that hyper-cultivated world, civilized to morbid excess and to the 'deterioration of the species'—but without hoping for or attempting the cure of the incurable.

But man proposes, and genius disposes. Once the pen was in his hand, he could not bring himself to stop, and he had to go on to the end. His flow of ideas, increased by the unprecedented triumph of his first 'Discours,' threw him into 'a ferment of heroism and virtue,' of which 'the seed had been planted in his childhood by his father, his country, and Plutarch.'

We should note that his 'illumination' of 1749 coincided with the irruption of the bladder disease which was thenceforward to torture and intoxicate him until his death. His case seemed hopeless. In 1749 the doctors gave him not more than six months to live. We can imagine into what a frenzy this conviction would throw a sincere and courageous soul! Rousseau no longer had anything to withhold.

He withheld nothing. He saw only 'error and folly in the teachings' of those philosophers he had previously treated with respect and who considered him as their ally. He saw 'only oppression and misery in the social order.' And he said this without attenuation. He considered that 'to be listened to, he should make his conduct in accordance with his principles.' And he did so. He changed his costume, renouncing white stockings and fine shirts, he sold his watch, discarded his sword, and clothed himself in a commonplace suit of thick cloth, and a round wig; he gave up his position as cashier and claimed to earn his living as a labourer, a copyist of music. It was a revolution which took place within him, as it did a century later in Tolstoi, who was inspired by Rousseau's example and lessons—'I was really transformed.' Nobody recognized him; he was no longer the embarrassed, shamefaced little foreigner, frightened by everything. 'Audacious, proud, intrepid, full of scorn for the morals, maxims, and prejudices of his century, insensible to the scorn of those who had such prejudices, he crushed their little witticisms with his sentences as if he had crushed, he said, an insect between his fingers. What a change! All Paris repeated the acrid and biting sarcasms of this man who two years before and ten years afterward could never find what he had to say nor words in which to say it. . . .'

If later on he said that he was persecuted, it was in this period of war, declared and waged by him without quarter on all the society of his time, that one must seek the source of the implacable bitterness which he aroused.

The Discourse on the evils of science, art, and civilization was followed in 1753 by the *Discours sur l'origine de l'inégalité parmi les hommes*, whose social significance and revolutionary bitterness went far beyond the first discourse. Rousseau found himself carried away by the spirit of revolt burning within him and by the implacable logic of his thought, to denounce the idea of Property, which gives rise to inequality, the necessity for the regulation of this inequality by the State, and the fatal deterioration of States wherein power is arbitrarily usurped by rich men who end by reducing the human race to slavery. He denounced the plutocratic democracy of the future.[1] Many philosophers of the eighteenth century had already touched on these daring ideas; but none of them had applied the slightest will power to giving active form to their speculations. Rousseau did nothing by halves. For him thought was not a game. He was terribly serious. Fear was aroused when he hurled his anathema against the rich, and again when he declared revolt a *'juridical action'* when it strangled or dethroned the tyrant of *'despotism which was gradually raising its hideous head.'*

Added to the danger of such ideas, was the fact that by his genius as an orator he disposed of a tremendous means of influencing the masses. He created for himself an out-of-door style, forged to excite the masses, and wiping out every other style used by the desk-bound writers of the day.[2]

This can be seen in his third letter (to d'Alembert) *Sur les Spectacles* (1758)—283 pages—a torrent of passionate eloquence which highly inflamed public opinion. Parts of it were already a Revolutionary speech. d'Alembert, intimidated—he, the illustrious savant, member of five or six learned societies—was fearful of crossing swords with this hitherto unknown man who had no other title than that of *'citizen of Geneva.'*

'It would be very dangerous to struggle against such a pen as yours. . . . You know how to please the masses, by the very scorn which you show for them. . . .'

[1] *'In a monarchy the opulence of a private individual never places him above a prince; but in a republic it could easily place him above the law. Then a government has power no longer, and the rich are always the real sovereigns.'* (Letter to d'Alembert.)

[2] *'It was no longer a question of speaking to the few, but to the (general) public. . . . A change of style became necessary; to make myself better understood by all the world, I said fewer things in more words.'* (Preface of a Letter to d'Alembert.)

And he compared him to Luther!

Rousseau wished for nothing so much as to bid farewell to the public and to the world, to leave Paris and retire into nature, alone. And he did this. He availed himself of an invitation extended to him by the wife of a *fermier-général*, the sprightly Madame d'Epinay, to come and live in a 'Hermitage' in the forest of Montmorency. Here he took up his abode, 9th April 1756. '*It was only on that day*,' he said, '*that I began to live.*'

His erstwhile friends, his colleagues, could understand nothing of this. They accused him of acting only to make people talk, or of inveterate misanthropy; and Rousseau thought it necessary to explain himself in his letters to Malesherbes (1762). The real cause of his retirement, he said, was '*that unconquerable spirit of liberty, which nothing could overcome, and before which honours, fortune, and even reputation were as nothing.*' He added with sincerity that '*this spirit of liberty sprang in him, moreover, less from pride than from indolence; but this indolence is incredible; everything terrifies him; the slightest duties of civil life are insupportable; a word to say, a letter to write, a visit to be made, when these are necessary, are a torture for me. . . .*' All his youthful efforts to arrive, had but one object: '*retirement and repose.*' From the moment he could enjoy these, he hastened to avail himself of them. . . .

His own demon was the cause of their destruction.

Alone at last in his 'Hermitage,' and savouring with great satisfaction what his sons, the German romanticists, were to call '*Sehnsucht*,' '*Wonne der Wehmut*,' '*the happiness of tears*,' etc.—the erotic melancholy which he described in admirable pages, of feeling himself '*in the decline of life*' (he was forty-four years old!) —and '*overcome by the need of loving which he had never been able to satisfy*,' he abandoned himself to his erotic dreams.

'*It was June beneath the shady groves, there was the song of the nightingale, the babbling of the brook. . . .*' He surrounded himself '*with a seraglio of houris.*' He called himself '*The extravagant Shepherd*' of this band. Soon his dreams took shape; there appeared to him the heroines of his immortal romance—*La Nouvelle Héloïse*—blonde Julie and brown-haired Claire. He wandered with them in the forest of Montmorency. To make himself master of his dreams, he began by writing, without any plan, several scanty letters, the first two parts of the book. He

was immersed in this work when a passion for Madame
d'Houdetot, Madame d'Epinay's sister-in-law, set him on fire
(the spring of 1757). But in those hours when he again assumed
control of his work, he blushed, he was ashamed of perpetrating
by his *Julie* so flagrant a denial of all his fine sermons against the
world and the literature of love. '*After the severe principles which
he had proclaimed with such vigour, after so many biting invectives
against effeminate books, inspired by love and indolence,*' he gave
himself over to the enemy. He tried in vain to free himself; he
was completely subjugated. He tried to redeem himself by
'*turning his erotic reveries to a moral end,*' and in this he succeeded
to the point that it is not possible to dispute the high morality of
his works. This mixture of free passion and of sermonizing
morality which to-day appears to us to make his romance
weighty and stiff, added in his day to its indescribable success.
Well could writers of his day attack him from jealousy—Voltaire
descended to the lowest outrages—but public opinion was intoxicated, and above all, the ladies of the court. *Julie* caused the
shedding of torrents of tears. All criticism was swept aside by a
great wave of enthusiasm.

Nevertheless, Rousseau's tranquillity was troubled, and
storms, partly sentimental, caused him to leave his Thebaid.
He quarrelled with his hostess, Madame d'Epinay, and moved
into another house in the forest of Montmorency, at Montlouis,
then to Montmorency itself where members of the highest
nobility—the duke and duchess of Luxembourg—offered him
the most delicate hospitality.

Again a fine target for the envious slanders of the literary
men, who did not fail to deride bitterly this hermit, this man of
nature, this scorner of society, who always managed to find
lodgings with the masters of finance or members of the court!
Rousseau himself suffered from these contradictions; but he
could not refrain from accepting, with affectionate gratitude, the
benefactions which his noble friends offered him with such
generosity. During the four or five years which he passed under
their wing, he wrote his greatest works: *La Nouvelle Héloïse*
was finished there, the *Lettre à d'Alembert sur les Spectacles*, the
Contrat social, and *Emile*.

He had planned that this was to be the end of his literary
career. He had estimated that *Emile* and the *Contrat* would net

him a capital of eight to ten thousand francs with which he would purchase a life annuity for himself and his Thérèse. After which he would go and live in the retirement of the provinces, writing at his leisure the memoirs of his life. He wished to make of this life '*a work unique for its unparalleled veracity, in order that at least once a man might be seen as he is within.*' These *Confessions* were not to be published in his lifetime, and were to be written as a monologue, filling a happy solitude, apart from all worldly tumult.

He suspected nothing of the frightful storm which was gathering over him, a storm that was to uproot him from his shelter in Montmorency and pursue him until the end of his life.

He had made numerous enemies: La Pompadour, the king's favourite; the formidable Premier and Minister, Choiseul; the moulders of opinion in Paris, Madame du Deffand, and Mademoiselle de Lespinasse; the 'philosophers' who saw in him a renegade from their secret society, and at their head Voltaire, full of jealousy and malice; the Parisian magistrature, represented by the Parlement, which began to suspect the danger latent within the audacious and revolutionary ideas of this foreigner; finally, that strange coalition of atheists and bigots who, irresolute up to that time, were now swarming about a book whose danger Rousseau himself did not suspect.

This book was not, as one might think to-day, the *Contrat social* which thirty years later was to become Robespierre's breviary, and which at that time passed relatively unnoticed,[1] but the most beautiful, the purest and most benevolent book he ever wrote, the gospel of toleration and charitable belief, free from all the prejudices of the Churches—*La Profession de foi du vicaire savoyard*, which formed the fourth part of *Emile*. This work was to seal the alliance against Rousseau of what he called the '*fanaticism of atheists*' and '*fanaticism of the bigots.*' Passions mounted to a paroxysm, and there were symptoms of a furious civil war. The publication of the '*Encyclopédie*' had kindled the flame. The two parties unleashed, Christians and philosophers, tore each other to pieces '*like mad wolves.*' '*Perhaps there was only*

[1] At least in France, for it was burned in Geneva. And Rousseau had every reason to be indignant. '*My book,*' he said, '*attacks all governments and is not proscribed under any of them. It praises one government only and proposes it as an example; it is under this one that it is burned. The magistrate of Geneva punishes its own citizen for preferring the laws of his own country to those of any other!*' (Lettres de la montagne, L. vi.)

lacking on both sides,' wrote Rousseau, *'capable and trustworthy leaders for it to degenerate into a civil war, and God knows what a civil and religious war would have led to, when the most cruel intolerance prevailed on both sides.'* Rousseau, who suffered from this poisonous atmosphere, had wished by his *Nouvelle Héloïse*, his *Emile*, and his *Profession de foi* to bring peace to the two opposing camps, and to preach tolerance to them—he only turned them all against himself.

It took him a long time to realize his danger. He, usually so ready to harbour groundless fears, refused to understand the many warnings of his friends, alarmed by the approaching publication of *Emile*. Rousseau was bathed in the ecstasy in which he had written this book which replaced for him the sons he had had and lost. In the charming little château presented him by the Luxembourgs, surrounded by water like an 'Isola Bella,' for company his Thérèse, his cat and his dog, he did not hear the thunder on the edge of the forest of Montmorency. When he began to take fright, he fell from his heights and lost his head, seeing danger everywhere it was not, and accusing the Jesuits who had other things to think of at that moment, for they were being persecuted and expelled from all the Catholic countries. Physicians who have studied Rousseau's case, date from the end of the year 1761 the first grave crisis in his persecution mania. It was provoked by this unexpected blow, and was accompanied by a violent attack of his urinary disease, the torture of which led him for a moment to think of suicide.

It was in this state that there fell upon him the terrible decree of the Parlement of Paris. Less than twenty days after *Emile* had appeared in Holland, and before there had been time to distribute it in France, without preliminary warning, the Parlement condemned the book to be burned, and the author to arrest (9th June 1762). On 11th June, the book was mutilated and publicly burned at the foot of the great stairway of the Palais de Justice in Paris; and it was said openly that it was not enough to burn the book, that the author should be burned too. Rousseau's protectors, the highest nobility of France—the Luxembourgs, the Boufflers, and the Conti—were themselves fearful of being compromised with him, and urged him to flee. This he did, not without regret, on 11th June. A fine passage in his *Confessions* recalls, with moving details, the night of his leave-taking and flight. He succeeded in reaching Swiss soil, and, prostrating himself, kissed '*the land of liberty*' with great emotion.

He was not long in being disillusioned on the score of Swiss 'liberty.' His enemies pursued him with unbelievable relentlessness. Nine days later than Paris, Geneva in its turn burned *Emile*. Berne followed, then Neuchâtel. '*Throughout all Europe, a cry of malediction was raised against me, a fury of which the equal has never been seen. I was an infidel, an atheist, a madman, a ferocious beast, a wolf.*' He believed that the world had gone crazy.

It is scarcely surprising that a weak and soft-hearted man, unarmed, the prey of a torturing and poisoning disease, should have lost the balance of reason under the avalanche of hate which engulfed him, and that henceforth he was to become the prey of a persecution mania that only increased with the years! It seemed to him that the whole world was leagued against him; and in his solitude and excitement, his imagination wove the absurd web of a universal conspiracy; in its centre he believed he saw an unknown power—a power he avoided naming—which was bent upon causing him to suffer the most frightful tortures.

He sought and found temporary refuge in the land of the king of Prussia, in the district of Neuchâtel—although he found it distasteful to be under obligation to Frederick II for whom he felt an aversion—in this differing greatly from the French philosophers who fawned upon him (it is remarkable that the solitary dreamer had in political matters a much surer judgment than Voltaire). He took up his domicile in Motiers, in the Val-Travers, on 9th June 1762, and remained there two and a half years under the protection of the Prussian king's intelligent governor, Lord Keith (Earl Marischal)—such great noblemen, independent of opinion and personally enlightened, were always Rousseau's best defenders. But he lost this support by the departure of Lord Keith and, with extreme imprudence, at the very moment he should have contrived to be forgotten, he gaily re-entered the battle with his *Lettres écrites de la montagne* (June to October 1764), in which he strongly attacked his enemies, the Church and State of Geneva, and in which in the name of true Christianity he made the case against the Pharisees of reformed Protestantism.

All the pastors rose up in arms. The church of Motiers was

closed to him, communion refused, he was denounced from the pulpit as the Antichrist, the people were aroused against him, in the fields stones were thrown at him, he was threatened with a gun. In September 1765, a nocturnal attack on his house forced him to leave precipitately, and after a month's stay on the Ile de St. Pierre, in the lake of Bienne, where he would have liked to pass the rest of his days (he wrote an account of this too brief sojourn in one of the most beautiful of the *Rêveries du promeneur solitaire*), Berne ordered him to leave. Again he had to fly, to fly from Switzerland, his fatherland, which repudiated him and which he now called a 'murderous land.'

He crossed Paris where he did not have the right to remain, and accepting the invitation extended him by the Scottish historian David Hume, crossed to England, to London (January 1766), then to Wootton in Derbyshire. But Hume and Rousseau were little able to understand one another; and Hume, by his ironical coldness, his ambiguous attitude and his hidden dealings with the greatest English and French enemies of his guest, alarmed and then maddened the morbidly sensitive Rousseau. He imagined in Hume one of the agents in the conspiracy against him; and Hume's culpable indiscretion in unhesitatingly handing over to the implacable animosity of the Encyclopædists and the malevolence of the entire world, the secret of the derangement and the confidences of Rousseau, justified the suspicions of the latter.

This last blow distracted the poor delirious brain. In a panic of terror, he fled from England (May 1767), across France from place to place, like a hunted man.[1] At the height of his madness he ended each of his letters with the cry: '*I am innocent!*' He was allowed to return to Paris where he took up lodging in a poor house on the rue Plâtrière, earning his living as a copyist of music.

He had written his *Confessions*; the last page is pure madness; and he had read it to several friends. But they, fearing to be denounced—and Madame d'Epinay first among them—caused his readings to be forbidden by the police; and the *cabinet noir*

---

[1] He thought of fleeing to America, to the islands of the Archipelago, to Cyprus, or any other forgotten corner of Greece, under the protection of the Grand Turk, safe from the 'cruelty of Christian charity.' (Letter of 5th Oct. 1768.)

As a matter of fact he was still under the decree of arrest; and his friends, even the Prince de Conti, were worried. He had to change his name.

intercepted his letters. This was not the way to calm his frenzy! Alone—'*More alone in the midst of Paris than Robinson on his island*'—believing himself spied upon as the enemy of the entire world, Rousseau wrote his hallucinated *Dialogues de Rousseau avec Jean-Jacques*, the most piercing analysis he ever made of himself, but giving the wildest account of the conspiracy against him. Imagining no human being capable of hearing his despairing cry, he called out to God, and decided to deliver his manuscript directly to him, by laying it on the high altar of Notre Dame in Paris. He found the grille to the choir closed! This was the supreme blow. It seemed to him that God himself had turned against him. . . .[1]

Then, his deep piety convinced him that if God permitted him to be persecuted, that persecution must then have been written '*in the eternal decrees*,' and there was nothing for him to do but bow before them, sorrowfully but with confidence. . . .

He was thus calmed, but his mental health was not restored. And the last work that occupied him, *Les Rêveries du promeneur solitaire* (begun in the autumn of 1776, and interrupted by his death in 1778), showed him no less mad than the *Dialogues*, but a tranquil madman, tender and sad, wandering in his mind. He was no longer irritated, it seemed to him he was living in a nightmare (and it was too true!), he awaited with resignation the hour when he would awaken. Now he knew, he believed, that he could look forward to no reparation on earth. . . . '*Here I am alone on the earth, no brother, neighbour, friend, society, save myself. The most sociable and the most loving of human beings has been proscribed by unanimous accord.*' He was alone, eternally, '*calm at the bottom of the abyss, poor mortal, unfortunate, but impassive like God himself. . . .*'

Nevertheless, his art had lost nothing; it was even purified. And these last *Rêveries* are like the beautiful song of an old and melancholy nightingale in the silence of the forest. He muses over the few happy days of his life: they were above all those in which he was absorbed into nature, one with the Cosmos. More

---

[1] He also caused to be printed a great many copies of an appeal: 'To all Frenchmen who still love justice and truth'; and distributed them in the streets. In April 1776, he remitted the manuscript of the *Dialogues* to a young English visitor, who seemed to him to have been sent from heaven; and this friend had the work printed in London in 1780. The original is in the British Museum.

than any man of the West, he realized complete ecstasy in the Oriental sense, *the feeling of being stripped bare of any other affection,* that concentration in the depths of Being, *in which he was entwined with himself.* The great relaxation of his last days was botany: what he most liked in this was not the satisfaction of scientific knowledge, but contact with the life of the earth and all the memories it evoked, *the fields, the water, the woods, solitude, above all, peace and rest. . . .* He also beguiled himself with music, with the melodies he sang. They were later collected under the title: *Les Consolations des misères de ma vie.*

For the last month of his life, he was lucky enough to be taken away from his poor Paris lodging and transported to the most beautiful of country places, Ermenonville, nine leagues from the capital, by the generosity of a rich gentleman, M. de Girardin. He was installed here on 20th May 1778, and he fully enjoyed this little Paradise Regained. Even his health seemed improved. At the end of June, an English visitor, J. H. de Magellan, heard him accompany on the piano the *canzonetta* 'Saul,' in *Othello,* which was the last of his compositions. On Thursday morning, 2nd July 1778, he was stricken. The doctors diagnosed a cerebral œdema—*ictus apoplectique consécutif à grande urémie.*[1]

The unfortunate man, who in dying thought himself *alone on the earth* and condemned to remain so *for eternity,* did not know that he had conquered the present and the future. During the last years of his life, from 1770 to 1778, six editions of his complete works had appeared, ten of *La Nouvelle Héloïse.* In 1782 were published the first part of his *Confessions* and the *Rêveries* which excited the imagination of readers already intrigued by the mystery of his sudden death in the romantic setting of Ermenonville. From 1780, half of France made pilgrimage to the Ile des Peupliers where rested the ashes of the mad sage—even the Queen and all the Princes. Visitors abandoned themselves to transports of adoration and love. In vain was the hatred of the 'philosophers' shown by venomous attacks and

[1] A study by Dr. S. Elosu, *La Maladie de J.-J. Rousseau* (1929, Fischbacher), gives the best account of all Rousseau's illnesses in the course of his life. It is the most complete and reasonable résumé of all that has been written on the subject.

Rousseau's enemies spread a rumour of suicide. This rumour should absolutely be rejected. All the testimony of the autopsy is conclusive. Moreover, Rousseau was profoundly opposed to suicide.

attempts to destroy a reputation detracting from their own. All opposition was broken. The rising revolutionary generation invoked the republican of Geneva, who—in contrast to the great lord of Ferney, Voltaire, who died a month before (30th May 1778) —faithful to his principles, had led to the end the life of a man of the people, a little country bourgeois. The future leaders of the French Revolution, of every party, who were later to devour one another—Barnave, Danton, Carnot, Billaud-Varenne, Couthon, Madame Roland—were united in the cult rendered Rousseau. Brissot went to the Bastille for having developed the consequences of the *Discours sur l'inégalité*. Robespierre, who had seen Rousseau during the last days of his life, consecrated his life to him in a sort of *ex-voto*, on the eve of his entrance into political action. He stressed Rousseau's teaching in the tribune, and, arrived at the height of his power, exalted him in his famous speech of the 18th Floréal (7th May 1794). In this oration he avenged Rousseau for the hostility of the *Encyclopædists*, paying him the homage of '*this Revolution of which he was the precursor, and which carried him to the Pantheon.*' He bestowed upon him, with the crown of oak leaves, '*the ministry of preceptor of the human race.*' In the hall of the Constituent Assembly, the bust of Jean-Jacques faced those of Franklin and Washington.

But the influence of Rousseau extended beyond politics. It permeated and fructified German philosophy. Kant was overcome by reading *Emile*; he vowed he could never re-read it without being transported. '*There was a time,*' he said, '*when I proudly imagined that knowledge constituted the honour of humanity, and I looked down upon the ignorant people. It was Rousseau who unsealed my eyes. This illusory superiority vanished: I learned to honour man.*' The *Contrat social* had no less an effect upon him. In it he found his own moral illumination, his principle of '*that liberty which is man's characteristic.*' Later the founders of Marxism, who appropriated the dialectics of Hegel, showed its workings by examples taken from Rousseau.

All the German geniuses of the great *Sturm und Drang* movement, beginning with Lessing, its precursor, and with Herder, down to Goethe and Schiller who composed an *Ode to Rousseau*, were members of the Rousseau cult.

It was not only his thought which was revolutionary. His very writing brought about a revolution in the manner of feeling and of expressing feeling; and it transformed the art of the future. Rousseau was several men in one, several different artists, and all of the first order. He was a powerful orator, with no equal in France save Bossuet; without seeking to do so, he revived the eloquence of the classic Forum; certain of his writings are overwhelming orations. He had the harmony, the pitch, the burning flow of a Demosthenes.

And at the same time he was the master of an intimate art, of the reverie which speaks half-aloud, of the confession which pierces to the bottom of the soul. His psycho-physiological peculiarities, which were at once the cause of his genius and of his ills, were essentially derived from his egotism. With no regard for the usages of society or of modish literature, he spoke only of himself. He had discovered the real '*I.*' He had worked, as he said, in the '*dark chamber,*' with no other art than '*to follow exactly the lines which he saw marked.*' He was never tired of observing himself. Up to his time, no one had yet done this to the same degree, with the exception of Montaigne: Rousseau even taxed him with having posed for the public.

Now in thus shamelessly expressing himself, he stripped bare and exposed what thousands of beings of his time were forced to repress. He freed the modern soul, he taught it to burst its fetters, to know and to express itself.

We may add that, in order to express this new world, he had to create a new language, which was free and more supple.

'*I choose my own style as I choose other things. I do not try to make it uniform; I will always have that which comes to me, I will use it as I like, without scruple; I will say each thing that I feel, as I see it, without studied effect, without constraint, without attempting to be uniform. In throwing myself into the memory of the impression received and of the feeling that is present, I will give a double painting of the state of my soul; namely at the moment the event took place, and at the moment I describe it: my uneven and natural style, at times rapid and at others diffuse, sometimes wise and sometimes mad, sometimes grave and again gay, will itself form a part of my story. . . .*'

This richness of rhythm and emotion might easily have degenerated into confusion, if the born musician within him had not wielded a conductor's bâton. He wrote in 1760 to his printer Rey that he was above all a musician for whom '*harmony was of so great importance in style that he placed it immediately after clarity, and even before accuracy.'* If the need arose, he would have sacrificed to it the truthfulness of the story; he deliberately sacrificed grammar in order not to compromise harmony. With him, ideas came after rhythm. He first sang within himself his periods and his sentences, without giving them words. Without doubt he was a great prose poet and a precursor of French romanticism, no less by his metre and rhythm than by his sensitiveness and his ideas. Chateaubriand and Lamartine sprang from him, Michelet and George Sand were impregnated with Rousseau.

All modern pedagogic theory is inspired by his *Emile* and his knowledge of the child. The most celebrated institute of new education in Geneva bears his name. He, so weak towards himself, proved an admirable director of conscience, firm and lucid, without harshness. He had a generous instinct for true morality, sane and alive, not dogmatic nor abstract, nor subject to any principles or *Credo,* but adapted to just needs and weakness, profoundly humane.

A thing both singular and remarkable in a mind so classic, disposed towards absolute judgments, his rigour as a maker of rules was entirely imbued by a relativism that is modern and in accord with his passion for tolerance. In his *Lettre à d'Alembert* will be found clearly stated the principle of relative right, of the relativity of judgment and of historical relativism. He had an acute sense of movement, of πάντα ρεῖ and by this dynamism, contrasting with the static rationalism of preceding times, he prepared the way for modern thought, for the 'Die and become!' (*Stirb und Werde!*) of Goethe.

He opened into literature the riches of the subconscious, the secret movements of being, hitherto ignored and repressed, and their constant fermentations, the *libido*. He was one of the sources of Freudianism.

From him, Tolstoi received the thunderbolt in his youth. As a young man he wore about his neck a medal bearing Rousseau's portrait, like a holy image. His moral reform and his school of Iasnaia Poliana were based upon the teachings and example of Jean-Jacques. To his last days, he continued to invoke him. Their resemblance is no less striking in the field of art than that of religion. '*So much do the pages of Rousseau touch my heart,*' said Tolstoi, '*I believe that I might have written them.*' In truth, he did re-write them. He was the Jean-Jacques of the nineteenth century.

May I be permitted, in ending, to speak of my personal gratitude to the great musician-poet. I have often encountered his shade in my walks about the shore of beautiful Lake Leman 'around which,' he wrote, 'his heart has never ceased to roam'—and from the window of the dwelling at Villeneuve where I write these lines, I see the bay and slopes of Clarens; at its summit between the trees, the rose-coloured house of Julie stands dreaming.

OF the three Discourses of Jean-Jacques Rousseau—the first, upon the _Arts and Sciences_ (1749); the second, upon the Origin of Inequalities among Mankind (1753); the third (_Letter to d'Alembert_), upon the Theatre (1758): the first, although it created the greatest excitement and founded the reputation of Jean-Jacques, is by far the most superficial. One feels that it was written in a few hours, literally to have flowed from the pen: and despite the author's state of exaltation while writing it, it gives the impression of being a paradoxical play of the mind, similar to the philosophical literature of the salons. Jean-Jacques does not yet appear to have entirely understood the seriousness of the question, nor above all to have taken his own powers fully into account. He only shows the distrust and dislike of a young provincial Genevese toward Parisian society, against the 'treacherous uniformity' it imposed, and against 'the perfidious veil of politeness' which surrounded it. He reproached science, letters, and art with having allowed themselves to be dominated and tamed by power and of 'spreading garlands of flowers over the iron chains with which men are laden.' _His criticisms of these things lacked weight._ Although his Discourse appeared to be only an exercise in oratory for the diversion of men of letters, it also threatened to lead ill-adjusted minds to dangerous excesses: thus, for example, the condemnation of the printing press and of the 'frightful disorders' it caused—which led to the logical conclusion that the libraries too must be burned. If Jean-Jacques later complained that his first Discourse was ill understood, and gave added explanation of his thesis, it can also be said that the Discourse of 1749 readily lent itself to misunderstanding.

The first Discourse was, besides, too literary and not solid enough to cause anxiety. It could be attributed to a young and brilliant college 'rhetorician' who set forth his prosopopœia in the style of a Latin discourse. It is that success which, revealing to Jean-Jacques the power of his pen, inspired him with a just pride in his extraordinary personality; and he finally dared 'to appear as he really was.' Between the first and the second Discourse, he became another man who boldly threw down the gauntlet to the society of his day.

The second Discourse upon a question proposed by the Academy *of Dijon,* 'What is the origin of inequality among men, and is it authorized by natural law?' *is dedicated to the Republic of Geneva: and the dedication contains, together with a eulogy of the Republic, the ideal picture of the country and government under which Jean-Jacques would wish to live.*

A DISCOURSE

ON A SUBJECT PROPOSED BY THE
ACADEMY OF DIJON:

WHAT IS THE ORIGIN OF INEQUALITY AMONG MEN,
AND IS IT AUTHORIZED BY NATURAL LAW?

I CONCEIVE THAT THERE ARE TWO KINDS OF INEQUALITY AMONG
the human species; one, which I call natural or physical,
because it is established by nature, and consists in a difference
of age, health, bodily strength, and the qualities of the mind or
of the soul: and another, which may be called moral or political
inequality, because it depends on a kind of convention, and is
established, or at least authorized by the consent of men. This
latter consists of the different privileges, which some men enjoy
to the prejudice of others; such as that of being more rich, more
honoured, more powerful or even in a position to exact
obedience.

The subject of the present discourse, therefore, is more precisely this. To mark, in the progress of things, the moment at
which right took the place of violence and nature became subject
to law, and to explain by what sequence of miracles the strong
came to submit to serve the weak, and the people to purchase
imaginary repose at the expense of real felicity.

There is a very specific quality which distinguishes man from
the brute and which will admit of no dispute. This is the faculty
of self-improvement, which, by the help of circumstances,
gradually develops all the rest of our faculties, and is inherent in
the species as in the individual. In all the nations of the world,
the progress of the understanding has been exactly proportionate
to the wants which the peoples had received from nature, or
been subjected to by circumstances, and in consequence to the
passions that induced them to provide for those necessities.

The more we reflect on this subject, it is impossible indeed
to conceive how a man, by his own powers alone, without the
aid of communication and the spur of necessity, could have
bridged so great a gap.

[26]

I think I need not fear contradiction in holding man to be possessed of the only natural virtue, which could not be denied him by the most violent detractor of human virtue. I am speaking of compassion, which is a disposition suitable to creatures so weak and subject to so many evils as we certainly are: by so much the more universal and useful to mankind, as it comes before any kind of reflection; and at the same time so natural, that the very brutes themselves sometimes give evident proofs of it.

In spite of all their morality, men would have never been better than monsters, had not nature bestowed on them a sense of compassion, to aid their reason: but the detractor did not see that from this quality alone flow all those social virtues, of which he denied man the possession. But what is generosity, clemency or humanity but compassion applied to the weak, to the guilty, or to mankind in general? Even benevolence and friendship are, if we judge rightly, only the effects of compassion, constantly set upon a particular object: for how is it different to wish that another person may not suffer pain and uneasiness and to wish him happy? Compassion must, in fact, be the stronger, the more the animal beholding any kind of distress identifies himself with the animal that suffers. Now, it is plain that such identification must have been much more perfect in a state of nature than it is in a state of reason. It is reason which engenders self-respect, and reflection that confirms it: it is reason which turns man's mind back upon itself, and divides him from everything that could disturb or afflict him.

It is then certain that compassion is a natural feeling, which, by moderating the violence of love of self in each individual, contributes to the preservation of the whole species. It is this compassion that hurries us without reflection to the relief of those who are in distress: it is this which in a state of nature supplies the place of laws, morals, and virtues, with the advantage that none are tempted to disobey its gentle voice.

The inequality of mankind is hardly felt in a state of nature.

The first man who, having enclosed a piece of ground, bethought himself of saying *This is mine,* and found people simple enough to believe him, was the real founder of civil society. From how many crimes, wars, and murders, from how many horrors and misfortunes might not anyone have saved mankind, by pulling up the stakes, or filling up the ditch, and crying to his fellows, 'Beware of listening to this impostor; you are undone if you once forget that the fruits of the earth belong to us all, and the earth itself to nobody.' But there is great probability that things had then already come to such a pitch, that they could no longer continue as they were; for the idea of property depends on many prior ideas, which could only be acquired successively, and cannot have been formed all at once in the human mind. Men must have made very considerable progress, and acquired considerable knowledge and industry which they must also have transmitted and increased from age to age, before they arrived at this last point of the state of nature.

From the moment one man began to stand in need of the help of another; from the moment it appeared advantageous to any one man to have enough provisions for two, equality disappeared, property was introduced, work became indispensable, and vast forests became smiling fields, which man had to water with the sweat of his brow, and where slavery and misery were soon seen to germinate and grow up with the crops.

Metallurgy and agriculture were the two arts which produced this great revolution. The poets tell us it was gold and silver, but, for the philosophers, it was iron and corn, which first civilized men, and ruined humanity.

The cultivation of the earth necessarily brought about its distribution; and property, once recognized, gave rise to the first rules of justice.

In this state of affairs, equality might have been sustained, had the talents of individuals been equal, and had, for example, the use of iron and the consumption of commodities always exactly balanced each other; but, as there was nothing to preserve this balance, it was soon disturbed; the strongest did most work; the most skilful turned his labour to best account; the most ingenious devised methods of diminishing his labour: the husbandman wanted more iron, or the smith more corn, and, while both laboured equally, the one gained a great deal by his work, while the other could hardly support himself. Thus natural inequality unfolds itself insensibly with that of combination.

On the other hand, free and independent as men were before,

they were now, in consequence of a multiplicity of new wants, brought into subjection, as it were, to all nature, and particularly to one another; and each became in some degree a slave even in becoming the master of other men: if rich, they stood in need of the services of others; if poor, of their assistance; and even a middle condition did not enable them to do without one another. Man must now, therefore, have been perpetually employed in getting others to interest themselves in his lot, and in making them, apparently at least, if not really, find their advantage in promoting his own. Thus he must have been sly and artful in his behaviour to some, and imperious and cruel to others; being under a kind of necessity to ill-use all the persons of whom he stood in need, when he could not frighten them into compliance, and did not judge it his interest to be useful to them. There arose rivalry and competition on the one hand, and conflicting interests on the other, together with a secret desire on both of profiting at the expense of others. All these evils were the first effects of property, and the inseparable attendants of growing inequality.

It is impossible that men should not at length have reflected on so wretched a situation, and on the calamities that overwhelmed them. The rich, in particular, must have felt how much they suffered by a constant state of war, of which they bore all the expense. Destitute of valid reasons to justify and of sufficient strength to defend himself, able to crush individuals with ease, but easily crushed himself by a troop of bandits, one against all, and incapable, on account of mutual jealousy, of joining with his equals against numerous enemies united by the common hope of plunder, the rich man, thus urged by necessity, conceived at length the profoundest plan that ever entered the mind of man: this was to employ in his favour the forces of those who attacked him, to make allies of his adversaries, to inspire them with different maxims, and to give them other institutions as favourable to himself as the law of nature was unfavourable.

With this view, after having represented to his neighbours the horror of a situation which armed every man against the rest, and made their possessions as burdensome to them as their wants, and in which no safety could be expected either in riches or in poverty, he readily devised plausible arguments to make them close with his design. 'Let us join,' said he, 'to guard the weak from oppression, to restrain the ambitious, and secure to every man the possession of what belongs to him: let us institute rules of justice and peace, to which all without exception may be obliged to conform; rules that may in some measure make amends for the caprices of fortune, by subjecting equally the powerful and the weak to the observance of reciprocal obligations. Let us, in a word, instead of turning our forces against ourselves, collect them in a supreme power which may govern us by wise laws.'

All ran headlong to their chains, in hopes of securing their liberty; for they had just wit enough to perceive the advantages of political institutions, without experience enough to enable them to foresee the dangers. The most capable of foreseeing the dangers were the very persons who expected to benefit by them.

Such was, or may well have been, the origin of society and law, which bound new fetters on the poor, and gave new powers to the rich; which irretrievably destroyed natural liberty, eternally fixed the law of property and inequality, converted clever usurpation into unalterable right, and, for the advantage of a few ambitious individuals, subjected all mankind to perpetual labour, slavery, and wretchedness. It is easy to see how the establishment of one community made that of all the rest necessary, and how, in order to make head against united forces, the rest of mankind had to unite in turn. Societies soon multiplied and spread over the face of the earth, till hardly a corner of the world was left in which a man could escape the yoke, and withdraw his head from beneath the sword which he saw perpetually hanging over him by a thread. Civil right having thus become the common rule among the members of each community, the law of nature maintained its place only between different communities, where, under the name of the right of nations, it was qualified by certain tacit conventions, in order to make commerce practicable, and serve as a substitute for natural compassion, which lost, when applied to societies, almost all the influence it had over individuals, and survived no longer except in some great cosmopolitan spirits, who, breaking down the imaginary barriers that separate different peoples, follow the example of our Sovereign Creator, and include the whole human race in their benevolence.

Hence arose national wars, battles, murders, and reprisals, which shock nature and outrage reason; together with all those horrible prejudices which class among the virtues the honour of shedding human blood. The most distinguished men hence learned to consider cutting each other's throats a duty; at length men massacred their fellow-creatures by thousands without so much as knowing why. Such were the first effects which we can see to have followed the division of mankind into different communities.

It is beyond dispute, and indeed the fundamental maxim of all political right, that people have set up chiefs to protect their liberty, and not to enslave them. *If we have a prince,* said Pliny to Trajan, *it is to save ourselves from having a master.*

I consider the establishment of the political body as a real contract between the people and the chiefs chosen by them: a contract by which both parties bind themselves to observe the laws therein expressed, which form the ties of their union. The people having in respect of their social relations concentrated all their wills in one, the several articles in which this will is explained, become so many fundamental laws, obligatory on all the members of the State without exception, and one of these articles regulates the choice and power of the magistrates appointed to watch over the execution of the rest. This power extends to everything which may maintain the constitution, without going so far as to alter it.

If we follow the progress of inequality in these various revolutions, we shall find that the establishment of laws and of the right of property was its first term, the institution of magistracy the second, and the conversion of legitimate into arbitrary power the third and last; so that the condition of rich and poor was authorized by the first period; that of powerful and weak by the second; and only by the third that of master and slave, which is the last degree of inequality, and the term at which all the rest remain, when they have got so far.

Political distinctions necessarily produce civil distinctions. These differences are of several kinds; but riches, nobility, or rank, power and personal merit being the principal distinctions by which men form an estimate of each other in society, I could prove that the harmony or conflict of these different forces is the surest indication of the good or bad constitution of a State. I could show that among these four kinds of inequality, personal qualities being the origin of all the others, wealth is the one to which they are all reduced in the end; for, as riches tend most immediately to the prosperity of individuals, and are easiest to communicate, they are used to purchase every other distinction. By this observation we are enabled to judge pretty exactly how far a people has departed from its primitive constitution, and of its progress towards the extreme term of corruption.

If we exposed all the different aspects, under which inequality has up to the present appeared, we should see oppression continually gain ground without it being possible for the oppressed to know where it would stop, or what legitimate means was left them of checking its progress. We should see the rights of citizens, and the freedom of nations slowly extinguished, and the complaints, protests, and appeals of the weak treated as seditious murmurings. We should see the honour of defending the common cause confined by statecraft to a mercenary part of the people. We should see taxes made necessary by such means, and the disheartened husbandman deserting his fields even in the midst of peace, and leaving the plough to gird on the sword. We should see the champions of their country sooner or later becoming its enemies, and for ever holding their daggers to the breasts of their fellow-citizens.

It is from the midst of this disorder and these revolutions, that despotism, gradually raising up its hideous head and devouring everything that remained sound and untainted in any part of the State, would at length trample on both the laws and the people, and establish itself on the ruins of the republic. The times which immediately preceded this last change would be times of trouble and calamity; but at length the monster would swallow up everything, and the people would no longer have either chiefs or laws, but only tyrants.

This is the last term of inequality, the extreme point that closes the circle, and meets that from which we set out. Here all private persons return to their first equality, because they are nothing; and, subjects having no law but the will of their master, and their master no restraint but his passions, all notions of good and all principles of equity again vanish. There is here a complete return to the law of the strongest, and so to a new state of nature.

The contract of government is so completely dissolved by despotism, that the despot is master only so long as he remains the strongest; as soon as he can be expelled, he has no right to complain of violence. The popular insurrection that ends in the death or deposition of a Sultan is as lawful an act as those by which he disposed, the day before, of the lives and fortunes of his subjects. As he was maintained by force alone, it is force alone that overthrows him. Thus everything takes place according to the natural order.

It follows from this survey that, as there is hardly any inequality in the state of nature, all the inequality which now prevails owes its strength and growth to the development of our faculties and the advance of the human mind, and becomes at last permanent and legitimate by the establishment of property and laws. Secondly, it follows that moral inequality, authorized by positive right alone, clashes with natural right, whenever it is not proportionate to physical inequality; a distinction which sufficiently determines what we ought to think of that species of inequality which prevails in all civilized countries; since it is plainly contrary to the law of nature, however defined, that children should command old men, fools wise men, and the privileged few should gorge themselves with superfluities, while the starving multitude are in want of the bare necessities of life.

J.-J. ROUSSEAU

CITIZEN OF GENEVA

to M. D'ALEMBERT

OF THE FRENCH ACADEMY, OF THE ROYAL ACADEMY OF SCIENCE OF PARIS, OF
THAT OF PRUSSIA, OF THE ROYAL SOCIETY OF LONDON, OF THE ROYAL ACADEMY
OF BELLES–LETTRES OF SWEDEN, AND OF THE INSTITUTE OF BOLOGNA

ON HIS ARTICLE

GENEVA

IN THE VII VOLUME OF THE ENCYCLOPÆDIA
AND ESPECIALLY

ON THE PLAN TO ESTABLISH A THEATRE OF COMEDY
IN THIS CITY

PREFACE

JUSTICE AND TRUTH ARE THE FIRST OBLIGATIONS OF MAN: humanity, his country, are his first affections! When private considerations make him invert this order, he commits a crime.

Solitude calms the soul, and assuages those passions which arise from the hurry and tumult of the world. Remote from the provocation of vice, we speak of it with less indignation: remote from the evils that affect us, we have less sensibility of heart. Since I no longer converse with mankind, I have almost ceased to detest the wicked. Besides, the ill they have done me deprives me of all right to say any harm of them: henceforward must I forgive them, that there may be no resemblance between us. I should substitute, without further thought, the love of reverence to that of justice: but it is much better to forget everything.

I think I have found a principle, which if fully demonstrated as it may be, would instantly disarm persecution and superstition, and assuage that fury for making proselytes, which seems to animate the ignorant. It is that human reason hath no common determinate measure, and that it is very wrong for any man to lay down his own sense of things as a rule for others.

Let us suppose the disputants to be sincere; otherwise all they say is idle prattle. So far as a certain point there are common principles, and common evidence; and besides, each man has his own reason to determine him; therefore his opinion does not lead to scepticism; but, on the other hand, as the general limits of reason are not fixed, and no man has a power or control over the understanding of another person, the proud dogmatism must be stopped short. If ever peace could be established, where interest, pride, and ambition reign at present, the quarrels of priests and philosophers would have an end.

But what method would you point out for keeping men within bounds? Severe laws, well executed. Severe laws, you say! The first is to suffer no such: if we violate this, what will become of the severity of the rest? Laws well executed? The question is whether that can be done: for the force of laws has its measure, and so has that of vice. We cannot be sure of executing the laws, till we have compared these two quantities, and find that the former surpasseth the latter. The knowledge of these two relations constitutes the proper science of a legislator: for if his business was no more than to publish edicts and regulations, with a view to redressing abuses as fast as they rise, no doubt but he would say very fine things; yet for the most part they would be ineffectual, and serve rather as hints towards excellent laws, than as a means to execute them. Upon the whole, the framing of laws is not such a great matter, but every sensible honest man may very well hit upon such institutions, as, when properly observed, shall be of great use to society. Where is the least student of the law, that is not capable to draw up a moral code as pure as that of Plato's republic? But that is not the only point in debate. The business is to suit this code in such a manner to the people for whom it is framed, and to the matters ordained therein, that the execution thereof shall follow naturally from the sole concurrence of these relations; which is, following Solon's example, in compiling such laws, as are not indeed the best in themselves but the best the people can bear and in such and such circumstances: otherwise it is much better that disorders should continue, than be prevented or provided against by laws which are not to be observed; for besides not redressing the evil, it is exposing the law to contempt.

Another, and not less important, observation is that matters of morality and universal justice are not regulated like those of particular justice and strict right, by laws and edicts: or if the laws have sometimes an influence on manners, it is when they derive their whole force from that spring. In such a case they return that very force, by a kind of reaction well known to true politicians.

How then can government have an influence on manners? My answer is, by the public opinion. As our habits arise from our opinions in retirement, in society they are owing to those of others. When we live in society, it is the judgment of our fellow-members that determines our actions: nothing appears good or desirable to private people, but what the public has judged such; and the only happiness most men know, is to be esteemed happy.

With regard to the choice of proper means for directing the public opinion, this is another question—and this is not the proper place to resolve it. These means are neither laws nor punishments, nor any sort of coercive methods.

Therefore it is all in vain; neither reason, nor virtue, nor laws will prevail over the public opinion, so long as there is no contrivance to change it. Once more I say it, force will not do.

Opinion, queen of the world, is in no wise subject to the power of kings; they themselves are her first slaves.

If a government can greatly influence the manners of the people, it is only by its primitive institution: when once it has determined those manners, not only it has no longer the power to alter them, unless it undergoes a revolution itself; but it will find a very great difficulty in preserving them against the unavoidable accidents by which they are continually attacked, and their natural bias to change. Public opinions, though so difficult to govern, are in themselves of a very mutable nature. Chance, a thousand fortuitous causes, and unforeseen circumstances, will bring about what force and reason cannot; or rather, it is because chance directs them that force is ineffectual: just as in a throw of dice, let the impulse of the hand be never so strong, it will not be in the least the more effectual towards hitting the lucky point.

The most that human wisdom can do, is to prevent changes, and carefully to guard against everything that is likely to produce them; but as soon as they are suffered or authorized, it is very seldom that the magistrates can control, and indeed they are never sure of controlling their effects.

In monarchies, never can private wealth raise a man above the prince; but in a republic it may easily set him above the laws. Then the government has no longer any weight, and the rich man is the real sovereign.

Must there be then, say you, no shows nor sports in a republic? Yes, there must and a great many. It is republics that first instituted them, and it is in republics that they are exhibited with a genuine air of festivity. Who are the people whom it most becomes to have frequent meetings, and to enter into agreeable parties of pleasure and mirth, but they who have so many reasons to love each other, and to continue for ever united? We have many of these public festivals already; and were we to have more, I should still be pleased. But let us not adopt those exclusive entertainments which hold only a small number of people, locked up, as it were, in a gloomy cavern, where they sit timid and motionless in pensive silence; where the eye is offended with such disagreeable objects as partition walls, iron spikes, soldiers, and striking images of servitude and inequality. No, happy people, these are not your festivals! You are to assemble in the open air, under the canopy of heaven, and there you are to feast on the contemplation of your happiness. Let your pleasures be neither mercenary nor effeminate; let no constraint nor interest adulterate them; let them be free and generous like yourselves; let the sun dart its rays on your innocent spectacles and then you will form one yourselves, the finest that eyes can behold.

But you want to know the nature of these festivals, and what is to be shown there: nothing, if you will. Wherever liberty and affluence reign, there is the seat of true happiness. You may plant a maypole in the middle of a square and crown it with flowers; let the people then be assembled round, and this shall be called a festival. You may do better still: let the spectators be exhibited as a show; let them be actors themselves; let each man see and love himself in others, to the end that they may be all the more intimately united. I have no occasion to refer to the games of the ancient Greeks; there are others of modern date, which still exist, and are in use with us. Every year we have reviews, and public prizes, such as the crowning of those who are excellent in shooting at a mark, or in artillery and navigation. Institutions so useful,[1] and so agreeable, cannot be too numerous; there cannot be too many coronations of this sort. Why should not we do as much to render ourselves hearty and robust, as to learn the military exercise? Hath the republic less need of artists than soldiers? Why should not we, on the plan of the military rewards, found other gymnastic prizes, for wrestling, for races, for the disc, and for various bodily exercise? Why should not we excite our watermen by rowing for wagers on the lake? Can there be in the universe a more splendid sight than to behold a hundred boats, elegantly rigged, on that spacious magnificent basin, putting off at a signal given, in order to seize a flag hoisted at a mark, and attending on the victor to receive the merited prize?

I gave the feasts of the Lacedemonians as a model of those which I should be glad to see established among fellow-citizens. It was not only their object, but likewise their simplicity that recommended them: there was no pomp, no luxury, or parade; a secret charm of patriotism rendered them engaging, and they breathed a kind of military spirit becoming free men:[2] engaged

[1] It is not enough that the people have bread, and live according to their station; they must also live agreeably; to the end that they may be more able to discharge their respective duties, and less eager to alter their condition; as also that the public order may be the better established. Good morals depend more than we imagine on every man's being pleased with his condition of life. Briguing and intrigues are owing to restlessness and discontent: everything goes amiss, when one person covets another's employment. To do well in life, a man must love his profession. The state is never rightly fixed, till each individual being seated in his place, their whole force is united, and concurs to the general good, instead of being employed to their mutual prejudice, as it must happen in every ill-constituted government. This being premised, what are we to think of those who would deprive the people of festivals, pleasures, and every kind of amusement, as tending to divert them from their work? This maxim is barbarous, is false. So much the worse, if the people have no time left but to earn their bread: they must be allowed some to eat it in comfort; otherwise they will not earn it long. That just and beneficent Deity, who is willing they should work, is willing also they should divert themselves: nature equally subjects them to exercise and repose, to pleasure and pain. The dislike to work hurts the poor wretches more than work itself. Therefore if you would have people active and industrious, give them festivals, give them amusements, which shall render them fond of their condition of life, and hinder their envying those of an easier situation. A few days lost in this manner, will enhance the value of the rest. Preside over their pleasures in order to render them decent; this is the right method to encourage them to work.

[2] I remember, when I was a boy, to have been struck with a very simple sight, which has been imprinted ever since in my memory, notwithstanding the passage of time, and the multiplicity of other objects. The regiment of St. Gervais had performed their exercise, and according to custom they sat down to supper in companies; most

neither in business, nor pleasures, or at least what are so called with us, they passed, in that delightful uniformity, the whole day without finding it too long, and their whole life without finding it too short. Each evening they came home, gay and good humoured, to take their frugal repast, content with their country, with their fellow-citizens, and with themselves. If you desire an example of these public diversions, I will give you one mentioned by Plutarch. There were, he says, three companies of dancers, according to the three several ages of nature, and each company made a chorus to the dance. That of the old men began the first, singing the following couplet:

> That active courage youthful blood contains
> Did once with equal vigour warm our veins.

Next came that of the young men, who sang in their turn, beating their arms in cadence:

> Valiant and bold we are, let who will try:
> Who dare accept our challenge, soon shall die.

---

of the regiment met after supper in the Square of St. Gervais, and all went dancing, officers and soldiers together, round the fountain, on the basin of which there were drums, fifes, and men with flambeaux in their hands. When people have been exhilarated with feasting, their dancing does not seem to offer anything very enjoying to the eye; and yet the concerted motion of five or six hundred men in uniform holding one another by the hand, and forming a long band, which played in cadence, and without the least confusion, with a thousand turns and returns, a thousand sorts of figured evolutions, the choice songs that spirited them, the noise of drums, the light of flambeaux and a certain military pomp amidst a scene of pleasure, all this together formed a very agreeable spectacle, which it was impossible not to be affected with. It was late, the women were gone to bed; they all got up. The windows were soon full of female gapers who inspired the actors with fresh ardour; but they could not confine themselves long to their windows, they came down; the wives flocked about their husbands; the servants brought wine, and the children, awakened by the noise ran half-naked to their fathers and mothers. The dance was suspended; nothing now passed but embracing, laughing, healths, caresses. From all this there resulted a general rapture, which I cannot describe, and which, in times of universal joy, we naturally feel, when surrounded by everything dear to us. My father embracing me, was seized with a palpitation which I think I feel and share with him still. 'Jean,' said he to me, 'love thy country. See here thy honest countrymen; they are all friends, all brothers; joy and concord are in their hearts. Thou art a Genevois; some time or other thou wilt see other people; but when thou hast travelled as far as thy father, thou wilt say thou never didst see their fellows.'

They wanted to recommence the dance, but it was no longer possible: they did not so much as know what they were doing; their heads were all turned with an inebriation sweeter far than that of wine. After staying some time on the square to laugh and chat, they were obliged to separate: each retired quietly with his family; and thus it was that those amiable prudent women brought back their husbands, not by disturbing, but going to share their pleasures. I am very sensible that this sight, which so greatly affected me, would have had no charm to a thousand others: one must have eyes made on purpose to see it, and a heart to feel it. No, there is no pure joy, but that of a community; and the genuine sentiments of nature are felt only by the people. O dignity, daughter of pride, and parent of corroding care, did ever thy gloomy slaves taste such a moment as this in all their lives?

Afterwards came the children, who answered them, singing with a loud voice:

> Those seeds which nature in our breast did sow,
> Shall soon to generous fruits of virtue grow:
> Then all those valiant deeds, which you relate,
> We will excel, and scorn to imitate.

These, Sir, are the entertainments proper for republics.

THE REVERIES OF A SOLITARY WALKER

EVERYTHING ON EARTH IS A CONTINUAL EBB. NOTHING CAN keep a fixed and constant form; and our affections, attached to external things, necessarily change with them. Always before or behind us, they recall the past, which is no more, or anticipate the future, which perhaps will never be: in all there is nothing solid to which the heart can cleave. Neither have we here below scarcely any other than passing pleasure; as to continual happiness, I doubt if it is known. There is hardly a single instant of our liveliest enjoyments of which the heart can truly say, *I wish this instant would last for ever*. And how then can we call a fugitive state happy which leaves uneasiness and void in the heart, which leaves regret for something preceding, and hope for something after it?

But if there is a state in which the soul finds a seat solid enough entirely to repose and collect there its whole being, without being obliged to have recourse to the past, or stretch towards the future; where time is to her a void; where the present continually lasts, without, however, denoting its duration, and without the least sign of succession, without any other sense of privation or enjoyment, of pleasure or pain, hope or fear, than solely that of our existence, and that that sentiment alone is able wholly to occupy it; as long as that state lasts, he who finds himself in it may call himself happy, not from a poor, imperfect, relative happiness, like that we feel in the pleasures of life, but from a full, perfect, and sufficient happiness, which does not leave the least void in the soul it would be glad to fill. This is the state in which I often found myself on St. Peter's island, during my solitary reveries, whether stretched in my boat, seated on the shores of the agitated lake, or else on the banks of a beautiful river, or a brook murmuring through the gravel.

In what consists the enjoyment of a like situation? In nothing external, nothing but one's self, and our own existence; as long as this state lasts, we are sufficient to ourselves, like God. The sense of existence, stripped of every other affection, is of itself a precious sense of contentment and peace, which alone would suffice to render this existence lovely and sweet, to him who

C [41]

knows to remove from his mind all those terrestrial and sensual impressions which incessantly arise to distract and to trouble our comfort here below. But the greatest part of mankind, agitated by continual passions, are little acquainted with this state, and, having imperfectly tasted it a few moments, preserve an obscure and confused idea of it only, which does not enable them to feel its charms.

It is necessary the heart should be at peace, and that no passion should arise to trouble the calm. It is necessary that he who feels it should have dispositions adapted to it; they are likewise necessary in the concourse of surrounding objects. It does not demand an absolute repose, or too great an agitation, but an uniform and moderate movement, without fits or intervals. Without motion, life is a lethargy. If the movement is unequal or too violent, it awakens; in showing us surrounding objects, it destroys the charms of thought and tears us from ourselves, instantly to restore us to the bonds of fortune and man, and brings us back to a sense of our misfortunes. An absolute silence leads to sadness: it represents the image of death. Then the succour of a happy imagination is necessary, and offers itself naturally enough to those who have received that blessing from Heaven. The movements, which do not externally arise, are then felt within us.

On awakening from any long and peaceful reverie, perceiving myself surrounded by flowers, birds, and verdure, permitting my wandering sight to rove remote over romantic shores, by which a vast extent of waters clear and crystalline was shut in, I assimilated every lovely object to my fictions, and, having at last a knowledge of myself, and that which surrounded me, I was unable to guess the point which separated fiction from reality; so much did all combine to render dear the retired and solitary life I led in my beloved abode.

THE SOCIAL CONTRACT

*I*N *his* Discourse on the Origin of Inequalities among Mankind (1753), *Rousseau put down as demonstrated the establishment* 'of a true contract between the people and the leaders chosen by them,' *but he added that he would postpone until later* 'investigations still to be made upon the nature of the fundamental pact of all government.'

Hardly was he installed in his Hermitage at Montmorency, in April 1756, when he resumed these investigations. They seemed to him the most important of the tasks assigned to him. He said this in his Confessions, *Book IX.* 'Of the various works which I had planned, the one I had considered the longest, which appealed most strongly to my taste, on which I wanted to work all my life, and which in my opinion should have placed the seal upon my reputation, was my *Political Institutions.* . . . I conceived the first idea of the book thirteen or fourteen years ago when I was at Venice. Since that time my views had been greatly enlarged by the historical study of morals (*i.e.* mainly by his *Discourse on the Origin of Inequalities*). I had come to see that in the last resort everything depends upon Politics; and that, whatever men may do, no nation will ever be anything but what the nature of its government may make it; thus the great question of the best possible government appears to me to be reduced to this: what is the nature of the government best adapted to train a nation to become the most virtuous, the most enlightened, the wisest, the best? . . . I thought I saw that this question was most closely united to this other question: what is the government which by its nature holds itself nearest to the law; from this question, what is the law? and a whole chain of questions of the same importance. I saw that all this led to great truths, useful for the happiness of humankind, but above all to that of my fatherland, where I had not found in the journey I had just made (1754) notions of law and liberty that seemed to me sufficiently exact and clear. . . .'

He worked on this slowly, for several years, avoiding any mention of the work to anyone, even his then closest adviser—Diderot. He feared to introduce any spirit of satire into a work in which he intended 'to put only the whole force of reason, without any trace of ill-humour or partiality.' *After his* Letter to d'Alembert (1758), *he went back to his* Political Institutions, *but saw that it would take years to finish; he abandoned the project, extracting only* The Social Contract, *which he wrote at the same time he was engaged upon* Emile. The Social Contract *appeared in Amsterdam, one or two months before* Emile, *therefore in the spring of 1762, shortly before Rousseau's flight into Switzerland, where the works were burned at Geneva almost immediately after their appearance, on 18th June 1762.*

THE SOCIAL CONTRACT

OR

PRINCIPLES OF POLITICAL RIGHT

BOOK I

MAN IS BORN FREE; AND EVERYWHERE HE IS IN CHAINS. Since no man has a natural authority over his fellow, and force creates no right, we must conclude that conventions form the basis of all legitimate authority among men.

We cannot invoke any voluntary alienation of liberty, as Grotius claims.

To renounce liberty is to renounce being a man, to surrender the rights of humanity and even its duties. Such a renunciation is incompatible with man's nature. The words *slave* and *right* contradict each other, and are mutually exclusive.

We must always go back to a first convention.

'The Social Compact' arises from the necessity of co-operation among men against natural forces.

'The problem is to find a form of association which will defend and protect with the whole common force the person and goods of each associate, and in which each, while uniting himself with all, may still obey himself alone, and remain as free as before.' This is the fundamental problem of which the *Social Contract* provides the solution.

If we discard from the social compact what is not of its essence, we shall find that it reduces itself to the following terms:

'*Each of us puts his person and all his power in common under the supreme direction of the general will, and, in our corporate capacity, we receive each member as an indivisible part of the whole.*

At once, in place of the individual personality of each contracting party, this act of association creates a moral and collective body, composed of as many members as the assembly contains

[45]

votes, and receiving from this act its unity, its common identity, its life and its will. This public person, so formed by the union of all other persons, takes the name of sovereign.

As soon as this multitude is so united in one body, it is impossible to offend against one of the members without attacking the body, and still more to offend against the body without the members resenting it.

In order that the social compact may not be an empty formula, it tacitly includes the undertaking, which alone can give force to the rest, that whoever refuses to obey the general will shall be compelled to obey by the whole body. This means nothing less than that he will be forced to be free; for this is the condition which, by giving each citizen to his country, secures him against all personal dependence.

What man loses by the social contract is his natural liberty and an unlimited right to everything he tries to get and succeeds in getting; what he gains is civil liberty and the proprietorship of all he possesses.

We might add to what man acquires in the civil state, moral liberty, which alone makes him truly master of himself; for the mere impulse of appetite is slavery, while obedience to a law which we prescribe to ourselves is liberty.

I shall end this book by remarking on a fact on which the whole social system should rest: *i.e.* that, instead of destroying natural inequality, the fundamental compact substitutes, for such physical inequality as nature may have set up between men, an equality that is moral and legitimate, and that men, who may be unequal in strength or intelligence, become every one equal by convention and legal right.[1]

BOOK II

The first and most important deduction from the principles we have so far laid down is that the general will alone can direct the State according to the object for which it was instituted, *i.e.* the common good.

---

[1] Under bad governments, this equality is only apparent and illusory: it serves only to keep the pauper in his poverty and the rich man in the position he has usurped. In fact, laws are always of use to those who possess and harmful to those who have nothing: from which it follows that the social state is advantageous to men only when all have something and none too much.

Sovereignty, being nothing less than the exercise of the general will, can never be alienated, and the Sovereign, who is no less than a collective being, cannot be represented except by himself.

The moment a master exists, there is no longer a Sovereign, and from that moment the body politic has ceased to exist.

Sovereignty, for the same reason as makes it inalienable, is indivisible; for will either is, or is not, general;[1] it is the will either of the body of the people, or only of a part of it. In the first case, the will, when declared, is an act of Sovereignty and constitutes law: in the second, it is merely a particular will, or act of magistracy—at the most a decree.

It follows that the general will is always right and tends to the public advantage; but it does not follow that the deliberations of the people are always equally correct. Our will is always for our own good, but we do not always see what that is; the people is never corrupted, but it is often deceived, and on such occasions only does it seem to will what is bad.

There is often a great deal of difference between the will of all and the general will; the latter considers only the common interest, while the former takes private interest into account, and is no more than a sum of particular wills.

As nature gives each man absolute power over all his members, the social compact gives the body politic absolute power over all its members also; and it is this power which, under the direction of the general will, bears, as I have said, the name of Sovereignty.

Each man alienates, I admit, by the social compact, only such part of his powers, goods and liberty as it is important for the community to control; but it must also be granted that the Sovereign is sole judge of what is important.

Every service a citizen can render the State he ought to render as soon as the Sovereign demands it; but the Sovereign, for its part, cannot impose upon its subjects any fetters that are useless to the community, nor can it even wish to do so; for no more by the law of reason than by the law of nature can anything occur without a cause.

[1] To be general, a will need not always be unanimous; but every vote must be counted: any exclusion is a breach of generality.

We can see from this that the sovereign power, absolute, sacred and inviolable as it is, does not and cannot exceed the limits of general conventions, and that every man may dispose at will of such goods and liberty as these conventions leave him; so that the Sovereign never has a right to lay more charges on one subject than on another, because, in that case, the question becomes particular, and ceases to be within its competency.

The social treaty has for its end the preservation of the contracting parties. He who wills the end wills the means also, and the means must involve some risks, and even some losses. He who wishes to preserve his life at others' expense should also, when it is necessary, be ready to give it up for their sake. Furthermore, the citizen is no longer the judge of the dangers to which the law desires him to expose himself; and when the prince says to him: 'It is expedient for the State that you should die,' he ought to die, because it is only on that condition that he has been living in security up to the present, and because his life is no longer a mere bounty of nature, but a gift made conditionally by the State.

The death-penalty inflicted upon criminals may be looked on in much the same light: it is in order that we may not fall victims to an assassin that we consent to die if we ourselves turn assassins.

Again, every malefactor, by attacking social rights, becomes on forfeit a rebel and a traitor to his country; by violating its laws he ceases to be a member of it; he even makes war upon it. In such a case the preservation of the State is inconsistent with his own, and one or the other must perish; in putting the guilty to death, we slay not so much the citizen as an enemy.

We may add that frequent punishments are always a sign of weakness or remissness on the part of the government. There is not a single ill-doer who could not be turned to some good. The State has no right to put to death, even for the sake of making an example, anyone whom it can leave alive without danger.

[*Rousseau then examines the* 'laws which are, properly speaking, only the conditions of civil association,' *and of which the people ought to be the author.*]

[48]

Good laws are not those which are good in themselves, but those which are well made for that particular people.

A thousand nations have achieved earthly greatness, that could never have endured good laws; even such as could have endured them could have done so only for a very brief period of their long history. Most peoples, like most men, are docile only in youth; as they grow old they become incorrigible. When once customs have become established and prejudices inveterate, it is dangerous and useless to attempt their reformation; the people, like the foolish and cowardly patients who rave at sight of the doctor, can no longer bear that anyone should lay hands on its faults to remedy them.

Useful revolutions are rare; they are exceptions, the cause of which is always to be found in the particular constitution of the State concerned. They cannot even happen twice to the same people, for it can make itself free as long as it remains barbarous, but not when the civic impulse has lost its vigour. Then disturbances may destroy it, but revolutions cannot mend it; it needs a master, and not a liberator. Free peoples, be mindful of this maxim: 'Liberty may be gained, but can never be recovered.'

As nature has set bounds to the stature of a well-made man, and, outside those limits, makes nothing but giants or dwarfs, similarly, for the constitution of a State to be at its best, it is possible to fix limits that will make it neither too large for good government, nor too small for self-maintenance. In every body politic there is a *maximum* strength which it cannot exceed and which it only loses by increasing in size. Every extension of the social tie means its relaxation; and, generally speaking, a small State is stronger in proportion than a great one.

If we ask in what precisely consists the greatest good of all, which should be the end of every system of legislation, we shall find it reduce itself to two main objects, liberty and equality —liberty, because all particular dependence means so much force taken from the body of the State, and equality, because liberty cannot exist without it.

I have already defined civil liberty; by equality, we should understand, not that the degrees of power and riches are to be absolutely identical for everybody; but that power shall never be great enough for violence, and shall always be exercised by virtue of rank and law; and that, in respect of riches, no citizen shall ever be wealthy enough to buy another, and none poor enough to be forced to sell himself.[1]

BOOK III

The public force needs an agent of its own to bind it together and set it to work under the direction of the general will, to serve as a means of communication between the State and the Sovereign. Here we have what is, in the State, the basis of government, often wrongly confused with the Sovereign, whose minister it is.

What then is government? An intermediate body set up between the subjects and the Sovereign, to secure their mutual correspondence, charged with the execution of the laws and the maintenance of liberty, both civil and political.

Those who hold that the act, by which a people puts itself under a prince, is not a contract, are certainly right. It is simply and solely a commission, an employment, in which the rulers, mere officials of the Sovereign, exercise in their own name the power of which it makes them depositaries. This power it can limit, modify, or recover at pleasure.

In the first place, the Sovereign may commit the charge of the government to the whole people or to the majority of the people, so that more citizens are magistrates than are mere private individuals. This form of government is called *democracy*.

Or it may restrict the government to a small number, so that there are more private citizens than magistrates; and this is named *aristocracy*.

Lastly, it may concentrate the whole government in the hands of a single magistrate from whom all others hold their power. This third form is the most usual, and is called *monarchy*, or royal government.

If we take the term in the strict sense, there never has been a real democracy, and there never will be. It is against the natural order for the many to govern and the few to be governed. It

---

[1] If the object is to give the State consistency, bring the two extremes as near to each other as possible; allow neither rich men nor beggars. These two estates, which are naturally inseparable, are equally fatal to the common good; from the one come the friends of tyranny, and from the other tyrants. It is always between them that public liberty is put up to auction; the one buys, and the other sells.

is unimaginable that the people should remain continually assembled to devote their time to public affairs, and it is clear that they cannot set up commissions for that purpose without the form of administration being changed.

Besides, how many conditions that are difficult to unite does such a government presuppose! First, a very small State, where the people can readily be got together and where each citizen can with ease know all the rest; secondly, great simplicity of manners, to prevent business from multiplying and raising thorny problems; next, a large measure of equality in rank and fortune, without which equality of rights and authority cannot long subsist; lastly, little or no luxury—for luxury either comes of riches or makes them necessary; it corrupts at once rich and poor, the rich by possession and the poor by covetousness; it sells the country to softness and vanity, and takes away from the State all its citizens, to make them slaves one to another, and one and all to public opinion.

It may be added that there is no government so subject to civil wars and intestine agitations as democratic or popular government, because there is none which has so strong and continual a tendency to change to another form, or which demands more vigilance and courage for its maintenance as it is. Under such a constitution above all, the citizen should arm himself with strength and constancy, and say, every day of his life, what a virtuous Count Palatine said in the Diet of Poland: 'Malo periculosam libertatem quam quietum servitium.'

Were there a people of gods, their government would be democratic. So perfect a government is not for men.

There are three sorts of aristocracy—natural, elective, and hereditary. The first is only for simple peoples; the third is the worst of all governments; the second is the best, and is aristocracy properly so called.

Besides the advantage that lies in the distinction between the two powers, it presents that of its members being chosen; for, in popular government, all the citizens are born magistrates; but here magistracy is confined to a few, who become such only by election. By this means uprightness, understanding, experience and all other claims to pre-eminence and public esteem become so many further guarantees of wise government.

In a word, it is the best and most natural arrangement that

the wisest should govern the many, when it is assured that they will govern for its profit, and not for their own. There is no need to multiply instruments, or get twenty thousand men to do what a hundred picked men can do even better. But it must not be forgotten that corporate interest here begins to direct the public power less under the regulation of the general will, and that a further inevitable propensity takes away from the laws part of the executive power.

MONARCHY

So far, we have considered the prince as a moral and collective person, unified by the force of the laws, and the depositary in the State of the executive power. We have now to consider this power when it is gathered together into the hands of a natural person, a real man, who alone has the right to dispose of it in accordance with the laws. Such a person is called a monarch or king.

If no government is more vigorous than this, there is also none in which the particular will holds more sway and rules the rest more easily. Everything moves towards the same end indeed, but this end is by no means that of the public happiness, and even the force of the administration constantly shows itself prejudicial to the State.

Kings desire to be absolute, and men are always crying out to them from afar that the best means of being so is to get themselves loved by their people. This precept is all very well, and even in some respects very true. Unfortunately, it will always be derided at court. The power which comes of a people's love is no doubt the greatest; but it is precarious and conditional, and princes will never rest content with it. The best kings desire to be in a position to be wicked, if they please, without forfeiting their mastery.

If it is hard for a great State to be well governed, it is much harder for it to be so by a single man; and everyone knows what happens when kings substitute others for themselves.

An essential and inevitable defect, which will always rank monarchical below republican government, is that in a republic the public voice hardly ever raises to the highest positions men who are not enlightened and capable, and such as to fill them with honour; while in monarchies those who rise to the top are most often merely petty blunderers, petty swindlers, and petty intriguers, whose petty talents cause them to get into the highest positions at Court, but, as soon as they have got there, serve only to make their ineptitude clear to the public.

Crowns have been made hereditary in certain families, and an order of succession has been set up, to prevent disputes from arising on the death of kings. That is to say, the disadvantages of regency have been put in place of those of election, apparent tranquillity has been preferred to wise administration, and men have chosen rather to risk having children, monstrosities, or imbeciles as rulers to having disputes over the choice of good kings.

Everything conspires to take away from a man who is set in authority over others the sense of justice and reason. Much trouble, we are told, is taken to teach young princes the art of reigning; but their education seems to do them no good. It would be better to begin by teaching them the art of obeying. If royal education necessarily corrupts those who receive it, what is to be hoped from a series of men brought up to reign? It is, then, wanton self-deception to confuse royal government with government by a good king. To see such government as it is in itself, we must consider it as it is under princes who are incompetent or wicked: for either they will come to the throne wicked or incompetent, or the throne will make them so.

Liberty, not being a fruit of all climates, is not within the reach of all peoples. The more this principle, laid down by Montesquieu, is considered, the more its truth is felt; the more it is combated, the more chance is given to confirm it by new proofs.

In fact, the more we reflect, the more we find the difference between free and monarchical States to be this: in the former, everything is used for the public advantage; in the aristocratic, the public forces and those of individuals are affected by each other, and either increases as the other grows weak; finally, instead of governing subjects to make them happy, despotism makes them wretched in order to govern them.

We find then, in every climate, natural causes according to

which the form of government which it requires can be assigned, and we can even say what sort of inhabitants it should have.

As the particular will acts constantly in opposition to the general will, the government continually exerts itself against the Sovereignty. The greater this exertion becomes, the more the constitution changes; and, as there is in this case no other corporate will to create an equilibrium by resisting the will of the prince, sooner or later the prince must inevitably suppress the Sovereign and break the social treaty. This is the unavoidable and inherent defect which, from the very birth of the body politic, tends ceaselessly to destroy it, as age and death end by destroying the human body.

There are two general courses by which government degenerates: *i.e.* when it undergoes contraction, or when the State is dissolved.

Government undergoes contraction when it passes from the many to the few, that is, from democracy to aristocracy, and from aristocracy to royalty. To do so is its natural propensity.

When the State is dissolved, the abuse of government, whatever it is, bears the common name of *anarchy*. To distinguish, democracy degenerates into *ochlocracy,* and aristocracy into *oligarchy*; and I would add that royalty degenerates into *tyranny*; but this last word is ambiguous and needs explanation.

In vulgar usage, a tyrant is a king who governs violently and without regard for justice and law. In the exact sense, a tyrant is an individual who arrogates to himself the royal authority without having a right to it. *Tyrant* and *usurper* are thus perfectly synonymous terms.

Such is the natural and inevitable tendency of the best constituted governments. If Sparta and Rome perished, what State can hope to endure for ever?

The body politic, as well as the human body, begins to die as soon as it is born, and carries in itself the causes of its destruction. Both may have a constitution that is more or less robust and suited to preserve them a longer or a shorter time. The constitution of man is the work of nature; that of the State the work of art. It is not in men's power to prolong their own lives; but it is for them to prolong as much as possible the life of the State, by giving it the best possible constitution. The best constituted State will have an end; but it will end later than any other, unless some unforeseen accident brings about its untimely destruction.

The life-principle of the body politic lies in the sovereign authority. The legislative power is the heart of the State; the executive power is its brain, which causes the movement of all the parts. The brain may become paralysed and the individual still live. A man may remain an imbecile and live; but as soon as the heart ceases to perform its functions, the animal is dead.

The Sovereign, having no force other than the legislative power, acts only by means of the laws; and the laws being solely the authentic acts of the general will, the Sovereign cannot act save when the people is assembled.

As soon as public service ceases to be the chief business of the citizens, and they would rather serve with their money than with their persons, the State is not far from its fall. When it is necessary to march out to war, they pay troops and stay at home: when it is necessary to meet in council, they name deputies and stay at home. By reason of idleness and money, they end by having soldiers to enslave their country and representatives to sell it.

The lukewarmness of patriotism, the activity of private interest, the vastness of States, conquest, and the abuse of government suggested the method of having deputies or representatives of the people in the national assemblies. These are what, in some countries, men have presumed to call the Third Estate. Thus the individual interest of two orders is put first and second; the public interest occupies only the third place.

Sovereignty, for the same reason that makes it inalienable, cannot be represented; it lies essentially in the general will, and will does not admit of representation: it is either the same, or other; there is no intermediate possibility. The deputies of the people, therefore, are not and cannot be its representatives: they are merely its stewards, and can carry through no definite acts. Every law the people has not ratified in person is null and void —is, in fact, not a law. The moment a people allows itself to be represented, it is no longer free: it no longer exists.

The legislative power once well established, the next thing is to establish similarly the executive power. It has been held that this act of establishment was a contract between the people and the rulers it sets over itself. There is only one contract in the State, and that is the act of association, which in itself excludes the existence of a second.

The institution of government is not a contract, but a law; the depositaries of the executive power are not the people's masters, but its officers; it can set them up and pull them down when it likes; for them there is no question of contract, but of obedience; and in taking charge of the functions the State imposes on them they are doing no more than fulfilling their duty as citizens, without having the remotest right to argue about the conditions.

When therefore the people sets up an hereditary government, whether it be monarchical and confined to one family, or aristocratic and confined to a class, what it enters into is not an undertaking; the administration is given a provisional form, until the people chooses to order it otherwise.

There is in the State no fundamental law that cannot be revoked, not excluding the social compact itself; for if all the citizens assembled of one accord to break the compact, it is impossible to doubt that it would be very legitimately broken.

BOOK IV

There is but one law which, from its nature, needs unanimous consent. This is the social compact; for civil association is the most voluntary of all acts. Every man being born free and his own master, no one, under any pretext whatsoever, can make any man subject without his consent.

If then there are opponents when the social compact is made, their opposition does not invalidate the contract, but merely prevents them from being included in it. They are foreigners among citizens. When the State is instituted, residence constitutes consent; to dwell within its territory is to submit to the Sovereign.

Apart from this primitive contract, the vote of the majority always binds all the rest. This follows from the contract itself. The constant will of all the members of the State is the general will; by virtue of it they are citizens and free. When in the popular assembly a law is proposed, what the people is asked is not exactly whether it approves or rejects the proposal, but whether it is in conformity with the general will, which is their will. Each man, in giving his vote, states his opinion on that point; and the general will is found by counting votes.

[*In the rest of Book IV Rousseau examines the institutions of ancient Rome, as examples of the management of public affairs in a great Republic. Finally, he treats of the relation of religion with the State.*]

Religion, considered in relation to society, which is either general or particular, may also be divided into two kinds: the religion of man, and that of the citizen. The first, which has neither temples, nor altars, nor rites, and is confined to the purely internal cult of the supreme God and the eternal obligations of morality, is the religion of the Gospel pure and simple, the true theism, what may be called natural divine right or law. The other, which is codified in a single country, gives it its gods, its own tutelary patrons; it has its dogmas, its rites, and its external cult prescribed by law; outside the single nation that follows it, all the world is in its sight infidel, foreign and barbarous; the duties and rights of man extend for it only as far as its own altars. Of this kind were all the religions of early peoples, which we may define as civil or positive divine right or law.

There is a third sort of religion of a more singular kind, which gives men two codes of legislation, two rulers, and two countries, renders them subject to contradictory duties, and makes it impossible for them to be faithful both to religion and to citizenship. Such are the religions of the Lamas and of the Japanese, and such is Roman Christianity, which may be called the religion of the priest. It leads to a sort of mixed and anti-social code which has no name.

In their political aspect, all these three kinds of religion have their defects. The third is so clearly bad, that it is waste of time to stop to prove it such. All that destroys social unity is worthless; all institutions that set man in contradiction to himself are worthless.

There remains the religion of man or Christianity—not the Christianity of to-day, but that of the Gospel, which is entirely different. By means of this holy, sublime, and real religion all

[57]

men, being children of one God, recognize one another as brothers, and the society that unites them is not dissolved even at death.

But this religion, having no particular relation to the body politic, leaves the laws in possession of the force they have in themselves without making any addition to it; and thus one of the great bonds that unite society considered in severalty fails to operate. Nay, more, so far from binding the hearts of the citizens to the State, it has the effect of taking them away from all earthly things. I know of nothing more contrary to the social spirit.

Christianity as a religion is entirely spiritual, occupied solely with heavenly things; the country of the Christian is not of this world. He does his duty, indeed, but does it with profound indifference to the good or ill success of his cares. Provided he has nothing to reproach himself with it matters little to him whether things go well or ill here on earth.

Christianity preaches only servitude and dependence. Its spirit is so favourable to tyranny that it always profits by such a *régime*. True Christians are made to be slaves, and they know it and do not much mind: this short life counts for too little in their eyes.

But let us come back to what is right, and settle our principles on this important point. The right which the social compact gives the Sovereign over the subjects does not, we have seen, exceed the limits of public expediency.[1] The subjects then owe the Sovereign an account of their opinions only to such an extent as they matter to the community. Now, it matters very much to the community that each citizen should have a religion. That will make him love his duty; but the dogmas of that religion concern the State and its members only so far as they have reference to morality and to the duties which he who professes them is bound to do to others. Each man may have, over and above, what opinions he pleases, without it being the Sovereign's business to take cognizance of them; for, as the Sovereign has no authority in the other world, whatever the

[1] 'In the republic,' says the Marquis d'Argenson, 'each man is perfectly free in what does not harm others.' This is the invariable limitation, which it is impossible to define more exactly.

lot of its subjects may be in the life to come, that is not its business, provided they are good citizens in this life.

There is therefore a purely civil profession of faith of which the Sovereign should fix the articles, not exactly as religious dogmas, but as social sentiments without which a man cannot be a good citizen or a faithful subject. While it can compel no one to believe them, it can banish from the State whoever does not believe them—it can banish him, not for impiety, but as an anti-social being, incapable of truly loving the laws and justice, and of sacrificing, at need, his life to his duty. If anyone, after publicly recognizing these dogmas, behaves as if he does not believe them, let him be punished by death: he has committed the worst of all crimes, that of lying before the law.

The dogmas of civil religion ought to be few, simple, and exactly worded, without explanation or commentary. The existence of a mighty, intelligent and beneficent Divinity, possessed of foresight and providence, the life to come, the happiness of the just, the punishment of the wicked, the sanctity of the social contract and the laws: these are its positive dogmas. Its negative dogmas I confine to one, intolerance, which is a part of the cults we have rejected.

Now that there is and can be no longer an exclusive national religion, tolerance should be given to all religions that tolerate others, so long as their dogmas contain nothing contrary to the duties of citizenship. But whoever dares to say: *Outside the Church is no salvation*, ought to be driven from the State.

EMILE

ROUSSEAU *had always shown a leaning toward the vocation of teacher. In* 1735, *when he was* 23 *years old, he wrote to his father that, of all the states he could consider, the only one for which he had 'some predilection' was that of tutor to young men of rank. He made several trials of this occupation without too much success—at Lyons in* 1740–1741, *and in Paris in* 1743. *And as early as* 1740 *he had put his educational theories on paper in a 'Plan' which foreshadowed certain characteristics of his* Emile: *but at that time he had not undergone his moral reformation so antagonistic to the society of his day. During his stay at the Hermitage and at Montmorency, he passionately attacked the problem of education. Since civilization appeared to him to have betrayed 'the natural man,' it was necessary that it be reconstructed:—a problem with which the Encyclopædists, his former friends, now his enemies, did not occupy themselves.*

'The literature and science of our day,' *he wrote in his Preface,* 'tend rather to destroy than to build up. We find fault after the manner of a master; to suggest, we must adopt another style, a style less in accordance with the pride of the philosopher. In spite of all those books, whose only aim, so they say, is public utility, the most useful of all arts, the art of training men, is still neglected.'

Rousseau worked on Emile *at the same time as on* The Social Contract. *The two works are related. The principles set forth in both are based on the essential liberty of natural man which should be safeguarded by education—and really assured by the lawmaker. Both are the boldest and most fruitful works to have come from Rousseau's pen, or to have been conceived by the pre-revolutionary spirit of the* 18th *century. Also, both of them were condemned to be burned, almost immediately after their appearance at the bookseller's.* Emile, *finished in* 1760, *was published—and burned—in* 1762.

EMILE

OR EDUCATION

IN THE NATURAL ORDER MEN ARE ALL EQUAL AND THEIR COMMON calling is that of manhood, so that a well-educated man cannot fail to do well in that calling and those related to it. It matters little to me whether my pupil is intended for the army, the church, or the law. Before his parents chose a calling for him nature called him to be a man. Life is the trade I would teach him. The real object of our study is man and his environment.

Life is not breath, but action, the use of our senses, our mind, our faculties, every part of ourselves which makes us conscious of our being. Life consists less in length of days than in the keen sense of living.

Our wisdom is slavish prejudice, our customs consist in control, constraint, compulsion. Civilized man is born and dies a slave. The infant is bound up in swaddling-clothes, the corpse is nailed down in his coffin. All his life long man is imprisoned by our institutions.

Fix your eyes on nature, follow the path traced by her. She keeps children at work, she hardens them by all kinds of difficulties, she soon teaches them the meaning of pain and grief. Accustom them therefore to the hardships they will have to face.

By slow and careful stages man and child learn to fear nothing.

All wickedness comes from weakness. The child is only naughty because he is weak; make him strong and he will be good; if we could do everything we should never do wrong. Of all the attributes of the Almighty, goodness is that which it would be hardest to dissociate from our conception of Him.

I shall not take pains to prevent Emile hurting himself; far from it, I should be vexed if he never hurt himself, if he grew up unacquainted with pain. To bear pain is his first and most useful lesson. Instead of keeping him mewed up in a stuffy room, take him out into a meadow every day; let him run about, let him struggle and fall again and again, the oftener the better; he will learn all the sooner to pick himself up.

What do you mean when you say, 'Man is weak'? The term weak implies a relation, a relation of the creature to whom it is applied. An insect or a worm whose strength exceeds its needs is strong; an elephant, a lion, a conqueror, a hero, a god himself whose needs exceed his strength is weak.

O man! live your own life and you will no longer be wretched. Keep to your appointed place in the order of nature and nothing can tear you from it. Do not kick against the stern law of necessity.

That man is truly free who desires what he is able to perform, and does what he desires. This is my fundamental maxim. Apply it to childhood, and all the rules of education spring from it.

There are two kinds of dependence: dependence on things, which is the work of nature; and dependence on men, which is the work of society. Dependence on things, being non-moral, does no injury to liberty and begets no vices; dependence on men, being out of order, gives rise to every kind of vice, and through this master and slave become mutually depraved.

Keep the child dependent on things only. Let his wishes meet with physical obstacles only, or the punishment which results from his own actions, lessons which will be recalled when the same circumstances occur again. It is enough to prevent him from wrongdoing without forbidding him to do wrong. Experience or lack of power should take the place of law.

Your child must not get what he asks, but what he needs; he must never act from obedience, but from necessity.

The words *obey* and *command* will be excluded from his vocabulary, still more those of *duty* and *obligation*; but the words strength, necessity, weakness, and constraint must have a large place in it.

Thus you will make him patient, equable, calm, and resigned, even when he does not get all he wants; for it is in man's nature to bear patiently with the nature of things, but not with the ill-will of another.

[62]

Let us lay it down as an incontrovertible rule that the first impulses of nature are always right; there is no original sin in the human heart; the how and why of the entrance of every vice can be traced.

The education of the earliest years should be merely negative. It consists, not in teaching virtue or truth, but in preserving the heart from vice and from the spirit of error.

The only moral lesson which is suited for a child—the most important lesson for every time of life—is this: 'Never hurt anybody.' The very rule of well-doing, if not subordinated to this rule, is dangerous, false and contradictory. Who is there who does no good? Everyone does some good, the wicked as well as the righteous; he makes one happy at the cost of the misery of a hundred, and hence spring all our misfortunes.

Human intelligence is finite, and not only can no man know everything, he cannot even acquire all the scanty knowledge of others. Since the contrary of every false proposition is a truth, there are as many truths as falsehoods. We must, therefore, choose what to teach. The small store which really contributes to our welfare alone deserves the study of a wise man, and therefore of a child whom one would have wise. He must know not merely what is, but what is useful.

Keep this truth ever before you—Ignorance never did anyone any harm, error alone is fatal, and we do not lose our way through ignorance but through self-confidence.

Let us transform our sensations into ideas, but do not let us jump all at once from the objects of sense to objects of thought. The latter are attained by means of the former. Let the senses be the only guide for the first workings of reason. No book but the world, no teaching but that of fact.

Teach your scholar to observe the phenomena of nature; if you would have it grow, do not be in too great a hurry to satisfy this curiosity. Let him know nothing because you have told him, but because he has learnt it for himself. If ever you substitute authority for reason he will cease to reason; he will be a mere plaything of other people's thoughts.

If he goes wrong let him alone, do not correct his mistakes; hold your tongue till he finds them out for himself and corrects them, or at most arrange something, as opportunity offers, which may show him his mistakes. If he never makes mistakes he will never learn anything thoroughly.

This is the essential point in my method—Do not teach the child many things, but never let him form inaccurate or confused ideas. I care not if he knows nothing provided he is not mistaken, and I only acquaint him with truths to guard him against the errors he might put in their place. Reason and judgment come slowly, prejudices flock to us in crowds, and from these he must be protected.

It is not your business to teach him the various sciences, but to give him a taste for them and methods of learning them when this taste is more mature. That is a fundamental principle of all good education.

The notions of things thus acquired for oneself are clearer and much more convincing than those acquired from the teaching of others; and not only is our reason not accustomed to a slavish submission to authority, but we develop greater ingenuity in discovering relations and connecting ideas.

Our real teachers are experience and emotion, and man will never learn what befits a man except under its own conditions.

As soon as we have contrived to give our pupil an idea of the word 'Useful,' we have got an additional means of controlling him.

'What is the use of that?' This is the sacred formula, the formula by which he and I test every action of our lives.

I do not like verbal explanations. Young people pay little heed to them, nor do they remember them. Things! Things! I cannot repeat it too often. We lay too much stress upon words; we teachers babble, and our scholars follow our example.

I hate books; they only teach us to talk about things we know nothing about. But since we must have books, there is one book which, to my thinking, supplies the best treatise of an education according to nature. What is this wonderful book? Is it Aristotle? Pliny? Buffon? No; it is *Robinson Crusoe*.

Your main object should be to keep out of your scholar's way all idea of such social relations as he cannot understand, but when the development of knowledge compels you to show him the mutual dependence of mankind, instead of showing him its moral side, turn all his attention at first towards industry and the mechanical arts which make men useful to one another.

The value set by the general public on the various arts is in inverse ratio to their real utility. They are even valued directly according to their uselessness.

What will become of your pupils if you let them acquire this foolish prejudice, if you share it yourself? If, for instance, they see you show more politeness in a jeweller's shop than in a locksmith's. What idea will they form of the true worth of the arts and the real value of things when they see, on the one hand, a fancy price and, on the other, the price of real utility, and that the more a thing costs the less it is worth? As soon as you let them get hold of these ideas, you may give up all attempt at further education; in spite of you they will be like all the other scholars—you have wasted fourteen years.

In everything the art which is most generally useful and necessary, is undoubtedly that which most deserves esteem.

Agriculture is the earliest and most honourable of arts; metal work I put next, then carpentry, and so on. This is the order in which the child will put them, if he has not been spoilt by vulgar prejudices. What valuable considerations Emile will derive from his Robinson in such matters.

Thus the idea of social relations is gradually developed in the child's mind, before he can really be an active member of human society. Emile sees that to get tools for his own use, other people must have theirs, and that he can get in exchange what he needs and they possess. I easily bring him to feel the need of such exchange and to take advantage of it.

Every man must live; this argument, which appeals to everyone with more or less force in proportion to his humanity, strikes me as unanswerable when applied to oneself.

If in this world there is any condition so miserable that one cannot live without wrong-doing, where the citizen is driven into evil, you should hang, not the criminal, but those who drove him into crime.

You reckon on the present order of society, without considering that this order is itself subject to inscrutable changes, and that you can neither foresee nor provide against the revolution which may affect your children. The great become small, the rich poor, the king a commoner. Does fate strike so seldom that you can count on immunity from her blows? The crisis is approaching, and we are on the edge of a revolution.

Outside the pale of society, the solitary, owing nothing to any man, may live as he pleases, but in society either he lives at the cost of others, or he owes them in labour the cost of his keep. Man in society is bound to work; rich or poor, weak or strong, every idler is a thief.

Stoop to the position of a working man, to rise above your own.

Emile shall learn a trade. 'An honest trade, at least,' you say. What do you mean by honest? Is not every useful trade honest? I would not make an embroiderer, a gilder, a polisher of him, like Locke's young gentleman. Neither would I make him a musician, an actor, or an author. I would rather have him a shoemaker than a poet, I would rather he paved streets than painted flowers on china. 'But,' you will say, 'policemen, spies, and hangmen are useful people.' There would be no use for them if it were not for the government.

Emile will not long be a workman before he discovers those social inequalities he had not previously observed.

We have made him a worker and a thinker; we have now to make him loving and tender-hearted, to perfect reason through feeling. But before we enter on this new order of things, let us cast an eye over the stage we are leaving behind us, and perceive as clearly as we can how far we have got.

Emile knows little, but what he knows is really his own; he has no half-knowledge. Among the few things he knows and knows thoroughly this is the most valuable, that there are many things he does not know now but may know some day, many more that other men know but he will never know, and an infinite number which nobody will ever know. He is large-minded, not through knowledge, but through the power of acquiring it; he is open-minded, intelligent, ready for anything. I am content if he knows the 'Wherefore' of his actions and the 'Why' of his beliefs. For once more my object is not to supply him with exact knowledge, but the means of getting it when required, to teach him to value it at its true worth, and to love truth above all things.

Emile is industrious, temperate, patient, steadfast, and full of courage. His imagination is still asleep, so he has no exaggerated ideas of danger; the few ills he feels he knows how to endure in patience, because he has not learnt to rebel against fate. As to death, he knows not what it means; but accustomed as he is to submit without resistance to the law of necessity, he will die, if die he must, without a groan and without a struggle; that is as much as we can demand of nature, in that hour which we all abhor. To live in freedom, and to be independent of human affairs, is the best way to learn how to die.

Do you think that the earlier years of a child, who has reached his fifteenth year in this condition, have been wasted?

Our passions are the chief means of self-preservation; to try to destroy them is therefore as absurd as it is useless; this would be to overcome nature, to reshape God's handiwork.

I consider those who would prevent the birth of the passions almost as foolish as those who would destroy them.

But should we reason rightly, if from the fact that passions are natural to man, we inferred that all the passions we feel in ourselves and behold in others are natural? All those which enslave and destroy us have another source; nature does not bestow them on us; we seize on them in her despite.

The people are mankind; those who do not belong to the people are so few in number that they are not worth counting. Man is the same in every station of life; if that be so, those ranks to which most men belong deserve most honour.

Society must be studied in the individual and the individual in society; those who desire to treat politics and morals apart from one another will never understand either.

Since it is impossible in the state of nature that the difference between man and man should be great enough to make one dependent on another, there is in fact in this state of nature an actual and indestructible equality. In the civil state there is a vain and chimerical equality of right; the means intended for its maintenance themselves serve to destroy it; and the power of the community, added to the power of the strongest for the oppression of the weak, disturbs the sort of equilibrium which nature has established between them. From this first contradiction spring all the other contradictions between the real and the apparent, which are to be found in the civil order. The many will always be sacrificed to the few, the common weal to private interest; those specious words—justice and subordination—will always serve as the tools of violence and the weapons of injustice.

I would have you so choose the company of a youth that he should think well of those among whom he lives, and I would have you so teach him to know the world that he should think ill of all that takes place in it. Let him know that man is by nature good, let him feel it, let him judge his neighbour by himself; but let him see how men are depraved and perverted by society; let him find the source of all their vices in their preconceived opinions.

Shall we make of Emile a knight-errant, a redresser of wrongs, a paladin? He will do all that he knows to be useful and good. He will do nothing more, and he knows that nothing is useful and good for him which is unbefitting his age. He knows that his first duty is to himself; that young men should distrust themselves; that they should act circumspectly; that they should show respect to those older than themselves, reticence and discretion in talking without cause, modesty in things indifferent, but courage in well-doing, and boldness to speak the truth. Such were those illustrious Romans who, having been admitted into public life, spent their days in bringing criminals to justice and in protecting the innocent, without any motives beyond those of learning, and of the furtherance of justice and of the protection of right conduct.

Emile is not fond of noise or quarrelling, not only among men, but among animals. This peaceful spirit is one of the results of his education, which has never stimulated self-love or a high opinion of himself, and so has not encouraged him to seek his pleasure in domination and in the sufferings of others. The sight of suffering makes him suffer too; this is a natural feeling.

When I want to train a natural man, I do not want to make him a savage and to send him back to the woods, but living in the whirl of social life it is enough that he should not let himself be carried away by the passions and prejudices of men; let him see with his eyes and feel with his heart, let him own no sway but that of reason.

I am aware that many of my readers will be surprised to find me tracing the course of my scholar through his early years without speaking to him of religion. At fifteen he will not even know that he has a soul, at eighteen even he may not be ready to learn about it. For if he learns about it too soon, there is the risk of his never really knowing anything about it.

'We must believe in God if we would be saved.' This doctrine wrongly understood is the root of bloodthirsty intolerance and the cause of all the futile teaching which strikes a deadly blow at human reason by training it to cheat itself with mere words.

The obligation of faith assumes the possibility of belief.

There are circumstances in which one can be saved without belief in God, and these circumstances occur in the case of children or madmen when the human mind is incapable of the operations necessary to perceive the Godhead. From the same principle it is plain that any man having reached old age without faith in God will not, therefore, be deprived of God's presence in another life if his blindness was not wilful; and I maintain that it is not always wilful.

Let us beware of proclaiming the truth to those who cannot as yet comprehend it, for to do so is to try to inculcate error. It would be better to have no idea at all of the Divinity than to have mean, grotesque, harmful, and unworthy ideas; to fail to perceive the Divine is a lesser evil than to insult it.

The neglect of all religion soon leads to the neglect of man's duty.

PROFESSION OF FAITH OF
A SAVOYARD VICAR

*T*HE Profession of Faith of a Savoyard Vicar *which is suddenly interpolated into Book IV of Emile is like a different work altogether. In its amplitude and fervour, these pages form the great illumination in the life of Rousseau and in philosophical and religious thought in the* 18th *century.*

Later telling of 'the great revolution' *which came about in him following the thunderbolt in* 1749—*when* 'another moral world unveiled itself to my gaze,' *and he felt himself* 'obliged to undertake this great review of his thought'—*Rousseau spoke of the repulsion which came over him with regard to the Encyclopædists, his contemporaries*—'ardent missionaries of Atheism, and very imperious dogmatists, they did not endure without anger that on any point there might exist anyone who dared to think otherwise than they. . . .' 'Never,' *he affirmed,* 'did I adopt their desolating doctrine; and this resistance to men so intolerant, who moreover had their own views, was not one of the least causes for attracting their animosity.'—*He undertook to formulate his own philosophy. This was a difficult labour, and he was often on the verge of giving it up. Nevertheless he persisted.* 'For the first time in my life I had courage.' *To him it was a question of the* 'eternal fate of his soul.'

'The result of my painful researches was practically that which I gave out in the *Profession of Faith of a Savoyard Vicar*, a work unworthily prostituted and profaned in the present generation, but which some day may make a revolution among men, if ever good sense and good faith are born again among them.' (*Third* Reverie of a Solitary Stroller, *written in* 1777, *on the eve of his death.*)

It is indeed true that this little work, so vast in scope, which aroused the anger of both Catholics and Protestants and led to the author's persecution by both—had incalculable reverberations in the heart of the generation that followed his.

PROFESSION OF FAITH OF
A SAVOYARD VICAR

I CANNOT UNDERSTAND HOW ANYONE CAN BE A SCEPTIC sincerely and on principle. Either such philosophers do not exist or they are the most miserable of men. Doubt with regard to what we ought to know is a condition too violent for the human mind; it cannot long be endured; in spite of itself the mind decides one way or another, and it prefers to be deceived rather than to believe nothing.

I consulted the philosophers, I examined their various theories; I found them all alike proud, assertive, dogmatic, professing, even in their so-called scepticism, to know everything, proving nothing, scoffing at each other. Weigh their arguments, they are all destructive; they are only agreed in arguing with each other. I could find no way out of my uncertainty by listening to them.

I suppose this prodigious diversity of opinion is caused, in the first place, by the weakness of the human intellect; and, in the second, by pride. We have no means of measuring this vast machine, we are unable to calculate its workings; we know neither its guiding principles nor its final purpose; we do not know ourselves, we know neither our nature nor the spirit that moves us; we scarcely know whether man is one or many; we are surrounded by impenetrable mysteries. These mysteries are beyond the region of sense, we think we can penetrate them by the light of reason, but we fall back on our imagination. Through this imagined world each forces a way for himself which he holds to be right; none can tell whether his path will lead him to the goal. Yet we long to know and understand it all. A fragment of some vast whole whose bounds are beyond our gaze, a fragment abandoned by its Creator to our foolish quarrels, we are vain enough to want to determine the nature of that whole and our own relations with regard to it.

The first thing I learned from these considerations was to restrict my enquiries to what directly concerned myself, to rest in profound ignorance of everything else, and not even to trouble myself to doubt anything beyond what I required to know.

I also realized that the philosophers, far from ridding me of my vain doubts, only multiplied the doubts that tormented me and failed to remove any one of them. So I chose another guide and said, 'Let me follow the Inner Light; it will not lead me so far astray as others have done, or if it does it will be my own fault, and I shall not go so far wrong if I follow my own illusions as if I trusted to their deceits.'

I exist, and I have senses through which I receive impressions. This is the first truth that strikes me and I am forced to accept it. Not only do I exist, but other entities exist also, that is to say, the objects of my sensations; and even if these objects are merely ideas, still these ideas are not me.

Everything outside myself, everything which acts upon my sense, I call matter, and all the particles of matter which I suppose to be united into separate entities I call bodies. Thus all the disputes of the idealists and the realists have no meaning for me; their distinctions between the appearance and the reality of bodies are wholly fanciful.

I am now as convinced of the existence of the universe as of my own. I next consider the objects of my sensations, and I find that I have the power of comparing them, so I perceive that I am endowed with an active force of which I was not previously aware.

There is not a being in the universe who may not be regarded as in some respects the common centre of all, around which they are grouped, so that they are all reciprocally end and means in relation to each other. The mind is confused and lost amid these innumerable relations, not one of which is itself confused or lost in the crowd. What absurd assumptions are required to deduce all this harmony from the blind mechanism of matter set in motion by chance!

I believe that the world is governed by a wise and powerful will; I see it or rather I feel it, and it is a great thing to know this. But has this same world always existed, or has it been created? Is there one source of all things? Are there two or many? What is their nature? I know not; and what concern is it of mine?

Whether matter is eternal or created, whether its origin is passive or not, it is still certain that the whole is one, and that it proclaims a single intelligence; for I see nothing that is not part of the same ordered system, nothing which does not co-operate to the same end, namely, the conservation of all within the established order. This being who wills and can perform his

will, this being active through his own power, this being, whoever he may be, who moves the universe and orders all things,
is what I call God. To this name I add the ideas of intelligence,
power, will, which I have brought together, and that of kindness
which is their necessary consequence; but for all this I know
no more of the being to which I ascribe them. He hides himself
alike from my senses and my understanding; the more I think
of him, the more perplexed I am; I know full well that he
exists, and that he exists of himself alone; I know that my
existence depends on his, and that everything I know depends
upon him also. I see God everywhere in his works; I feel him
within myself; I behold him all around me; but if I try to ponder
him himself, if I try to find out where he is, what he is, what is
his substance, he escapes me and my troubled spirit finds nothing.

Convinced of my unfitness, I shall never argue about the
nature of God unless I am driven to it by the feeling of his
relations with myself. But when, in my desire to discover my
own place within my species, I consider its different ranks and
the men who fill them, where am I now? What a sight meets
my eyes! Where is now the order I perceived? Nature showed
me a scene of harmony and proportion; the human race shows
me nothing but confusion and disorder. The elements agree
together; men are in a state of chaos. I behold the earth, and
there is evil upon it.

Man is free to act, and as such he is animated by an immaterial
substance; that is the third article of my creed.

If man is at once active and free, he acts of his own accord;
what he does freely is no part of the system marked out by
Providence and it cannot be imputed to Providence. Providence
does not will the evil that man does when he misuses the freedom
given to him; neither does Providence prevent his doing it,
either because the wrong done by so feeble a creature is as
nothing in its eyes, or because it could not prevent it without
doing a greater wrong and degrading his nature. Providence
has made him free that he may choose the good and refuse the
evil. It has made him capable of this choice if he uses rightly
the faculties bestowed upon him, but it has so strictly limited
his powers that the misuse of his freedom cannot disturb the
general order. The evil that man does reacts upon himself without
affecting the system of the world.

D   [73]

It is the abuse of our powers that makes us unhappy and wicked. Our cares, our sorrows, our sufferings are of our own making. Moral ills are undoubtedly the work of man, and physical ills would be nothing but for our vices which have made us liable to them. Death is the cure for the evils you bring upon yourself; nature would not have you suffer perpetually.

O Man! seek no further for the author of evil; thou art he. There is no evil but the evil you do or the evil you suffer, and both come from yourself. Evil in general can only spring from disorder, and in the order of the world I find a never-failing system.

Where all is well, there is no such thing as injustice. Justice and goodness are inseparable; now goodness is the necessary result of boundless power and of that self-love which is innate in all sentient beings. The omnipotent projects himself, so to speak, into the being of his creatures. Creation and preservation are the everlasting work of power; it does not act on that which has no existence; God is not the God of the dead; he could not harm and destroy without injury to himself. The omnipotent can only will what is good. Therefore he who is supremely good, because he is supremely powerful, must also be supremely just, otherwise he would contradict himself; for that love of order which creates order we call goodness and that love of order which preserves order we call justice.

If the soul is immaterial, it may survive the body; and if it so survives, Providence is justified. Had I no other proof of the immaterial nature of the soul, the triumph of the wicked and the oppression of the righteous in this world would be enough to convince me. I should seek to resolve so appalling a discord in the universal harmony. I should say to myself, 'All is not over with life, everything finds its place at death.' I should still have to answer the question, 'What becomes of man when all we know of him through our senses has vanished?' This question no longer presents any difficulty to me when I admit the two substances. When the union of soul and body is destroyed, I think one may be dissolved and the other may be preserved. Why should the destruction of the one imply the destruction of the other? On the contrary, so unlike in their nature, they were during their union in a highly unstable condition, and when this union comes to an end they both return to their natural state; the active vital substance regains all the force which it expended to set in motion the passive dead substance. Alas! my vices make me only too well aware that man is but half-alive during this life; the life of the soul only begins with the death of the body.

But what is that life? Is the soul of man in its nature immortal? I know not. My finite understanding cannot hold the infinite; what is called eternity eludes my grasp. What can I assert or deny, how can I reason with regard to what I cannot conceive? I believe that the soul survives the body for the maintenance of order; who knows if this is enough to make it eternal? However, I know that the body is worn out and destroyed by the division of its parts, but I cannot conceive a similar destruction of the conscious nature, and as I cannot imagine how it can die, I presume that it does not die. As this assumption is consoling and in itself not unreasonable, why should I fear to accept it?

Do not ask me whether the torments of the wicked will endure for ever, whether the goodness of their creator can condemn them to eternal suffering. All the same I find it hard to believe that they will be condemned to everlasting torments. If the supreme justice calls for vengeance, it claims it in this life.

Thus it is that, in the contemplation of God in his works, and in the study of such of his attributes as it concerned me to know, I have slowly grasped and developed the idea, at first partial and imperfect, which I have formed of this Infinite Being. When I hear it said that my soul is spiritual and that God is a spirit, I revolt against this abasement of the divine essence; as if God and my soul were of one and the same nature! As if God were not the one and only absolute being, the only really active, feeling, thinking, willing being, from whom we derive our thought, feeling, motion, will, our freedom and our very existence! We are free because he wills our freedom, and his inexplicable substance is to our souls what our souls are to our bodies.

The more I strive to envisage his infinite essence the less do I comprehend it; but it is, and that is enough for me; the less I understand, the more I adore. I abase myself, saying, 'Being of beings, I am because thou art; to fix my thoughts on thee is to ascend to the source of my being. The best use I can make of my reason is to resign it before thee; my mind delights, my weakness rejoices, to feel myself overwhelmed by thy greatness.'

Having thus deduced from the perception of objects of sense and from my inner consciousness, which leads me to judge of causes by my native reason, the principal truths which I require to know, I must now seek such principles of conduct as I can draw from them, and such rules as I must lay down for my guidance in the fulfilment of my destiny in this world, according to the purpose of my Maker. Still following the same method, I do not derive these rules from the principles of the higher philosophy, I find them in the depths of my heart, traced by nature in characters which nothing can efface. I need only consult myself with regard to what I wish to do; what I feel to be right is right, what I feel to be wrong is wrong; conscience is the best casuist; and it is only when we haggle with conscience that we have recourse to the subtleties of argument.

There is therefore at the bottom of our hearts an innate principle of justice and virtue, by which, in spite of our maxims, we judge our own actions or those of others to be good or evil; and it is this principle that I call conscience.

But it is not enough to be aware that there is such a guide; we must know her and follow her. If she speaks to all hearts, how is it that so few give heed to her voice? She speaks to us in the language of nature, and everything leads us to forget that tongue.

There is an age when the heart is eager, unquiet, greedy of a happiness which is still unknown, a happiness which it seeks, and, deceived by the senses, it settles at length upon the empty show of happiness and thinks it has found it where it is not. These illusions, if they lead me astray, I am at least no longer deceived by them; I know them for what they are, and even when I give way to them, I despise myself; far from regarding them as the goal of my happiness, I behold in them an obstacle to it. I long for the time when, freed from the fetters of the body, I shall be myself, at one with myself, no longer torn in two, when I myself shall suffice for my own happiness. Meanwhile I am happy even in this life, for I make small account of all its evils, in which I regard myself as having little or no part, while all the real good that I can get out of this life depends on myself alone.

To raise myself so far as may be even now to this state of happiness, strength, and freedom, I exercise myself in lofty contemplation. I consider the order of the universe, not to explain it by any futile system, but to revere it without ceasing, to adore the wise Author who reveals himself in it. I hold intercourse with him; I immerse all my powers in his divine essence; I am overwhelmed by his kindness, I bless him and his gifts, but I do not pray to him. What should I ask of him—to change the order of nature, to work miracles on my behalf? Should I, who am bound to love above all things the order which he has established in his wisdom and maintained by his providence, should I desire the disturbance of that order on my own account? No, that rash prayer would deserve to be punished rather than to be granted.

In my well-founded self-distrust the only thing that I ask of God, or rather expect from his justice, is to correct my error if I go astray, if that error is dangerous to me. To be honest I need not think myself infallible; my opinions, which seem to me true, may be so many lies; for what man is there who does not cling to his own beliefs; and how many men are agreed in everything? The illusion which deceives me may indeed have its source in myself, but it is God alone who can remove it. I have done all I can to attain the truth; but its source is beyond my reach.

In my exposition you find nothing but natural religion; strange that we should need more!

Do not let us confuse the outward forms of religion with religion itself. The service God requires is of the heart; and when the heart is sincere that is ever the same.

God desires to be worshipped in spirit and in truth; this duty belongs to every religion, every country, every individual. As to the form of worship, if order demands uniformity, that is only a matter of discipline and needs no revelation.

Let us therefore seek honestly after truth; let us yield nothing to the claims of birth, to the authority of parents and pastors, but let us summon to the bar of conscience and of reason all that they have taught us from our childhood. In vain do they exclaim, 'Submit your reason'; a deceiver might say as much; I must have reasons for submitting my reason.

[77]

Faith is confirmed and strengthened by understanding; the best religion is of necessity the simplest. He who hides beneath mysteries and contradictions the religion that he preaches to me, teaches me at the same time to distrust that religion. The God whom I adore is not the God of darkness, he has not given me understanding in order to forbid me to use it; to tell me to submit my reason is to insult the giver of reason. The minister of truth does not tyrannize over my reason, he enlightens it.

We have three principal forms of religion in Europe. One accepts one revelation, another two, and another three. Each hates the others, showers curses on them, accuses them of blindness, obstinacy, hardness of heart, and falsehood.

In all three revelations the sacred books are written in languages unknown to the people who believe in them.

I can never believe that every man is obliged to know what is contained in books, and that he who is out of reach of these books, and of those who understand them, will be punished for an ignorance which is no fault of his. Were not all these books written by men? Why then should a man need them to teach him his duty, and how did he learn his duty before these books were in existence? Either he must have learnt his duties for himself, or his ignorance must have been excused.

Two-thirds of mankind are neither Jews, Mahometans, nor Christians; and how many millions of men have never heard the name of Moses, Jesus Christ, or Mahomet?

I regard all individual religions as so many wholesome institutions which prescribe a uniform method by which each country may do honour to God in public worship; institutions which may each have its reason in the country, the government, the genius of the people, or in other local causes which make one preferable to another in a given time or place. I think them all good alike, when God is served in a fitting manner. True worship is of the heart. God rejects no homage, however offered, provided it is sincere.

While we await further knowledge, let us respect public order; in every country let us respect the laws, let us not disturb the form of worship prescribed by law; let us not lead its citizens into disobedience; for we have no certain knowledge that it is good for them to abandon their own opinions for others, and on the other hand we are quite certain that it is a bad thing to disobey the law.

Whatever decision you come to, remember that the real duties of religion are independent of human institutions; that a righteous heart is the true temple of the Godhead; that in every land, in every sect, to love God above all things and to love our neighbour as ourself is the whole law; remember there is no religion which absolves us from our moral duties; that these alone are really essential, that the service of the heart is the first of these duties, and that without faith there is no such thing as true virtue.

Shun those who, under the pretence of explaining nature, sow destructive doctrines in the hearts of men, those whose apparent scepticism is a hundredfold more self-assertive and dogmatic than the firm tone of their opponents. Under the arrogant claim, that they alone are enlightened, true, honest, they subject us imperiously to their far-reaching decisions, and profess to give us, as the true principles of all things, the unintelligible systems framed by their imagination. Moreover, they overthrow, destroy, and trample underfoot all that men reverence; they rob the afflicted of their last consolation in their misery; they deprive the rich and powerful of the sole bridle of their passions; they tear from the very depths of man's heart all remorse for crime, and all hope of virtue; and they boast, moreover, that they are the benefactors of the human race. Truth, they say, can never do a man harm. I think so too, and to my mind that is strong evidence that what they teach is not true.[1]

[1] Bayle has proved very satisfactorily that fanaticism is more harmful than atheism, and that cannot be denied; but what he has not taken the trouble to say, though it is none the less true, is this: Fanaticism, though cruel and bloodthirsty, is still a great and powerful passion, which stirs the heart of man, teaching him to despise death, and giving him an enormous motive power, which only needs to be guided rightly to produce the noblest virtues; while irreligion, and the argumentative philosophic spirit generally, on the other hand, assaults the life and enfeebles it, degrades the soul; concentrates all the passions in the basest self-interest, in the meanness of the human self, thus it saps unnoticed the very foundations of all society; for what is common to all these private interests is so small that it will never outweigh their opposing interests.

If atheism does not lead to bloodshed, it is less from love of peace than from indifference to what is good; as if it mattered little what happened to others, provided the sage remained undisturbed in his study. His principles do not kill men, but they prevent their birth, by destroying the morals by which they were multiplied, by detaching them from their fellows, by reducing all their affections to a secret selfishness, as fatal to population as to virtue. The indifference of the philosopher is like the peace in a despotic state; it is the repose of death; war itself is not more destructive.

Thus fanaticism, though its immediate results are more fatal than those of what is now called the philosophic mind, is much less fatal in its after effects.

Be honest and humble; learn how to be ignorant, then you will never deceive yourself or others. If ever your talents are so far cultivated as to enable you to speak to other men, always speak according to your conscience, without caring for their applause. The abuse of knowledge causes incredulity. The learned always despise the opinions of the crowd; each of them must have his own opinion. A haughty philosophy leads to atheism just as blind devotion leads to fanaticism. Avoid these extremes; keep steadfastly to the path of truth, or what seems to you truth, in simplicity of heart, and never let yourself be turned aside by pride or weakness. Dare to confess God before the philosophers; dare to preach humanity to the intolerant. It may be you will stand alone, but you will bear within you a witness which will make the witness of men of no account with you. Let them love or hate, let them read your writings or despise them; no matter. Speak the truth and do the right; the one thing that really matters is to do one's duty in this world; and when we forget ourselves we are really working for ourselves.

JULIE

OR THE NEW HÉLOÏSE

*R*OUSSEAU *had fled from Paris in April* 1756. *He took up his abode in the country, in the little house of the Hermitage, on the edge of the forest of Montmorency. It was spring and Rousseau lived in his dreams.* 'Devoured by a need of loving, which he had never been able to satisfy, he saw himself on the verge of old age and death without ever really having lived,' *Rousseau took pity on himself and indulged his melancholy. His imagination peopled his loneliness with charming beings of his own creation. He imagined to himself* 'the love, the friendship, the two idols of his heart under the most delightful aspect. . . .' *He imagined two friends* 'of similar character, but different . . . not perfect but to his taste, lovingly generous and full of sensibility.' 'I made one dark and the other fair,' *he said,* 'one lively and the other gentle, one wise and the other weak, but of a weakness so touching that it almost became virtue. To one of the two I gave a lover who was the dear friend of the other, and even something more; but I allowed no rivalry, no quarrels, no jealousy, because I wished to spoil nothing of this cheerful picture by anything that degraded nature. Under the sway of my two charming models, I identified myself with the lover and friend; but I made him young and lovable, giving him moreover the virtues and defects which I felt I possessed.—In order to place my personages in a setting suitable to them, I passed over in my mind the most beautiful spots I had seen in my travels. For a long time I thought of the Borromean Islands, whose delightful aspect had transported me; but I found there too much of ornament and art for my personages. Nevertheless I had to have a lake, and I ended by choosing that one around which my heart has never ceased to roam. I decided on the part of this lake (Léman) where I have long fixed my residence in that imaginary happiness to which I have been restricted by my fate. I established my young wards at Vevey. . . . I first jotted down upon paper several scanty letters. . . . The first two parts of the book were written

D* [81]

almost entirely in this manner, without my having any well-formed plan. . . . After much effort, powerless to rid myself of all these imaginings, I delivered myself over entirely to them, and occupied myself in trying to put enough order and continuity in my story to make a novel. . . .' (*Confessions, Book IX.*)

JULIE

OR THE NEW HÉLOÏSE

I AM OF OPINION, WHEN ONCE THE UNDERSTANDING IS A LITTLE developed by reflection, it is better to reason for ourselves than to depend upon books for the discovery of truth; for by that means it will make a much stronger impression; whilst on the contrary, by taking things for granted, we view objects by halves and in a borrowed light. We are richer than we think; yet, says Montaigne, our whole education consists in borrowing. We are taught rather to use the wealth of other men than break into our own store.

The grand error of young students is a too implicit dependence upon books, and too much diffidence in their own capacity; without reflecting that they are much less liable to be misled by their own reason, than by the sophistry of systematical writers. If we would but consult our own feelings, we should easily distinguish virtue and beauty: we do not want to be taught either of these; but examples of extreme virtue and superlative beauty are less common, and these are therefore more difficult to be understood. Our vanity leads us to mistake our own peculiar imbecility for that of nature and to think those qualities chimerical which we do not perceive within ourselves; idleness and vice rest upon pretended impossibility, and men of little genius conclude that things which are uncommon have no existence. These errors we must endeavour to eradicate, and by using ourselves to contemplate grand objects, destroy the notion of their impossibility. Thus by degrees, our emulation is roused by example, our taste refines, and everything indifferent becomes intolerable.

But let us not have recourse to books for principles which may be found within ourselves. What have we to do with the idle disputes of philosophers concerning virtue and happiness? Let us rather employ that time in being virtuous and happy, which others waste in fruitless inquiries after the means: let us rather imitate great examples, than busy ourselves with systems and opinions.

I always believed that virtue was in reality active beauty; or

[83]

at least that they were intimately connected, and sprang from the same source in nature. From this idea it follows that wisdom and taste are to be improved by the same means, and that a mind truly sensible of the charms of virtue must receive an equal impression from every other kind of beauty. Yet accurate and refined perception are to be acquired only by habit; and hence it is that we see a painter, in viewing a fine prospect or a good picture, in raptures at certain objects, which a common observer would not even have seen. How many real impressions do we perceive, which we cannot account for? how many *je-ne-sais-quoi* frequently occur, which taste only can determine? Taste is, in some degree, the microscope of judgment; it brings small objects to our view, and its operations begin where those of judgment end. How then shall we proceed in its cultivation? By exercising our sight as well as feeling, and by judgment of the beautiful from inspection, as we judge of virtue from sensation.

In what is called honour, there is a material distinction between that which is founded on the opinion of the world, and that which is derived from self-esteem. The first is nothing but the loud voice of foolish prejudice, which has no more stability than the wind; but the basis of the latter is fixed in the eternal truth of morality. The honour of the world may be of advantage with regard to fortune; but as it cannot reach the soul, it has no influence on real happiness. True honour, on the contrary, is the very essence of felicity; for it is that alone that inspires the permanent interior satisfaction which constitutes the happiness of a rational being.

What wretch dares preach that virtue which he will not practise? Whosoever suffers himself to be thus blinded by his passions will soon find himself punished in a loathing for those very sensations to which he sacrificed his honour. There can be no pleasure in any enjoyment which the heart cannot approve, and which tends to sink in our estimation the object of our love. Abstract the idea of perfection and our enthusiasm vanishes; take away our esteem, and love is at an end. How is it possible for a woman to honour a man who dishonours himself? and how can he adore the person who was weak enough to abandon herself to a vile seducer? Mutual contempt therefore is the consequence; their very passions will grow burdensome, and they will have lost their honour without finding happiness.

Ah, Julie, too much sensibility, too much tenderness, proves the bitterest curse instead of the most fruitful blessing: vexation and disappointment are its certain consequences. The temperature of the air, the change of the seasons, the brilliancy of the sun, or thickness of the fogs, are so many moving springs to the unhappy possessor, and he becomes the wanton sport of their arbitration: his thoughts, his satisfaction, his happiness depend on the blowing of the winds. Swayed as he is by prejudices, and distracted by passions, the sentiments of his heart find continual opposition from the axioms of his head. Should he perchance square his conduct to the undeviable rule of right, and set up truth for his standard, instead of profit and convenience, he is sure to fall a martyr to the maxims of his integrity; the world will join in the cry, and hunt him down as a common enemy. He will search for supreme happiness, without taking into account the infirmities of his nature; thus his affections and his reason will be engaged in a perpetual warfare, and unbounded ideas and desires must pave the way for endless disappointments.

Forbear then to give way to a self disesteem more dangerous and destructive than any weakness of which you could be guilty. Does true love debase the soul? No: nor can any crime, which is the result of that love, ever rob you of that enthusiastic ardour for truth and honour, which so raised you above yourself.

True love is the chastest of all human connections; and the sacred flame of love should purify our natural inclinations by concentring them in one object. It is love that secures us from temptation, and makes the whole sex indifferent, except the beloved individual. To a woman indifferent to love, every man is the same, and all are men; but to her whose heart is truly susceptible of that refined passion, there is no other man in the world but her lover. What do I say? Is a lover no more than a man? He is a being far superior! There exists not a man in the creation with her who truly loves: her lover is more, and all others are less; they live for each other, and are the only beings of their species. They have no desires; they love. The heart is not led by, but leads the senses, and throws over their errors the veil of delight. There is nothing obscene but in lewdness and its gross language. Real love, always modest, seizes not impudently its favours, but steals them with timidity. Its flame purifies all caresses.

Can we be deprived of virtues we really possess by false aspersions of calumny? Do the insults of a drunken man prove such insults deserved? Or does the honour of the virtuous and prudent lie at the mercy of the first brute he meets? Will you tell me that fighting a duel shows a man to have courage, and that this is sufficient to efface the dishonour, and prevent the reproach, due to all other vices? I would ask you, what kind of honour can dictate such a decision? Or what arguments justify it? On such principles a knave needs only fight to cease to be a knave; the assertions of a liar become true when they are maintained at the point of the sword; and, if you were even accused of killing a man, you have only to kill a second, to prove the accusation false. Thus virtue, vice, honour, infamy, truth, and falsehood all derive their existence from the event of a duel. There is no other law than violence, no other argument than murder: all the reparation due to the insulted, is to kill them, and every offence is equally washed away by the blood of the offender or the offended. If wolves themselves could reason, would they entertain maxims more inhuman than these?

Beware then of confounding the sacred name of honour with that barbarous prejudice, which subjects every virtue to the decision of the sword, and is only adapted to make men daring villains. Do you not see that the crimes which shame and a sense of honour have not prevented, are screened and multiplied by a false shame and the fear of reproach? It is this fear which makes men hypocrites and liars: it is this which makes them imbrue their hands in the blood of their friends, for an indiscreet word, which should have been forgotten, for a merited reproach too severe to be borne. It is this which transforms the abused and fearful maid into an infernal fury.

Do you know any crime equal to wilful murder? If humanity also be the basis of every virtue, what must be thought of the man whose bloodthirsty and depraved disposition prompts him to seek the life of his fellow-creature?

What though it be true, that a man is despised who refuses to fight; which contempt is most to be feared, that of others for doing well, or that of ourselves for having acted ill? He who has a proper esteem for himself is little sensible to the unjust reproach cast on him by others, and is only afraid of deserving it. Probity and virtue depend not on the opinion of the world, but on the nature of things; and though all mankind should approve of the action you are about, it would not be the less shameful in itself. But it is a false notion, that to refrain from it, through a virtuous motive, would be bringing yourself into contempt. The virtuous man, whose whole life is irreproachable, and who never betrayed any marks of cowardice, will refuse to stain his hands with blood, and will be only the more respected for such refusal. Always ready to serve his country, to protect the weak, to discharge his duty on the most dangerous occasions, and to defend in every just and reasonable cause whatever is dear to him, at the hazard of his life, he displays throughout the whole of his conduct that unshaken fortitude, which is inseparable from true courage. Animated by the testimony of a good conscience, he appears undaunted, and neither flies from, nor seeks, his enemy. It is easily observed that he fears less to die than to act basely; that he dreads the crime, but not the danger. If at any time the mean prejudices of the world raise a clamour against him, the conduct of his whole life is his testimony, and every action is approved by a behaviour so uniformly irreproachable.

I would have courage exerted only on lawful occasions, and not an idle parade made of it when it is unnecessary, as if there was some fear of not having it ready when it should be called for. There are cowards who will make one effort to exert their courage, that they may have a pretence to avoid danger the rest of their lives. True courage is more constant and less impetuous; it is always what it ought to be, and wants neither the spur nor the rein; the man of real magnanimity carries it always about him; in fighting he exerts it against his enemy; in company against backbiting and falsehood, and on a sickbed against the attacks of pain and the horrors of death. That fortitude of mind which inspires true courage is always exerted; it places virtue out of the reach of events, and does not consist in braving danger, but in not fearing it.

All other pretences to bravery are wild, extravagant, and brutal; it is even cowardice to submit to them; and I despise as much the man who runs himself into needless danger, as him who turns his back on what he ought to encounter.

All this, added to my natural aversion to cruelty, fills me with such horror at duels, that I regard them as instances of the lowest degree of brutality into which mankind can possibly descend. I look upon those who go cheerfully to a duel in no other light than as wild beasts going to tear each other to pieces; and if there remain the least sentiments of humanity within them, I think the murdered less to be pitied than the murderer.

How many great families would sink into oblivion, if we respected only those which descended from truly respectable originals? Judge of the past by the present: for two or three honest citizens ennobled by virtuous means, a thousand knaves find every day the way to aggrandize themselves and families. But to what end serves that nobility of which their descendants are so proud unless it be to prove the injustice and infamy of their ancestors? There are, I must confess, a great number of bad men among the common people; but the odds are always twenty to one against a gentleman, that he is descended from a rascal.

In what consists the honour, then, of that nobility of which you are so tenacious? How does it affect the glory of one's country or the good of mankind? A mortal enemy to liberty and the laws, what did it ever produce in most of those countries where it has flourished, but the rod of tyranny and the oppression of the people?

Justice and the fitness of things require that everyone should be disposed of in a manner the most advantageous to himself and to society. These two amiable minds were doubtless formed by the hands of nature for each other. In a peaceful and happy union, at liberty to exert their talents and display their virtues, they might have enlightened the world with the splendour of their examples. Why should an absurd prejudice, then, cross the eternal directions of nature, and subvert the harmony of thinking Beings? Why should the vanity of a cruel father thus hide their light under a bushel, and wound those tender and benevolent hearts, which were formed to soothe the pangs of others? Are not the ties of marriage the most free, as well as the most sacred of all engagements? Yes, every law to lay a constraint on them is unjust. Every father, who presumes to form or break them, is a tyrant. This chaste and holy tie of nature is neither subjected to sovereign power nor paternal authority; but to the authority only of that common parent who hath the power over our hearts, and, by commanding their union, can at the same time make them love each other.

To what end are natural conveniences sacrificed to those of opinion? A disagreement in rank and fortune loses itself in marriage, nor doth any equality therein tend to make the marriage state happy; but a disagreement in person and disposition ever remains, and is that which makes it necessarily miserable. A child that hath no rule of conduct but her fond passion, will frequently make a bad choice; but the father who has no other rule for his than the opinion of the world, will make a worse. A daughter may want knowledge and experience to form a proper judgment of the discretion and conduct of men; a good father ought doubtless in that case to advise her. He has a right, it is even his duty to say, 'My child, this is a man of probity, or that man is a knave. This is a man of sense, or that is a fool.' Thus far ought the father to judge, the rest belongs to the daughter. The tyrants, who exclaim that such maxims tend to disturb the good order of society, are those who, themselves, disturb it most. Let men rank according to their merit; and let those hearts be united, that are objects of each other's choice. This is what the good order of society requires; those who would confine it to birth or riches are the real disturbers of that order; and ought to be rendered odious to the public, or punished, as enemies to society.

Justice requires that such abuses should be redressed; it is the duty of every man to set himself in opposition to violence, and to strengthen the bonds of society.

If love be not predominant, prudence only directs the choice; if passion prevail, nature has already determined it. So sacred is the law of nature, that no human being is permitted to transgress it, or can transgress it with impunity; nor can any consideration of rank or fortune abrogate it, without involving mankind in guilt and misfortune.

I will content myself to recommend to you two things. Be virtuous and remember Julie.

I will not make use of any of those subtle arguments you have taught me to despise; and which, though they fill so many volumes, never yet made one man virtuous. Peace to those gloomy reasoners! To what ravishing delights their hearts are strangers! Leave, my friend, those idle moralists and consult your own breast. It is there you will always find a spark of sacred fire, which hath so often inflamed us with love for the sublimest virtue. It is there you will trace the lasting image of true beauty, the contemplation of which inspires us with a sacred enthusiasm; an image which the passions may continually defile, but never can efface. . . . Would you know which is most truly desirable, riches or virtue? Think on that which interests us most in the perusal of history. Did you never covet the riches of Crœsus, the honours of Cæsar, the power of Nero, nor the pleasures of Heliogabalus? If they were happy, why did you not wish to be placed in the same situation? But they were not, you were sensible they were not happy; you were sensible they were vile and contemptible; and that bad men, however fortunate, are not objects of envy. What characters did you then contemplate with the greatest pleasure? What examples did you most admire? Which did you most desire to imitate? Inexpressible are the charms of ever-blooming virtue: it was the condemned Athenian drinking hemlock; it was Brutus, dying for his country; it was Regulus, in the midst of tortures; it was Cato, plunging his dagger in his breast. Those were the unfortunate heroes whose virtues excited your envy, while your own sensations bore witness of that real felicity they enjoyed, under their apparent misfortunes. Think not this sentiment peculiar to yourself; it is the sentiment of all mankind, and that frequently in spite of themselves. That divine image of virtue, imprinted universally on the mind, displays irresistible charms even to the least virtuous. No sooner doth passion permit us to contemplate its beauty, but we wish to resemble it; and if the most wicked of mankind could but change his being, he would choose to be virtuous.

But though it is not expected you should be put to the trials of a Cato, or a Regulus, yet every man ought to cherish a love for his country, resolution and integrity, and to keep his promise inviolable, even at the expense of his life. Private virtues are often the more sublime, as they less aspire to public approbation, but have their end in the testimony of a good conscience, which gives the virtuous a more solid satisfaction than the loudest applauses of the multitude. Hence you may see true greatness is confined to no one station of life, and that no man can be happy who is not the object of his own esteem.

I am convinced it is not good for man to be alone. Human minds must be united to exert their greatest strength, and the united force of friendly souls like that of the collateral bars of an artificial magnet, is incomparably greater than the sum of their separate forces. This is thy triumph, celestial friendship! But what is even friendship itself compared to that perfect union of souls which connects the most perfect, the most harmonious amity, with ties a hundred times more sacred? Where are the men whose ideas, gross as their appetites, represent the passion of love only as a fever in the blood, the effect of brutal instinct?

I enter with a secret horror on this vast desert, the world; whose confused prospect appears to me only as a frightful scene of solitude and silence. In vain my soul endeavours to shake off the universal restraint it lies under. It was the saying of a celebrated ancient that he was never less alone than when he was by himself: for my part, I am never alone but when I mix with the crowd, and am neither with you nor with anybody else. My heart would speak, but it feels there is none to hear: it is ready to answer, but no one speaks anything that regards it. I understand not the language of the country, and nobody here understands mine.

They talk about everything because everyone has something to say; they examine nothing to the bottom, for fear of being tedious, but propose matters in a cursory manner, and treat them with rapidity: everyone gives his opinion and supports it in a few words; no one attacks with virulence that of another, nor obstinately defends his own; they discuss the point only for the sake of improvement, and stop before it comes to a dispute: everyone improves, everyone amuses himself, and they all part satisfied with each other; even the philosopher himself carrying away something worthy his private meditation.

But, after all, what kind of knowledge do you think is to be gained from such agreeable conversation? To form a just judgment of life and manners; to make a right use of society; to know, at least, the people with whom we converse; there is nothing, Julie, of all this: all they teach is to plead artfully the cause of falsehood, to confound by their philosophy, all the principles of virtue; to throw a false colour, by the help of sophistry, on the passions and prejudices of mankind; and to give a certain turn to error, agreeable to the fashionable mode of thinking. It is not necessary to know the characters of men, but their interests, to guess their sentiments on any occasion. When a man talks on any subject, he rather expresses the opinions of his garb or his fraternity, than his own, and will change them as often as he changes his situation and circumstances. Thus men do not speak their own sentiments, but those they would instil into others, and the zeal which they affect is only the mask of interest.

You may imagine, however, that such persons as are unconnected and independent have, at least, a personal character and an opinion of their own. Not at all, they are only different machines, which never think for themselves, but are set a-going by springs.

As everyone considers his own particular interest, and none of them that of the public, and as the interests of individuals are always opposed, there is amongst them a perpetual clashing of parties and cabals, a continual ebb and flow of prepossessions and contrary opinions. Every club has its rules, its opinions, its principles, which are nowhere else admitted. An honest man at one house is a knave at the next door. The good, the bad, the beautiful, the ugly, truth, and even virtue itself have all only a limited and local existence. Such are the notions I have formed of great societies.

It was not the French in particular on whom I intended to animadvert. For if the characters of nations can be determined only by their difference, how can I, who have as yet no acquaintance with any other, pretend to draw the character of this? I should not besides have been so indifferent as to fix on the metropolis for the place of observation. I am not ignorant that capital cities differ less from each other, than the national characters of the people, which are there in a great measure lost and confounded, as well from the influence of courts, all which bear a great resemblance to each other, as from the common consequence of living in a close and numerous society, which is everywhere nearly the same for all men, and prevails over the original and peculiar character of the country.

Were I to study the national characteristics of a people, I would repair to some of the more distant provinces, where the inhabitants still pursue their natural inclinations. I would proceed slowly and carefully through several of those provinces, and those at greatest distance from each other: from the difference

I might observe between them, I would then trace the peculiar genius of each province; from what was theirs in common and not customary to other countries, I would trace the genius of the nation in general, and what appeared common to all nations, I should regard as characteristics of mankind in general.

The only way to come at the true manners of a nation is to study the private life of the most numerous order among them; for to confine your observations to those who only personate assumed characters, is only to observe the actions of a company of comedians.

How comes it that in so opulent a city the poor people are so miserable? This question is well worth your asking: but it is not the people you converse with that are to resolve it. It is in the splendid apartments of the rich that the novice goes to learn the manners of the world; but the man of sense and experience betakes himself to the cottages of the poor. These are the places for the detection of those iniquitous practices, that in polite circles are varnished over, and hid beneath a specious show of words. These are the places where one learns by what base and secret arts the rich and powerful snatch a crumb of black bread from the oppressed whom they feign to pity in public. You will learn many things in the garrets of a fifth floor, which are buried in profound silence in the suburbs of St. Germain! You will find that many fine talkers would be struck dumb, if all those they have made unhappy were present to contradict their boasted pretensions to humanity.

I know the sight of misery that excites only fruitless pity is disagreeable; and that even the rich turn away their eyes from the unhappy objects to whom they refuse relief: but money is not the only thing the unfortunate stand in need of; and they are but indolent in well-doing who can exert themselves only with their purse in their hands. Consolation, advice, concern, friends, protection, these are all so many resources which compassion points out to those who are not rich, for the relief of the indigent. The oppressed often stand in need only of a tongue, to make known their complaints. They often want no more than a word they cannot speak, a reason they are ashamed to give, entrance at the door of a great man which they cannot obtain. The intrepid countenance of disinterested virtue may remove infinite obstacles, and the eloquence of a man of probity makes even a tyrant tremble in the midst of his guards.

If you would then act as a man, learn to descend again. Humanity, like a poor salutary stream, flows always downwards to its level; fertilizing the humble vales, while it leaves dry those barren rocks, whose threatening heads cast a frightful shade, or tumbling headlong down involve the plain in ruins.

True love, as well as virtue, has this advantage, that it is rewarded by every sacrifice we make to it, and that we in some measure enjoy the privations we impose on ourselves, in the very idea of what they cost us, and of the motives by which we were induced.

Besides, if it is true that love is the most delightful sensation that can enter into the human heart, everything that prolongs and fixes it, even at the expense of a thousand vexations, is still a blessing. If love is a desire, that is increased by obstacles, it ought never to be satisfied; it is better to preserve it, at any rate, than that it should be extinguished in pleasure.

The idea of extinguished love is more terrifying to a tender heart, than that of an unhappy flame; and to feel a disgust for what we possess, is an hundred times worse than regretting what is lost.

I invoked that Being enthroned on high, whose pleasure supports or destroys, by means of our own strength, what free-will he has bestowed. 'I eagerly,' said I, 'embrace the proffered good, of which thou art alone the author. I will be faithful because it is the chief duty which unites private families and society in general. I will be chaste, because it is the parent virtue which nourishes all the rest. I will adhere to everything relative to the order of nature which thou hast established, and to the dictates of reason which I derive from thee. I recommend my heart to thy protection, and my desires to thy guidance. Render all my actions conformable to my steadfast will, which is ever thine, and never more permit momentary error to triumph over the settled choice of my life.'

Having finished this short prayer, I clearly perceived where I must hereafter resort for that power to resist my inclinations, which I could not derive from myself. I had never been devoid of religion, but perhaps I had better have been wholly so, than to have possessed one which was external and mechanical; and which falsified the conscience without affecting the heart; one which was confined to set forms; and taught me to believe in God at stated hours, without thinking of him the remainder of my time.

Adore the Supreme Being, my worthy and prudent friend; with one puff of breath you will be able to dissipate those chimeras of reason which have a visionary appearance and which fly like so many shadows, before immutable truth. Nothing exists but through him, who is self-existent; it is he who directs the tendency of justice, fixes the basis of virtue, and gives a recompense to a short life spent according to his will; it is he who proclaims aloud to the guilty that their secret crimes are detected, and gives assurance to the righteous in obscurity, that their virtues are not without witness; it is he, it is his inalterable substance that is the true model of those perfections, of which we all bear the image within us. It is in vain that our passions disfigure it; its traces which are allied to the Infinite Being, ever present themselves to our reason, and serve to re-establish what error and imposture have perverted. These distinctions seem to me extremely natural; common sense is sufficient to point them out. Everything which we cannot separate from the idea of divine essence, is God, all the rest is the work of men. It is by the contemplation of this divine model that the soul becomes refined and exalted, that it learns to despise low desires, and to triumph over base inclinations. A heart impressed with these sublime truths is superior to the mean passions of human nature; the idea of infinite grandeur subdues the pride of man; the delight of contemplation abstracts him from gross desires; and if the immense Being who is the subject of his thoughts had no existence, it would nevertheless be of use to exercise his mind in such meditations, in order to make him more master of himself, more vigorous, more discreet and more happy.

Do you require a particular instance of those vain subtleties framed by that self-sufficient reason, which only relies on its own strength? Let us examine the arguments of those philosophers, those worthy advocates of a crime. Might one not conclude that, by a direct attack of the most holy and most solemn of all contracts, these dangerous disputants were determined at one stroke to annihilate human society in general, which is founded on the faith of engagements? But let us consider how they exculpate secret adultery. It is because, say they, no mischief arises from it; not even to the husband, who is ignorant of the wrong. But can they be certain that he will always remain ignorant of the injury offered him? Is it sufficient to authorize perjury and infidelity, that they do no wrong to others? Is the mischief which the guilty do to themselves not sufficient to create an abhorrence of guilt? Is it no crime to be false to our word, to destroy, as far as we are able, the obligation of oaths and the most inviolable contracts? Is it no crime to form attachments, which occasion you to desire the misfortune, and to wish the death of another? Even the death of one whom we ought to love above others, and with whom we have sworn to live? Is not that state in itself an evil, which is productive of a thousand consequential crimes? Even good itself, if attended with so many mischiefs, would, for that reason only, be an evil.

It is not only the interest of husband and wife, but it is the common benefit of mankind, that the purity of marriage be preserved unsullied. The public are in some measure guarantees of a contract which passes in their presence; and we may venture to say that the honour of a modest woman is under the special protection of all good and worthy people. Whoever therefore dares to seduce her, sins; first because he has tempted her to sin, and that everyone is an accomplice in those crimes which he persuades others to commit; in the next place, he sins directly himself, because he violates the public and sacred faith of matrimony, without which no order or regularity can subsist in society.

The crime, say they, is secret consequently no injury can result from it to anyone. If these philosophers believe in the existence of a God and the immortality of the soul, can they call that crime secret which has for its witness the Being principally offended and the only righteous judge? . . . If they do not however admit the omnipresence of the Divinity, yet how can they dare affirm that they do injury to no one? How can they prove that it is a matter of indifference to a parent to educate heirs who are strangers to his blood; to be encumbered perhaps with more children than he would otherwise have had, and to be obliged to distribute his fortune among those pledges of his dishonour, without feeling for them any sensations of parental tenderness and natural affection? If we suppose these philosophers to be materialists, we have then a stronger foundation for opposing their tenets by the gentle dictates of nature, which plead in every breast against the principles of a vain philosophy. In short, if the body alone produces cogitation, and sentiment depends entirely on organs, will there not be a strict analogy between two beings of the same blood; will they not have a more violent attachment to each other?

Is it doing no injury therefore, in your opinion, to destroy or disturb this natural union by the mixing of adulterate blood, and to pervert the principle of that mutual affection, which ought to cement all the members of one family? Who would not shudder with horror at the thought of having one infant changed for another by a nurse? and is it a less crime to make such a change before the infant is born?

With regard to the pretended connections which may be formed in families by means of adultery and infidelity, it cannot be considered as a serious argument, but rather as an absurd and brutal mockery, which deserves no other answer than disdain and indignation. The treasons, the quarrels, the battles, the murders, with which this irregularity has in all ages pestered the earth, are sufficient proofs how far the peace and union of mankind is to be promoted by attachments founded in guilt. If any social principle results from this vile and despicable commerce, it may be compared to that which invites a band of robbers, and which ought to be destroyed and annulled, in order to ensure the safety of lawful communities.

Every man has a right by nature to pursue what he thinks good, and avoid what he thinks evil, in all respects which are not injurious to others. When our life therefore becomes a misery to ourselves, and is of advantage to no one, we are at liberty to put an end to our being.

Let us hear what the philosophers say on this subject. First, they consider life as something which is not our own, because we hold it as a gift; but because it has been given to us, it is for that reason our own. Has not God given these sophists two arms? Nevertheless, when they are under fear of gangrene, they do not scruple to amputate one, or both if it is necessary.

They consider a man living upon earth as a soldier placed

on duty. God, say they, has fixed you in this world: why do you quit it without his leave? But you who argue thus, has he not stationed you in the town where you were born; why therefore do you quit it without his leave? Is not misery, of itself, a sufficient permission? Whatever station Providence has assigned me, whether it be in a regiment, or on the earth at large, he intended me to stay there while I found my station agreeable, and to leave it when it became intolerable. This is the voice of nature and the voice of God. I agree that we must wait for an order; but when I die a natural death, God does not order me to quit life, he takes it from me: it is by rendering life insupportable that he orders me to quit it. In the first case, I resist with all my force; in the second, I have the merit of obedience.

The grand error lies in making life of too much importance; as if our existence depended on it, and that death was a total annihilation. Our life is of no consequence in the sight of God; it is of no importance in the eyes of reason, neither ought it to be of any in our sight; and when we quit our body, we only lay aside an inconvenient habit.

The same sophists make it a question whether life can ever be an evil. But when we consider the multitude of errors, torments and vices with which it abounds, one would rather be inclined to doubt whether it can ever be a blessing. Guilt incessantly besieges the most virtuous of mankind. Every moment he lives, he is in danger of falling a prey to the wicked, or of being wicked himself. To struggle, and to endure, is his lot in this world; that of the dishonest man is to do evil, and to suffer. What is the chief occupation of a wise man in his life, but, if I may be allowed the expression, to collect himself inwardly and endeavour, even while he lives, to be dead to every object of sense? The only way by which wisdom directs us to avoid the miseries of human nature, is it not to detach ourselves from all earthly objects, from everything that is gross in our composition, to retire within ourselves, and to raise our thoughts to sublime contemplations? If therefore our misfortunes are derived from our passions and our errors, with what eagerness should we wish for a state which will deliver us from both the one and the other?

But admitting it, in general, a benefit to mankind to crawl upon the earth with gloomy sadness; I do not mean to intimate that the human race ought with one common consent to destroy themselves, and make the world one immense grave. While life is agreeable to us, we earnestly wish to prolong it, and nothing but a sense of extreme misery can extinguish the desire of existence; for we naturally conceive a violent dread of death, and this dread conceals the miseries of human nature from our sight. We drag a painful and melancholy life for a long time before we can resolve to quit it; but when once life becomes so unsupportable as to overcome the horror of death, then existence is evidently a great evil, and we cannot disengage ourselves from it too soon. Therefore, though we cannot exactly ascertain the point at which it ceases to be a blessing, yet at least we are certain that it is an evil long before it appears to be such, and with every sensible man the right of quitting life is by a great deal precedent to the temptation.

That is not all. After they have denied that life can be an evil, in order to bar our right of making away with ourselves, they confess immediately afterwards that it is an evil, by reproaching us with want of courage to support it. According to them it is cowardice to withdraw ourselves from pain and trouble, and they are none but dastards who destroy themselves. O Rome! thou victrix of the world, what a race of cowards did thy empire produce! Brutus, Cassius, and thou, great and divine Cato! That paltry rhetoricians should ever attempt to prove that thou wert a coward, for having preferred death to a shameful existence!

Without doubt, it is an evidence of great fortitude to bear with firmness the misery which we cannot shun; none but a fool, however, will voluntarily endure evils which he cannot avoid without a crime, to suffer pain unnecessarily. He who has not resolution to deliver himself from a miserable being by a speedy death, is like one who would rather suffer a wound to mortify than trust to the surgeon's knife for a cure.

Why should we be allowed to cure ourselves of the gout, and not to get rid of the misery of life? Do not both evils proceed from the same hand? Let them prove therefore that it is more justifiable to cure a transient disorder by the application of remedies, than to free ourselves from an incurable evil by putting an end to life. If we consider the object in view, it is in both cases to free ourselves from painful sensations; if we regard the means, both one and the other are equally natural; if we attend to the will of Providence, can we struggle against any evil, of which he is not the author? Can we deliver ourselves from any torment which his hand has not inflicted? What are the bounds which limit his power, and when is resistance lawful? Are we then to make no alteration in the condition of things, because everything is in the state he appointed? Must we do nothing in this life for fear of infringing his laws, or is it in our power to break them if we would? No, the occupation of man is more great and noble. God did not give him life that he should remain supinely in a state of constant inactivity. But he gave him freedom to act, conscience to will, and reason to choose what is good. He has constituted him sole judge of all his actions. He has engraved the precept in his heart, ' Do whatever you conceive to be for your own good, provided you thereby do injury to no one.' If my sensations tell me that death is eligible, I resist his orders by an obstinate resolution to live, for by making death desirable, he directs me to put an end to my being.

According to you, you have a right to put an end to your being. Your proof is of a very singular nature; 'Because I am disposed to die,' say you, 'I have a right to destroy myself.' This is certainly a very convenient argument for villains of all kinds: they ought to be very thankful to you for the arms with which you have furnished them; there can be no crimes, which, according to your arguments, may not be justified by the temptation to perpetrate them, and as soon as the impetuosity of passion shall prevail over the horror of guilt, their disposition to do evil will be considered as a right to commit it.

Is it lawful therefore for you to quit life? What! Were you placed here on earth to do nothing in this world? Did not heaven, when it gave you existence, give you some task or employment? If you have accomplished your day's work before evening, rest yourself for the remainder of the day, you have a right to do it; but let us see your work. What answer are you prepared to make the supreme judge, when he demands an account of your time? Thou unhappy wretch! Point out to me that just man who can boast that he has lived long enough; let me learn from him in what manner I ought to have spent my days, to be at liberty to quit life.

You say: 'Life is an evil.' But search, examine into the order of things; and see whether you can find any good which is not intermingled with evil. Does it therefore follow that there is no good in the universe, and can you confound what is in its own nature evil, with that which is only an evil accidentally? You have confessed yourself, that the transitory and passive life of man is of no consequence and only bears respect to matter from which he will soon be disencumbered; but his active and moral life, which ought to have most influence over his nature, consists in the exercise of free will. Life is an evil to a wicked man in prosperity, and a blessing to an honest man in distress; for it is not its casual modification, but its relation to some final object, which makes it either good or bad.

You are weary of living; and you say: 'Life is an evil.' Sooner or later you will receive consolation, and then you will say: 'Life is a blessing.' You will speak more truth, though not with better reason; for nothing will have altered but yourself. Begin the alteration then from this day, and since all the evil you lament is in the disposition of your own mind, correct your irregular appetites and do not set your house on fire, to avoid the trouble of putting it in order.

'I endure misery,' say you; 'is it in my power to avoid suffering?' You are wretched, you naturally endeavour to extricate yourself from misery. Let us see whether, for that purpose, it is necessary to die. . . . Quiet, disquietude, regret and despair, are evils of short duration, which never take root in the mind, and experience always falsifies that bitter reflection, which makes us imagine our misery will have no end. I will go further; I cannot imagine that the vices which contaminate us are more inherent in our nature than the troubles we endure; I not only believe that they perish with the body that gives them birth, but I think, beyond all doubt, that a longer life would be sufficient to reform mankind, and that many ages of youth would teach us that nothing is preferable to virtue.

However this may be, as the greatest part of our physical evils are incessantly increasing, the acute pains of the body, when they are incurable, may justify a man's destroying himself; for all his faculties being distracted with pain, he ceases to be a man before he is dead, and does nothing more in taking away his life than quit a body which encumbers him, and in which his soul is no longer resident.

But it is otherwise with the afflictions of the mind; which let them be ever so acute, always carry their remedy with them. In fact, what is it that makes any evil tolerable? nothing but its duration. What occasion is there therefore for any operation to remove troubles which die of course by their duration, the only circumstance which could render them supportable? Have patience, and you will be cured.

Oh! you will say, it doubles my afflictions, to reflect that they will cease at last! This is the vain sophistry of grief! an apophthegm void of reason, or propriety, and perhaps of sincerity. What an absurd motive of despair is the hope of terminating misery. And admitting any charm in grief, to make us in love with suffering, when we release ourselves from it by putting an end to our being, do we not at that instant incur all that we apprehend hereafter?

Reflect thoroughly, young man; what are ten, twenty, thirty years, in comparison with immortality? Pain and pleasure pass like a shadow! Life slides away in an instant; it is nothing of itself; its value depends on the use we make of it. The good that we have done is all that remains, and it is that alone which marks its importance.

You talk of the duties of a magistrate, and of a father of a family; and because you are not under those circumstances, you think yourself absolutely free. And you are then under no obligations to society, to whom you are indebted for your preservation, your talents, your understanding: do you owe nothing to your native country, and to those wretches who may need your assistance? Among the obligations you have enumerated, you have only omitted those of a man and a citizen.

You endeavour to justify yourself by examples. You presume to mention the Romans! Tell me, did Brutus die a lover in despair, and did Cato tear out his entrails for his mistress? Thou weak and abject man, what resemblance is there between Cato and thee?

How meanly you judge of the Romans, if you imagine that they thought themselves at liberty to quit life so soon as it became a burden to them. When Rome was no more, it was lawful for the Romans to give up their lives; they had discharged their duties on earth, they had no longer any country to defend, they were therefore at liberty to dispose of their lives, and to obtain that freedom for themselves which they could not recover for their country. Their death was an additional tribute to the glory of the Roman name, since none of them beheld a sight above all others most dishonourable, that of a true citizen stooping to an usurper.

But thou, what art thou? What hast thou done? Know that a

death such as you meditate is shameful and surreptitious. It is a theft committed on mankind in general. Before you quit life, return the benefits you have received from every individual. But, say you, I have no attachments, I am useless in the world. O thou young philosopher! art thou ignorant that thou canst not move a single step without finding some duty to fulfil; and that every man is useful to society, even by means of his existence alone?

What a pleasing and affecting scene is a simple and well-regulated family, where order, peace, and innocence reign throughout; where, without pomp or retinue, everything is assembled which can contribute to the real felicity of mankind!

It is no longer a house for show, but for convenience. Everything here is pleasant and agreeable; everything breathes an air of plenty and propriety, without an appearance of pomp and luxury. They have throughout substituted the useful in the place of the agreeable, and yet the agreeable has gained by the alteration.

Having a great deal of land, which they cultivate with the utmost industry, they require, besides the servants in the yard, a great number of day labourers, which procures them the pleasure of maintaining a great number of people without any inconvenience to themselves.

Mme de Wolmar does not think it sufficient to reward their industry by giving them money, but she thinks herself bound to do further services to those who have contributed to hers. Labourers, domestics, all who serve her, if it be but for a day, become her children.

Here, the choice of domestics is considered as an article of importance. They do not regard them merely as mercenaries, from whom they only require a stipulated service, but as members of a family, which, should they be ill-chosen, might be ruined by that means. The first thing they require of them is to be honest, the next is to love their master, and the third to serve him to his liking. They employ some days in teaching them their duty with a great deal of care and patience. The service is so simple, so equal and so uniform, the master and mistress are so little subject to whims and caprice, and the servants so soon conceive an affection for them, that their business is soon learned. Their condition is agreeable, but they are not suffered to be enervated by idleness, the parent of all vice.

When a domestic first enters into their service, he receives the common wages; but those wages are augmented every year by a twentieth part: so that at the end of twenty years, they will be more than doubled. This is a certain expedient of making servants grow continually more and more careful, and of attaching them to you by attaching yourself to them. There is not only prudence but justice in such a provision.

Though there is but one table among all the servants, yet there is but little communication between the men and the women, and this they consider as a point of great importance. Too close a connection between the two sexes frequently occasions mischief.

They do not, to prevent any dangerous intimacy between the two sexes, restrain them by positive rules which they might be tempted to violate in secret, but without seeming intention they establish good customs, which are more powerful than authority itself. They do not forbid any intercourse between them, but it is contrived in such a manner that they have no occasion or inclination to see each other. This is effectuated by making their business, their habits, their tastes, and their pleasures entirely different. Julie insists that neither love nor conjugal union is the result of a continual commerce between the sexes. In her opinion, husband and wife were designed to live together, but not to live in the same manner. They ought to act in concert, but not to do the same things. 'The kind of life,' says she, 'which would delight the one, would be insupportable to the other; the inclinations which nature has given them are as different as the occupations she has assigned them: they differ in their amusements as much as in their duties. In a word, each contributes to the common good by different ways, and the proper distribution of their several cares and employments is the strongest tie that cements their union.'

Every Sunday, after evening service, the women meet again. They chat, sing, run or play at some little game of skill. Refreshment is brought. Wine is almost always excluded, and the men, who are rarely admitted to this little female party, never are present at this collation.

To keep the women in order would signify nothing, if the men were not likewise under proper regulations. In the commonwealth, citizens are kept in order by principles of morality and virtue; but how are we to keep servants and mercenaries under proper regulations, otherwise than by force and constraint? The art of a master consists in disguising this restraint under the veil of pleasure and interest. The habit of frequenting public houses, the company of loose women, soon render them unserviceable to their masters, and unprofitable to themselves, and by teaching them a thousand vices, make them unfit for servitude, and unworthy of liberty.

To remedy this inconvenience, it is endeavoured to keep them at home by the same motives that induce them to go abroad. Why do they go abroad? To drink and play at a public house. They drink and play at home. All the difference is that the wine costs them nothing, that they do not get drunk, and that there are some winners at play, without any losers.

Behind the house is a shady walk, where they have fixed the lists. There, in summer time, the men meet every Sunday after sermon time, to play in little detached parties, not for money, for it is not allowed, nor for wine, which is given them, but for a prize furnished by their master's generosity. They are not confined to one particular game, but they change them, that one man, who happens to excel in a particular game, may not carry off all the prizes, and that they may grow stronger and more dexterous by a variety of exercises. At one time, the contest is who shall first reach a mark at the other end of the walk; at another time it is who shall throw the same stone farthest; then again it is who shall carry the same weight longest. This custom has imperceptibly become a kind of show in which the actors, being animated by the presence of the spectators, prefer the glory of applause to the lucre of the prize. As these exercises make them more active and vigorous, they set a greater value on themselves, and being accustomed to estimate their importance from their own intrinsic worth, they prize honour beyond money.

In the winter, their pleasures vary as well as their labours. On a Sunday, all the servants in the family and even the neighbours, men and women indiscriminately, meet after service time in a hall where there is a good fire, some wine, fruits, cakes and a fiddle to which they dance.

It has been said that no man is a hero in the eyes of his *valet de chambre*; perhaps not; but every worthy man will enjoy his servants' esteem: which sufficiently proves that heroism is only a vain phantom and that nothing is solid but virtue.

There is not only a proper subordination among those of

E

inferior station, but a perfect harmony among those of equal rank; and this is not the least difficult part of domestic economy.

Who does not see, that in this family, they have not even an idea of any such difficulty, so much does the union among the several members proceed from their attachment to the head. Is it not very natural, that the children of the same father should live together like brethren? This is what they tell us every day at church, without making us feel the sentiment; and this is what the domestics in this family feel, without being told it.

This disposition to good fellowship is owing to a choice of proper subjects. After having made the best assortment in their power, they unite them as it were by the services which they oblige each to render the other, and they contrive that it shall be the real interest of everyone to be beloved by his fellow servants.

Riches do not make a man rich, as is well observed in some romance. The wealth of a man is not in his coffers, but in the use he makes of what he draws out of them; for our possessions do not become our own, but by the uses to which we allot them, and abuses are always more inexhaustible than riches; whence it happens that our enjoyments are not in proportion to our expenses but depend on the best regulation of them. An idiot may toss ingots of gold into the sea, and say he has enjoyed them: but what comparison is there between such an extravagant enjoyment, and that which a wise man would have derived from the least part of their value? Order and regularity, which multiply and perpetuate the use of riches, are alone capable of converting the enjoyment of them into felicity.

Are the most wealthy the most happy? No: how then does wealth contribute to felicity? But every well-regulated family is emblematic of the master's mind. Gilded ceilings, luxury, and magnificence only serve to show the vanity of those who display such parade; whereas whenever you see order without melancholy, peace without slavery, plenty without profusion, you may say with confidence, the master of this house is a happy being.

For my own part, I think the most certain sign of true content is a domestic and retired life, and that they who are continually resorting to others in quest of happiness, do not enjoy it at home.

There are many simple and sublime duties, which few people can relish and fulfil. Such are those of the master of a family, for which the air and bustle of the world give him a disgust, and which he never discharges properly when he is only inflamed by motives of avarice and interest. Some think themselves excellent masters, and are only careful economists; their income may thrive, and their family nevertheless be in a bad condition. They ought to have more enlarged views to direct an administration of such importance, so as to give it a happy issue. The first thing to be attended to in the due regulation of a family, is to admit none but honest people, who will not have any secret intention to disturb that regularity. But are honesty and servitude so compatible, that we may hope to find servants who are honest men? No, if we would have them, we must not enquire for them, but we must make them; and none who are not men of integrity themselves are capable of making others honest.

The grand art by which the masters make their servants what they would desire them to be, is to appear themselves before them what they really are. Their behaviour is always frank and open. As their servants never see them do anything but what is just, reasonable, and equitable, they do not consider justice as a tax on the poor, as a yoke on the unhappy, and as one of the evils of their condition. The care they take never to let the labourers come in vain, and lose their day's work in seeking after their wages, teaches their servants to set a just value on time.

You never perceive any sullenness or mutiny in the discharge of their duty, because there is never any haughtiness or capriciousness in the orders they receive; nothing is required of them but what is reasonable and expedient, and their master and mistress have too much respect for the dignity of human nature, even in a state of servitude, to put them upon any employment which may debase them. Moreover, nothing here is reckoned mean but vice, and whatever is reasonable and necessary is deemed honourable and becoming.

It requires a sound mind to be able to enjoy the pleasures of retirement; the virtuous, only, being capable of amusing themselves with their family concerns; and of voluntarily secluding themselves from the world: if there be on earth any such thing as happiness, they undoubtedly enjoy it in such a state. But the means of happiness are nothing to those who know how to make use of them; and we never know in what true happiness consists, till we have acquired a taste for its enjoyment.

If I were desired to speak with precision as to the reason why the inhabitants of this place are happy, I should think I could not answer with greater propriety than to say, it is because *they here know how to live*; not in the sense in which these words would be taken in France, where it would be understood that they had adopted certain customs and manners in vogue: no, but they have adopted such manners as are most agreeable to human life; to that life which extends beyond itself, and is not given up for lost even in the hour of death.

Julie has a father who is anxious for the honour and interests of his family: she has children for whose subsistence it is necessary to provide. This ought to be the chief care of man in a state of society; and was therefore the first in which Julie and her husband were united. When they began housekeeping they examined into the state of their fortunes; not considering so much whether they were proportioned to their rank, as to their wants; and seeing that they were sufficient for the provision of an honourable family, they had not so bad an opinion of their children as to be fearful lest the patrimony they had to leave would not content them. They applied themselves therefore rather to improve their present, than acquire a larger fortune.

It is true that an estate which is not augmented is liable to many accidents by which it will naturally diminish: but if this were a sufficient motive to begin increasing, when would it cease to be a pretext for a constant augmentation? Must it be divided among several children? Be it so, must they be all idle? Will not the industry of each be a supplement to his share, and ought it not to be considered in the partition? It is thus that insatiable avarice makes its way under the mask of prudence and leads to vice under the cloak of its own security.

The master of this house possesses but a moderate fortune, according to the estimation of the world; but in reality I hardly know anybody more opulent. There is indeed no such thing as absolute wealth: that term signifying only the relation between the wants and possessions of those who are rich. One man is rich, though possessing only an acre of land; another is a beggar in the midst of heaps of gold. Luxury and caprice have no bounds, and make more persons poor than real wants.

I was at first struck with a peculiarity in the economy of this house, where there appeared so much ease, freedom, and gaiety in the midst of order and diligence; the great fault of well-regulated houses being that they always wear an air of gloominess and restraint. The extreme solicitude also of the heads of the family looks too much like avarice. Everything about them seems constrained. Such slavish fathers of families cannot be said to live for themselves, but for their children; without considering that they are not only fathers but men, and that they ought to set their children an example how to live prudent and happy. More judicious maxims are adopted here. M. de Wolmar thinks one of the principal duties of a father of a family is to make his house, in the first place, agreeable, that his children may delight in their home, and that seeing their father happy, they may be tempted to tread in his footsteps. Another of his maxims, and which he often repeats, is that the gloomy and sordid lives of fathers and mothers are almost always the first cause of the ill-conduct of children.

As to Julie, she obeys, without scruple, the dictates of her heart. Can a mind so susceptible as hers be insensible of pleasure? On the contrary, she delights in every amusement, nor refuses to join in any diversion that promises to be agreeable; but her pleasures are the pleasures of Julie. She neglects neither her own convenience nor the satisfaction of those who are dear to her. She esteems nothing superfluous that may contribute to the happiness of a sensible mind: but censures everything as such, that serves only to make a figure in the eyes of others.

As the first step to virtue is to forbear doing ill, so the first step to happiness is to be free from pain. These two maxims which, well understood, would render precepts of morality in a degree useless, are favourable ones with Mme de Wolmar. She is extremely affected by the misfortunes of others; and it would be as difficult for her to be happy with wretched objects about her, as it would be for an innocent man to preserve his virtue and live in the midst of vice. She has none of that barbarous piety, which is satisfied with turning away its eye from the miserable objects it might relieve. On the contrary, she makes it her business to seek out such objects: it is the existence, and not the presence, of the unhappy which gives her affliction. It is not sufficient for her to be ignorant that there are any such; it is necessary to her quiet that she should be assured there are none miserable; at least within her sphere of charity: for it would be unreasonable to extend her concern beyond her own neighbourhood, and to make her happiness depend on the welfare of all mankind. She takes care to inform herself of the necessities of all that live near her, and interests herself in their relief as if their wants were her own. She knows everyone personally, includes them all, as it were, in her family, and spares no pains to banish, or alleviate, those misfortunes and afflictions to which human life is subject.

What pleases me most in the solicitude which prevails here regarding the happiness of others is, that their benevolence is always exerted with prudence, and is never abused. We do not always succeed in our benevolent intentions; but on the contrary, some people imagine they are doing great services, who are, in reality, doing great injuries, and with a view to a little manifest good, are guilty of much unforeseen evil. Mme de Wolmar indeed possesses, in an eminent degree, a qualification very rare, even among women of the best character; I mean an exquisite discernment in the distribution of her favours. Who ever hath committed an infamous or wicked action, hath nothing to hope for from her but justice, and her pardon, if he has offended her; but never that favour and protection, which she can bestow on a worthier object.

Her protection is never refused to anyone who really stands in need of, and deserves to obtain it: but for those who desire to raise themselves through fickleness or ambition only, she can very seldom be prevailed upon to give herself any trouble. The natural business of man is to cultivate the earth and subsist on its produce. The peaceful inhabitant of the country need only know in what happiness consists, to be happy. His situation is the only necessary, the only useful one in life. He is never unhappy but when others tyrannize over him or seduce him by their vices. In agriculture and husbandry consists the real prosperity of a country, the greatness and strength which a people desire from themselves, that which depends not on other nations, which is not obliged to attack others for its own preservation, but is productive of the surest means of its own defence. In making an estimate of the strength of a nation, a superficial observer would visit the court, the prince, his ports, his troops, his magazines, and his fortified towns; but the true politician would take a survey of the country, and visit the cottages of the husbandmen. The former would only see what is already executed, but the latter what was capable of being put into execution.

On this principle they contribute as much as possible to make the peasants happy in their condition, without ever assisting them to change it. Care is exerted in teaching them to honour their native condition, by seeming to honour it themselves.

Mme de Wolmar's great maxim is, therefore, never to encourage anyone to change his condition, but to contribute all in her power to make everyone happy in his present station; being particularly solicitous to prevent the happiest of all situations, that of a peasant in a free state, from being despised in favour of other employments.

I, one day, made an objection on this subject, founded on the different talents which nature seems to have bestowed on mankind, in order to fit them for different occupations, without any regard to their birth. This she obviated, however, by observing that there were two more material things to be consulted, before talents: these were virtue and happiness. 'Man,' said she, 'is too noble a being to be made a mere tool of for the use of others: he ought not to be employed in what he is fit for, without consulting how far such employment is fit for him; for we are not made for our stations, but our stations for us. In the right distribution of things, therefore, we should not adapt men to circumstances, but circumstances to men; we should not seek that employment for which a man is best adapted, but that which is best adapted to make him virtuous and happy. For it can never be right to destroy one human soul for the temporal advantage of others, nor to make any man a villain for the use of honest people.

'In order to pursue our talents, we must know what they are and it is no easy matter to discover the talents with which nature hath severally endowed us. There is nothing so equivocal as the genius frequently attributed to youth. Real talent, or true genius, is attended with a certain simplicity of disposition, which makes it less restless and enterprising, less ready to thrust itself forward, than a superficial and false one; which is nevertheless generally mistaken for the true, and consists only in a vain desire of making a figure without talents to support it. One of these geniuses hears the drum beat, and is immediately in idea a general; another sees a palace, and imagines himself an architect. But it is not enough to be sensible of the bent of our genius, unless we are willing to pursue it. Will a prince turn coachman because he is expert at driving a set of horses? Will a duke turn cook because he is ingenious at inventing ragouts? Our talents all tend to preferment; no one pretends to those which would fit him for an inferior station: do you think this is agreeable to the order of nature? Suppose everyone sensible of his own talents, and as willing to employ them, how is it possible? How could they surmount so many obstacles? He who finds in himself the want of abilities would call in subtlety and intrigue to his aid, which another, more sure of himself, would disdain. In multiplying indiscreetly the number of professors and academicians, true merit is lost in the crowd, and the honours, due to the most ingenious, are always bestowed on the most intriguing. Did there exist a society wherein the rank and employment of its respective members were exactly calculated to their talents and personal merit, everyone might there aspire to the place he should be most fit for; but it is necessary to conduct ourselves by other rules, and give up that of abilities, in societies where the vilest of all talents is the only one that leads to fortune.

'I will add further: I cannot be persuaded of the utility of having so many different talents displayed. It seems necessary, the number of persons so qualified should be exactly proportionate to the wants of society. I am apt to think, therefore, that great talents in men are like great virtues in drugs, which nature has provided to cure our maladies, though its intention certainly was that we should never stand in need of them. In the vegetable kingdom there are plants which are poisonous; in the brutal, animals that would tear us to pieces; and among mankind there are those who possess talents no less destructive to their species. Besides, if everything were to be put to that use for which its qualities seem best adapted, it might be productive of more harm than good in the world. There are thousands of simple, honest people who have no occasion for a diversity of great talents; supporting themselves better by their simplicity than others with all their ingenuity. But, in proportion as their morals are corrupted, their talents are displayed, as if to serve as a supplement to the virtues they have lost, and to oblige the vicious to be useful in spite of themselves.'

Another subject on which we differed, was the relieving of beggars. I represented to her that this practice tended to multiply beggars and vagabonds, who take pleasure in that idle life, and by rendering themselves a burden on society, deprive it of their labour.

'I see very well,' says she, 'you have imbibed prejudices by living in great cities, and some of those maxims by which you complaisant reasoners love to flatter the hard-heartedness of the wealthy. My husband has always appeared to despise these arguments. "We permit," says he, "and even support at a great expense, a multitude of useless professions; many of which serve only to spoil and corrupt our manners. Now, to look upon the profession of a beggar as a trade, it serves to excite in us those sentiments of humanity which ought to unite all mankind. A great number of beggars may be burthensome to a state: but of how many professions, which are tolerated and encouraged, may we not say the same? It belongs to the legislature and administration to take care there should be no beggars; but, in order to make them lay down their trade, is it necessary to make all other ranks of people inhuman and unnatural?" For my part,' continued Julie, 'without knowing what the poor may be to the state, I know they are all my brethren, and that I cannot, without thinking myself inexcusable, refuse them the small relief they ask of me. I know too much of life, to be ignorant how many misfortunes may reduce an honest man to such a situation; and how can I be sure that an unhappy stranger, who comes, in the name of God, to implore my assistance, and to beg a poor morsel of bread, is not such an honest man, ready to perish for want, and whom my refusal may drive to despair? A halfpenny and a piece of bread are refused to nobody; should they meet with the same relief at every house which can afford it, it would be sufficient to support them on their journey. But supposing this was not enough to yield them any real help, it is at least a proof that we take some part in their distress; a sort of salutation that softens the rigour of refusing them more. A halfpenny and a morsel of bread cost little more and are a more civil answer than a mere *God help you*; which is too often the only thing bestowed, as if the gifts of Providence were not in the hands of men, or that Heaven had any other store on earth than what is laid up in the coffers of the rich. In short, whatever we ought to think of such unfortunate wretches, and though nothing should in justice be given to common beggars, we ought at least, out of respect to ourselves,

E*

to take some notice of suffering humanity, and not harden our hearts at the sight of the miserable.'

Julie's mind and body are equally sensible. The same delicacy prevails as well in her senses as her sentiments. She was formed to know and taste every pleasure; but then her method of enjoyment resembles the austerity of self-denial: not indeed of that afflicting and painful self-denial, which is hurtful to nature, and which its author rejects as ridiculous homage; but of that slight and moderate restraint, by which the empire of reason is preserved; and which serves as a whet to pleasure by preventing disgust. Thus her mind preserves its first vigour: her taste is not spoiled by use; she has no need to excite it by excess.

A still nobler object, which she proposes to herself from the exercise of this virtue, is that of remaining always mistress of herself, and to subject her inclinations to rule. This is a new way to be happy; for it is certain that we enjoy nothing with so little inquietude as what we can part from without pain; and if the philosopher be happy, it is because he is the man from whom fortune can take the least.

'Life is indeed short,' says she, 'which is a reason for enjoying it to the end, and managing its duration in such a manner as to make the most of it. If one day's indulgence and satiety deprives us of a whole year's taste for enjoyment, it is bad philosophy to pursue our desires so far as they may be ready to lead us.'

'Besides the constitution common to its species, every child at birth possesses a peculiar temperament, which determines its genius and character; and which it is improper either to prevent or restrain; the business of education being only to model and bring to perfection. Nature makes no mistakes. All the vices imputed to malignity of disposition are only the effect of the bad form it hath received. There is not a villain upon earth, whose natural propensity, well directed, might not have been productive of great virtues; nor is there a wrong-head in being, that might not have been of use to himself in society, had his natural talents taken a certain bias, just as deformed and monstrous images are rendered beautiful and proportionable, by placing them in a proper point of view. Everything tends to the common good in the universal system of nature. Every man has the place assigned in the best order and arrangement of things; the business is to find out that place, and not to disturb such order. What must be the consequence then of an education begun in the cradle, and carried on always in the same manner, without regard to the vast diversity of temperaments and geniuses in mankind? Useless or hurtful instructions would be given to the greater part, while at the same time they are deprived of such as would be most useful and convenient; nature would be confined on every side, and the greatest qualities of the mind defaced, in order to substitute in their place mean and little ones, of no utility. By using indiscriminately the same means with different talents, the one serves to deface the other and all are confounded together. In a word, in return for so much pains indiscreetly taken, all these little prodigies become wits without sense, and men, without merit, remarkable only for their weakness and insignificancy.'

Learn not always to depend on your own sagacity on difficult occasions; but on that Being whose omnipotence is equal to his wisdom, and who knows how to direct us in everything aright. The greatest defect in human wisdom, even in that which has only virtue for its object, is a too great confidence, which makes us judge by the present of the future, and of our whole lives from the experience of a single moment. We perceive ourselves resolute one instant, and therefore conclude we shall always be so. The modest language of true fortitude is: '*I had resolution on this or that occasion*'; but he who boasts of his present security knows not how weak he may prove on the next trial.

How vain are all our projects, how absurd our reasonings in the eyes of that Being who is not confined to time or space! Man is so weak as to disregard things which are placed at a distance from him: he sees only the objects which immediately surround him; change his notions of things as the point of sight is changed from whence he views them. We judge of the future from what agrees with us now, without knowing how far that which pleases to-day may be disagreeable to-morrow; we depend on ourselves, as if we were always the same, and yet are changing every day. Who can tell if they shall always desire what they wish for? If they shall be to-morrow what they are to-day, if external objects and even a change in the constitution of the body may not vary the modification of their minds, and if we may not be made miserable by the very means we have concerted for our happiness?

I have heard a good deal of argument against the free-agency of man, and despise all its sophistry. A casuist may take what pains he will to prove that I am no free agent, my innate sense of freedom constantly destroys his arguments: for whatever choice I make after deliberation, I feel plainly that it depended only on myself to have made the contrary. Indeed, all the scholastic subtilties I have heard on this head are futile and frivolous; because they prove too much, are equally used to oppose truth and falsehood, and whether a man be a free agent or not, serve equally to prove one or the other. With this kind of reasoners, the Deity himself is not a free agent, and the word liberty is in fact a term of no meaning. They triumph, not in having solved the difficulty, but in having substituted a chimera in its room.

I don't believe that after having provided in every shape for the wants of man in his formation, God interests himself in an extraordinary manner for one person more than another. Those who abuse the common aids of Providence are unworthy such assistance, and those who make good use of them have no occasion for any other. Such a partiality appears to me injurious to divine justice. You will say this severe and discouraging doctrine may be deduced from the Holy Scripture. Be it so. Is it not my first duty to honour my Creator? In whatever veneration then I hold the sacred text, I hold its author in a still greater; and I could sooner be induced to believe the Bible corrupted or unintelligible, than that God can be malevolent or unjust.

But does it follow from thence that prayer is useless? God forbid that I should deprive myself of that resource. Every act of the understanding which raises us to God carries us above ourselves; in imploring his assistance we learn to experience it. It is not his immediate act that operates on us, it is we that improve ourselves by raising our thoughts in prayer to him. All that we ask aright, he bestows; and we acquire strength in confessing our weakness. But if we abuse this ordinance and turn mystics instead of raising ourselves to God, we are lost in our own wild imaginations; in seeking grace, we renounce reason; in order to obtain of heaven one blessing, we trample underfoot another, and in obstinately persisting that Heaven should enlighten our hearts, we extinguish the light of our understandings. But who are we that we should insist on the Deity's performing miracles, when we please, in our favour?

I have heard you often censure the ecstasies of the pietists: but do you know from whence they arise? From allotting a longer time to prayer than is consistent with the weakness of human nature. Hence the spirits are exhausted, the imagination takes fire, they see visions, they become inspired and prophetical; nor is it then in the power of the understanding to stop the progress of fanaticism.

I have condemned indeed the ecstasies of the mystics, and condemn them still, when they serve to detach us from our duty; and by raising in us a disgust against an active life by the charm of contemplation, seduce us into that state of quietism which you imagine me so near, and from which I believe myself nevertheless to be as far distant as yourself.

I know very well that to serve God is not to pass our lives on our knees in prayer; that it is to discharge on earth those obligations which our duty requires.

We ought first to perform the duties of our station, and then pray when we have time.

I have lived and I die in the Protestant communion whose maxims we deduced from scripture and reason; concerning which my heart hath always confirmed what my lips uttered. I have always sincerely sought what was most conformable to truth, and the glory of my Creator. I may have been deceived in my research; I have not the vanity to think I have always been in the right. I may, indeed, have been constantly in the wrong; but my intention has been invariably good. If God did not vouchsafe to enlighten my understanding further, he is too merciful and just to demand of me an account of what he has not committed to my care.

God is more merciful than I am criminal, and my confidence increases as I find I approach nearer to him.

To what punishment can a just God condemn me? The reprobates, it is said, hate him. Must he not first make me not to love him? No, I fear not to be found one of that number. O thou great Eternal Being! Supreme intelligence! Source of life and happiness! Creator! Preserver! Father! Lord of nature! God powerful and good, of whose existence I never doubted a moment, and under whose eye I have always delighted to live! I know, I rejoice, that I am going to appear before thy throne. In a few days, my soul, delivered from its earthly tabernacle, shall begin to pay thee more worthily that immortal homage which will constitute my happiness to all eternity. I look upon what I shall be, till that moment comes, as nothing. Those who sleep on the bosom of a father, are in no fear of being awakened.

THE CONFESSIONS

*W*HILE *he was still at Montmorency, after the success of* The New Héloïse, *and while he was finishing* Emile, *from which he expected to make a little money, Rousseau, dreaming of retirement, reserved for himself 'an occupation which would fill his empty solitude,' with no intention of publication during his lifetime. This was to be 'the memoirs of my life.' He wished to make of them 'a work unique for its truthfulness, so that the world might possess for the first time the portrait of a man "painted after nature" . . .' The events which made necessary his flight interrupted this plan and deprived him of a great part of his documents, upon which he counted for refreshing his wavering memory, too often led astray by his perpetual reveries. Nevertheless, he started this work in 1765 in the solitude of Motiers-Travers in Switzerland. He then gave to his Memoirs the name of* Confessions. *Again interrupted by his flight from Switzerland to London, then by the mental panic which followed, he returned to the* Confessions, *in April 1769, and finished them in December 1770, in Paris. But the story does not go farther than the end of October 1770, the time of his departure from Switzerland. He gave up writing of what followed, in order not to have to relive the sufferings of those years. By an admirable mastery over his mind, he was able to keep the last parts of his work free from any suggestion of the deliriums of anguish which possessed him; we only catch a glimpse of them in the last page; and it is perhaps because they were perceptible then that he decided not to continue. A still higher strength of character kept him from taking revenge on his enemies, whom he could easily have pilloried, and who expected this as was shown by the slanderous fury of certain among them. The* Confessions *were published after Rousseau's death, the first six books in 1782; the other six in 1789.*

No other of Rousseau's works had so much influence on the French literature of the following century. His book was the mother of the Confessions *of the first romanticists, of the* René *of Chateaubriand and the* Adolphe *of Benjamin Constant. It opened into the art of the novel the recesses of the inner life.*

[119]

I FELT BEFORE I THOUGHT; 'TIS THE COMMON FATE OF HUMANITY. Figure to yourself a timid and docile character in common life, but ardent, haughty, invincible in his passions; a child always governed by the voice of reason, always treated with mildness, equity, and complaisance; who has not even the idea of injustice, and who, for the first time, experiences a terrible one, from those, precisely, he most cherishes and respects. What a perverting of ideas! what a disorder in the sentiments! what confusion in the heart, in the brain, in all one's little being, intelligent and moral! I say, let anyone imagine to himself all this, if possible; for as to myself, I am not capable of discovering or following the least trace of what passed in me at the time.

I had not sense enough to feel how much appearances condemned me, and to put myself in the place of others; I kept to my own, and all I felt was the rigour of a dreadful chastisement for a crime I had not committed. The soreness of my body, though severe, I scarcely felt; I only felt indignation, rage, and despair. My cousin, in almost a like case, who had been punished for an involuntary fault as a premeditated act, grew furious by my example, and raised himself in a manner to unite with me. Both in the same bed embraced each other with convulsive transports; we were suffocated; and when our young hearts, a little eased, could breathe out their indignation, we sat up in our bed, and began both of us crying out an hundred times, with all our force: *Carnifex! Carnifex! Carnifex!*

I feel in writing this my pulse still rise; these moments would be continually present, were I to live an hundred thousand years. This first sentiment of violence and of injustice is so deeply graven on my soul, that every resembling idea brings back my first emotion; and this sentiment, relative to me in its origin, has taken such a consistence, and is so far from personal interest, that my heart is inflamed at the sight or recital of an unjust action, whatever may be its object or wheresoever it may be committed, as if the effect fell on me. When I read the history of a cruel tyrant, the subtle black actions of a knavish priest, I could set off heartily to stab these miscreants, though I should perish an hundred times in the attempt. I have often sweated in pursuing and stoning a cock, a cow, a dog, an animal I saw torment another, only because he knew himself to be the strongest. This emotion may be natural to me, and I believe it is; but the profound remembrance of the first injustice I suffered, was too long and too strongly annexed not to have greatly strengthened it.

Reflections on myself have not a little contributed to keep my heart sound. I drew from them this great maxim of morality, the only one perhaps in practical use, to shun those situations which put our duty in opposition with our interests, and which show us our good in the misfortunes of others; and that in such situations, however sincere a love for virtue we bear, we weaken sooner or later without perceiving it, and become unjust and wicked in fact, without ceasing to be just and innocent at the heart.

This maxim, strongly imprinted on my heart and put in practice in all my conduct, though a little late, is one of those which have given me the most whimsical and foolish appearance, not only among the public, but more particularly among my acquaintance. I have been charged with being original, and not doing like others. In fact, I thought little of doing either like others or otherwise than they did. I sincerely desired to do what was right. I avoided, as much as possible, those situations which procured me an interest contrary to that of another man, and consequently a secret, though involuntary, desire of hurting that man.

The sophism which more than once ruined me is that of the greatest part of mankind, who complain of want of power, when it is too late to make use of it. Virtue is dearly bought by our own fault; if we were always prudent, we should seldom have occasion of virtue. But inclinations which might be easily surmounted, drag us without resistance; we yield to light temptations whose danger we despise. Insensibly we fall into perilous situations from which we might easily have preserved ourselves, but from which we cannot extricate ourselves without heroic efforts which affright us; so we fall at last into the abyss, in saying to God, 'Why hast thou made me so weak?' But, in spite of us, he replies to our consciences, 'I made you too weak to get out of the gulf, because I made you strong enough not to fall into it.'

In the successive order of my inclinations I had always been too high or too low; Achilles or Thersites; sometimes a hero, sometimes a villain. M. Gaime took the pains to put me in my proper place, and to show me to myself without sparing or discouraging me. He spoke to me very honourably of my talents and my genius; but he added that he saw obstacles arise from them which would prevent me from making the best of them, so that they would, according to him, serve me much less in the attainment of fortune than in resources to do without it. He painted me the true picture of human life, of which I had but wrong ideas: he explained to me, how in adversity a wise man may always attain happiness, and gain that wind which blows him there; how there is no happiness without prudence, and how it is that prudence belongs to every condition. He greatly deadened my admiration for grandeur, in proving to me that those who lorded it over others were neither wiser nor happier than they were. He told me one thing which often occurs to my memory; and that is, if each man could read the hearts of others, there would be more people would wish to descend than ascend. This reflection, whose reality strikes, and has nothing forced, has been very useful to me in the course of my life, in making me keep to my lot peaceably. He gave me the first true ideas of honesty, which my bombastic genius had only known to excess. He made me understand, that the enthusiasm for sublime virtue was of little use in society; that in aiming too high you are liable to fall; that the continuity of little duties well fulfilled demanded no less strength than heroic actions; that you find your account in it much better, in respect to both reputation and happiness; and that the esteem of mankind was infinitely better than sometimes their admiration.

In my opinion, idleness is no less the pest of society than solitude. Nothing contracts the mind, nothing engenders trifles, tales, backbitings, slander and falsities, so much as being shut up in a room opposite others, reduced to no other occupation than the necessity of continually chattering. When everyone is employed, they speak only when they have something to say; but if you are doing nothing, you must absolutely talk incessantly, and this of all constraints is the most troublesome and the most dangerous. I dare go even further, and maintain, that, to render a circle truly agreeable, everyone must be not only doing something, but something which requires a little attention.

When I was at Motiers, I sat down with my neighbours to make laces: should I once more mix with the world, I will carry in my pocket a cup and ball, to play with it the whole day, to dispense with talking when I have nothing to say. If everyone did so, mankind would be less wicked, their friendship more certain and I believe more agreeable. In fine, let wags laugh if they will: I maintain that the only moral within the reach of the present age is the cup and ball moral.

Believers generally make God as they are themselves: good people make him good, the wicked make him mischievous; choleric and spiteful bigots see nothing but hell, because they would be glad to damn everybody; mild and friendly souls believe little of it, and one of the astonishments I can't get the better of is, to perceive the good Fénelon speak of it, in his *Telemachus*, as if he readily believed it: but I hope he told a lie; for, in fact, however veridical a man may be, he must lie a little sometimes if he is a bishop. Mamma did not do so with me; and her soul without spleen, which could not imagine a vindictive and continually angry God, saw nothing but clemency and mercy where bigots saw nothing but justice and punishment. She often said, that there would be no justice in God in being equitable towards us; for not having given us that which must make us so, it would be demanding more of us than He has given. The most whimsical of all was her believing in purgatory, but not in hell. This proceeded from her not knowing how to dispose of the wicked, as she could neither damn them nor place them with the good until they were become so; it must be owned the wicked are, both in this world and the next, extremely troublesome.

When a man has a little true relish for the sciences, the first thing he finds in his pursuit is their connection, which causes them mutually to attract, assist, and enlighten each other, and that one cannot do without the other. Though the human mind is not sufficient to all, and must always prefer one as the principal, yet if it has not some notion of the others, it often finds itself in obscurity even with that it has chosen. I knew that what I had undertaken was good and useful in itself, and that nothing but a change of method was necessary. Beginning with the Encyclopædia, I went on, dividing it into branches; I saw the contrary was necessary, to take (them) each one separately, and follow (them) each one by itself to the point at which they unite. Thus I came back to the ordinary synthesis; but I came back as a man who knows what he is doing.

I was never so near wisdom as at this happy period. Without great remorse for the past, delivered from the care of futurity, the ruling sentiment of my mind was to enjoy the present. Bigots have in general a little sensuality, extremely keen, which makes them favour with delight the innocent pleasures permitted them. Worldlings impute it to them as a crime. I don't know why; or rather I do know. It is because they envy them the enjoyment of pleasures for which they have lost all taste. I had this taste, and found it pleasing to falsify it in surety of conscience. My heart as yet new gave itself into all with the pleasure of a child, or rather, if I dare say so, with the voluptuousness of an angel; for really these tranquil enjoyments have the serenity of those of Paradise. Dinners on the grass, suppers in the arbour, gathering in the fruits, vintage, peeling flax in the evening with our people, these things were to us so many holidays. More solitary walks had still greater charms, because the mind could expand itself more freely.

I courageously renounced a sinful pleasure, with a few sighs, I own; but also with that inward satisfaction I tasted for the first time in my life, when I could say to myself, I deserve my own esteem; I can prefer my duty to my pleasures. This was the first real obligation I had to reading. 'Twas that which taught me to reflect and compare. After having adopted principles so pure not long before; after those rules of wisdom and virtue I had made myself, and that I felt myself so ambitious to follow; the shame of being so little consistent with myself, to belie so soon and so openly my own maxims, got the better of pleasure: pride had, perhaps, as great a share in my resolution as virtue, it produces effects so like it, the mistake is pardonable.

One of the advantages of good actions is to raise the soul and dispose it to better: for such is human weakness, one must add to the number of good actions an abstinence from the evil we are tempted to commit.

I thought that the gospel being the same for every Christian, and the only difference in religious opinions the result of the explanations given by men to that which they did not understand, it was the exclusive right of the sovereign power in every country to fix the mode of worship, and this unintelligible dogma; and that consequently it was the duty of a citizen to admit the one and conform to the other in the manner prescribed by the law. The conversation of the Encyclopædists, far from staggering my faith, gave it a new strength by my natural aversion to disputes and party. The study of man and the universe had everywhere shown me the final causes and the wisdom by which they were directed. The reading of the Bible, and especially of the New Testament, to which I had for several years past applied myself, had given me a sovereign contempt for the base and stupid interpretations given to the words of Jesus Christ by persons the least worthy of understanding his divine doctrine. In a word, philosophy, while it attached me to the essential part of religion, had detached me from the trash of the little formularies with which men had rendered it obscure. Judging that for a reasonable man there were not two ways of being a Christian I was also of opinion that in each country everything relative to form and discipline was within the jurisdiction of the laws. From this principle so social and pacific, and which has brought upon me such cruel persecutions, it followed that, if I wished to be a citizen of Geneva, I must become a Protestant, and conform to the mode of worship established in my country.

I felt that writing for bread would soon have extinguished my genius and destroyed my talents, which were less in my pen than in my heart, and solely proceeded from an elevated and noble manner of thinking, by which alone they could be cherished and preserved. Nothing vigorous or great can come from a pen totally venal. Necessity, nay even avarice, would have made me write rather rapidly than well. If the desire of success had not led me into cabals, it might have made me endeavour to publish fewer true and useful works than those which might be pleasing to the multitude; and instead of a distinguished author, which I might possibly become, I should have been nothing more than a scribbler. No, no! I have always felt that the profession of letters was illustrious in proportion as it was less a trade. It is too difficult to think nobly when we think for a livelihood. To be able, to dare even to speak great truths, an author must be independent of success. I gave my books to the public with a certainty of having written for the general good of mankind, without giving myself the least concern about what was to follow. If the work was thrown aside, so much the worse for such as did not choose to profit by it. Their approbation was not necessary to enable me to live; my profession was sufficient to maintain me had not my works had a sale; for which reason, alone, they all sold.

I had perceived everything to be radically connected with politics, and that, upon whatever principles these were founded, a people would never be more than that which the nature of the government made them; therefore the great question of the best government possible appeared to me to be reduced to this: what is the nature of the government properest to form the most virtuous and enlightened, the wisest and best people, taking the last epithet in its most extensive meaning? I thought this question was much if not quite of the same nature with that which follows: What government is that which by its nature always maintains itself nearest to the laws? Hence, what is the law? and a series of questions of similar importance. I perceived these led to great truths, useful to the happiness of mankind.

It has been remarked that most men are in the course of their lives frequently unlike themselves, and seem to be transformed into others very different from what they were. It was not to establish a thing so generally known that I wished to write a book; I had a newer and more important object. This was to search for the cause of these variations, and, by confining my observations to those which depend on ourselves, to demonstrate in what manner it might be possible to direct them, in order to render us better and more certain of our dispositions. For it is undoubtedly more painful to an honest man to resist desires already formed, and which it is his duty to subdue, than to prevent, change, or modify the same desires in their source, were he capable of tracing them to it. A man under temptation resists once because he has strength of mind, he yields another time because this is overcome; had it been the same as before he would again have triumphed.

By examining within myself, and searching in others what could be the cause of these different manners of being, I discovered that, in a great measure, they depended on the anterior impression of external objects; and that, continually modified by our senses and organs, we, without knowing it, bore in our ideas, sentiments, and even actions, the effect of these modifications. The striking and numerous observations I had collected were beyond all manner of dispute, and by their natural principles seemed proper to furnish an exterior regimen, which, varied according to circumstances, might place and support the mind in the state most favourable to virtue. From how many mistakes would reason be preserved, how many vices would be stifled in their birth, were it possible to force animal economy to favour moral order, which it so frequently disturbs! Climates, seasons, sounds, colours, light, darkness, the elements, ailments, noise, silence, motion, rest, all act on the animal machine, and consequently on the mind; all offer us a thousand means, almost certain of directing in their origin the sentiments by which we suffer ourselves to be governed.

Being past the age of romantic projects, and having been more stunned than flattered by the trumpet of fame, my only hope was that of living at ease, and constantly at leisure. This is the life of the blessed in the world to come, and for the rest of mine here below I made it my supreme happiness.

They who reproach me with so many contradictions will not fail here to add another to the number. I have observed that the indolence of great companies made them insupportable to me, and I am now seeking solitude for the sole purpose of abandoning myself to inaction. This, however, is my disposition; if there be in it a contradiction, it proceeds from nature and not from me; but there is so little that it is precisely on that account that I am always consistent. The indolence of company is burdensome because it is forced. That of solitude is charming because it is free, and depends upon the will. In company I suffer cruelly by inaction because this is of necessity. I must there remain nailed to my chair, or stand upright like a picket, suffering at the same time the fatigue of inaction and all the torment of constraint; obliged to pay attention to every foolish thing uttered, and to all the idle compliments paid, and constantly to keep my mind upon the rack that I may not fail to introduce in my turn my jest or my lie. And this is called idleness! It is the labour of a galley slave.

The indolence I love is not that of a lazy fellow who sits with his arms crossed in total inaction, and thinks no more than he acts, but that of a child which is incessantly in motion doing nothing. I love to amuse myself with trifles, by beginning a hundred things, and never finishing one of them, by going and coming as I take either into my head, by changing my project at every instant, by following a fly through all its windings, in wishing to overturn a rock to see what is under it, by undertaking with ardour the work of ten years, and abandoning it without regret at the end of ten minutes; finally, in musing from morning until night without order or coherence, and in following in everything the caprice of the moment.

Botany, such as I have always considered it, and of which after my own manner I began to become passionately fond, was precisely an idle study, proper to fill up the void of my leisure, without leaving room for the delirium of imagination or the weariness of total inaction. Carelessly wandering in the woods and the country, mechanically gathering here a flower and there a branch, observing a thousand and a thousand times the same things, and always with the same interest, were to me the means of passing an eternity without a weary moment.

I know no homage more worthy of the Divinity than the silent admiration excited by the contemplation of his works. I can easily comprehend the reason why the inhabitants of great cities, who see nothing but walls, streets, and crimes, have but little faith; but not whence it happens that people in the country, and especially such as live in solitude, can possibly be without it. How comes it to pass these do not a hundred times a day elevate their minds in ecstasy to the author of the wonders which strike their senses? For my part, it is especially at rising, wearied by a want of sleep, that long habit inclines me to this elevation which imposes not the fatigue of thinking. But to this effect I must be struck with the ravishing beauties of nature. In my chamber I pray less frequently, and not so fervently; but at the view of a fine landscape I feel myself moved, but by what I am unable to tell. I have somewhere read of a wise bishop who on a visit to his diocese, found an old woman, whose only prayer consisted in the sole interjection, Oh! 'Good mother,' said he to her, 'continue to pray in this manner; your prayer is better than ours.' This better prayer is mine also.

THE WORKS OF

JEAN-JACQUES ROUSSEAU

(1712–1778)

Discourse on the Arts and Sciences (1749)
The Village Soothsayer (1753)
Discourse on the Origin of Inequality (1753)
Letter on French Music (1753)
Letter to d'Alembert on the Theatre (1758)
Discourse on Political Economy (1758)
Julie, or The New Héloïse (1761)
The Social Contract (1762)
Emile, or Education (1762)
The Confessions (1765–1770)
The Reveries of a Solitary Walker (1778)

VOLTAIRE

FRANÇOIS MARIE AROUET, who took the name of VOLTAIRE, the son of a lawyer, was born in Paris on the 21st of November 1694. He received a first-class education, and at an early age was taken up by Parisian literary circles as a young man of exceptional promise. His first writings were lampoons of the Regent, and he quickly found himself in the Bastille. This was the beginning of a long life of rebellion against every kind of authority and oppressive autocracy, whether King, Church, or the Law. He was almost continually in exile, and he used his brilliant talents, his enormous reputation as a playwright and poet, and his great wealth made as an army contractor, in a constant war on behalf of the oppressed. A number of people, unjustly condemned, owed their lives to him. In his lifetime he was regarded as the equal of Corneille and Racine as a writer of plays, and as a poet he took a place in the first rank. But to-day we remember him for his bitterly satirical short novels, of which the most famous, *Candide*, appeared in 1759. He returned to Paris in 1778 to see his last play produced, and killed himself by receiving and shaking hands with all his friends and acquaintances in the capital whom he had not seen for many years: a ceremony which lasted for two days. He died immediately after, on the 30th of May. During the Revolution the people, for whom he was a hero, removed his remains with great pomp to the Panthéon.

VOLTAIRE

by ANDRÉ MAUROIS

I

IN 1694 THERE WAS BORN INTO THE FAMILY OF A PARISIAN notary a puny child who was baptized François Marie Arouet, and who later rechristened himself Monsieur de Voltaire. We must remember that Voltaire's physical weakness was always yoked to a marvellously ardent and active temperament. For more than eighty years he said he was dying, but his ills never prevented him from working, from battling, from writing, or from mocking. It was an age when the English bourgeoisie were turning to Puritanism, while the French bourgeoisie were being tempted by Jansenism. Voltaire was brought up with a fanatical brother by a devout father. In reaction he acquired a horror of religious practices. Nevertheless his father had him educated by the Jesuits; but if they succeeded admirably in teaching him a love of the classics, they certainly did not manage to inspire him with a respect for religion.

What was to be done with this gifted child? Monsieur Arouet tried to make a lawyer of him, but the son had other ambitions. He knew some great lords. He wished to become an ambassador's page, and he left for Holland. There he committed a thousand follies, tried to carry off a girl with whom he was in love, and was sent back to France.

This was under the Regency, a weak and discredited government. It rained pamphlets and songs. Voltaire wrote some; it was known. In those days a *lettre de cachet* was enough to put a man in prison; suddenly Voltaire found himself condemned to the Bastille for a year. It was a severe lesson, and one which made him ponder the dangers of despotism. As a matter of fact, the régime at the Bastille was very mild. The prisoners were allowed freedom to work. While he was there Voltaire composed poems and tragedies; when he came out he had his *Œdipe* performed, and became famous.

Fame at thirty is a delightful thing. He enjoyed it, lived

among the great, made love to actresses, and became a man of the world; then a rude incident awoke him from his dream, and flung him on thornier paths. In revenge for a bold riposte a certain Chevalier de Rohan-Chabot had Voltaire thrashed by his lackeys. Voltaire tried to get justice, and attempted to fight the offender; but he was a mere commoner, and the Rohans had him thrown into the Bastille. When he came out he had declared war on a society which tolerated such injustice.

A new Voltaire was born. He left for England. His stay there quite transformed his thinking. He saw that there the bourgeois could aspire to any dignity, that liberty did not seem incompatible with order, that religion was tolerant of philosophy. The multiplicity of Protestant sects increased his scepticism. From reading Locke he took a philosophy, from Swift a model, from Newton a scientific doctrine. The Bastille had made him wish for a new society; England showed him what that society might be.

Returning to France in 1729, he soon regained fame and fortune. His tragedies were triumphs; his business undertakings prospered. But his whole conception of the world had changed, and he soon surreptitiously set it forth in his *Lettres Philosophiques sur les Anglais*. By describing English institutions he undertook to make the French reconsider their religious and political ideas. Thus roundabout he gave a preliminary sketch of his doctrine: civil and religious liberty, the importance of trade, the value of science. This book made him the champion of the middle classes in the struggle ahead. The police realized it, and prosecuted the book, which was burned by parliamentary decree in the court of the Palais de Justice. As for the author, he had to flee; he soon found asylum at the château of Cirey, which belonged to his friend and admirer the Marquise du Châtelet. She was a scholar herself. During a liaison of sixteen years she and Voltaire together studied astronomy, mechanics, chemistry, and even history; it was for her that he wrote a universal history which he called *Essai sur les Mœurs*.

Mme du Châtelet, like all women who love great men, wanted to see hers recognized by the world. She tried to reconcile him with the Court, succeeded in getting him into the Académie Française in 1746, and shone at his side in the miniature court of the Duchesse de Maine. It was for her that he began to write such stories as *Micromegas* and *Zadig*. They were tales written for fun, and he attached little importance to them, yet they added much to his fame.

Another little court, at Lunéville, where Stanislas Lesczinski, former King of Poland, reigned over a mistress and a professor, saw the great tragedy in Voltaire's life. Mme du Châtelet was led astray by young St.-Lambert, handsome and sensitive. She was surprised by Voltaire, who stormed, and then, like a true philosopher, forgave. But the lady conceived, and died in child-bed. Voltaire's grief was unfeigned.

Deprived of his refuge at Cirey, he sought shelter with the King of Prussia, Frederick II, with whom he had long maintained a friendly correspondence. All his life Voltaire dreamed of the 'enlightened despot'; he thought he had found one in Frederick, as later in Catherine of Russia. A stay at Potsdam soon showed him that the ways of philosopher kings were devilishly like those of tyrant kings. Where could he escape from both? He took the road for Switzerland; in that republican land he would be safe from the royal police (1754). But he soon learned that fanaticism was a menace in Geneva or Lausanne, just as at Paris. Protestant pastors preached against him. One could not be entirely secure in either France or Switzerland, and the safe thing was to have a foot in each country. With two houses on the shore of the lake and two along the frontier, he was able to flee at the slightest alarm, and wait for the storm to pass. In France he had the château of Ferney and the estate (comté) of Tournai; in Switzerland, a fine house at Lausanne and the Ermitage des Délices in Genevan territory. 'Thus crawling from one lair to the other, I escape from kings and armies.'

It was his long old age at Ferney which gave Voltaire's fame a chance to spread both wide and deep. Feeling himself in safety and free at last to say whatever he thought on the affairs of the world, he became the greatest journalist of his time, perhaps of all time. From Ferney a rain of pamphlets, of tracts, of facetiæ poured over Europe, now seriously attacking abuses, now turning them to ridicule. Several times Voltaire was led to take sides against official justice for accused persons whom he thought innocent. By winning the rehabilitation of Calas, an unfortunate Protestant who had been tortured and put to death for a crime he did not commit, by defending another Protestant, Sirven, and the unhappy Chevalier de la Barre, victim of the judges of

Abbeville, Voltaire won and deserved a reputation for courage and humanity that made him renowned in thousands of homes which his writings had never reached.

Soon he became a legend. All Europe knew the emaciated old man with the keen eyes, wrapped in a flowered dressing-gown, always dying and always the most active of the living; as eager to cultivate his garden as to compose tragedies; making clocks and silk stockings, casually tossing off a masterpiece like *Candide*; defending a victim as adroitly as he attacked an enemy; turning his château into a theatre, a tribunal, and a philosophers' council; corresponding with four kings, and wrangling with his neighbours; dangerous, amusing, and apparently immortal. This superhuman existence came to an end after all, but it came, as was fitting, by deification. On his last journey to Paris he was acclaimed by an immense crowd shouting: 'Room for Voltaire! Long live Voltaire! Glory to the defender of Calas!' On the stage of the Comédie Française he saw his bust crowned by the actors to the plaudits of the spectators who stood in a body to do him honour. A few weeks later he died (30th May 1778). He had had a happy life and a triumphant end.

II

Voltaire's life, his personal adventures and his position in the world allow us to predict pretty nearly what his philosophy will be. Because he had suffered intolerance, *lettres de cachet* and the insolence of grandees, and because he had imagination and a heart, he would be a stubborn opponent of all fanaticism and all despotism. Because he was a bourgeois and an excellent business man, he would admire the constitution adopted in England by 'a nation of shopkeepers.' Because by intelligence, shrewdness and talent he had amassed a great fortune, this reformer would never be a revolutionary. Finally, because he was at once admirably intelligent, interested in all the sciences from theology to politics and from astronomy to history, and able to explain the most obscure questions with simple lucidity, he would exercise on the men of his time and even on those of the following century a greater influence than any other writer.

We might well give to his complete works the celebrated

title, '*De omni re scibili et de quibusdam aliis,*' but though he does indeed speak 'of all things knowable and even of some others,' he is famous chiefly for his philosophy of religion, or rather of irreligion. His name has given us a substantive, *voltaireanism,* which dictionaries define as 'an attitude of mocking incredulity toward religion.' Throughout the nineteenth century adversaries of Christianity and sceptics of all religions invoked Voltaire. Monsieur Homais, Flaubert's anti-clerical pharmacist, believed he was drawing on Voltaire for his witticisms and his ideas. It is not certain, however, that Voltaire would have approved of M. Homais. If he made sport of the superstitions of established religion, he was so much preoccupied with religious problems that he devoted a great part of his works to them. If we are to study Voltaire's philosophy we must begin by indicating his answers to the principal metaphysical questions posed by religion.

In the first place, does God exist? No doubt of it: Voltaire believes that a divine mechanic planned, built and regulated the universe. His grand proof is the order in the world, 'the simple and sublime laws by which the celestial globes march in the abyss of space.' The clock proves the existence of the clock-maker, the marvellous work which is our universe shows a workman, and all the constant laws show a legislator.

There have, however, been thinkers who maintained that these regular laws of Nature might be due to chance. Nature exists to all eternity; everything in it changes continually. But if everything is for ever changing, all possible combinations are bound to occur. Thus in the infinity of centuries such a combination as the present order of the universe is not impossible.

This explanation of the world as chance Voltaire finds prodigiously illusory, 'in the first place because intelligent beings exist in the universe, and you cannot prove it possible for mere motion to produce intelligence; secondly, because by your own reasoning the odds are infinity to one that an intelligent cause animates the universe. A man alone facing infinity is poor indeed. When we see a fine machine, we say that there is a mechanic, and that the mechanic has an admirable understanding. The world is certainly an admirable machine; hence there is in the world an admirable intelligence, wherever it may be. This argument is an old one, and none the worse for that. . . .'

Objection; This world is not such a great success. We have

F   [137]

said it is an admirable machine whose perfection proves the existence of a God, but fundamentally is this true? And has not the machine tremendous defects which prove the very opposite of this doctrine? Voltaire never tires of painting the fearful ills to which poor man is heir. From the ulcers that ate the face of Pangloss to the Lisbon earthquake, from the slaughter of the battlefields to the furnace of the auto-da-fé, he takes pleasure in showing the horror of man's fate. Is it thinkable that a lord and father would invent such tortures to crush a few miserable little creatures? 'We are absolutely imperceptible animals, and yet we are borne down by everything that surrounds us. After all the countless cities destroyed, rebuilt, destroyed again like ant-hills, what shall we say of the seas of sand, of plagues, of inundations, of volcanoes, of earthquakes, of diseases, wars, and crimes?'

Voltaire sees the force of the objection, but he answers that God created the world by universal laws, that He does not concern himself with individual destinies, and that in any case there is in favour of God's existence an argument of an entirely different nature, and an irrefutable one—the moral argument.

'Belief in a God who rewards good deeds and punishes bad ones,' Voltaire asserts, 'is the belief most useful to mankind. It is the only curb on powerful men; it is the only curb on men who skilfully commit secret crimes. Fifteenth-century Italy swarmed with atheists. What happened? It was as common to poison a man as to give him supper, and to sink a stiletto in your friend's heart as to embrace him. . . . I do not ask you to mingle with this necessary faith the superstitions which dishonour it. The atheist is a monster; the victim of superstition is another monster. . . . The narrow zone of virtue lies between atheism and fanaticism. Believe in a good God, and be good. . . . I should hate to deal with an atheist prince who found it to his interest to have me pounded in a mortar; I am very sure I should be pounded. If I were a sovereign I should hate to deal with atheist courtiers. It is necessary to princes and peoples that the idea of a Supreme Being should be deeply engraved in their minds. . . .'

It cannot be said that this proof of God's existence is a very solid one, for it proves equally well the necessity of believing, with certain Oriental peoples, in the divinity of the sovereign.

'If you cease to believe that the King is a God, what will become of the State?' But it was not for himself that Voltaire liked this argument; it was for the people. What would become of the lord of Ferney if his servants ceased to believe in the punishments and recompenses of the other world?

III

Agreed, then, that we believe in God, that is, in a marvellously powerful mind which has built the wonderful machine of the universe, and which has imposed moral laws upon us. But we will not wring from our arguments more than is in them, and we will recognize that if the existence of the world proves the existence of a God, it by no means proves the existence of the God of Jews and Christians, any more than of any other particular God. Our deist is also an agnostic.

'What is the nature of God? Is He corporeal or spiritual? How,' replies Voltaire, 'do you expect me to know?' We see that each people has created its gods in its own image. Before arguing the nature of God we must meditate on the following story: 'One day,' says Voltaire, 'I heard a mole arguing with a May-beetle in front of a summer-house which I had just put up at the bottom of my garden. "That is a fine structure," said the mole; "it must have been a powerful mole indeed that produced such a work." "You're joking," said the May-beetle. "A May-beetle replete with genius was the architect of that building." Since then I have resolved never to argue the matter.' We believe, then, in a God, but not in the God of the religions, and we will talk freely and quite gaily of the absurd tales they have made up. Voltaire's whole *Dictionnaire Philosophique* is one long string of pleasantries about Moses, Abraham, and the biblical heroes.

What is man's position before God? Does Voltaire believe in free will? Like his friends the scientists, he admits that the world is subject to fixed laws. These laws are immutable: 'Bodies fall toward the centre of the earth. . . . Pear trees can never bear pineapples. . . . The instinct of a spaniel cannot be the instinct of an ostrich. . . . Everything is arranged, interlocked, limited. . . . Man can have but a certain number of teeth, of hairs, and of ideas. A time is bound to come when he loses teeth, hair, and ideas. . . . If one could interfere in the destiny of a fly, one could shape the destiny of all flies, of all men, of all Nature. Only imbeciles say, "My doctor pulled my aunt through a mortal illness. He added ten years to her life." Your doctor saved your aunt. But by so doing he certainly did not defy the order of Nature; he followed it. It is plain that your aunt could not avoid being born in such-and-such a city, having such-and-such a disease at such-and-such a time, that the doctor could not be elsewhere than in the city where he was, that your aunt was bound to call him, that he was bound to prescribe the drugs which cured her. Hence the order of Nature was not disturbed by the cure of your aunt. The man who called us "puppets of Providence" seems to have aptly described us.'

But could not God himself, by means of miracles, modify His own laws in favour of those who deserve it? No. God is the slave of His own will, of His wisdom, of His inherent nature. He cannot violate the laws of Nature because he cannot be fickle and inconstant like us. The Eternal Being cannot become a weathercock.

If God can make no changes in the laws of this world, what is the use of addressing prayers to Him? This is, as a matter of fact, perfectly vain, and Voltaire would not have us pray. 'A fine thing, your prayers and petitions to God! One praises a man because one thinks him vain, weak, and because one hopes to make him change his mind. Let us do our duty to God: let us be just. That is the only true prayer.'

Voltaire, then, is a determinist. But he finds himself led to re-establish free will, as he re-establishes God, for moral reasons; for want of belief in free will we would fall back into social chaos. To deny liberty is to destroy all the bonds of human society. 'What is to be gained by regarding ourselves as turn-spits, when we act like free beings?' Liberty is but the illusion we have of it, but this illusion is necessary to keep us in a state where we can believe and act. 'The welfare of society demands that man should believe himself a free agent. I begin to think more of happiness than of a truth.' Here he finds an argument which reconciles everything. 'We are wheels in an immense machine, but everything goes on in our minds as if we were free agents, because this feeling of freedom is itself one of the wheels of the machine.'

Does Voltaire believe in the existence of the soul and in immortality? He believes there is a force distinct from matter, subtler than matter, which, if you like, might be called the soul;

but he does not believe in immortality at all. 'About the soul we know nothing. Everyone should say to himself: Who are you? Whence do you come? What are you doing? You are thinking and feeling something, and if you feel and think for a thousand million years you will never know more than this by your own lights. God gave you understanding to do right, and not to penetrate to the essence of things which He created. Besides, what would immortality mean, and what could a soul be which felt with no body, heard without ears, smelled without a nose, and touched without hands?'

Here we are on dangerous ground again. If souls are not immortal, how can they be punished or rewarded after death? What becomes of the belief in Hell and Paradise? There Voltaire is not far from agreeing with a Catholic priest whose story he tells. The priest said to a too-indulgent Huguenot minister, 'My friend, I don't believe in eternal hell any more than you do, but it is a good thing for your maid, your tailor, and even your lawyer to believe in it.'

In short, Voltaire entirely subordinates metaphysics to morals, that is to daily practice. There you have the whole sense of that admirable little novel, Candide. Candide is a most pessimistic picture of the universe as we know it. We are exposed to fearful ills; we are condemned without having done anything very wrong, or, on the contrary, are pardoned despite our faults. Men are massacred by the Bulgars or burned by the Inquisition; women are violated by pirates or by the grand inquisitors. It is all absurd, and the world as it is resembles the nightmare of a madman. Let us not try to understand, and 'let us cultivate our garden.' This phrase, with which Candide ends, must be taken in a very general sense. It is an engineer's morality. Cultivating our garden means: let us build clean cities, let us try to improve the production of the goods necessary to mankind, let us till the soil; in short, let us live as Voltaire himself lived at Ferney, and not trouble about the rest. Life is neither good nor bad. It is what it is. We must accept it, and try to improve it to the extent of our poor abilities. How? By work, by moderation, by patience. The arguments of metaphysicians are useless; the gardener's spade-strokes are more effective. *We must cultivate our garden.*

The only weakness of this so reasonable Voltairean pragmatism is that it takes no account of spiritual needs. It is easy enough to tell men, 'Believe in God, or your morality will collapse.' But it is almost impossible to maintain a real belief in that fashion. It is easy enough to tell them, 'Believe in liberty and in the immortality of the soul, or no civilized society will be possible.' But that is the surest way of turning them from those two beliefs. Finally, it is easy enough to say, 'Cultivate your garden,' and even to do it. But it is impossible to dispel metaphysical doubts by this mechanical labour alone. Voltaire's doctrine does not explain why religion is. Why, when one religion loses its authority, do men always rebuild it under nearly similar forms? Voltaire does not even set himself this historical problem.

IV

Nevertheless he is a historian, and undoubtedly the greatest historian of his century. Not only did he write the history of Louis XIV and that of Charles XII, but above all he was among the first, with his *Essai sur les Mœurs*, to attempt a universal history, or as we would say to-day an Outline of History. Bossuet had been before him in daring to undertake a *Discours sur l'Histoire Universelle*. But the intentions of the two works are diametrically opposed. Bossuet wanted to show that history is the result of the will of Providence which interferes unceasingly to regulate the fate of empires; Voltaire, on the contrary, strives to push the supernatural out of history. He takes pleasure in showing that great events come from small causes—for example that if the Duchess of Marlborough has been more receptive to the Queen of England's fondness for her, the fate of Europe would have been changed. Voltaire believes that historical events are but results of chance, and that the march of destiny is occasionally turned aside only by men of genius.

He was the first to include in universal history the history of the great peoples of Asia—India, Japan, China. His idea was to show the unimportance of the small Jewish-Christian adventure, and of the sacred scriptures, in the history of our planet. His *Essai sur les Mœurs* is above all else a pamphlet against supernatural history. For the prejudices of the sacred historians he merely substitutes his own no less dangerous prejudices. In the whole history of the Middle Ages, he sees but 'a mass of crimes, follies, and misfortunes.' He understood the nature of feudalism extremely ill.

He makes of modern history one long struggle between secular and clerical powers, between Church and State; and he rashly believes that the victory of the State will be beyond a doubt the end of all persecution. That is indeed but slight understanding of human nature; and the State, having triumphed over the Church, was to persecute its adversaries in the name of a doctrine as savagely as, and sometimes more savagely than, the Church had done in the name of a faith.

But Voltaire is admirable when he discovers behind the variety of customs and beliefs the profound identity of institutions. Everywhere he sees laws established to preserve what is essential to the human species, what prevents its total ruin: family life, property, security, and a curb imposed upon arbitrary power by law, or at least by custom. 'Asiatic ceremonies are bizarre. Asiatic beliefs are absurd, but their precepts are just. . . . Dervish, fakir, Buddhist, and priest all say, Be just and kind.' 'From this picture we see that everything belonging intimately to human nature is alike from one end of the universe to the other, while everything depending on custom is different. Custom produces variety; nature, unity. The soil is everywhere the same, and cultivation produces different fruits.'

This conclusion was quite new at the time, and Voltaire drew from his historical studies a political credo which amounts to a very wise liberalism. What Voltaire passionately admired in his youth, and continued to admire all his life, was the England of the Whigs: liberty of thought and expression, toleration, supremacy of civil over religious authority; a chance for men of an inferior class to rise to a higher class, constitutional and limited monarchy—such is the political theory of Voltaire. If he had lived to see the Revolution he would have advocated maintaining Louis XVI, but setting an English-style parliament to watch over him.

To sum up, what he wants is to make our poor race as little unhappy as possible. He does not believe it can be preserved from inequality, and he expresses himself on the subject with a certain harshness. 'On our unhappy globe it is impossible for men living in society not to be divided into two classes, one of oppressors, the other of the oppressed. The human species as it is cannot subsist without an infinite number of useful men who have nothing, for a man at his ease will not quit his own land to till

[143]

yours, and if you need a pair of boots it is not the Attorney-General who will make them for you. Equality, the most natural of ideas, is at the same time also the most illusory. . . .'

He has a horror of war. He describes it a hundred times, with harsh and realistic imagery, in the manner of Goya. He hates cruelty in every form, and torture in particular. He believes we must struggle against it, but that man is a dangerous animal, and that it will always be difficult to keep him from fighting. He believes in the possibility not of making men good but of so governing them that their wickedness shall do the least possible harm. We cannot change the laws of nature, but we can try to command nature by obeying it, just as a skilful engineer does not destroy the torrent, but succeeds in harnessing it.

One day as he was writing the article on *Civil and Ecclesiastical Law* for his *Dictionnaire Philosophique*, he asked himself what were the essential rules of free government, and he came to wish 'that no ecclesiastical law should be valid without the express sanction of the government; that all ecclesiastics should always be subject to the government, since they are subjects of the State; that there should be but one weight, one measure, one tax; that all law should be clear, uniform, and precise; that nothing should be held infamous but vice; that all imposts should be proportional.' These desires were to figure in almost all the *cahiers* of demands presented by the Third Estate in 1789, and almost all have passed into law among the best governed nations.

It has been said that this political theory of Voltaire's was predominantly negative; but all government must begin by being negative, since it is essentially a control and a limit imposed on human passions. The good which Voltaire did at Ferney proves that he was also capable of imagining the constructive and positive task of government. He had good sense, wit, admirable intelligence, pity for the unfortunate, all mixed with a great hatred of oppressors and a great fear of the mob. Those are excellent ingredients for a liberal and prudent statesman, which is just what he was.

V

'Despite the faults with which one may reproach Voltaire,' writes the Duchess of Choiseul, 'he will always be the author whom I shall read and re-read with most pleasure, because of his taste and his universality. What is it to me that he tells me nothing new, if he develops what I have thought, and if he tells me better than anyone else what others have already said? I do not need to have him teach me more than anyone else knows, and what author can tell me so passing well as he what everyone knows?' Here Mme de Choiseul translates to perfection the feeling which Voltaire's contemporaries had for his clarity and his universality. This man who knew everything, who talked competently of science, of economics, of politics, of history, and of religion, who illuminated the most recondite questions and gave his readers the feeling that like him they were qualified to understand everything —this man wielded a tremendous influence over the nobility and the cultivated bourgeoisie of his time. He imbued them with a liberalism healthy in itself, but bound to lead to the excesses of the Revolution because it too soon broke down barriers in whose necessity Voltaire after all believed more than anyone else.

After the Revolution, when France returned to her old traditions, when she found her kings and her religion again, the new philosophers, Bonald and Joseph de Maistre, considered Voltaire one of the powers of darkness. The liberal opposition to the new régime, on the contrary, adopted him as their inspiration, and between 1815 and 1830 he was read more than during his lifetime. This was the period when his writings created the French anticlerical petty bourgeoisie of which M. Homais is one type, and which toward the end of the century made up the Radical party. His influence on literature was also great, but was exercised chiefly by the best part of his work, namely by his novels. The spirit of *Candide* inspired Renan, Anatole France, and even such Rightest authors as Charles Maurras and Jacques Bainville, while Voltaire's style, swift, brilliant, clear, and simple, remained the ideal of a whole clan of French writers—those who did not adopt the master of the rival school, Chateaubriand. Even abroad such writers as Byron owed much to Voltaire's irony. Bernard Shaw's great ambition was later to be that of playing in England the rôle played by Voltaire in France, and close to our own day Lytton Strachey was to offer the odd spectacle of an English humorist seated in Voltaire's reclining arm-chair.

We must set against the judgment just quoted from Mme de Choiseul that of another woman, Empress Eugénie. 'Voltaire . . .' she said. 'I shall never forgive him for having made

F*   [145]

me understand things which I shall never understand.' This is an admirable *mot,* for it finds the one chink in the armour of the Voltarean spirit. That in human nature and in the universe there is an immense share of mystery, that men have feelings and cling to beliefs which words are powerless to describe, that nations live as much by traditions and memories as by clear ideas—this Voltaire never recognized. And that is why, after his nineteenth-century triumphs (which were triumphs of opposition), he has lost favour, at least so far as his dogmatic works go, with many cultivated people. But human thought is condemned to swing for ever to and fro between excess of credulity and excess of scepticism. A Voltaire, with his brilliant, lucid mockery, was necessary to reduce to impotence the fanatics of his age; a reaction was necessary in its turn to calm and subdue the fanatics of Voltaireanism; soon a new Voltaire must write a new *Candide* about fanatics of a kind unknown to Ferney, who are hatching misery for man to-day, snatching him from the cultivation of his garden.

CANDIDE

OR OPTIMISM[1]

HOW CANDIDE WAS BROUGHT UP IN A FINE CASTLE, AND HOW HE WAS EXPELLED FROM THENCE

THERE LIVED IN WESTPHALIA, IN THE CASTLE OF MY LORD THE Baron of Thunder-ten-tronckh, a young man, on whom nature had bestowed the most agreeable manners. His face was the index to his mind. He had an upright heart, with an easy frankness; which, I believe, was the reason he got the name of *Candide*. He was suspected, by the old servants of the family, to be the son of my Lord the Baron's sister, by a very honest gentleman of the neighbourhood, whom the young lady declined to marry, because he could only produce seventy-one armorial quarterings; the rest of his genealogical tree having been destroyed through the injuries of time.

The Baron was one of the most powerful lords in Westphalia; his castle had both a gate and windows; and his great hall was even adorned with tapestry. The dogs of his outer yard composed his hunting pack upon occasion, his grooms were his huntsmen, and the vicar of the parish was his chief almoner. He was called My Lord by everybody, and everyone laughed when he told his stories.

My Lady the Baroness, who weighed about twenty-five stone, attracted, by that means, very great attention, and did the honours of the house with a dignity that rendered her still more respectable. Her daughter Cunegonde, aged about seventeen years, was of a ruddy complexion, fresh, plump, and well calculated to excite the passions. The Baron's son appeared to be in every respect worthy of his father. The preceptor, Pangloss, was the oracle of the house, and little Candide listened to his lectures with all the simplicity that was suitable to his age and character.

Pangloss taught metaphysico-theologo-cosmolonigology. He proved most admirably, that there could not be an effect without

---

[1] *Editor's Note:* Voltaire gave this novel the fictitious sub-title: 'Translated from the German of Dr. Ralph, with the additions found in the doctor's pocket when he died at Minden, in the year of grace 1759.'

a cause; that, in this best of possible worlds, my Lord the Baron's castle was the most magnificent of castles, and my Lady the best of Baronesses that possibly could be.

'It is demonstrable,' said he, 'that things cannot be otherwise than they are: for all things having been made for some end, they must necessarily be for the best end. Observe well, that the nose has been made for carrying spectacles; therefore we have spectacles. The legs are visibly designed for stockings, and therefore we have stockings. Stones have been formed to be hewn, and make castles; therefore my Lord has a very fine castle; the greatest baron of the province ought to be the best accommodated. Swine were made to be eaten; therefore we eat pork all the year round: consequently, those who have merely asserted that all is good, have said a very foolish thing; they should have said all is the best possible.'

Candide listened attentively, and believed implicitly; for he thought Miss Cunegonde extremely handsome, though he never had the courage to tell her so. He concluded, that next to the good fortune of being Baron of Thunder-ten-tronckh, the second degree of happiness was that of being Miss Cunegonde, the third to see her every day, and the fourth to listen to the teachings of Master Pangloss, the greatest philosopher of the province, and consequently of the whole world.

One day Cunegonde having taken a walk in the environs of the castle, in a little wood, which they called a park, espied Doctor Pangloss giving a lesson in experimental philosophy to her mother's chambermaid; a little brown wench, very handsome, and very docile. As Miss Cunegonde had a strong inclination for the sciences, she observed, without making any noise, the reiterated experiments that were going on before her eyes; she saw very clearly the sufficient reason of the Doctor, the effects and the causes; and she returned greatly flurried, quite pensive, and full of desire to be learned; imagining that she might be a sufficient reason for young Candide, who also might be the same to her.

On her return to the castle, she met Candide, and blushed; Candide also blushed; she wished him good morrow with a faltering voice, and Candide answered her, hardly knowing what he said. The next day, after dinner, as they arose from table, Cunegonde and Candide happened to get behind the screen.

Cunegonde dropped her handkerchief, and Candide picked it up; she, not thinking any harm, took hold of his hand; and the young man, not thinking any harm either, kissed the hand of the young lady, with an eagerness, a sensibility, and grace, very particular; their lips met, their eyes sparkled, their knees trembled, their hands strayed. The Baron of Thunder-ten-tronckh happening to pass close by the screen, and observing this cause and effect, thrust Candide out of the castle, with lusty kicks. Cunegonde fell into a swoon and as soon as she came to herself, was heartily cuffed on the ears by my Lady the Baroness. Thus all was thrown into confusion in the finest and most agreeable castle possible.

WHAT BECAME OF CANDIDE AMONG THE BULGARIANS

Candide being expelled from the terrestrial paradise, rambled a long while without knowing where, weeping, and lifting up his eyes to heaven, and sometimes turning them towards the finest of castles, which contained the handsomest of baronesses. He laid himself down, without his supper, in the open fields, between two furrows, while the snow fell in great flakes. Candide, almost frozen to death, crawled next morning to the neighbouring village, which was called Waldberghoff-trarbk-dikdorff. Having no money, and almost dying with hunger and fatigue, he stopped in a dejected posture before the gate of an inn. Two men, dressed in blue, observing him in such a situation, 'Brother,' says one of them to the other, 'there is a young fellow well built, and of a proper height.' They accosted Candide, and invited him very civilly to dinner.

'Gentlemen,' replied Candide, with an agreeable modesty, 'you do me much honour, but I have no money to pay my shot.'

'O sir,' said one of the blues, 'persons of your appearance and merit never pay anything; are you not five feet five inches high?'

'Yes, gentlemen, that is my height,' returned he, making a bow.

'Come, sir, sit down at table; we will not only treat you, but we will never let such a man as you want money; men are made to assist one another.'

'You are in the right,' said Candide; 'that is what Pangloss always told me, and I see plainly that everything is for the best.'

[149]

They entreated him to take a few crowns, which he accepted, and would have given them his note; but they refused it, and sat down to table.

'Do not you tenderly love——?'

'O yes,' replied he, 'I tenderly love Miss Cunegonde.'

'No,' said one of the gentlemen; 'we ask you if you do tenderly love the King of the Bulgarians?'

'Not at all,' said he, 'for I never saw him.'

'How! he is the most charming of kings, and you must drink his health.'

'Oh, with all my heart, gentlemen,' and drinks.

'That is enough,' said they to him; 'you are now the bulwark, the support, the defender, the hero of the Bulgarians; your fortune is made, and you are certain of glory.' Instantly they put him in irons, and carried him to the regiment. They made him turn to the right, to the left, draw the rammer, return the rammer, present, fire, step double; and they gave him thirty blows with a cudgel. The next day, he performed his exercises not quite so badly, and received but twenty blows; the third day the blows were restricted to ten, and he was looked upon by his fellow-soldiers, as a kind of prodigy.

Candide, quite stupefied, could not well conceive how he had become a hero. One fine Spring day he took it into his head to walk out, going straight forward, imagining that the human, as well as the animal species, were entitled to make whatever use they pleased of their limbs. He had not travelled two leagues, when four other heroes, six feet high, came up to him, bound him, and put him into a dungeon. He is asked by a Court-martial whether he chooses to be whipped six and thirty times through the whole regiment, or receive at once twelve bullets through the forehead? He in vain argued that the will is free, and that he chose neither the one nor the other; he was obliged to make a choice; he therefore resolved, in virtue of God's gift called *free-will*, to run the gauntlet six and thirty times. He underwent this discipline twice. The regiment being composed of two thousand men, he received four thousand lashes, which laid open all his muscles and nerves, from the nape of his neck to the back. As they were proceeding to a third course, Candide, being quite spent, begged as a favour that they would be so kind as to shoot him; he obtained his request; they hoodwinked him, and made him kneel; the King of the Bulgarians passing by, enquired into the crime of the delinquent; and as this prince was a person of great penetration, he discovered from what he heard of Candide, that he was a young metaphysician, entirely ignorant of the things of this world; and he granted him his pardon, with a clemency which will be extolled in all histories, and throughout all ages. An experienced surgeon cured Candide in three weeks, with emollients prescribed by no less a master than Dioscorides. His skin had already begun to grow again, and he was able to walk, when the King of the Bulgarians gave battle to the King of the Abares.

HOW CANDIDE MADE HIS ESCAPE FROM THE BULGARIANS, AND WHAT AFTERWARDS BEFEL HIM

Nothing could be so fine, so neat, so brilliant, so well ordered, as the two armies. The trumpets, fifes, hautboys, drums, and cannon, formed an harmony superior to what hell itself could invent. The cannon swept off at first about six thousand men on each side; afterwards, the musketry carried away from the best of worlds, about nine or ten thousand rascals that infected its surface. The bayonet was likewise the sufficient reason of the death of some thousands of men. The whole number might amount to about thirty thousand souls. Candide, who trembled like a philosopher, hid himself as well as he could, during this heroic butchery.

At last, while the two kings were causing *Te deums*—glory to God—to be sung in their respective camps, he resolved to go somewhere else, to reason upon the effects and causes. He walked over heaps of the dead and dying; he came at first to a neighbouring village belonging to the Abares, but found it in ashes; for it had been burnt by the Bulgarians, according to the law of nations. Here were to be seen old men full of wounds, casting their eyes on their murdered wives, who were holding their infants to their bloody breasts. You might see in another place virgins, outraged after they had satisfied the natural desires of some of those heroes, breathing out their last sighs. Others, half-burnt, praying earnestly for instant death. The whole field was covered with brains, and with legs and arms lopped off.

Candide betook himself with all speed to another village. It belonged to the Bulgarians, and had met with the same treatment from the Abarian heroes. Candide, walking still forward over quivering limbs, or through rubbish of houses, got at last out of the theatre of war, having some small quantity of provisions in his knapsack, and never forgetting Miss Cunegonde. His provisions failed him when he arrived in Holland; but having heard that everyone was rich in that country, and that they were Christians, he did not doubt but he should be as well treated there as he had been in my Lord the Baron's castle, before he had been expelled thence on account of Miss Cunegonde's sparkling eyes.

He asked alms from several grave-looking persons, who all replied, that if he continued that trade, they would confine him in a house of correction, where he should learn to earn his bread.

He applied afterwards to a man, who for a whole hour had been discoursing on the subject of charity, before a large assembly. This orator, looking at him askance, said to him:

'What are you doing here? Are you for the good cause?'

'There is no effect without a cause,' replied Candide, modestly; 'all is necessarily linked, and ordered for the best. A necessity banished me from Miss Cunegonde; a necessity forced me to run the gauntlet; another necessity makes me beg my bread, till I can get into some business by which to earn it. All this could not be otherwise.'

'My friend,' said the orator to him, 'do you believe that the Anti-Christ is alive?'

'I never heard whether he is or not,' replied Candide; 'but whether he is, or is not, I want bread!'

'You do not deserve to eat any,' said the other; 'get you gone, you rogue; get you gone, you wretch; never in thy life come near me again!'

The orator's wife, having popped her head out of the chamber window, and seeing a man who doubted whether Anti-Christ was alive, poured on his head a full vessel of dirty water. Oh heavens! to what excess does religious zeal transport the fair sex!

A man who had not been baptized, a good Anabaptist, named *James*, saw the barbarous and ignominious manner with which they treated one of his brethern, a being with two feet, without feathers, and endowed with a rational soul. He took him home with him, cleaned him, gave him bread and beer, made him a present of two florins, and offered to teach him the method of working in his manufactories of Persian stuffs, which are fabricated in Holland. Candide, prostrating himself almost to the ground, cried out, 'Master Pangloss argued well when he said, that everything is for the best in this world; for I am infinitely more affected with your very great generosity, than by the hard-heartedness of that gentleman with the cloak, and the lady, his wife.'

Next day, as he was taking a walk, he met a beggar, all covered over with sores, his eyes half dead, the tip of his nose eaten off, his mouth turned to one side of his face, his teeth black, speaking through his throat, tormented with a violent cough, with gums so rotten, that his teeth came near falling out every time he spat.

HOW CANDIDE MET HIS OLD MASTER OF PHILOSOPHY, DR. PANGLOSS, AND WHAT HAPPENED TO THEM

Candide, moved still more with compassion than with horror, gave this frightful mendicant the two florins which he had received of his honest Anabaptist James. The spectre fixed his eyes attentively upon him, dropt some tears, and was going to fall upon his neck. Candide, affrighted, drew back.

'Alas!' said the one wretch to the other, 'don't you know your dear Pangloss?'

'What do I hear! Is it you, my dear master! You in this dreadful condition! What misfortune has befallen you? Why are you no longer in the most magnificent of castles? What has become of Miss Cunegonde, the nonpareil of the fair sex, the masterpiece of nature?'

'I have no more strength,' said Pangloss.

Candide immediately carried him to the Anabaptist's stable, where he gave him a little bread to eat. When Pangloss was refreshed a little, 'Well,' said Candide, 'what has become of Cunegonde?'

'She is dead,' replied the other.

Candide fainted away at this word; but his friend recovered his senses, with a little bad vinegar which he found by chance in the stable.

Candide opening his eyes, cried out, 'Cunegonde is dead!

[153]

Ah, best of worlds, where art thou now? But of what distemper did she die? Was not the cause, her seeing me driven out of the castle by my Lord, her father, with such hard kicks on the breech?'

'No,' said Pangloss, 'she was gutted by some Bulgarian soldiers, after having been barbarously ravished. They knocked my Lord the Baron on the head, for attempting to protect her; my Lady the Baroness was cut in pieces; my poor pupil was treated like his sister; and as for the castle, there is not one stone left upon another, nor a barn, nor a sheep, nor a duck, nor a tree. But we have been sufficiently revenged; for the Abarians have done the very same thing to a neighbouring barony, which belonged to a Bulgarian Lord.'

At this discourse, Candide fainted away a second time; but coming to himself, and having said all that he ought to say, he enquired into the cause and the effect, and into the sufficient reason that had reduced Pangloss to so deplorable a condition. 'Alas,' said the other, 'it was love; love, the comforter of the human race, the preserver of the universe, the soul of all sensible beings, tender love.' 'Alas!' said Candide, 'I know this love, the sovereign of hearts, the soul of our soul; yet it never cost me more than a kiss, and twenty kicks. But how could this charming cause produce in you so abominable an effect?'

Pangloss made answers as follows: 'Oh my dear Candide, you know Paquetta, the pretty attendant on our noble Baroness; I tasted in her arms the delights of Paradise, which produced those torments of hell with which you see me devoured. She was infected, and perhaps she is dead. Paquetta received this present from a very learned monk, who had it from an old countess, who received it from a captain of horse, who was indebted for it to a marchioness, who got it from a Spaniard. For my part, I shall give it to nobody, for I am dying.'

'Oh Pangloss!' cried Candide, 'what a strange genealogy! Was not the devil at the head of it?'

'Not at all,' replied the great man; 'it was a thing indispensable; a necessary ingredient in the best of worlds; for if the Spaniard had not caught, in an island of America, this distemper, we should have had neither chocolate nor cochineal. It may also be observed, that to this day, upon our continent, this malady is as peculiar to us, as is religious controversy. The Turks, the Indians, the Persians, the Chinese, the Siamese, and the

Japanese, know nothing of it yet. But there is sufficient reason why they, in their turn, should become acquainted with it, a few centuries hence. In the meantime, it has made marvellous progress among us, and especially in those great armies composed of honest hirelings, well disciplined, who decide the fates of states; for we may rest assured, that when thirty thousand men in a pitched battle fight against troops equal to them in number, there are about twenty thousand of them on each side who have the pox.'

'That is admirable,' said Candide; 'but you must be cured.' 'Ah! how can I?' said Pangloss; 'I have not a penny, my friend; and throughout the whole extent of this globe, we cannot get anyone to bleed us, or give us a glister, without paying for it, or getting some other person to pay for us.'

This last speech determined Candide. He went and threw himself at the feet of his charitable Anabaptist James, and gave him so touching a description of the state his friend was reduced to, that the good man did not hesitate to entertain Dr. Pangloss, and had him cured at his own expense. During the cure, Pangloss lost only an eye and an ear. As he wrote well, and understood arithmetic perfectly, the Anabaptist made him his bookkeeper. At the end of two months, being obliged to go to Lisbon on account of his business, he took the two philosophers along with him, in his ship. Pangloss explained to him how everything was such as it could not be better; but James was not of this opinion. 'Mankind,' said he, 'must have somewhat corrupted their nature; for they were not born wolves, and yet they have become wolves; God has given them neither cannon of twenty-four pounds, nor bayonets; and yet they have made cannon and bayonets to destroy one another, I might throw into the account bankrupts; and the law which seizes on the effects of bankrupts only to bilk the creditors.' 'All this was indispensable,' replied the one-eyed doctor, 'and private misfortunes constitute the general good; so that the more private misfortunes there are, the whole is the better.' While he was thus reasoning, the air grew dark, the winds blew from the four quarters of the world, and the ship was attacked by a dreadful storm, within sight of the harbour of Lisbon.

TEMPEST, SHIPWRECK, EARTHQUAKE AND WHAT BECAME OF
DR. PANGLOSS, CANDIDE, AND JAMES THE ANABAPTIST

One half of the passengers being weakened, and ready to breathe their last, with the inconceivable anguish which the rolling of the ship conveyed through the nerves and all the humours of the body, which were quite disordered, were not capable of being alarmed at the danger they were in. The other half uttered cries and made prayers; the sails were rent, the masts broken, and the ship became leaky. Everyone worked that was able, nobody cared for anything and no order was kept. The Anabaptist contributed his assistance to work the ship. As he was upon deck, a furious sailor rudely struck him, and laid him sprawling on the planks; but with the blow he gave him, he himself was so violently jolted, that he tumbled overboard with his head foremost, and remained suspended by a piece of a broken mast. Honest James ran to his assistance, and helped him on deck again; but in the attempt, he fell into the sea, in the sight of the sailor, who suffered him to perish, without deigning to look upon him. Candide drew near and saw his benefactor, one moment emerging, and the next swallowed up for ever. He was just going to throw himself into the sea after him, when the philosopher Pangloss hindered him, by demonstrating to him, that the road to Lisbon had been made on purpose for this Anabaptist to be drowned in. While he was proving this, *a priori*, the vessel foundered, and all perished except Pangloss, Candide, and the brutal sailor, who drowned the virtuous Anabaptist. The villain luckily swam ashore, whither Pangloss and Candide were carried on a plank.

When they had recovered themselves a little, they walked towards Lisbon. They had some money left, with which they hoped to save themselves from hunger, after having escaped from the storm.

Scarce had they set foot in the city, bewailing the death of their benefactor, when they perceived the earth to tremble under their feet, and saw the sea swell in the harbour, and dash to pieces the ships that were at anchor. The whirling flames and ashes covered the streets and public places, the houses tottered, and their roofs fell to the foundations, and the foundations were scattered; thirty thousand inhabitants of all ages and sexes were crushed to death in the ruins. The sailor, whistling and swearing, said, 'There is some booty to be got here.' 'What can be the sufficient reason of this phenomenon?' said Pangloss. 'This is certainly the last day of the world,' cried Candide. The sailor ran quickly into the midst of the ruins, encountered death to find money, found it, laid hold of it, got drunk, and having slept himself sober, purchased the favours of the first willing girl he met with, among the ruins of the demolished houses, and in the midst of the dying and the dead. While he was thus engaged, Pangloss pulled him by the sleeve; 'My friend,' said he, 'this is not right; you trespass against universal reason, you choose your time badly.' 'Brains and blood!' answered the other; 'I am a sailor, and was born at Batavia; you have mistaken your man, this time, with your universal reason.'

Some pieces of stone having wounded Candide, he lay sprawling in the street, and covered with rubbish. 'Alas!' said he to Pangloss, 'get me a little wine and oil; I am dying.' 'This trembling of the earth is no new thing,' answered Pangloss. 'The City of Lima, in America, experienced the same concussions last year; the same cause has the same effects; there is certainly a train of sulphur under the earth, from Lima to Lisbon.' 'Nothing is more probable,' said Candide; 'but, for God's sake, a little oil and wine.' 'How probable?' replied the philosopher; 'I maintian that the thing is demonstrable.' Candide lost all sense, and Pangloss brought him a little water from a neighbouring fountain.

The day following, having found some provisions, in rummaging through the rubbish, they recruited their strength a little. Afterwards, they employed themselves like others, in administering relief to the inhabitants that had escaped from death. Some citizens that had been relieved by them, gave them as good a dinner as could be expected amidst such a disaster. It is true that the repast was mournful, and the guests watered their bread with their tears. But Pangloss consoled them by the assurance that things could not be otherwise; 'For,' said he, 'all this must necessarily be for the best. For if this volcano is at Lisbon, it could not be elsewhere; for it is impossible that things should not be where they are, for all is good.'

A little man clad in black, who belonged to the Inquisition, and sat at his side, took him up very politely, and said: 'It seems, sir, you do not believe in original sin; for if all is for the best, then there has been neither Fall nor punishment.'

'I most humbly ask your Excellency's pardon,' answered Pangloss, still more politely; 'for the fall of man and the curse necessarily entered into the best of worlds possible.' 'Then, sir, you do not believe there is liberty,' said the inquisitor. 'Your Excellency will excuse me,' said Pangloss; 'liberty can consist with absolute necessity; for it was necessary we should be free; because, in short, the determinate will——'

Pangloss was in the middle of his proposition, when the inquisitor made a signal with his head to the tall armed footman in a cloak, who waited upon him, to bring him a glass of port wine.

HOW A FINE INQUISITION WAS CELEBRATED TO PREVENT EARTHQUAKES, AND HOW CANDIDE WAS WHIPPED

After the earthquake, which had destroyed three-fourths of Lisbon, the sages of the country could not find any means more effectual to prevent a total destruction, than to give the people a splendid Inquisition. It had been decided by the university of Coimbra, that the spectacle of some persons burnt to death by a slow fire, with great ceremony, was an infallible antidote for earthquakes.

In consequence of this resolution, they had seized a Biscayan, convicted of having married his godmother, and two Portuguese, who, in eating a pullet, had stripped off the lard. After dinner, they came and secured Dr. Pangloss, and his disciple Candide; the one for having spoke too freely, and the other for having heard with an air of approbation. They were both conducted to separate apartments, extremely damp, and never incommoded with the sun. Eight days after, they were both clothed with a gown and had their heads adorned with paper crowns. Candide's crown and gown were painted with inverted flames, and with devils that had neither tails nor claws; but Pangloss's devils had claws and tails, and the flames were pointed upwards. Being thus dressed, they marched in procession, and heard a very pathetic speech followed by fine music on a squeaking organ. Candide was whipped on the back in cadence, while they were singing; the Biscayan, and the two men who would not eat lard, were burnt; and Pangloss, though it was contrary to custom, was hanged. The same day, the earth shook anew, with a most dreadful noise.

Candide, affrighted, interdicted, astonished, all bloody, all panting, said to himself: 'If this is the best of possible worlds, what then are the rest? Supposing I had not been whipped now, I have been so, among the Bulgarians; but, Oh, my dear Pangloss; thou greatest of philosophers, that it should be my fate to see thee hanged without knowing for what! Oh! my dear Anabaptist! thou best of men, that it should be thy fate to be drowned in the harbour! Oh! Miss Cunegonde! the jewel of ladies, that it should be thy fate to have been outraged and slain!'

He returned, with difficulty, supporting himself, after being lectured, whipped, absolved, and blessed, when an old woman accosted him, and said: 'Child, take courage, and follow me.'

HOW AN OLD WOMAN TOOK CARE OF CANDIDE, AND HOW HE FOUND THE OBJECT HE LOVED

Candide did not take courage, but he followed the old woman to a ruined house. She gave him a pot of pomatum to anoint himself, left him something to eat and drink, and showed him a very neat little bed, near which was a complete suit of clothes. 'Eat, drink, and sleep,' said she to him, 'and may God take care of you. I will be back to-morrow.' Candide, astonished at all he had seen, at all he had suffered, and still more at the charity of the old woman, offered to kiss her hand. 'You must not kiss my hand,' said the old woman, 'I will be back to-morrow. Rub yourself with the pomatum, eat, and take rest.'

Candide, notwithstanding so many misfortunes, ate, and went to sleep. Next morning, the old woman brought him his breakfast, looked at his back, and rubbed it herself with another ointment; she afterwards brought him his dinner; and she returned at night, and brought him his supper. The day following she performed the same ceremonies. 'Who are you?' would Candide always say to her. 'Who has inspired you with so much goodness? What thanks can I render you?' The good woman made no answer; she returned in the evening, but brought him no supper. 'Come along with me,' said she, 'and say not a word.' She took him by the arm, and walked with him into the country about a quarter of a mile; they arrived at a house that stood by itself, surrounded with gardens and canals. The old woman knocked at a little door, which being opened, she conducted Candide by a private staircase into a gilded closet, and leaving him on a brocade couch, shut the door and went her way. Candide thought he was in a revery, and looked upon all his life as an unlucky dream, but at the present moment, a very agreeable vision.

The old woman returned very soon, supporting with difficulty a woman trembling, of a majestic port, glittering with jewels, and covered with a veil. 'Take off that veil,' said the old woman to Candide. The young man approached and took off the veil with a trembling hand. What joy! what surprise! he thought he saw Miss Cunegonde; he saw her indeed! it was she herself. His strength failed him, he could not utter a word, but fell down at her feet. Cunegonde fell upon the carpet. The old woman applied aromatic waters; they recovered their senses, and spoke to one another. At first, their words were broken, their questions and answers crossed each other, amidst sighs, tears and cries. The old woman recommended them to make less noise, and then left them to themselves. 'How! is it you?' said Candide; 'are you still alive? do I find you again in Portugal? You were not ravished then, as the philosopher Pangloss assured me?' 'Yes, all this was so,' said the lovely Cunegonde; 'but death does not always follow from these two accidents.' 'But your father and mother! were they not killed?' 'It is but too true,' answered Cunegonde, weeping. 'And your brother?' 'My brother was killed too.' 'And why are you in Portugal? and how did you know that I was here? and by what strange adventure did you contrive to bring me to this house?' 'I will tell you all that, presently,' replied the lady; 'but first you must inform me of all that has happened to you, since the harmless kiss you gave me, and the rude kicking which you received for it.'

Candide obeyed her with the most profound respect; and though he was forbidden to speak, though his voice was weak and faltering, and though his back still pained him, yet he related to her in the most artless manner, everything that had befallen him since the moment of their separation.

[*Voltaire relates here how Candide lost Cunegonde a second time; how he had to flee to America, where, with his valet Cacambo, he visited the country of Eldorado; how he carried away from this country many sparkling gems which brought him some good luck; how he attached to his retinue the philosopher Martin, as pessimistic a man as Pangloss was optimistic; and how, accompanied by Martin, Candide visited Europe, searching everywhere for his Cunegonde.]*

THE VISIT TO SEIGNIOR POCOCURANTE, THE NOBLE VENETIAN

Candide and Martin went in a gondola on the Brenta, and arrived at the palace of the noble Pococurante. His gardens were very spacious and ornamented with fine statues of marble, and the palace itself was a piece of excellent architecture. The master of the house, a very rich man, of about three-score, received our two inquisitives very politely, but with very little heartiness; which, though it confused Candide, did not give the least uneasiness to Martin.

At first, two young girls, handsome, and very neatly dressed, served them with chocolate, which was frothed extremely well. Candide could not help dropping them a compliment on their beauty, their politeness, and their address. 'The creatures are well enough,' said the senator Pococurante: 'I sometimes make them sleep with me; for I am quite disgusted with the ladies of the town; their coquetry, their jealousies, quarrels, humours, monkey-tricks, pride, follies, and the sonnets one is obliged to make, or hire others to make for them; but, after all, these two girls begin to grow tiresome to me.'

After breakfast, Candide, taking a walk in a long gallery, was charmed with the beauty of the pictures. He asked by what master were the first two. 'They are by Raphael,' said the senator; 'I bought them at a very high price, merely out of vanity, some years ago. They are said to be the finest paintings in Italy: but they do not please me at all; the colours are dead, the figures not finished, and do not appear with *relief* enough; the drapery is very bad. In short, let people say what they will, I do not find there a true imitation of nature. I do not like a piece, unless it makes me think I see nature itself; but there are no such pieces to be met with. I have, indeed, a great many pictures, but I do not value them at all.'

While they were waiting for dinner, Pococurante entertained

them with a concert; Candide was quite charmed with the music. 'This *noise*,' said Pococurante, 'might divert one for half an hour or so; but if it were to last any longer, it would grow tiresome to everybody, though no soul durst own it. Music is, nowadays, nothing else but the art of executing difficulties; and what has nothing but difficulty to recommend it, does not please in the long run.

'I might, perhaps, take more pleasure in the opera, if they had not found out the secret of making such a monster of it as shocks me. Let those go that will to see wretched tragedies set to music, where the scenes are composed for no other end than to lug in by the head and ears two or three ridiculous songs, in order to show off the throat of an actress to advantage. Let who will, or can, swoon away with pleasure, at hearing a eunuch trill out the part of Cæsar and Cato, while strutting upon the stage with a ridiculous and affected air. For my part, I have long ago bid adieu to those paltry entertainments, which constitute the glory of Italy, and are purchased so extravagantly dear.' Candide disputed the point a little, but with great discretion. Martin was entirely of the same sentiments with the senator. They sat down to table, and after an excellent dinner, went into the library. Candide, casting his eyes upon a Homer very handsomely bound, praised his High Mightiness for the goodness of his taste. 'There,' said he, 'is a book that was the delight of the good Pangloss, the greatest philosopher in Germany.' 'It doesn't delight me,' said Pococurante, with utter indifference; 'I was made to believe formerly, that I took a pleasure in reading Homer. But his continued repetition of battles that resemble each other; his gods, who are always very busy without bringing anything to a decision; his Helen, who is the subject of the war, and has scarce anything to do in the whole piece; I say all these defects give me the greatest disgust. I have asked some learned men, if they perused him with as little pleasure as I did. Those who were candid confessed to me, that they could not bear to touch the book, but that they were obliged to give it a place in their libraries, as a monument of antiquity, as they do old rusty medals, which are of no use in commerce.'

'Your Excellence does not entertain the same opinion of Virgil?' said Candide. 'I confess,' replied Pococurante, 'that the second, the fourth, and the sixth book of his Æneid are excellent;

but as for his pious Æneas, his brave Cloanthus, his friend Achates, the little Ascanius, the infirm King Latinus, the burgess Amata, and the insipid Lavinia, I do not think anything can be more frigid or more disagreeable. I prefer Tasso, and Ariosto's soporiferous tales far before him.'

'Shall I presume to ask you, sir,' said Candide, 'whether you do not enjoy a great deal of pleasure in perusing Horace?' 'He has some maxims,' said Pococurante, 'which may be of a little service to a man who knows the world, and being delivered in expressive numbers, are imprinted more easily on the memory. But I set little value on his voyage to Brundisium, his description of his bad dinner, and the Billingsgate squabble between one Pupillus, whose speech, he said, was full of filthy stuff, and another whose words were as sharp as vinegar. I never could read without great disgust, his indelicate lines against old women and witches; and I cannot see any merit in his telling his friend Mæcenas, that if he should be ranked by him amongst the lyric poets, he would strike the stars with his sublime brow. Some fools admire everything in an author of reputation; for my part, I read only for myself; I approve nothing but what suits my own taste.' Candide, having been taught to judge of nothing for himself, was very much surprised at what he heard; but Martin looked upon the sentiment of Pococurante as very rational.

'Oh, there's Cicero,' said Candide; 'this great man, I fancy, you are never tired of reading.' 'I never read him at all,' replied the Venetian. 'What is it to me, whether he pleads for Rabirius or Cluentius? I have trials enough of my own. I might, indeed, have been a greater friend to his philosophical works, but when I found he doubted of everything, I concluded I knew as much as he did, and that I had no need of a tutor to learn ignorance.'

'Well! here are four and twenty volumes of the Academy of Sciences,' cried Martin; 'it is possible there may be something valuable in them.' 'There might be,' said Pococurante, 'if a single one of the authors of this hodgepodge had been even the inventor of the art of making pins; but there is nothing in all those volumes but chimerical systems, and scarce a single article of real use.'

'What a prodigious number of theatrical pieces you have got here,' said Candide, 'in Italian, Spanish, and French!' 'Yes,' said the senator, 'there are about three thousand, and not three dozen good ones among them all. As for that collection of sermons, which all together are not worth one page of Seneca, and all those huge volumes of divinity, you may be sure they are never opened either by me or anybody else.'

Martin perceiving some of the shelves filled with English books; 'I fancy,' said he, 'a republican, as you are, must certainly be pleased with compositions that are writ with so great a degree of freedom.' 'Yes,' said Pococurante, 'it is commendable to write what one thinks; it is the privilege of man. But all over our Italy they write nothing but what they don't think. Those who now inhabit the country of the Cæsars and Antonines, dare not have a single idea, without taking out a licence. I should be very well satisfied with the freedom that breathes in the English writers, if passion and the spirit of party did not corrupt all that was valuable in it.'

Candide, discovering a Milton, asked him if he did not look upon that author as a great genius. 'What!' said Pococurante, 'that blockhead, that has made a long commentary in ten books of rough verse, on the first chapter of Genesis? that gross imitator of the Greeks, who has disfigured the creation, and who, when Moses has represented the Eternal producing the world by a word, makes the Messiah take a large pair of compasses from the armoury of God, to mark out his work? How can I have any esteem for one who has spoiled the hell and devils of Tasso; who turns Lucifer sometimes into a toad, and sometimes into a pigmy; makes him deliver the same speech a hundred times over; represents him disputing on divinity; and who, by a serious imitation of Ariosto's comic invention of firearms, represents the devils letting off their cannon in heaven? Neither myself, nor anyone else in Italy, can be pleased at these outrages against common sense; but the marriage of Sin and Death, and the adders of which Sin was brought to bed, are enough to make every person of the least delicacy or taste vomit. This obscure, fantastical, and disgusting poem was despised at its first publication; and I only treat the author now in the same manner as he was treated in his own country by his contemporaries. By the by, I speak what I think; and I give myself no uneasiness whether other people think as I do, or not.'

Candide was vexed at this discourse; for he respected Homer, and was fond of Milton. 'Ah!' said he, whispering to Martin, 'I am very much afraid that this strange man has a sovereign contempt for our German poets.' 'There would be no great harm in that,' said Martin. 'Oh, what an extraordinary man!' said Candide, muttering to himself. 'What a great genius is this Pococurante! nothing can please him.'

After having thus reviewed all the books, they went down into the garden. Candide expatiated upon its beauties. 'I never knew anything laid out in such bad taste,' said the master; 'we have nothing but trifles here; but a day or two hence, I shall have one laid out upon a more noble plan.'

When our two inquisitives had taken their leave of his Excellency, 'Now, surely,' said Candide to Martin, 'you will confess that he is one of the happiest men upon earth, for he is above everything that he has.' 'Do not you see,' said Martin, 'that he is disgusted with everything that he has? Plato has said a long time ago, that the best stomachs are not those which cast up all sorts of victuals.' 'But,' said Candide, 'is not there pleasure in criticizing everything? in perceiving defects where other people fancy they see beauties?' 'That is to say,' replied Martin, 'that there is pleasure in having no pleasure.' 'Ah, well,' said Candide, 'no person will be so happy as myself, when I see Miss Cunegonde again.' 'It is always best to hope,' said Martin.

In the meantime, days and weeks passed away, but no Cacambo was to be found. And Candide was so immersed in grief, that he did not recollect that Paquetta and Girofflee never so much as once came to return him thanks.

OF CANDIDE AND MARTIN SUPPING WITH SIX STRANGERS,
AND WHO THEY WERE

One night as Candide, followed by Martin, was going to seat himself at table with some strangers who lodged in the same inn, a man with a face black as soot came behind him, and taking him by the arm, said, 'Get ready to start with us immediately; don't fail!' He turned his head and saw Cacambo. Nothing but the sight of Cunegonde could have surprised or pleased him more. He was ready to run mad for joy. Embracing his dear friend, 'Cunegonde is here,' said he, 'without doubt; where is she? Carry me to her, that I may die with joy in her company!' 'Cunegonde is not here,' said Cacambo, 'she is at Constantinople.' 'Oh, Heavens! at Constantinople? But, if she was in China, I would fly thither; let us begone.' 'We will go after supper,' replied Cacambo; 'I can tell you no more; I am a slave; my master expects me, and I must go and wait at table; say not a word; go to supper and hold yourself in readiness.'

Candide, distracted between joy and grief, charmed at having seen his trusty agent, astonished at beholding him a slave, full of the idea of finding his mistress again, his heart palpitating, and his understanding confused, set himself down at the table with Martin (who looked on all these adventures without the least emotion), and with six strangers that were come to spend the carnival at Venice.

Cacambo, who poured out wine for one of the six strangers, drew near to his master, towards the end of the repast, and whispered in his ear, 'Sire, your Majesty may set out when you think proper, the ship is ready.' On saying these words he went out. The guests looked at each other in surprise, without speaking a word; when another servant approaching his master, said to him, 'Sire, your Majesty's chaise is at Padua, and the yacht is ready.' The master gave a nod, and the domestic retired. All the guests stared at one another again, and their mutual surprise was increased. A third servant approaching the third stranger, said to him, 'Sire, believe me, your Majesty must not stay here any longer; I am going to get everything ready'; and immediately he disappeared.

Candide and Martin had by this time concluded that this was a masquerade of the carnival. A fourth domestic said to the fourth master: 'Your Majesty may depart whenever you please'; and went out as the others had done. The fifth servant said the same to the fifth master; but the sixth servant spoke in a different manner to the sixth stranger, who sat near Candide; ' 'Faith, Sire,' said he, 'no one will trust your Majesty any longer, nor myself either: and we may both be sent to jail this very night; I shall, however, take care of myself. Adieu.'

All the domestics having disappeared, the six strangers, with Candide and Martin, remained in a profound silence. At last Candide broke the silence; 'Gentlemen,' said he, 'this is something very droll; but why should you be all Kings? For my part, I own to you, that I am not, neither is Martin.'

Cacambo's master answered very gravely in Italian, 'I assure you that I am not in jest; I am Achmet III. I was Grand Sultan for several years; I dethroned my brother; my nephew dethroned me; my viziers were beheaded; I pass my life in the old seraglio. But my nephew, the Grand Sultan Mahmoud, permits me to take a voyage sometimes for the benefit of my health, and I have come to pass the carnival at Venice.'

A young man who sat near Achmet, spoke next: 'My name is Ivan; I was Emperor of all the Russias; I was dethroned in my cradle; my father and mother were imprisoned; I was brought up in prison. I have sometimes permission to travel, accompanied by two persons as guards; I am also come to pass the carnival at Venice.'

The third said, 'I am Charles Edward, King of England; my father ceded his rights to the throne to me. I have sought to defend them; eight hundred of my adherents had their hearts torn out alive, and their heads struck off. I myself have been in prison; I am going to Rome, to pay a visit to my father, who has been dethroned, as well as myself and my grandfather, and am come to Venice to celebrate the carnival.'

The fourth then said, 'I was King of Poland; the fortune of war has deprived me of my hereditary dominions; my father experienced the same reverse; I resign myself to Providence, like the Sultan Achmet, the Emperor Ivan, and Charles Edward, whom God long preserve; and I am come to pass the carnival at Venice.'

The fifth said, 'I was King of Poland; I lost my kingdom twice; but Providence has given me another government, in which I have done more good than all the kings of the Sarmatians put together, have been able to do on the banks of the Vistula. I resign myself to Providence, and am come to pass the carnival at Venice.'

It was now the sixth monarch's turn to speak. 'Gentlemen,' said he, 'I am not so great a prince as any of you; but for all that, I have been a King, as well as the best of you. I am Theodore; I was elected King of Corsica; I was once called *Your Majesty*, but at present am scarce allowed the title of *Sir*. I have caused money to be coined, but am not master at present of a farthing. I have had two secretaries of state, but now have scarce a single servant. I have been myself on a throne, and have for some time lain upon straw in a common jail in London. I am afraid I shall meet with the same treatment here, although I came hither, like your Majesties, to pass the carnival at Venice.'

The five other kings heard this speech with a noble compassion. Each of them gave King Theodore twenty sequins to buy him some clothes and shirts, and Candide made him a present of a diamond worth two thousand sequins. 'Who,' said the five kings, 'can this person be, who is able to give, and really has given an hundred times as much as any of us?' 'Sir, are you also a king?' 'No, gentlemen,' said Candide, 'nor have I any desire to be one.'

At the instant they rose from the table, there arrived at the same inn four Serene Highnesses, who had also lost their dominions by the fortune of war, and were come to pass the carnival at Venice. But Candide took no notice of these new-comers, his thoughts being wholly taken up with going to Constantinople in search of his dear Cunegonde.

CANDIDE'S VOYAGE TO CONSTANTINOPLE

The faithful Cacambo had already prevailed on the Turkish captain who was going to carry Sultan Achmet back again to Constantinople, to receive Candide and Martin on board. They both of them embarked, after they had prostrated themselves before his miserable Highness. As Candide was on his way, he said to Martin, 'There were six dethroned kings that we supped with; and what is still more, among these six kings, there was one that I gave alms to. Perhaps there may be a great many other princes more unfortunate still. For my own part, I have lost only one hundred sheep, and am flying to the arms of Cunegonde. My dear Martin, I must still say, Pangloss was in the right; all things are for the best.' 'I wish they were,' said Martin. 'But,' said Candide, 'the adventure we met with at Venice is something romantic. Such a thing was never before either seen or heard of, that six dethroned kings should sup together at a common inn.' 'This is not more extraordinary,' replied Martin, 'than most of the things that have happened to us. It is a common thing for kings to be dethroned; and with respect to the honour that we had of supping with them, it is a trifle that does not merit our attention.'

Scarce had Candide got on board, when he fell on the neck of his old servant and friend Cacambo. 'Well,' said he, 'what news of Cunegonde? is she still a miracle of beauty? does she love me still? how does she do? No doubt but you have bought a palace for her at Constantinople?'

'My dear master,' replied Cacambo, 'Cunegonde washes dishes on the banks of the Propontis, for a prince who has very few to wash; she is a slave in the house of an ancient sovereign named *Ragotsky*, to whom the Grand Turk allows three crowns a day to support him in his asylum; but, what is worse than all, she has lost her beauty, and is become shockingly ugly.' 'Well, handsome or ugly,' replied Candide, 'I am a man of honour, and it is my duty to love her still. But how came she to be reduced to so abject a condition, with the five or six millions that you carried her?' 'Well,' said Cacambo, 'was I not to give two millions to Signor Don Fernandes d'Obaraa, y Figuero, y Mascarenes, y Lampourdos, y Souza, the governor of Buenos-Ayres, for permission to take Miss Cunegonde back again? and did not a pirate rob us of all the rest? Did not this pirate carry us to Cape Matapan, to Milo, to Nicaria, to Samos, to Dardanelles, to Marmora, to Scutari? Cunegonde and the old woman are servants to the prince I told you of, and I am a slave of the dethroned sultan.' 'What a chain of shocking calamities!' said Candide. 'But, after all, I have some diamonds, I shall easily purchase Cunegonde's liberty. It is a pity that she is grown so ugly.'

Then, turning himself to Martin, 'Who do you think,' says he, 'is most to be pitied; the Sultan Achmet, the Emperor Ivan, King Charles Edward, or myself?' 'I cannot tell,' said Martin, 'I must look into your hearts to be able to tell.' 'Ah!' said Candide, 'if Pangloss were here, he would know and tell us.' 'I know not,' replied Martin, 'in what sort of scales your Pangloss would weigh the misfortunes of mankind, and how he would appraise their sorrows. All that I can venture to say is, that there are millions of men upon earth a hundred times more to be pitied than King Charles Edward, the Emperor Ivan, or Sultan Achmet.' 'That may be so,' said Candide.

In a few days they reached the Black Sea. Candide began with ransoming Cacambo at an extravagant price; and, without loss of time, he got into a galley with his companions, to go to the banks of the Propontis, in search of Cunegonde, however ugly she might have become.

Among the crew, there were two slaves that rowed very badly, to whose bare shoulders the Levant trader would now and then apply severe strokes with a bull's pizzle. Candide, by a natural sympathy, looked at them more attentively than at the rest of the galley-slaves, and went up to them with a heart full of pity. The features of two of their faces, though very much disfigured, seemed to bear some resemblance to those of Pangloss and the unfortunate Baron, the brother of Miss Cunegonde. This fancy made him feel very sad. He looked at them again more attentively. 'Really,' said he to Cacambo, 'if I had not seen the good Pangloss hanged, and had not had the misfortune to kill the Baron myself, I should think it was they who are rowing in this galley.'

At the names of the Baron and Pangloss, the two galley-slaves gave a loud shriek, became as if petrified in their seats, and let their oars drop. The master of the Levanter ran up to them, and redoubled the lashes of the bull's pizzle upon them. 'Hold! hold! Signior,' cried Candide, 'I will give you what money you please.' 'What! it is Candide!' said one of the galley-slaves; 'Oh! it is Candide!' said the other. 'Do I dream?' said Candide; 'am I awake? am I in this galley? is that Master Baron whom I killed? is that Master Pangloss whom I saw hanged?'

'It is ourselves! It is our very selves!' they exclaimed. 'What! is that the great philosopher?' said Martin. 'Harkee, Master Levant Captain,' said Candide, 'what will you take for the ransom of Monsieur Thunder-ten-tronckh, one of the first Barons of the Empire, together with Master Pangloss, the most profound metaphysician of Germany?' 'You Christian dog,' said the Levant captain, 'since these two dogs of Christian slaves are a baron and a metaphysician, which, without doubt, are high dignities in their own country, you shall give me fifty thousand sequins.' 'You shall have the money, sir; carry me back again, like lightning, to Constantinople, and you shall be paid directly. But stop, carry me to Miss Cunegonde first.' The Levant captain, on the first offer of Candide, had turned the head of the vesssel towards the city, and made the other slaves row faster than a bird cleaves the air.

Candide embraced the Baron and Pangloss a hundred times.

'How happened it that I did not kill you, my dear Baron? and, my dear Pangloss, how came you to life again, after being hanged? and how came both of you to be galley-slaves in Turkey?' 'Is it true that my dear sister is in this country?' said the Baron. 'Yes,' replied Cacambo. 'Then I see my dear Candide once more,' said Pangloss.

Candide presented Martin and Cacambo to them; the whole party mutually embraced, and all spoke at the same time. The galley flew like lightning, and they were already in the port. A Jew was sent for, to whom Candide sold a diamond for fifty thousand sequins, which was worth a hundred thousand, the Israelite swearing by Abraham that he could not give any more. He immediately paid the ransom of the Baron and Pangloss. The latter threw himself at the feet of his deliverer, and bathed them with his tears; as for the other, he thanked him with a nod and promised to repay him the money the first opportunity. 'But is it possible that my sister is in Turkey?' said he. 'Nothing is more possible,' replied Cacambo; 'for she scours dishes in the house of a prince of Transylvania!' Two more Jews were instantly sent for, to whom Candide sold some more diamonds; and he and his party all set out again, in another galley, to go and deliver Cunegonde.

WHAT HAPPENED TO CANDIDE, CUNEGONDE, PANGLOSS, MARTIN, ETC.

'I ask your pardon once more,' said Candide to the Baron. 'I ask pardon for having thrust my sword through your body.' 'Don't let us say any more about it,' said the Baron; 'I was a little too hasty, I must confess. But since you desire to know by what fatality I came to be a galley-slave, I will inform you. After I was cured of my wound, by a brother who was an apothecary, I was attacked and carried off by a party of Spaniards, who confined me in prison at Buenos-Ayres, at the very time my sister was setting out from thence. I demanded leave to return to Europe. I was nominated to go as almoner to Constantinople, with the French ambassador. I had not been eight days engaged in this employment, when one day I met with a young, well-made Icoglan. It was then very hot; the young man went to bathe himself, and I took the opportunity to bathe myself too. I did not know that it was a capital crime for a Christian to be found naked with a young Mussulman. A cadi ordered me to receive a hundred strokes of the bastinado on the soles of my feet, and condemned me to the galleys. I do not think there ever was a greater act of injustice. But I should be glad to know how it comes about, that my sister is dish-washer in the kitchen of a Transylvania prince, who is a refugee among the Turks.'

'But you, my dear Pangloss,' said Candide, 'how came I ever to set eyes on you again!' 'It is true, indeed,' said Pangloss, 'that you saw me hanged; I ought naturally to have been burnt; but you may remember, that it rained prodigiously when they were going to roast me; the storm was so violent that they despaired of lighting the fire. I was therefore hanged because they could do no better. A surgeon bought my body, carried it home with him and began to dissect me. He first made a crucial incision. No one could have been more slovenly hanged than I was. The executioner of the Inquisition burnt people marvellously well, but he was not used to the art of hanging them. The cord being wet did not slip properly, and the noose was badly tied: in short, I still drew my breath. The crucial incision made me give such a dreadful shriek, that my surgeon fell down backwards, and fancying he was dissecting the devil, he ran away, ready to die with the fright, and fell down a second time on the staircase, as he was making off. His wife ran out of an adjacent closet, on hearing the noise, saw me extended on the table with my crucial incision, and being more frightened than her husband, fled also, and tumbled over him. When they were come to themselves a little, I heard the surgeon's wife say to him, "My dear, how came you to be so foolish as to venture to dissect a heretic? Don't you know that the devil always takes possession of the bodies of such people? I will go immediately and fetch a priest to exorcise him.' I shuddered at this proposal, and mustered up what little strength I had left to cry out, "Oh! have pity upon me"! At length the Portuguese barber took courage, sewed up my skin, and his wife nursed me so well, that I was upon my feet again in about fifteen days. The barber got me a place, to be footman to a knight of Malta, who was going to Venice; but my master not being able to pay me my wages, I engaged in the service of a Venetian merchant, and went along with him to Constantinople.

'One day I took a fancy to go into a mosque. There was nobody there but an old imam, and a very handsome young devotee saying her prayers. Her throat was uncovered; she had in her bosom a beautiful nosegay of tulips, anemones, ranunculuses, hyacinths, and auriculas; she let her nosegay fall; I took it up, and presented it to her with the most profound reverence. However, I was so long in handing it to her, that the imam fell into a passion, and seeing I was a Christian, called out for help. They carried me before the cadi, who ordered me a hundred bastinadoes, and to be sent to the galleys. I was chained to the same galley and the same bench with the Baron. There were on board this galley, four young men from Marseilles, five Neapolitan priests, and two monks of Corfu, who told us that the like adventures happened every day. The Baron pretended that he had suffered more injustice than I; and I insisted that it was far more innocent to put a nosegay into a young woman's bosom, than to be found stark naked with an Icoglan. We were perpetually disputing, and we received twenty lashes every day with a bull's pizzle, when the concatenation of events in this universe brought you to our galley, and you ransomed us.'

'Well, my dear Pangloss,' said Candide, 'when you were hanged, dissected, severely beaten, and tugging at the oar in the galley, did you always think that things in this world were all for the best?' 'I am still as I always have been, of my first opinion,' answered Pangloss; 'for as I am a philosopher, it would be inconsistent with my character to contradict myself; especially as Leibnitz could not be in the wrong; and his pre-established harmony is certainly the finest system in the world, as well as his gross and subtle matter.'

HOW CANDIDE FOUND CUNEGONDE AND THE OLD WOMAN AGAIN

While Candide, the Baron, Pangloss, Martin, and Cacambo were relating their adventures to each other, and disputing about the contingent and non-contingent events of this world, and while they were arguing upon effects and causes, on moral and physical evil, on liberty and necessity, and on the consolations a person may experience in the galleys in Turkey, they arrived on the banks of the Propontis, at the house of the Prince of Transylvania. The first objects which presented themselves were Cunegonde and the old woman, hanging out some table-linen on the line to dry.

The Baron grew pale at this sight. Even Candide, the affectionate lover, on seeing his fair Cunegonde awfully tanned, with her eye-lids reversed, her neck withered, her cheeks wrinkled, her arms red and rough, was seized with horror, jumped near three yards backwards, but afterwards advanced to her, but with more politeness than passion. She embraced Candide and her brother, who, each of them, embraced the old woman, and Candide ransomed them both.

There was a little farm in the neighbourhood, which the old woman advised Candide to hire till they could meet with better accommodation for their whole company. As Cunegonde did not know that she had grown ugly, nobody having told her of it, she put Candide in mind of his promise to marry her, in so peremptory a manner, that he durst not refuse her. But when this thing was intimated to the Baron, he said, 'I will never suffer such meanness on her part, nor such insolence on yours. With this infamy I will never be reproached. The children of my sister could never be enrolled in the chapters of Germany. No; my sister shall never marry any but a Baron of the empire.' Cunegonde threw herself at her brother's feet, and bathed them with her tears, but he remained inflexible. 'You ungrateful puppy, you,' said Candide to him, 'I have delivered you from the galleys; I have paid your ransom; I have also paid that of your sister, who was a scullion here, and is very homely; I have the goodness, however, to make her my wife, and you are fool enough to oppose it; I have a good mind to kill you again, you make me so angry.' 'You may indeed kill me again,' said the Baron; 'but you shall never marry my sister while I have breath.'

CONCLUSION

Candide had no great desire, at the bottom of his heart, to marry Cunegonde. But the extreme impertinence of the Baron determined him to conclude the match, and Cunegonde pressed it so earnestly, that he could not retract. He advised with Pangloss,

Martin, and the trusty Cacambo. Pangloss drew up an excellent memoir, in which he proved that the Baron had no right over his sister, and that she might, according to all the laws of the empire, espouse Candide with her left hand. Martin was for throwing the Baron into the sea: Cacambo was of opinion that it would be best to send him back again to the Levant captain, and make him work at the galleys. This advice was thought good; the old woman approved it, and nothing was said to his sister about it. The scheme was put in execution for a little money, and so they had the pleasure of punishing the pride of a German Baron.

It is natural to imagine that Candide, after so many disasters, married to his sweetheart, living with the philosopher Pangloss, the philosopher Martin, the discreet Cacambo, and the old woman, and especially as he had brought so many diamonds from the country of the ancient Incas, must live the most agreeable life of any man in the whole world. But he had been so cheated by the Jews, that he had nothing left but the small farm; and his wife, growing still more ugly, turned peevish and insupportable. The old woman was very infirm, and worse humoured than Cunegonde herself. Cacambo, who worked in the garden, and went to Constantinople to sell its productions, was worn out with labour, and cursed his fate. Pangloss was ready to despair, because he did not shine at the head of some university in Germany. As for Martin, as he was firmly persuaded that all was equally bad throughout, he bore things with patience. Candide, Martin, and Pangloss disputed sometimes about metaphysics and ethics. They often saw passing under the windows of the farm-house boats full of effendis, bashaws, and cadis, who were going into banishment to Lemnos, Mitylene, and Erzerum. They observed that other cadis, other bashaws, and other effendis, succeeded to the posts of those who were exiled, only to be banished themselves in turn. They saw heads nicely impaled, to be presented to the Sublime Porte. These spectacles increased the number of their disputations; and when they were not disputing, their *ennui* was so tiresome that the old woman would often say to them, 'I want to know which is the worst: to be ravished an hundred times by negro pirates, to run the gauntlet among the Bulgarians, to be whipped and hanged, to be dissected, to row in the galleys; in a word, to have suffered all the miseries

we have undergone, or to stay here, without doing anything?'
'That is a great question,' said Candide.

This discourse gave rise to new reflections, and Martin concluded upon the whole, that mankind were born to live either
in the distractions of inquietude, or in the lethargy of disgust.
Candide did not agree with that opinion, but remained in a
state of suspense. Pangloss confessed that he had always suffered
dreadfully; but having once maintained that all things went
wonderfully well, he still kept firm to his hypothesis, though
it was quite opposed to his real feelings.

There lived in the neighbourhood a very famous dervish,
who passed for the greatest philosopher in Turkey. They went
to consult him. Pangloss was chosen speaker, and said to him,
'Master, we are come to desire you would tell us why so strange
an animal as man was created.'

'What's that to you?' said the dervish; 'is it any business of
thine?' 'But, my reverend father,' said Candide, 'there is a horrible
amount of evil in the world.' 'What signifies,' said the dervish,
'whether there be good or evil? When his Sublime Highness
sends a vessel to Egypt, does it trouble him whether the mice
on board are at their ease or not?' 'What would you have one
do then?' said Pangloss. 'Hold your tongue,' said the dervish.
'I promised myself the pleasure,' said Pangloss, 'of reasoning with
you upon effects and causes, the best of possible worlds, the
origin of evil, the nature of the soul, and the pre-established
harmony.'—The dervish, at these words, shut the door in their
faces.

During this conference, news was brought that two viziers
and a mufti were strangled at Constantinople, and a great many
of their friends impaled. This catastrophe made a great noise for
several hours. Pangloss, Candide, and Martin, on their way back
to the little farm, met a good-looking old man, taking the air
at his door, under an arbour of orange trees. Pangloss, who had
as much curiosity as philosophy, asked him the name of the
mufti who was lately strangled. 'I know nothing at all about it,'
said the good man; 'and what's more, I never knew the name
of a single mufti, or a single vizier, in my life. I am an entire
stranger to the story you mention; and presume that, generally
speaking, they who trouble their heads with state affairs, sometimes die shocking deaths, not without deserving it. But I never

trouble my head about what is doing at Constantinople; I content myself with sending my fruits thither, the produce of my garden, which I cultivate with my own hands!' Having said these words, he introduced the strangers into his house. His two daughters and two sons served them with several kinds of sherbet, which they made themselves, besides caymac, enriched with the peels of candied citrons, oranges, lemons, bananas, pistachio nuts, and Mocha coffee, unadulterated with the bad coffee of Batavia and the isles. After which, the two daughters of this good Mussulman perfumed the beards of Candide, Pangloss, and Martin.

'You must certainly,' said Candide to the Turk, 'have a very large and very opulent estate!' 'I have only twenty acres,' said the Turk; 'which I, with my children, cultivate. Labour keeps us free from three of the greatest evils: tiresomeness, vice, and want.'

As Candide returned to his farm, he made deep reflections on the discourse of the Turk. Said he to Pangloss and Martin, 'The condition of this good old man seems to me preferable to that of the six kings with whom we had the honour to sup.' 'The grandeurs of royalty,' said Pangloss, 'are very precarious, in the opinion of all philosophers. For, in short, Eglon, king of the Moabites, was assassinated by Ehud; Absalom was hung by the hair of his head, and pierced through with three darts; King Nadab, the son of Jeroboam, was killed by Baasha; King Elah by Zimri; Ahaziah by Jehu; Athaliah by Jehoiadah; the kings Joachim, Jechonias, and Zedekias were carried into captivity. You know the fates of Crœsus, Astyages, Darius, Dionysius of Syracuse, Pyrrhus, Perseus, Hannibal, Jugurtha, Ariovistus, Cæsar, Pompey, Nero, Otho, Vitellius, Domitian, Richard II, Edward II, Henry VI, Richard III, Mary Stuart, Charles I of England, the three Henrys of France, and the Emperor Henry IV. You know——' 'I know very well,' said Candide, 'that we ought to look after our garden.' 'You are in the right,' said Pangloss, 'for when man was placed in the garden of Eden, he was placed there, *ut operatur cum,* to cultivate it; which proves that mankind are not created to be idle.' 'Let us work,' said Martin, 'without disputing; it is the only way to render life supportable.'

All their little society entered into this laudable design, according to their different abilities. Their little piece of ground produced a plentiful crop. Cunegonde was indeed very homely, but she became an excellent pastry cook. Paquetta worked at embroidery, and the old woman took care of the linen. There was no idle person in the company, not excepting even Girofflee; he made a very good carpenter, and became a very honest man.

As to Pangloss, he evidently had a lurking consciousness that his theory required unceasing exertions, and all his ingenuity, to sustain it. Yet he stuck to it to the last; his thinking and talking faculties could hardly be diverted from it for a moment. He seized every occasion to say to Candide, 'All the events in this best of possible worlds are admirably connected. If a single link in the great chain were omitted, the harmony of the entire universe would be destroyed. If you had not been expelled from that beautiful castle, with those cruel kicks, for your love to Miss Cunegonde; if you had not been imprisoned by the Inquisition; if you had not travelled over a great portion of America on foot; if you had not plunged your sword through the Baron; if you had not lost all the sheep you brought from that fine country, Eldorado, together with the riches with which they were laden, you would not be here to-day, eating preserved citrons and pistachio nuts.'

'That's very well said, and may all be true,' said Candide; 'but let's cultivate our garden.'

THE WORLD AS IT IS:

BABOUC'S VISION [1]

AMONG THE GENII WHO PRESIDE OVER THE EMPIRES OF THE earth, Ithuriel held one of the first ranks, and had the department of Upper Asia. He one morning descended into the abode of Babouc, the Scythian, who dwelt on the banks of the Oxus, and said to him:

'Babouc, the follies and vices of the Persians have drawn upon them our indignation. Yesterday an assembly of the genii of Upper Asia was held, to consider whether we would chastise Persepolis or destroy it entirely. Go to that city; examine everything; return and give me a faithful account; and, according to thy report, I will then determine whether to correct or extirpate the inhabitants.'

'But, my lord,' said Babouc, with great humility, 'I have never been in Persia, nor do I know a single person in that country.'

'So much the better,' said the angel, 'thou wilt be the more impartial: thou hast received from Heaven the spirit of discernment, to which I now add the power of inspiring confidence. Go, see, hear, observe, and fear nothing. Thou shalt everywhere meet with a favourable reception.'

Babouc mounted his camel, and set out with his servants. After having travelled some days, he met, near the plains of Senaar, the Persian army, which was going to attack the forces of India. He first addressed himself to a soldier, whom he found at a distance from the main army, and asked him what was the occasion of the war.

'By all the gods,' said the soldier, 'I know nothing of the matter. It is none of my business. My trade is to kill and to be killed, to get a livelihood. It is of no consequence to me whom I serve. To-morrow, perhaps, I may go over to the Indian camp; for it is said that they give their soldiers nearly half a copper

---

[1] *Editor's Note: Babouc's Vision* is, so to speak, a first sketch of *Candide*, valuable for us for its very conciseness, and because we find in it, in compact form, all of Voltaire's philosophy. 'If all is not well, all is passable.' We must take the world 'as it is.'

drachma a day more than we have in this cursed service of Persia. If thou desirest to know why we fight, speak to my captain.'

Babouc, having given the soldier a small present, entered the camp. He soon became acquainted with the captain, and asked him the cause of the war.

'How canst thou imagine that I should know it?' said the captain, 'or of what importance is it to me? I live about two hundred leagues from Persepolis: I hear that war is declared: I instantly leave my family, and, having nothing else to do, go, according to our custom, to make my fortune, or to fall by a glorious death.'

'But are not thy companions,' said Babouc, 'a little better informed than thee?'

'No,' said the officer, 'there are none but our principal satraps that know the true cause of our cutting one another's throats.'

Babouc, struck with astonishment, introduced himself to the generals, and soon became familiarly acquainted with them. At last one of them said:

'The cause of this war, which for twenty years past hath desolated Asia, sprang originally from a quarrel between a eunuch belonging to one of the concubines of the great king of Persia, and the clerk of a factory belonging to the great king of India. The dispute was about a claim which amounted nearly to the thirtieth part of a daric. Our first minister, and the representative of India, maintained the rights of their respective masters with becoming dignity. The dispute grew warm. Both parties sent into the field an army of a million of soldiers. This army must be recruited every year with upwards of four hundred thousand men. Massacres, burning of houses, ruin and devastation, are daily multiplied; the universe suffers; and their mutual animosity still continues. The first ministers of the two nations frequently protest that they have nothing in view but the happiness of mankind; and every protestation is attended with the destruction of a town, or the desolation of a province.'

Next day, on a report being spread that peace was going to be concluded, the Persian and Indian generals made haste to come to an engagement. The battle was long and bloody. Babouc beheld every crime, and every abomination. He was witness to the arts and stratagems of the principal satraps, who did all that lay in their power to expose their general to the disgrace of a defeat. He saw officers killed by their own troops, and soldiers stabbing their already expiring comrades in order to strip them of a few bloody garments torn and covered with dirt. He entered the hospitals to which they were conveying the wounded, most of whom died through the inhuman negligence of those who were well paid by the king of Persia to assist these unhappy men.

'Are these men,' cried Babouc, 'or are they wild beasts? Ah! I plainly see that Persepolis will be destroyed.'

Full of this thought, he went over to the camp of the Indians, where, according to the prediction of the genii, he was as well received as in that of the Persians; but he saw there the same crimes which had already filled him with horror.

'Oh!' said he to himself, 'if the angel Ithuriel should exterminate the Persians, the angel of India must certainly destroy the Indians.'

But being afterward more particularly informed of all that passed in both armies, he heard of such acts of generosity, humanity, and greatness of soul, as at once surprised and charmed him:

'Unaccountable mortals, as ye are,' cried he, 'how can you thus unite so much baseness and so much grandeur, so many virtues and so many vices?'

Meanwhile the peace was proclaimed; and the generals of the two armies, neither of whom had gained a complete victory, but who, for their own private interest, had shed the blood of so many of their fellow-creatures, went to solicit their courts for rewards. The peace was celebrated in public writings which announced the return of virtue and happiness to the earth.

'God be praised,' said Babouc, 'Persepolis will now be the abode of spotless innocence, and will not be destroyed, as the cruel genii intended. Let us haste without delay to this capital of Asia.'

He entered that immense city by the ancient gate, which was entirely barbarous, and offended the eye by its disagreeable rusticity. All that part of the town savoured of the time when it was built; for, notwithstanding the obstinacy of men in praising ancient at the expense of modern times, it must be owned that the first essays in every art are rude and unfinished.

Babouc mingled in a crowd of people composed of the most ignorant, dirty and deformed of both sexes, who were thronging with a stupid air into a large and gloomy enclosure. By the constant hum; by the gestures of the people; by the money which some persons gave to others for the liberty of sitting down, he imagined that he was in a market, where chairs were sold; but observing several women fall down on their knees with an appearance of looking directly before them, while in reality they were leering at the men by their sides, he was soon convinced that he was in a temple. Shrill, hoarse, savage and discordant voices made the vault re-echo with ill-articulated sounds, that produced the same effect as the braying of asses, when, in the plains of Pictavia, they answer the cornet that calls them together. He stopped his ears; but he was ready to shut his mouth and hold his nose, when he saw several labourers enter into the temple with picks and spades, who removed a large stone, and threw up the earth on both sides, from whence exhaled a pestilential vapour. At last some others approached, deposited a dead body in the opening, and replaced the stone upon it.

'What!' cried Babouc, 'do these people bury their dead in the place where they adore the deity? What! are their temples paved with carcasses? I am no longer surprised at those pestilential diseases that frequently depopulate Persepolis. The putrefaction of the dead, and the infected breath of such numbers of the living, assembled and crowded together in the same place, are sufficient to poison the whole terrestrial globe. Oh! what an abominable city is Persepolis! The angels probably intend to destroy it in order to build a more beautiful one in its place, and to people it with inhabitants who are more virtuous and better singers. Providence may have its reasons for so doing; to its disposal let us leave all future events.'

Meanwhile the sun approached his meridian height. Babouc was to dine at the other end of the city with a lady for whom her husband, an officer in the army, had given him some letters: but he first took several turns in Persepolis, where he saw other temples, better built and more richly adorned, filled with a polite audience, and resounding with harmonious music. He beheld public fountains, which, though ill-placed, struck the eye by their beauty; squares where the best kings that had governed Persia seemed to breathe in bronze, and others where he heard the people crying out:

'When shall we see our beloved master?'

He admired the magnificent bridges built over the river; the superb and commodious quays; the palaces raised on both sides; and an immense house, where thousands of old soldiers, covered with scars and crowned with victory, offered their daily praises to the god of armies. At last he entered the house of the lady, who, with a set of fashionable people, waited his company to dinner. The house was neat and elegant; the repast delicious; the lady, young, beautiful, witty, and engaging; and the company worthy of her; and Babouc every moment said to himself:

'The angel Ithuriel has little regard for the world, or he would never think of destroying such a charming city.'

In the meantime he observed that the lady, who had begun by tenderly asking news about her husband, spoke more tenderly to a young magi, toward the conclusion of the repast. He saw a magistrate, who, in presence of his wife, paid his court with great vivacity to a widow; the indulgent widow had one arm round the magistrate's neck while she held out the other hand to a very handsome and very modest young citizen. The magistrate's wife was the first to leave the table in order to converse in the neighbouring room with her spiritual director who arrived very late after having been expected for dinner; and the eloquent spiritual director exhorted her in the neighbouring room with so much vehemence and unction that when the lady returned her eyes were swimming, her cheeks inflamed, her walk uncertain, and her speech trembling.

Babouc then began to fear that the angel Ithuriel had but too much reason for destroying Persepolis. The talent he possessed of gaining confidence let him that same day into all the secrets of the lady. She confessed to him her affection for the young magi, and assured him that in all the houses in Persepolis he would meet with similar examples of attachment. Babouc concluded that such a society could not possibly survive: that jealousy, discord and vengeance must desolate every house; that tears and blood must be daily shed; that husbands would certainly kill their wives' lovers or be killed by them; and, in fine, that Ithuriel would do well to destroy immediately a city abandoned to continual disasters.

Such were the gloomy ideas that possessed his mind, when a grave man in a black gown appeared at the gate and humbly begged to speak to the young magistrate. This stripling, without rising or taking the least notice of the old gentleman, gave him some papers with a haughty and careless air and then dismissed him. Babouc asked who this man was. The mistress of the house said to him in a low voice:

'He is one of the best advocates in the city, and hath studied the law these fifty years. The other, who is but twenty-five years of age, and has only been a satrap of the law for two days, hath ordered him to make an extract of a process he is going to determine, though he has not as yet examined it.'

'This giddy youth acts wisely,' said Babouc, 'in asking counsel of an old man. But why is not the old man himself the judge?'

'Thou art surely in jest,' said she; 'those who have grown old in laborious and inferior posts are never raised to places of dignity. This young man has a great post because his father is rich; and the right of dispensing justice is purchased here like a farm.'

'O unhappy city!' cried Babouc, 'this is surely the height of anarchy and confusion. Those who have thus purchased the right of judging will doubtless sell their judgments; nothing do I see here but an abyss of iniquity!'

While he was thus expressing his grief and surprise a young warrior, who that very day had returned from the army, said to him:

'Why wouldst thou not have seats in the courts of justice offered for sale? I myself purchased the right of braving death at the head of two thousand men who are under my command. It has this year cost me forty darics of gold to lie on the earth thirty nights successively in a red dress, and at last to receive two wounds with an arrow, of which I still feel the smart. If I ruin myself to serve the emperor of Persia, whom I never saw, the satrap of the law may well pay something for enjoying the pleasure of giving audience to pleaders.'

Babouc was filled with indignation, and could not help condemning a country where the highest posts in the army and the law were exposed for sale. He at once concluded that the inhabitants must be entirely ignorant of the art of war and the laws of equity; and that, though Ithuriel should not destroy them, they must soon be ruined by their detestable administration.

He was still further confirmed in his bad opinion by the arrival of a fat man, who, after saluting all the company with great familiarity, went up to the young officer and said:

'I can only lend thee fifty thousand darics of gold; for indeed the taxes of the empire have this year brought me in but three hundred thousand.'

Babouc inquired into the character of this man who complained of having gained so little, and was informed that in Persepolis there were forty plebeian kings who held the empire of Persia by lease, and paid a small tribute to the monarch.

After dinner he went into one of the most superb temples in the city, and seated himself amidst a crowd of men and women who had come thither to pass away the time. A magi appeared in a machine elevated above the heads of the people, and talked a long time of vice and virtue. He divided into several parts what needed no division at all: he proved methodically what was sufficiently clear, and he taught what everybody knew. He threw himself into a passion with great composure, and went away perspiring and out of breath. The assembly then awoke and imagined they had been present at a very instructive discourse. Babouc said:

'This man has done his best to tire two or three hundred of his fellow-citizens; but his intention was good, and there is nothing in this that should occasion the destruction of Persepolis.'

Upon leaving the assembly he was conducted to a public entertainment, which was exhibited every day in the year. It was in a kind of great hall, at the end of which appeared a palace. The most beautiful women of Persepolis and the most considerable satraps were ranged in order, and formed so fine a spectacle that Babouc at first believed that this was all the entertainment. Two or three persons, who seemed to be kings and queens, soon appeared in the vestibule of their palace. Their language was very different from that of their people; it was measured, harmonious and sublime. Nobody slept. The audience kept a profound silence which was only interrupted by expressions of sensibility and admiration. The duty of kings, the love of virtue and the dangers arising from unbridled passions were all described by such lively and affecting strokes that Babouc shed tears. He doubted not but that these heroes and heroines, these kings and queens whom he had just heard, were the preachers of the empire; he even purposed to engage Ithuriel to come and hear them, being confident that such a spectacle would forever reconcile him to the city.

As soon as the entertainment was finished he resolved to visit the principal queen, who had recommended such pure and noble morals in the palace. He desired to be introduced to her majesty, and was led up a narrow staircase to an ill-furnished apartment in the second storey where he found a woman in a mean dress who said to him with a noble and pathetic air:

'This employment does not afford me a sufficient maintenance; one of the princes you saw has left me with child; I must soon lie in. I have no money, and without money one cannot lie in.'

Babouc gave her an hundred darics of gold, saying:

'Had there been no other evil in the city but this, Ithuriel would have been to blame for being so much offended.'

From thence he went to spend the evening at the house of a tradesman who dealt in magnificent trifles. He was conducted thither by a man of sense, with whom he had contracted an acquaintance. He bought whatever pleased his fancy; and the toy man with great politeness sold him everything for more than it was worth. On his return home his friends showed him how much he had been cheated. Babouc set down the name of the tradesman in his pocketbook, in order to point him out to Ithuriel as an object of peculiar vengeance on the day when the city should be punished. As he was writing he heard somebody knock at the door: this was the toy man himself, who came to restore him his purse, which he had left by mistake on the counter.

'How canst thou,' cried Babouc, 'be so generous and faithful, when thou hast had the assurance to sell me these trifles for four times their value?'

'There is not a tradesman,' replied the merchant, 'of ever so little note in the city, that would not have returned thee thy purse; but whoever said that I sold thee these trifles for four times their value is greatly mistaken: I sold them for ten times their value; and this is so true, that wert thou to sell them again in a month hence, thou wouldst not get even this tenth part. But nothing is more just. It is the variable fancies of men that set a value on these baubles; it is this fancy that maintains an hundred workmen whom I employ; it is this that gives me a fine house and a handsome chariot and horses; it is this, in fine, that excites industry, encourages taste, promotes circulation and produces abundance.

'I sell the same trifles to the neighbouring nation at a much higher rate than I have sold them to thee, and by these means I am useful to the empire.'

Babouc, after having reflected a moment, erased the trades-man's name from his tablets.

Babouc, not knowing as yet what to think of Persepolis, resolved to visit the magi and the men of letters; for, as the one studied wisdom and the other religion, he hoped that they in conjunction would obtain mercy for the rest of the people. Accordingly, he went next morning into a college of magi. The archimandrite confessed to him that he had an hundred thousand crowns a year for having taken the vow of poverty, and that he enjoyed a very extensive empire in virtue of his vow of humility; after which he left him with an inferior brother, who did him the honours of the place.

While the brother was showing him the magnificence of this house of penitence, a report was spread abroad that Babouc was come to reform all these houses. He immediately received petitions from each of them, the substance of which was, 'Preserve us and destroy all the rest.' On hearing their apologies, all these societies were absolutely necessary: on hearing their mutual accusations, they all deserved to be abolished. He was surprised to find that all the members of these societies were so extremely desirious of edifying the world, that they wished to have it entirely under their dominion.

Soon after, a little man appeared, who was a demi-magi, and who said to him:

'I plainly see that the work is going to be accomplished; for Zerdust is returned to earth; and the little girls prophesy, pinching and whipping themselves. We therefore implore thy protection against the great lama.'

'What!' said Babouc, 'against the royal pontiff, who resides at Tibet?'

'Yes, against him, himself.'

'What! you are then making war upon him, and raising armies!'

'No, but he says that man is a free agent, and we deny it.

We have written several pamphlets against him which he never read. Hardly has he heard our name mentioned. He has only condemned us in the same manner as a man orders the trees in his garden to be cleared from caterpillars.'

Babouc was incensed at the folly of these men who made profession of wisdom; and at the intrigues of those who had renounced the world; and at the ambition, pride and avarice of such as taught humility and a disinterested spirit; from all which he concluded that Ithuriel had good reason to destroy the whole race.

On his return home he sent for some new books to alleviate his grief, and in order to exhilarate his spirits, invited some men of letters to dine with him; when, like wasps attracted by a pot of honey, there came twice as many as he desired. These parasites were equally eager to eat and to speak; they praised two sorts of persons, the dead and themselves; but none of their contemporaries, except the master of the house. If any of them happened to drop a smart and witty expression, the rest cast down their eyes and bit their lips out of mere vexation that it had not been said by themselves. They had less dissimulation than the magi, because they had not such grand objects of ambition. Each of them behaved at once with all the meanness of a valet and all the dignity of a great man. They said to each other's face the most insulting things, which they took for strokes of wit. They had some knowledge of the design of Babouc's commission; one of them entreated him in a low voice to extirpate an author who had not praised him sufficiently about five years before; another requested the ruin of a citizen who had never laughed at his comedies; and the third demanded the destruction of the academy because he had not been able to get admitted into it. The repast being ended, each of them departed by himself; for in the whole crowd there were not two men that could endure the company or conversation of each other, except at the houses of the rich, who invited them to their tables. Babouc thought that it would be no great loss to the public if all these vermin were destroyed in the general catastrophe.

Having now got rid of these men of letters, he began to read some new books, where he discovered the true spirit by which his guests had been actuated. He observed with particular indignation those slanderous gazettes, those archives of bad taste, dictated by envy, baseness and hunger; those ungenerous satires, where the vulture is treated with lenity and the dove torn in pieces; and those dry and insipid romances, filled with characters of women to whom the author was an utter stranger.

All these detestable writings he committed to the flames, and went to pass the evening in walking. In this excursion he was introduced to an old man possessed of great learning, who had not come to increase the number of his parasites. This man of letters always fled from crowds; he understood human nature, availed himself of his knowledge and imparted it to others with great discretion. Babouc told him how much he was grieved at what he had seen and read.

'Thou hast read very despicable performances,' said the man of letters; 'but in all times, in all countries and in all kinds of literature, the bad swarm and the good are rare. Thou has received into thy house the very dregs of pedantry. In all professions, those who are least worthy of appearing are always sure to present themselves with the greatest impudence. The truly wise live among themselves in retirement and tranquillity; and we have still some men and some books worthy of thy attention.'

While he was thus speaking, they were joined by another man of letters; and the conversation became so entertaining and instructive, so elevated above vulgar prejudices and so comfortable to virtue, that Babouc acknowledged he had never heard the like.

'These are men,' said he to himself, 'whom the angel Ithuriel will not presume to touch, or he must be a merciless being indeed.'

Though reconciled to men of letters he was still enraged against the rest of the nation.

'Thou art a stranger,' said the judicious person who was talking to him; 'abuses present themselves to thy eyes in crowds, while the good, which lies concealed, and which is even sometimes the result of these very abuses, escapes thy observation.'

He then learned that among men of letters there were some who were free from envy; and that even among the magi themselves there were some men of virtue. In fine, he concluded that these great bodies, which by their mutual shocks seemed to threaten their common ruin, were at bottom very salutary institutions; that each society of magi was a check upon its rivals;

and that though these rivals might differ in some speculative points, they all taught the same morals, instructed the people, and lived in subjection to the laws; not unlike to those preceptors who watch over the heir of a family while the master of the house watches over them. He conversed with several of these magi, and found them possessed of exalted souls. He likewise learned that even among the fools who pretended to make war on the great lama there had been some men of distinguished merit; and from all these particulars he conjectured that it might be with the manners of Persepolis as it was with the buildings; some of which moved his pity, while others filled him with admiration.

He said to the man of letters:

'I plainly see that these magi, whom I at first imagined to be so dangerous, are in reality extremely useful; especially when a wise government hinders them from rendering themselves too necessary; but thou wilt at least acknowledge that your young magistrates, who purchase the office of a judge as soon as they can mount a horse, must display in their tribunals the most ridiculous impertinence and the most iniquitous perverseness. It would doubtless be better to give these places gratuitously to those old civilians who have spent their lives in the study of the law.'

The man of letters replied:

'Thou hast seen our army before thy arrival at Persepolis; thou knowest that our young officers fight with great bravery, though they buy their posts; perhaps thou wilt find that our young magistrates do not give wrong decisions, though they purchase the right of dispensing justice.'

He led him next day to the grand tribunal, where an affair of great importance was to be decided. The cause was known to all the world. All the old advocates that spoke on the subject were wavering and unsettled in their opinions. They quoted a hundred laws, none of which were applicable to the question. They considered the matter in a hundred different lights, but never in its true point of view. The judges were more quick in their decisions than the advocates in raising doubts. They were unanimous in their sentiments. They decided justly, because they followed the light of reason. The others reasoned falsely because they only consulted their books.

Babouc concluded that the best things frequently arose from abuses. He saw the same day that the riches of the receivers of the public revenue, at which he had been so much offended, were capable of producing an excellent effect; for the emperor having occasion for money, he found in an hour by their means what he could not have procured in six months by the ordinary methods. He saw that those great clouds, swelled with the dews of the earth, restored in plentiful showers what they had thence derived. Besides, the children of these new gentlemen, who were frequently better educated than those of the most ancient families, were sometimes more useful members of society; for he whose father hath been a good accountant may easily become a good judge, a brave warrior, and an able statesman.

Babouc was insensibly brought to excuse the avarice of the farmer of the revenues, who in reality was not more avaricious than other men, and besides was extremely necessary. He over-looked the folly of those who ruined themselves in order to obtain a post in the law or army; a folly that produces great magistrates and heroes. He forgave the envy of men of letters, among whom there were some that enlightened the world; and he was reconciled to the ambitious and intriguing magi, who were possessed of more great virtues than little vices. But he had still many causes of complaint. The gallantries of the ladies especially, and the fatal effects which these must necessarily produce, filled him with fear and terror.

As he was desirous of prying into the characters of men of every condition, he went to wait on a minister of state; but trembled all the way, lest some wife should be assassinated by her husband in his presence. Having arrived at the statesman's, he was obliged to remain two hours in the antechamber before his name was sent in, and two hours more after that was done. In this interval, he resolved to recommend to the angel Ithuriel both the minister and his insolent porters. The antechamber was filled with ladies of every rank, magi of all colours, judges, merchants, officers, and pedants; and all of them complained of the minister. The miser and the usurer said:

'Doubtless this man plunders the provinces.'

The capricious reproached him with fickleness; the voluptuary said:

'He thinks of nothing but his pleasure.'

[191]

The factious hoped to see him soon ruined by a cabal; and the women flattered themselves that they should soon have a younger minister.

Babouc heard their conversation, and could not help saying: 'This is surely a happy man; he hath all his enemies in his antechamber; he crushes with his power those that envy his grandeur; he beholds those who detest him grovelling at his feet.'

At length he was admitted into the presence-chamber, where he saw a little old man bending under the weight of years and business, but still lively and full of spirits.

The minister was pleased with Babouc, and to Babouc he appeared a man of great merit. The conversation became interesting. The minister confessed that he was very unhappy; that he passed for rich, while in reality he was poor; that he was believed to be all-powerful, and yet was constantly contradicted; that he had obliged none but a parcel of ungrateful wretches; and that, in the course of forty years' labour, he had hardly enjoyed a moment's rest. Babouc was moved with his misfortunes; and thought that if this man had been guilty of some faults, and Ithuriel had a mind to banish him, he ought not to cut him off, but to leave him in possession of his place.

While Babouc was talking to the minister, the beautiful lady with whom he had dined entered hastily, her eyes and countenance showing all the symptoms of grief and indignation. She burst into reproaches against the statesman; she shed tears; she complained bitterly that her husband had been refused a place to which his birth allowed him to aspire, and which he had fully merited by his wounds and his service. She expressed herself with such force; she uttered her complaints with such a graceful air; she overthrew objections with so much address, and enforced her arguments with so much eloquence, that she did not leave the chamber till she had made her husband's fortune.

Babouc gave her his hand, and said: 'Is it possible, madam, that thou canst take so much pains to serve a man whom thou dost not love, and from whom thou hast everything to fear?'

'A husband whom I do not love!' cried she; 'know, sir, that my husband is the best friend I have in the world; and there is nothing I would not sacrifice for him except my lover; and he would do anything for me except leave his mistress. I should like you to meet her; she is a charming woman, full of wit, of the most agreeable character; we are supping together this evening, with my husband and my little mage; come and share our joy.'

The lady conducted Babouc to her own house. The husband, who had at last arrived overwhelmed with grief, received his wife with transports of joy and gratitude. He embraced by turns his wife, his mistress, the little mage, and Babouc. Wit, harmony, cheerfulness, and all the graces, embellished the repast.

'Those who are sometimes called unvirtuous women,' said the fair lady with whom he was supping, 'almost always have the merits of a virtuous man. To convince you of this, come and dine with me to-morrow with the fair Teone. She is torn to pieces by a few old vestals, but she does more good than all of them together. She would not do a slight injustice to further her greatest interest; she gives her lover none but generous advice; she is concerned only for his fame; he would blush before her if he missed an occasion of doing good, for nothing encourages virtuous actions more than to have a mistress whose esteem one desires as witness and judge of one's conduct.'

Babouc kept the appointment. He found a house devoted to all the pleasures. Teone reigned over them; she could speak to everyone in his own language. Her natural intelligence set everyone at ease; she pleased almost without wishing it, she was as amiable as she was benevolent, and the value of all her good qualities was increased by the fact that she was beautiful.

Babouc, though a Scythian, and sent by a geni, found, that should he continue much longer in Persepolis, he would forget even the angel Ithuriel. He began to grow fond of a city, the inhabitants of which were polite, affable, and beneficent, though fickle, slanderous, and vain. He was much afraid that Persepolis would be condemned. He was even afraid to give in his account.

This, however, he did in the following manner. He caused a little statue, composed of different metals, of earth, and stones, the most precious and the most vile, to be cast by one of the best founders in the city, and carried it to Ithuriel.

'Wilt thou break,' said he, 'this pretty statue, because it is not wholly composed of gold and diamonds?'

Ithuriel immediately understood his meaning, and resolved

to think no more of punishing Persepolis, but to leave 'the world as it is.'

'For,' said he, 'if all is not well, all is passable.'

Thus Persepolis was suffered to remain; nor did Babouc complain like Jonah, who was highly incensed at the preservation of Nineveh. But when a man has been in the belly of a whale for three days, he is not so good-tempered as when he has been to the opera, to the theatre, and has supped in pleasant company.

MICROMEGAS:

PHILOSOPHICAL HISTORY[1]

A VOYAGE TO THE PLANET SATURN BY A NATIVE OF SIRIUS

IN ONE OF THE PLANETS THAT REVOLVE ROUND THE STAR KNOWN
by the name of Sirius, was a certain young gentleman of
promising parts, whom I had the honour to be acquainted
with in his last voyage to this our little ant-hill. His name was
Micromegas, an appellation admirably suited to all great men,
and his stature amounted to eight leagues in height, that is,
twenty-four thousand geometrical paces of five feet each.

Some of your mathematicians, a set of people always useful
to the public, will, perhaps, instantly seize the pen, and calculate
that Mr. Micromegas, inhabitant of the country of Sirius, being
from head to foot four and twenty thousand paces in length,
making one hundred and twenty thousand royal feet, that we,
denizens of this earth, being at a medium little more than five
feet high, and our globe nine thousand leagues in circumference:
these things being premised, they will then conclude that the
periphery of the globe which produced him must be exactly
one and twenty million six hundred thousand times greater than
that of this our tiny ball. Nothing in nature is more simple and
common. The dominions of some sovereigns of Germany or
Italy, which may be compassed in half an hour, when compared
with the empires of Ottoman, Russia, or China, are no other
than faint instances of the prodigious difference that nature hath
made in the scale of beings. The stature of his excellency being
of these extraordinary dimensions, all our artists will agree that
the measure around his body might amount to fifty thousand
royal feet—a very agreeable and just proportion.

His nose being equal in length to one-third of his face, and
his jolly countenance engrossing one-seventh part of his height,
it must be owned that the nose of this same Sirian was six
thousand three hundred and thirty-three royal feet to a hair,

---

[1] *Editor's Note:* Micromegas owes much to Swift and to *Gulliver's Travels,* but the
humour of the Frenchman is more personal and less stolid than that of the Englishman.
In effect, the traveller from Sirius is none other than Voltaire himself, that is, the spirit
which looks down from on high upon the stupidities and follies of man.

which was to be demonstrated. With regard to his understanding, it is one of the best cultivated I have known. He is perfectly well acquainted with abundance of things, some of which are of his own invention; for, when his age did not exceed two hundred and fifty years, he studied, according to the custom of the country, at the most celebrated university of the whole planet, and by the force of his genius discovered upwards of fifty propositions of Euclid, having the advantage by more than eighteen of Blaise Pascal, who (as we are told by his own sister), demonstrated two and thirty for his amusement and then left off, choosing rather to be an indifferent philosopher than a great mathematician.

About the four hundred and fiftieth year of his age, or latter end of his childhood, he dissected a great number of small insects not more than one hundred feet in diameter, which are not perceivable by ordinary microscopes, on which he composed a very curious treatise, which involved him in some trouble. The mufti of the nation, though very old and very ignorant, made shift to discover in his book certain lemmas that were suspicious, unseemly, rash, heretic, and unsound, and prosecuted him with great animosity; for the subject of the author's enquiry was whether, in the world of Sirius, there was any difference between the substantial forms of a flea and a snail.

Micromegas defended his philosophy with such spirit as made all the female sex his proselytes; and the process lasted two hundred and twenty years; at the end of which time, in consequence of the mufti's interest, the book was condemned by judges who had never read it, and the author expelled from court for the term of eight hundred years.

Not much affected at his banishment from a court that teemed with nothing but turmoils and trifles, he made a very humorous song upon the mufti, who gave himself no trouble about the matter, and set out on his travels from planet to planet, in order (as the saying is) to improve his mind and finish his education. Those who never travel but in a post-chaise or berlin, will, doubtless, be astonished at the equipages used above; for we that strut upon this little mole hill are at a loss to conceive anything that surpasses our own customs. But our traveller was a wonderful adept in the laws of gravitation, together with the whole force of attraction and repulsion, and made such seasonable use of his knowledge, that sometimes by the help of a sunbeam, and sometimes by the convenience of a comet, he and his retinue glided from sphere to sphere, as the bird hops from one bough to another. He in a very little time posted through the Milky Way, and I am obliged to own he saw not a twinkle of those stars supposed to adorn that fair empyrean, which the illustrious Dr. Derham brags to have observed through his telescope. Not that I pretend to say the doctor was mistaken. God forbid! But Micromegas was upon the spot, an exceeding good observer, and I have no mind to contradict any man. Be that as it may, after many windings and turnings, he arrived at the planet Saturn; and, accustomed as he was to the sight of novelties, he could not for his life repress a supercilious and conceited smile, which often escapes the wisest philosopher, when he perceived the smallness of that globe, and the diminutive size of its inhabitants; for really Saturn is but about nine hundred times larger than this our earth, and the people of that country mere dwarfs, about a thousand fathoms high. In short, he at first derided those poor pigmies, just as an Indian fiddler laughs at the music of Lully, at his first arrival in Paris: but as this Sirian was a person of good sense, he soon perceived that a thinking being may not be altogether ridiculous, even though he is not quite six thousand feet high; and therefore he became familiar with them, after they had ceased to wonder at his extraordinary appearance. In particular, he contracted an intimate friendship with the secretary of the Academy of Saturn, a man of good understanding, who, though in truth he had invented nothing of his own, gave a very good account of the inventions of others, and enjoyed in peace the reputation of a little poet and great calculator. And here, for the edification of the reader, I will repeat a very singular conversation that one day passed between Mr. Secretary and Micromegas.

THE CONVERSATION BETWEEN MICROMEGAS AND THE INHABITANT OF SATURN

His excellency having laid himself down, and the secretary approached his nose:

'It must be confessed,' said Micromegas, 'that nature is full of variety.'

[197]

'Yes,' replied the Saturnian, 'nature is like a parterre, whose flowers——'

'Pshaw!' cried the other, 'a truce with your parterres.'

'It is,' resumed the secretary, 'like an assembly of fair and brown women, whose dresses——'

'What a plague have I to do with your brunettes?' said our traveller.

'Then it is like a gallery of pictures, the strokes of which——'

'Not at all,' answered Micromegas, 'I tell you once for all, nature is like nature, and comparisons are odious.'

'Well, to please you,' said the secretary—

'I won't be pleased,' replied the Sirian, 'I want to be instructed; begin, therefore, without further preamble, and tell me how many senses the people of this world enjoy.'

'We have seventy and two,' said the academician, 'but we are daily complaining of the small number, as our imagination transcends our wants, for, with the seventy-two senses, our five moons and ring, we find ourselves very much restricted; and notwithstanding our curiosity, and the no small number of those passions that result from these few senses, we have still time enough to be tired of idleness.'

'I sincerely believe what you say,' cried Micromegas, 'for, though we Sirians have near a thousand different senses, there still remains a certain vague desire, an unaccountable inquietude incessantly admonishing us of our own unimportance, and giving us to understand that there are other beings who are much our superiors in point of perfection. I have travelled a little, and seen mortals both above and below myself in the scale of being, but I have met with none who had not more desire than necessity, and more want than gratification. Perhaps I shall one day arrive in some country where naught is wanting, but hitherto I have had no certain information of such a happy land.'

The Saturnian and his guest exhausted themselves in conjectures upon this subject, and after abundance of argumentation equally ingenious and uncertain, were fain to return to matter of fact.

'To what age do you commonly live?' said the Sirian.

'Lack-a-day! a mere trifle,' replied the little gentleman.

'It is the very same case with us,' resumed the other, 'the shortness of life is our daily complaint, so that this must be an universal law in nature.'

'Alas!' cried the Saturnian, 'few, very few on this globe outlive five hundred great revolutions of the sun (these, according to our way of reckoning, amount to about fifteen thousand years). So, you see, we in a manner begin to die the very moment we are born: our existence is no more than a point, our duration an instant, and our globe an atom. Scarce do we begin to learn a little, when death intervenes before we can profit by experience. For my own part, I am deterred from laying schemes when I consider myself as a single drop in the midst of an immense ocean. I am particularly ashamed, in your presence, of the ridiculous figure I make among my fellow-creatures.'

To this declaration, Micromegas replied:

'If you were not a philosopher, I should be afraid of mortifying your pride by telling you that the term of our lives is seven hundred times longer than the period of your existence: but you are very sensible that when the texture of the body is resolved, in order to reanimate nature in another form, which is the consequence of what we call death—when that moment of change arrives, there is not the least difference betwixt having lived a whole eternity, or a single day. I have been in some countries where the people live a thousand times longer than with us, and yet they murmured at the shortness of their time. But one will find everywhere some few persons of good sense, who know how to make the best of their portion, and thank the author of nature for his bounty. There is a profusion of variety scattered through the universe, and yet there is an admirable vein of uniformity that runs through the whole: for example, all thinking beings are different among themselves, though at bottom they resemble one another in the powers and passions of the soul. Matter, though interminable, hath different properties in every sphere. How many principal attributes do you reckon in the matter of this world?'

'If you mean those properties,' said the Saturnian, 'without which we believe this our globe could not subsist, we reckon in all three hundred, such as extent, impenetrability, motion, gravitation, divisibility, et cætera.'

'That small number,' replied the traveller, 'probably answers the views of the creator on this your narrow sphere. I adore his wisdom in all his works. I see infinite variety, but everywhere proportion. Your globe is small: so are the inhabitants. You have few sensations; because your matter is endued with few properties. These are the works of unerring providence. Of what colour does your sun appear when accurately examined?'

'Of a yellowish white,' answered the Saturnian, 'and in separating one of his rays we find it contains seven colours.'

'Our sun,' said the Sirian, 'is of a reddish hue, and we have no less than thirty-nine original colours. Among all the suns I have seen there is no sort of resemblance, and in this sphere of yours there is not one face like another.'

After divers questions of this nature, he asked how many substances, essentially different, they counted in the world of Saturn; and understood that they numbered but thirty: such as God; space; matter; beings endowed with sense and extension; beings that have extension, sense, and reflection; thinking beings who have no extension; those that are penetrable; those that are impenetrable, and also all others. But this Saturnian philosopher was prodigiously astonished when this Sirian told him they had no less than three hundred, and that he himself had discovered three thousand more in the course of his travels. In short, after having communicated to each other what they knew, and even what they did not know, and argued during a complete revolution of the sun, they resolved to set out together on a small philosophical tour.

THE VOYAGE OF THESE INHABITANTS OF OTHER WORLDS

Our two philosophers were just ready to embark for the atmosphere of Saturn, with a large provision of mathematical instruments, when the Saturnian's mistress, having got an inkling of their design, came all in tears to make her protests. She was a handsome brunette, though not above six hundred and three-score fathoms high; but her agreeable attractions made amends for the smallness of her stature.

'Ah! cruel man,' cried she, 'after a courtship of fifteen hundred years, when at length I surrendered, and became your wife, and scarce have passed two hundred more in thy embraces, to leave me thus, before the honeymoon is over, and go a rambling with a giant of another world! Go, go, thou art a mere virtuoso, devoid of tenderness and love! If thou wert a true Saturnian, thou wouldst be faithful and invariable. Ah! whither art thou going? what is thy design? Our five moons are not so inconstant, nor our ring so changeable as thee! But take this along with thee, henceforth I ne'er shall love another man.'

The little gentleman embraced and wept over her, notwithstanding his philosophy; and the lady, after having swooned with great decency, went to console herself with more agreeable company.

Meanwhile our two virtuosi set out, and at one jump leaped upon the ring, which they found pretty flat, according to the ingenious guess of an illustrious inhabitant of this our little earth. From thence they easily slipped from moon to moon; and a comet chancing to pass, they sprang upon it with all their servants and apparatus. Thus carried about one hundred and fifty millions of leagues, they met with the satellites of Jupiter, and arrived upon the body of the planet itself, where they continued a whole year; during which they learned some very curious secrets, which would actually be sent to the press, were it not for fear of the gentlemen inquisitors who have found among them some corollaries very hard of digestion.

But to return to our travellers. When they took leave of Jupiter, they traversed a space of about one hundred millions of leagues, and coasting along the planet Mars, which is well known to be five times smaller than our little earth, they descried two moons subservient to that orb, which have escaped the observations of all our astronomers. I know Castel will write, and that pleasantly enough, against the existence of these two moons; but I entirely refer myself to those who reason by analogy. Those worthy philosophers are very sensible that Mars, which is at such a distance from the sun, must be in a very uncomfortable situation, without the benefit of a couple of moons. Be that as it may, our gentlemen found their planet so small, that they were afraid they should not find room to take a little repose; so that they pursued their journey like two travellers who despise the paltry accommodation of a village, and push forward to the next market town. But the Sirian and his companion soon repented of their delicacy; for they journeyed a long time without finding a resting-place, till at length they discerned a small speck, which was the Earth. Coming from Jupiter, they could not but be moved with compassion at the sight of this miserable spot, upon which, however, they resolved to land, lest they should be a second time disappointed. They accordingly moved towards the tail of the comet, where, finding an Aurora Borealis ready to set sail, they embarked, and arrived on the northern coast of the Baltic on the fifth day of July, New Style, in the year 1737.

WHAT BEFELL THEM UPON THIS OUR GLOBE

Having taken some repose, and being desirous of reconnoitring the narrow field in which they were, they traversed it at once from north to south. Every step of the Sirian and his attendants measured about thirty thousand royal feet: whereas the dwarf of Saturn, whose stature did not exceed a thousand fathoms, followed at a distance quite out of breath; because, for every single stride of his companion, he was obliged to take twelve good steps at least. The reader may figure to himself (if we are allowed to make such comparisons) a very little rough spaniel dodging after a captain of the Prussian grenadiers.

As those strangers walked at a good pace, they compassed the globe in six and thirty hours; the sun, it is true, or rather the earth, describes the same space in the course of one day; but it must be observed that it is much easier to turn upon an axis than to walk afoot. Behold them then returned to the spot from whence they had set out, after having discovered that almost imperceptible sea, which is called the Mediterranean; and the other narrow pond that surrounds this molehill, under the denomination of the great ocean; in wading through which the dwarf had never wet his mid-leg, while the other scarce moistened his heel. In going and coming through both hemispheres, they did all that lay in their power to discover whether or not the globe was inhabited. They stooped, they lay down, they groped in every corner; but their eyes and hands were not at all proportioned to the small beings that crawled upon this earth; and, therefore, they could not find the smallest reason to suspect that we and our fellow-citizens of this globe had the honour to exist.

The dwarf, who sometimes judged too hastily, concluded at once that there was no living creature upon earth; and his chief reason was, that he had seen nobody. But Micromegas, in a polite manner, made him sensible of the unjust conclusion:

'For,' said he, 'with your diminutive eyes you cannot see

certain stars of the fiftieth magnitude. which I easily perceive; and do you take it for granted that no such stars exist?'

'But I have groped with great care' replied the dwarf.

'Then your sense of feeling must be bad' said the other.

'But this globe' said the dwarf 'is ill contrived; and so irregular in its form as to be quite ridiculous. The whole together looks like a chaos. Do but observe these little rivulets; not one of them runs in a straight line: and these ponds which are neither round, square, nor oval, nor indeed of any regular figure; together with these little sharp pebbles (meaning the mountains) that roughen the whole surface of the globe, and have torn all the skin from my feet. Besides, pray take notice of the shape of the whole, how it flattens at the poles, and turns round the sun in an awkward oblique manner, so as that the polar circles cannot possibly be cultivated. Truly, what makes me believe there is no inhabitant on this sphere, is a full persuasion that no sensible being would live in such a disagreeable place.'

'What then?' said Micromegas, 'perhaps the beings that inhabit it come not under that denomination; but, to all appearance, it was not made for nothing. Everything here seems to you irregular; because you fetch all your comparisons from Jupiter or Saturn. Perhaps this is the very reason of the seeming confusion which you condemn; have I not told you, that in the course of my travels I have always met with variety?'

The Saturnian replied to all these arguments; and perhaps the dispute would have known no end, if Micromegas, in the heat of the contest, had not luckily broken the string of his diamond necklace, so that the jewels fell to the ground; they consisted of pretty small unequal carats, the largest of which weighed four hundred pounds, and the smallest fifty. The dwarf, in helping to pick them up, perceived, as they approached his eye, that every single diamond was cut in such a manner as to answer the purpose of an excellent microscope. He therefore took up a small one, about one hundred and sixty feet in diameter, and applied it to his eye, while Micromegas chose another of two thousand five hundred feet. Though they were of excellent powers, the observers could perceive nothing by their assistance, so they were altered and adjusted. At length, the inhabitant of Saturn discerned something almost imperceptible moving between two waves in the Baltic. This was no other than a whale, which, in a dexterous manner, he caught with his little finger, and, placing it on the nail of his thumb, showed it to the Sirian, who laughed heartily at the excessive smallness peculiar to the inhabitants of this our globe. The Saturnian, by this time convinced that our world was inhabited, began to imagine we had no other animals than whales; and being a mighty debater, he forthwith set about investigating the origin and motion of this small atom, curious to know whether or not it was furnished with ideas, judgment, and free will. Micromegas was very much perplexed upon this subject. He examined the animal with the most patient attention, and the result of his inquiry was, that he could see no reason to believe a soul was lodged in such a body. The two travellers were actually inclined to think there was no such thing as mind in this our habitation, when, by the help of their microscope, they perceived something as large as a whale floating upon the surface of the sea. It is well known that, at this period, a flight of philosophers were upon their return from the polar circle, where they had been making observations, for which nobody has hitherto been the wiser. The gazettes record that their vessel ran ashore on the coast of Bothnia and that they with great difficulty saved their lives; but in this world one can never dive to the bottom of things. For my own part, I will ingenuously recount the transaction just as it happened, without any addition of my own; and this is no small effort in a modern historian.

THE TRAVELLERS CAPTURE A VESSEL

Micromegas stretched out his hand gently toward the place where the object appeared, and advanced two fingers, which he instantly pulled back, for fear of being disappointed, then opening softly and shutting them all at once, he very dexterously seized the ship that contained those gentlemen, and placed it on his nail, avoiding too much pressure, which might have crushed the whole in pieces.

'This,' said the Saturnian dwarf, 'is a creature very different from the former.'

Upon which the Sirian placed the supposed animal in the hollow of his hand, the passengers and crew, who believed themselves thrown by a hurricane upon some rock, began to put themselves in motion. The sailors having hoisted out some casks of wine, jumped after them into the hand of Micromegas: the mathematicians having secured their quadrants, sectors, and Lapland servants, went overboard at a different place, and made such a bustle in their descent, that the Sirian at length felt his fingers tickled by something that seemed to move. An iron bar chanced to penetrate about a foot deep into his forefinger; and from this prick he concluded that something had issued from the little animal he held in his hand; but at first he suspected nothing more: for the microscope, that scarce rendered a whale and a ship visible, had no effect upon an object so imperceptible as man.

I do not intend to shock the vanity of any person whatever; but here I am obliged to beg your people of importance to consider that, supposing the stature of a man to be about five feet, we mortals make just such a figure upon the earth as an animal the sixty thousandth part of a foot in height would exhibit upon a bowl ten feet in circumference. When you reflect upon a being who could hold this whole earth in the palm of his hand, and is provided with organs proportioned to those we possess, you will easily conceive that there must be a great variety of created substances: and pray, what must such beings think of those battles by which a conqueror gains a small village, to lose it again in the sequel?

I do not at all doubt, but if some captain of grenadiers should chance to read this work, he would add two large feet at least to the caps of his company; but I assure him his labour will be in vain; for, do what he will, he and his soldiers will never be other than infinitely diminutive and inconsiderable.

What wonderful address must have been inherent in our Sirian philosopher, that enabled him to perceive those atoms of which we have been speaking. When Leeuwenhoek and Hart-soecker observed the first rudiments of which we are formed, they did not make such an astonishing discovery. What pleasure, therefore, was the portion of Micromegas, in observing the motion of those little machines, in examining all their pranks, and following them in all their operations! With what joy did he put his microscope into his companion's hand; and with what transport did they both at once exclaim:

'I see them distinctly—don't you see them carrying burdens, lying down and rising up again?'

[205]

So saying, their hands shook with eagerness to see, and apprehension of losing such uncommon objects. The Saturnian, making a sudden transition from the most cautious distrust to the most excessive credulity, imagined he saw them engaged in their devotions and cried aloud in astonishment.

Nevertheless, he was deceived by appearances: a case too common, whether we do or do not make use of microscopes.

WHAT HAPPENED IN THEIR INTERCOURSE WITH MEN

Micromegas, being a much better observer than the dwarf, perceived distinctly that those atoms spoke; and made the remark to his companion, who was so much ashamed of being mistaken in his first suggestion, that he would not believe such a puny species could possibly communicate their ideas: for, though he had the gift of tongues, as well as his companion, he could not hear those particles speak; and therefore supposed they had no language.

'Besides, how should such imperceptible beings have the organs of speech? and what in the name of Jove can they say to one another? In order to speak, they must have something like thought, and if they think, they must surely have something equivalent to a soul. Now, to attribute anything like a soul to such an insect species appears a mere absurdity.'

'But just now,' replied the Sirian, 'you believed they were engaged in devotional exercises; and do you think this could be done without thinking, without using some sort of language, or at least some way of making themselves understood? Or do you suppose it is more difficult to advance an argument than to engage in physical exercise? For my own part, I look upon all faculties as alike mysterious.'

'I will no longer venture to believe or deny,' answered the dwarf: 'in short, I have no opinion at all. Let us endeavour to examine these insects, and we will reason upon them afterwards.'

'With all my heart,' said Micromegas, who, taking out a pair of scissors which he kept for paring his nails, cut off a paring from his thumb nail, of which he immediately formed a large kind of speaking trumpet, like a vast tunnel, and clapped the pipe to his ear: as the circumference of this machine included the ship and all the crew, the most feeble voice was conveyed along the circular fibres of the nail; so that, thanks to his industry, the philosopher could distinctly hear the buzzing of our insects that were below. In a few hours he distinguished articulate sounds, and at last plainly understood the French language. The dwarf heard the same, though with more difficulty.

The astonishment of our travellers increased every instant. They heard a nest of mites talk in a very sensible strain: and that *Lusus Naturæ* seemed to them inexplicable. You need not doubt but the Sirian and his dwarf glowed with impatience to enter into conversation with such atoms. Micromegas, being afraid that his voice, like thunder, would deafen and confound the mites, without being understood by them, saw the necessity of diminishing the sound; each, therefore, put into his mouth a sort of small toothpick, the slender end of which reached to the vessel. The Sirian, setting the dwarf upon his knees, and the ship and crew upon his nail, held down his head and spoke softly. In fine, having taken these and a great many more precautions, he addressed himself to them in these words:

'O ye invisible insects, whom the hand of the Creator hath deigned to produce in the abyss of infinite littleness! I give praise to his goodness, in that he hath been pleased to disclose unto me those secrets that seemed to be impenetrable.'

If ever there was such a thing as astonishment, it seized upon the people who heard this address, and who could not conceive from whence it proceeded. The chaplain of the ship repeated exorcisms, the sailors swore, and the philosophers formed a system: but, notwithstanding all their systems, they could not divine who the person was that spoke to them. Then the dwarf of Saturn, whose voice was softer than that of Micromegas, gave them briefly to understand what species of beings they had to do with. He related the particulars of their voyage from Saturn, made them acquainted with the rank and quality of Monsieur Micromegas; and, after having pitied their smallness, asked if they had always been in that miserable state so near akin to annihilation; and what their business was upon that globe which seemed to be the property of whales. He also desired to know if they were happy in their situation? if they were inspired with souls? and put a hundred questions of the like nature.

A certain mathematician on board, braver than the rest, and shocked to hear his soul called in question, planted his quadrant, and having taken two observations of this interlocutor, said: 'You believe then, Mr. What's your Name, that because you measure from head to foot a thousand fathoms——'

'A thousand fathoms!' cried the dwarf, 'good heavens! How should he know the height of my stature? A thousand fathoms! My very dimensions to a hair. What, measured by a mite! This atom, forsooth, is a geometrician, and knows exactly how tall I am: while I, who can scarce perceive him through a microscope, am utterly ignorant of his extent!'

'Yes, I have taken your measure,' answered the philosopher, 'and I will now do the same by your tall companion.'

The proposal was embraced: his excellency reclined upon his side; for, had he stood upright, his head would have reached too far above the clouds. Our mathematicians planted a tall tree near him, and then, by a series of triangles joined together, they discovered that the object of their observation was a strapping youth, exactly one hundred and twenty thousand royal feet in length. In consequence of this calculation, Micromegas uttered these words:

'I am now more than ever convinced that we ought to judge of nothing by its external magnitude. O God! who has bestowed understanding upon such seemingly contemptible substances, thou canst with equal ease produce that which is infinitely small, as that which is incredibly great: and if it be possible, that among thy works there are beings still more diminutive than these, they may nevertheless be endued with understanding superior to the intelligence of those stupendous animals I have seen in heaven, a single foot of whom is larger than this whole globe on which I have alighted.'

One of the philosophers assured him that there were intelligent beings much smaller than men, and recounted not only Virgil's whole fable of the bees; but also described all that Swammerdam hath discovered, and Réaumur dissected. In a word, he informed him that there are animals which bear the same proportion to bees, that bees bear to man; the same as the Sirian himself compared to those vast beings whom he had mentioned; and as those huge animals as to other substances, before whom they would appear like so many particles of dust. Here the conversation became very interesting, and Micromegas proceeded in these words:

'O ye intelligent atoms, in whom the Supreme Being hath

been pleased to manifest his omniscience and power, without all doubt your joys on this earth must be pure and exquisite: for, being unencumbered with matter, and, to all appearance, little else than soul, you must spend your lives in the delights of pleasure and reflection, which are the true enjoyments of a perfect spirit. True happiness I have nowhere found; but certainly here it dwells.'

At this harangue all the philosophers shook their heads, and one among them, more candid than his brethren, frankly owned, that excepting a very small number of inhabitants who were very little esteemed by their fellows, all the rest were a parcel of knaves, fools, and miserable wretches.

'We have matter enough,' said he, 'to do abundance of mischief, if mischief comes from matter; and too much understanding, if evil flows from understanding. You must know, for example, that at this very moment, while I am speaking, there are one hundred thousand animals of our own species, covered with hats, slaying an equal number of their fellow-creatures, who wear turbans; at least they are either slaying or being slain; and this hath usually been the case all over the earth from time immemorial.'

The Sirian, shuddering at this information, begged to know the cause of those horrible quarrels among such a puny race; and was given to understand that the subject of the dispute was a pitiful molehill (called Palestine), no larger than his heel. Not that any one of those millions who cut one another's throats pretends to have the least claim to the smallest particle of that clod. The question is, whether it shall belong to a certain person who is known by the name of Sultan, or to another whom (for what reason I know not) they dignify with the appellation of King. Neither the one nor the other has seen or ever will see the pitiful corner in question; and probably none of those wretches, who so madly destroy each other, ever beheld the ruler on whose account they are so mercilessly sacrificed!

'Ah, miscreants!' cried the indignant Sirian, 'such excess of desperate rage is beyond conception. I have a good mind to take two or three steps, and trample the whole nest of such ridiculous assassins under my feet.'

'Don't give yourself the trouble,' replied the philosopher, 'they are industrious enough in procuring their own destruction. At the end of ten years the hundredth part of those wretches will not survive; for you must know that, though they should not draw a sword in the cause they have espoused, famine, fatigue, and intemperance would sweep almost all of them from the face of the earth. Besides, the punishment should not be inflicted upon them, but upon those sedentary and slothful barbarians, who, from their palaces, give orders for murdering a million of men and then solemnly thank God for their success.'

Our traveller was moved with compassion for the entire human race, in which he discovered such astonishing contrast. 'Since you are of the small number of the wise,' said he, 'and in all likelihood do not engage yourselves in the trade of murder for hire, be so good as to tell me your occupation.'

'We anatomize flies,' replied the philosopher, 'we measure lines, we make calculations, we agree upon two or three points which we understand, and dispute upon two or three thousand that are beyond our comprehension.'

'How far,' said the Sirian, 'do you reckon the distance between the great star of the constellation Gemini and that called Caniculæ?'

To this question all of them answered with one voice: 'Thirty-two degrees and a half.'

'And what is the distance from hence to the moon?'

'Sixty semi-diameters of the earth.'

He then thought to puzzle them by asking the weight of the air; but they answered distinctly, that common air is about nine hundred times specifically lighter than an equal column of the lightest water, and nineteen hundred times lighter than current gold. The little dwarf of Saturn, astonished at their answers, was now tempted to believe those people sorcerers, who, but a quarter of an hour before, he would not allow were inspired with souls.

'Well,' said Micromegas, 'since you know so well what is without you, doubtless you are still more perfectly acquainted with that which is within. Tell me what is the soul, and how do your ideas originate?'

Here the philosophers spoke altogether as before; but each was of a different opinion. The eldest quoted Aristotle; another pronounced the name of Descartes; a third mentioned Malebranche; a fourth Leibnitz; and a fifth Locke. An old peripatecian lifting up his voice, exclaimed with an air of confidence, 'The soul is perfection and reason, having power to be such as it is, as Aristotle expressly declares, page 633, of the Louvre edition:

Ἐντελέχειά τίς ἐστι καὶ λύγος τοῦ σύναμιν ἔχοντος εἶναι τοιούτου

'I am not very well versed in Greek,' said the giant.

'Nor I either,' replied the philosophical mite.

'Why then do you quote that same Aristotle in Greek?' resumed the Sirian.

'Because,' answered the other, 'it is reasonable we should quote what we do not comprehend in a language we do not understand.'

Here the Cartesian interposing: 'The soul,' said he, 'is a pure spirit or intelligence, which hath received before birth all the metaphysical ideas; but after that event it is obliged to go to school and learn anew the knowledge which it hath lost.'

'So it was necessary,' replied the animal of eight leagues, 'that thy soul should be learned before birth, in order to be so ignorant when thou hast got a beard upon thy chin. But what does thou understand by spirit?'

'I have no idea of it,' said the philosopher, 'indeed, it is supposed to be immaterial.'

'At least, thou knowest what matter is?' resumed the Sirian.

'Perfectly well,' answered the other. 'For example: that stone is grey, is of a certain figure, has three dimensions, specific weight, and divisibility.'

'I want to know,' said the giant, 'what that object is, which, according to thy observation, hath a grey colour, weight, and divisibility. Thou seest a few qualities, but dost thou know the nature of the thing itself?'

'Not I, truly,' answered the Cartesian.

Upon which the Sirian admitted that he also was ignorant in regard to this subject. Then addressing himself to another sage, who stood upon his thumb, he asked, 'What is the soul? and what are her functions?'

'Nothing at all,' replied this disciple of Malebranche; 'God hath made everything for my convenience. In Him I see everything, by Him I act; He is the universal agent, and I never meddle in His work.'

'That is being a nonentity indeed,' said the Sirian sage; and then, turning to a follower of Leibnitz, he exclaimed: 'Hark ye, friend, what is thy opinion of the soul?'

'In my opinion,' answered this metaphysician, 'the soul is the hand that points at the hour, while my body does the office of the clock; or, if you please, the soul is the clock, and the body is the pointer; or again, my soul is the mirror of the universe, and my body the frame. All this is clear and uncontrovertible.'

A little partisan of Locke who chanced to be present, being asked his opinion on the same subject, said: 'I do not know by what power I think; but well I know that I should never have thought without the assistance of my senses. That there are immaterial and intelligent substances I do not at all doubt; but that it is impossible for God to communicate the faculty of thinking to matter, I doubt very much. I revere the eternal power, to which it would ill become me to prescribe bounds. I affirm nothing, and am content to believe that many more things are possible than are usually thought so.'

The Sirian smiled at this declaration, and did not look upon the author as the least sagacious of the company: and as for the dwarf of Saturn, he would have embraced this adherent of Locke, had it not been for the extreme disproportion in their respective sizes. But unluckily there was another animalcule in a square cap, who, taking the word from all his philosophical brethren, affirmed that he knew the whole secret. He surveyed the two celestial strangers from top to toe, and maintained to their faces that their persons, their fashions, their suns and their stars, were created solely for the use of man. At this wild assertion our two travellers were seized with a fit of that uncontrollable laughter, which (according to Homer) is the portion of the immortal gods: their bellies quivered, their shoulders rose and fell, and, during these convulsions, the vessel fell from the Sirian's nail into the Saturnian's pocket, where these worthy people searched for it a long time with great diligence. At length, having found the ship and set everything to rights again, the Sirian resumed the discourse with those diminutive mites, and promised to compose for them a choice book of philosophy which would demonstrate the very essence of things. Accordingly, before his departure, he made them a present of the book, which was brought to the Academy of Science at Paris, but when the old secretary came to open it he saw nothing but blank paper.

'Ay, ay,' said he, 'this is just what I suspected.'

LORD CHESTERFIELD'S EARS [1]

AH! FATE GOVERNS IRREMISSIBLY EVERYTHING IN THIS WORLD. I judge, as is natural, from my own experience.

Lord Chesterfield, who was very fond of me, had promised to be of help to me. A good living in his nomination fell vacant. I hastened up from the depths of the country to London; I presented myself before his lordship; I reminded him of his promises; he shook me warmly by the hand and said that indeed I did look ill. I replied that my greatest illness was poverty. He said he desired to cure me and immediately gave me a letter for Mr. Sidrac, near the Guildhall.

I had no doubt that Mr. Sidrac was the person to hasten the nomination to my living. I hastened to his house. Mr. Sidrac, who was his lordship's surgeon, at once began to examine me and assured me that if I had the stone, he would cut me very successfully.

You must know that his lordship had heard I was suffering great pain in the bladder and with his usual generosity had intended I should be cut at his expense. He had gone deaf, like his brother, and I had not been informed of it.

While I was wasting time in defending my bladder against Mr. Sidrac, who desired to cut me at all costs, one of the fifty-two competitors who wanted the same living reached his lordship, asked for my vicarage, and obtained it.

I was in love with Miss Fidler whom I was to marry as soon as I became a vicar; my rival had my post and my mistress.

The earl, hearing of my disaster and his mistake, promised to set everything right; but he died two days afterwards.

Mr. Sidrac pointed out to me, as clearly as daylight, that my good patron could not live a minute longer owing to the constitution of his organs, and proved to me that his deafness only came from the extreme dryness of the cord and drum of his ear. He even offered to harden my two ears with spirits of wine, and to make me deafer than any peer of the realm.

[1] *Editor's Note: Lord Chesterfield's Ears* is a work of Voltaire's old age. It does not reach the poetry of *Candide*. Nevertheless, it deserves a place here because it contains, in a very simple form, the essential of Voltaire's metaphysical ideas, just as the articles from the *Philosophical Dictionary* contain the essential of his moral and political ideas.

I realized that Mr. Sidrac was a very learned man. He inspired me with a taste for the science of Nature. Moreover, I saw that he was a charitable man who would cut me for nothing if necessary and who would aid me in every accident which might happen to me towards the neck of my bladder.

So I began to study Nature under his direction, to console myself for the loss of my vicarage and my mistress.

After many observations of Nature, made with my five senses, telescopes and microscopes, I said to Mr. Sidrac one day:

'They make fun of us; there is no such thing as Nature, everything is art; it is by an admirable art that all the planets dance regularly around the sun, while the sun turns round upon himself. Obviously some one as learned as the Royal Society of London must have arranged things in such a way that the square of the revolutions of each planet is always proportionate to the cube root of their distance from their centre; and a man must be a sorcerer to guess it.

'The ebb and flow of our Thames seems to me the constant result of an art not less profound and not less difficult to understand.

'Animals, vegetables, minerals, all seem to me arranged with weight, measure, number and movement; everything is a spring, a lever, a pulley, a hydraulic machine, a chemical laboratory, from the blade of grass to the oak, from the flea to man, from a grain of sand to our clouds.

'Certainly, there is nothing but art, and Nature is a delusion.'

'You are right,' replied Mr. Sidrac, 'but you are not the first in the field; that has already been said by a dreamer on the other side of the Channel,[1] but nobody has paid any attention to him.'

'What astonishes me and pleases me most of all is that, by means of this incomprehensible art, two machines always produce a third; and I am very sorry not to have made one with Miss Fidler; but I see it was arranged from all eternity that Miss Fidler should make use of another machine than mine.'

'What you say,' replied Mr. Sidrac, 'has been said before and said better; which is a probability that you think correctly. Yes, it is most amusing that two beings should produce a third; but it is not true of all beings; two roses do not produce a third

[1] Voltaire himself.

rose by kissing each other; two stones, or two metals, do not produce a third; and yet a metal and a stone are things which all human industry could not make. The great, the beautiful, continuous miracle is that a boy and a girl should make a child together, that a cock nightingale should make a little nightingale with his hen nightingale, and not with a lark. We ought to spend half our lives in imitating them, and the other half in blessing Him who invented this method. In generation there are a thousand vastly curious secrets. Newton says that Nature is everywhere like herself: *Natura est ubique sibi consona*. This is false in love; fish, reptiles and birds do not make love as we do; there is an infinite variety. The making of acting and sapient beings delights me. Vegetables have their value also. I am always amazed that a grain of wheat cast on to the ground should produce several others.'

'Ah!' said I, like the fool I then was, 'that is because the wheat must die to be born again, as they say in the schools.'

Mr. Sidrac laughed very circumspectly and replied:

'That was true in the time of the schools, but the meanest labourer to-day knows that the thing is absurd.'

'Ah! Mr. Sidrac, I beg your pardon; but I have been a theologian and a man cannot shake off his old habits immediately.'

Sometime after these conversations between poor parson Goodman and the excellent anatomist Sidrac, the surgeon met him in St. James's Park, pensive, preoccupied, with a more embarrassed look than a mathematician who has just made a bad mistake in calculation.

'What is the matter with you?' said Sidrac. 'Have you a pain in your bladder or your colon?'

'No,' said Goodman, 'but in the gall-bladder. I have just seen a carriage go by containing the Bishop of Gloucester, who is an insolent and whiffling pedant; I was on foot and it irritated me. I remembered that if I wanted to have a bishopric in this kingdom, 'tis ten thousand to one I should not obtain it, since there are ten thousand parsons in England. Since the death of Lord Chesterfield (who was deaf) I have had no patron. Let us suppose that the ten thousand Anglican parsons each have two patrons; in that event it is twenty thousand to one I shall not be a bishop. That is annoying when one thinks of it.

[215]

'I remembered that long ago it was suggested that I should go to India as a cabin-boy; I was assured I should make a great fortune, but I did not feel I was the kind of person to become an admiral. And, after having considered all professions, I have remained a parson without being good for anything.'

'Cease to be a priest,' said Sidrac, 'and make yourself a philosopher. It is an occupation which neither exacts nor gives wealth. What is your income?'

'I have only thirty guineas a year, and after the death of my old aunt, I shall have fifty.'

'My dear Goodman, that is enough to live in freedom and to think. Thirty guineas are six hundred and thirty shillings; that makes nearly two shillings a day. Philips only wanted one. With that amount of certain income a man can say everything he thinks about the East India Company, Parliament, the Colonies, the King, being in general, man and God; all of which is a great amusement. Come and dine with me, which will save you money; we will talk, and your thinking faculty will have the pleasure of communicating with mine by means of speech; a marvellous thing which men do not sufficiently admire.'

Conversation between Dr. Goodman and Sidrac the Anatomist concerning the Soul and Other Matters

Goodman: But, my dear Sidrac, why do you always speak of my thinking faculty? Why not just say my soul? It would be done more quickly and I should understand you just as well.

Sidrac: But I should not understand myself. I feel I know that God has given me the faculty of thinking and speaking; but I neither feel nor know whether He has given me an entity which is called a soul.

Goodman: Really, when I think about it, I perceive I know nothing more about it and that I have long been rash enough to think I did know. I have noticed that the eastern nations call the soul by a name which means life. Following their example, the Romans first meant the life of the animal by the word *anima.* Among the Greeks they spoke of the respiration of the soul. This respiration is a breath. The Latins translated the word breath by *spiritus;* whence comes the word equivalent to 'spirit' among nearly all modern nations. Since nobody has ever seen this breath, this spirit, it has been made an entity which no one can see or touch. It has been said to reside in our body without occupying any place there, to move our organs without touching them. What has not been said? It seems to me that all our talk is founded on ambiguities. I see the wise Locke felt that these ambiguities in all languages had plunged human reason into a chaos. He has no chapter on the soul in the only book of reasonable metaphysics ever written. And if he chances to use the word in certain passages, with him it only means our intelligence. Indeed everyone feels he has an intelligence, that he receives ideas, that he associates and dissociates them; but nobody feels he has within him another entity which gives him movement, sensations and thoughts. It is ridiculous to use words we do not understand and to admit entities of which we cannot have the slightest idea.

Sidrac: We are agreed then about a matter which has been the subject of dispute for so many centuries.

Goodman: And I am surprised that we are in agreement.

Sidrac: It is not surprising, we are honestly searching for the truth. If we were on the benches of the schools, we should argue like the characters of Rabelais. If we lived in the ages of terrible darkness which so long enveloped England, one of us would perhaps have the other burned. We live in an age of reason; we easily find what seems to us to be the truth and we dare to express it.

Goodman: Yes, but I am afraid this truth is a very paltry affair. In mathematics we have achieved prodigies which would astonish Apollonius and Archimedes, and would make them our pupils; but what have we discovered in metaphysics? Our own ignorance.

Sidrac: And is that nothing? You admit that the great Being has given you the faculty of feeling and thinking, as He has given your feet the faculty of walking, your hands the power of doing a thousand things, your entrails the power of digesting, your heart the power of urging your blood into your arteries. We hold everything from Him; we could not give ourselves anything, and we shall always be ignorant of the manner which the Master of the universe makes use of to guide us. For my part, I give Him thanks for having taught me that I know nothing of first principles. Men have always inquired how the soul acts upon the body. They ought first of all to have found out whether we have one. Either God has given us this present or He has communicated something which is its equivalent to us. However He went about it, we are under His hand. He is our Master, that is all I know.

Goodman: But tell me at least what you suspect. You have dissected brains, you have seen embryos and fœtuses; have you discovered any sign of the soul in them?

Sidrac: Not the least, and I have never been able to understand how an immortal, immaterial entity spent nine months uselessly hidden in an evil-smelling membrane between urine and excrement. It is difficult for me to conceive that this pretended simple soul existed before the formation of its body. For, if it were not a human soul, what use could it have been during the ages? And then how can we imagine a simple entity, a metaphysical entity, which waits during eternity the moment to animate matter for a few minutes? What becomes of this unknown entity, if the fœtus it should animate dies in the belly of its mother? It seems still more ridiculous to me that God should create a soul at the moment a man lies with a woman. It seems blasphemous that God should await the consummation of an adultery, of an incest, to reward these turpitudes by creating souls in their favour. It is still worse when I am told that God draws immortal souls from nothingness to make them suffer incredible tortures for eternity. What! Burn simple entities, entities which have nothing burnable! How should we go about burning the sound of a voice, a wind which has passed? Even then, this sound and this wind were material during the brief moment of their passage; but a pure spirit, a thought, a doubt? I am all at sea. Whichever way I turn, I find nothing but obscurity, contradiction, impossibility, ridiculousness, dreams, extravagance, fables, absurdity, stupidity, charlatanism.

But I am quite easy when I say: God is the Master. He who causes the innumerable stars to gravitate towards each other, He who made the light, is certainly powerful enough to give us feelings and ideas without our needing a small, foreign, invisible atom called soul. God has certainly given feeling, memory, and industry to all animals. He has given them life and it is as noble to give life as to give a soul. It is generally agreed that animals live; it is proved that they have feeling, since they have organs of feeling. And if they have all that without having a soul, why must we wish to have one at all costs?

Goodman: Perhaps from vanity. I am convinced that if a peacock could speak he would boast of having a soul and he would say his soul is in his tail. I am very much inclined to suspect with you that God made us to eat, to drink, to walk, to sleep, to feel, to think, to be full of passions, pride, and misery, without telling us one word of His secret. We do not know any more about this topic than the peacock I speak of; and he who said that we are born, live and die without knowing how, expressed a great truth.

He who calls us the puppets of Providence seems to me to have well defined us; since after all, for us to exist, there needs must be an infinity of movements. We did not make the movement; we did not establish its laws. There is someone who, having made the light, makes it move from the sun to our eyes and reach us in seven minutes. It is only through movement that my five senses are stirred; it is only through my five senses that I have ideas; therefore it is the Author of movement who gives me ideas. And when He tells me how He gives them to me, I shall render Him very humble thanks. Already I give Him great thanks for having allowed me to contemplate for a few years the magnificent spectacle of this world, as Epictetus says. It is true He might make me happier and let me have a good living and my mistress, Miss Fidler; but after all, even as I am, with my income of six hundred and thirty shillings, I am still greatly indebted to Him.

Sidrac: You say that God might have given you a good living and that He could make you happier than you are. There are some people who would not allow you to make such an assertion. Do you not remember that you yourself complained of Fate? A man who wished to be a parson must not contradict himself. Do you not see that, if you had had the parsonage and the woman you asked for, it would have been you who made Miss Fidler's child and not your rival? The child she would have had might have been a cabin-boy, have become an admiral, have won a naval battle at the mouth of the Ganges, and completed the dethronement of the Great Mogul. That alone would have changed the constitution of the universe. A world entirely different from ours would have been needed in order that your competitor should not have the living, should not marry Miss Fidler, and that you should not have been reduced to six hundred and thirty shillings while expecting the death of your aunt. Everything is linked up: and God will not break the eternal chain for the sake of my friend Goodman.

Goodman: I did not expect this line of reasoning when I spoke of Fate; but after all, if this is so, God is as much a slave as I am?

Sidrac: He is the slave of His will, of His wisdom, of the laws He made himself, of His necessary nature. He cannot infringe them, because He cannot be weak, inconstant, and flighty as we are, and the necessarily Eternal Being cannot be a weathercock.

Goodman: Mr. Sidrac, that leads straight to irreligion; for if God can change nothing in the affairs of this world, what is the use of singing His praises and addressing prayers to Him?

Sidrac: And who told you to pray to God, and praise Him? Much he cares for your praise and petitions! We praise a man because we think him vain; we pray to Him when we think Him weak and hope to make Him change His opinion. Let us do our duty to God, adore Him, act justly; that is true praise and true prayer.

Goodman: Mr. Sidrac, we have covered a lot of ground; for, without counting Miss Fidler, we have enquired whether we have a soul, whether there is a God, whether He can change, whether we are destined to two lives, whether . . . these are profound studies and perhaps I should never have thought of them if I had been a parson. I must go deeper into these necessary and sublime matters, since I have nothing else to do.

Sidrac: Well, Dr. Grou is coming to dine with me to-morrow; he is a very well-informed doctor; he went round the world with Banks and Solander. He must certainly understand God and the soul, the true and the false, the just and the unjust, far better than those who have never left Covent Garden. Moreover, Dr. Grou saw almost the whole of Europe in his youth; he witnessed five or six revolutions in Russia; he frequented the pasha Comte de Bonneval, who, as you know, became a complete Mohammedan at Constantinople. He was intimate with the Papist priest MacCarthy, the Irishman who had his prepuce cut off in honour of Mohammed, and with our Scotch Presbyterian, Ramsay, who did the same, and afterwards served in Russia and was killed in a battle against the Swedes in Finland. He has conversed with the reverend Father Malagrida, who has since been burned at Lisbon because the Holy Virgin revealed to him everything she did when she was in the womb of her mother, St. Anne. You can see that a man like Dr. Grou, who has seen so much, must be the greatest metaphysician in the world. To-morrow then, at my house for dinner.

Goodman: And the day after to-morrow, also, my dear Sidrac, for more than one dinner is needed to grow well informed.

Next day the three thinkers dined together; and as they became a little gayer towards the end of the meal, according to the custom of philosophers at dinner, they amused themselves by talking of all the miseries, all the follies, all the horrors which afflict the animal race from Australia to the Arctic Pole, and from Lima to Macao. This diversity of abominations is nevertheless very amusing. It is a pleasure unknown to stay-at-home burgesses and parish curates, who know nothing beyond their own church spire and who think that all the rest of the universe is like Change Alley in London, or the Rue de la Huchette in Paris.

'I have noticed,' said Dr. Grou, 'that in spite of the infinite variety of this globe, all the men I have seen, whether blacks with woolly hair, blacks with straight hair, the browns, the reds, the swarthy who are called whites, all have alike two legs, two eyes, and a head on their shoulders, despite St. Augustine, who asserts in his thirty-seventh sermon that he had seen acephalous men, that is headless men, monoculous men with only one eye, and monopeds who have only one leg. As to anthropophagi, I admit there are swarms of them and that everyone was once like them.

'I have often been asked if the inhabitants of the immense country called New Zealand, who are to-day the most barbarous of all barbarians, were baptized. I always reply that I do not know, but that it might be so; that the Jews, who were more barbarous than they, had two baptisms instead of one, the baptism of justice and the baptism of domicile.'

'I know them well,' said Mr. Goodman, 'and I have had long disputes with those who think we invented baptism. No, gentlemen, we have invented nothing; we have only introduced contractions. But pray tell me, Dr. Grou, among the eighty or hundred religions you saw in your travels, which seemed the most pleasant, that of the New Zealanders, or that of the Hottentots?'

Dr. Grou: That of the Island of Otaiti, without any doubt. I have travelled through the two hemispheres; I never saw anything like Otaiti and its religious queen. It is in Otaiti that Nature dwells. Elsewhere I saw nothing but masks; I saw only scoundrels deceiving fools, charlatans cheating others of their money to obtain authority, and cheating authority to have money with impunity; who sell you spiders' webs in order to eat your partridges; who sell you riches and pleasures when there is none, so that you will turn the spit while they exist.

By Heaven! It is not like that in the Island of Aiti, or of Otaiti. The island is much more civilized than New Zealand and the country of the Kafirs, and I dare to say, than our own England, because Nature has granted it a more fertile soil; she has given it the bread-fruit tree, a present as useful as it is wonderful, which she has only bestowed upon a few islands of the Southern Sea. Moreover, Otaiti possesses numerous edible birds, vegetables, and fruits. In such a country it is not necessary to eat one's neighbour; but there is a more natural, gentler, more universal necessity which the religion of Otaiti commands shall be satisfied in public. It is certainly the most respectable of all religious ceremonies; I have been an eyewitness to it, as well as the whole crew of our ship. These are not missionaries' fables, such as are to be found sometimes in the Edifying and Curious Letters of the Reverend Jesuit Fathers. Dr. John Hawkesworth is now completing the publication of our discoveries in the southern hemisphere. I have constantly accompanied that worthy young man, Banks, who has devoted his time and money to the observation of Nature, in the regions of the Antarctic Pole, while Dawkins and Wood returned from the ruins of Palmyra and Baalbek where they had excavated the most ancient monuments of the arts, and Hamilton taught the amazed Neapolitans the natural history of their Mount Vesuvius. With Banks, Solander, Cook, and a hundred others, I have seen what I am about to tell you.

The Princess Obeira, Queen of the Island of Otaiti . . .

At that moment the coffee was brought, and as soon as it was taken, Dr. Grou went on with his story as follows:

'The Princess Obeira,' I say, 'after having heaped us with presents with a politeness worthy of a queen of England was curious to be present one morning at our Anglican service. We celebrated it as pompously as we could. In the afternoon she invited us to hers; it was on the 14th May 1769. We found her surrounded by about one thousand persons of both sexes arranged in a semicircle and respectfully silent. A very pretty girl, simply dressed in light clothes, was lying on a platform which served as an altar. Queen Obeira ordered a fine young man of about twenty to make the sacrifice. He repeated a sort of prayer and got on to the altar. The two sacrificers were half naked. The Queen, with a majestic air showed the young victim the most convenient method of consummating the sacrifice. All the Otaitians were so attentive and so respectful that not one of our sailors dared to trouble the ceremony by an indecent laugh. That is what I have seen, I tell you; that is what our whole crew saw; it is for you to make deductions.'

' This sacred festival does not surprise me,' said Dr. Goodman. 'I am convinced that this is the first festival men have ever celebrated, and I do not see why we should not pray God when we are about to make a being in his image, as we pray to him before the meals which sustain our bodies. To labour to bring to life a reasonable creature is the most noble and holy action. Thus thought the early Indians, who revered the Lingam, the symbol of generation; the ancient Egyptians who carried the phallus in procession; the Greeks who erected temples to Priapus. If one may quote the miserable little Jewish nation, the clumsy imitator of all its neighbours, it is said in its books that this nation adored Priapus and that the queen-mother of the Jewish King Asa was the high priestess.

'However this may be, it is very probable that no race ever established or could establish a cult from libertinism. Debauchery sometimes slips in through the lapse of time; but the institution itself is always innocent and pure. Our earliest love-feasts, where boys and girls kissed each other innocently on the mouth, did not generate into rendezvous and infidelities until much later; and would to God I might sacrifice with Miss Fidler under Queen Obeira in all honour! It would assuredly be the finest day and the best action of my life.'

Mr. Sidrac, who had hitherto kept silence because Goodman

and Grou had been talking, at last abandoned his reserve and said:

'What I have just heard ravishes me with admiration. Queen Obeira seems to me the greatest queen in the southern hemisphere; I dare not say of both hemispheres; but among so much fame and happiness, there is one thing which makes me tremble and which Mr. Goodman mentioned without your replying. Is it true, Dr. Grou, that Captain Wallace, who anchored off that fortunate Island before you, brought to it the two most terrible scourges of the whole earth, the two poxes?'

'Alas!' replied Dr. Grou, 'the French accuse us and we accuse the French. Mr. Bougainville says that the accursed English gave the pox to Queen Obeira; and Mr. Cook asserts that the Queen obtained it from Mr. Bougainville himself. However this may be, the pox is like the fine arts, nobody knows who invented them, but eventually they ran through Europe, Asia, Africa, and America.'

'I have been a surgeon for a long time,' said Sidrac, 'and I confess I owe the greater part of my fortune to this pox; yet I do not detest it any the less. Mrs. Sidrac communicated it to me on the first night of her wedding; and, as she is an excessively delicate woman in all matters touching her honour, she published in all the London newspapers the statement that she was indeed attacked by an infamous disease but that she had contracted it in her mother's womb and that it was an old family habit.

'What was "Nature" thinking of when she poured this poison in the very source of life? It has been said, and I repeat it, that this is the most enormous and detestable of all contradictions. What! Man, they say, was made in God's image. *Finxit in effigiem moderantum cuncta deorum*, and it is in the spermatic vessels of this image that pain, infection, and death are placed! What becomes of Lord Rochester's fine verse:

> "*Love, in a land of infidels,*
> *Would lead to God.*" '

'Alas!' said the excellent Goodman, 'perhaps I have to thank Providence that I did not marry my dear Miss Fidler; for who knows what might have happened? We are never sure of anything in this world. In any case, Mr. Sidrac, you have promised me your help in everything concerning my bladder.'

'I am entirely at your service,' replied Sidrac, 'but you must get rid of these gloomy thoughts.'

Goodman, speaking in this way, seemed to foresee his fate.

As Mr. Sidrac spoke these wise words a servant came in to inform Mr. Goodman that the late Lord Chesterfield's steward was at the door in his carriage and wished to speak to him about a very urgent affair. Goodman ran down to receive the information and the steward invited him into the carriage and said:

'No doubt you know, sir, what happened to Mr. Sidrac on his wedding-night?'

'Yes, sir, he told me the story of that little adventure just now.'

'Well, the same thing occurred to the fair Miss Fidler and her parson husband. The morning after, they fought; the day after that, they separated and the parson has been deprived of his living. I am in love with Miss Fidler, I know that she loves you, but she does not hate me. I can rise superior to the little accident which was the cause of her divorce; I am in love and fearless. Give up Miss Fidler to me and I will see that you get the living, which is worth over a hundred and fifty guineas a year. You have only ten minutes to make up your mind.'

'This is a delicate proposition, sir; I must consult my philosophers Sidrac and Grou; I shall return to you immediately.'

He ran back to his two advisers.

'I see,' he said, 'that the affairs of this world are not decided by digestion alone, and that love, ambition, and money play a large part.'

He told them how he was situated, and begged them to decide at once. They both decided that with an income of a hundred and fifty guineas he could have all the girls in his parish and Miss Fidler as well.

Goodman felt the wisdom of this decision; he had the parsonage, he had Miss Fidler in secret, which was much more agreeable than having her as a wife. Mr. Sidrac was prodigal of good offices when they were needed; he became one of the most terrible priests in England and was more convinced than ever that fatality governs everything in this world.

DESTINY: Of all the books written in the western climes of the world, which have reached our times, Homer is the most ancient. In his works we find the manners of profane antiquity, coarse heroes, and material gods, made after the image of man, but mixed up with reveries and absurdities; we also find the seeds of philosophy, and more particularly the idea of destiny, or necessity, who is the dominatrix of the gods, as the gods are of the world.

When the magnanimous Hector determines to fight the magnanimous Achilles, and runs away with all possible speed, making the circuit of the city three times, in order to increase his vigour; when Homer compares the light-footed Achilles, who pursues him, to a man that is asleep! and when Madame Dacier breaks into a rapture of admiration at the art and meaning exhibited in this passage, it is precisely then that Jupiter, desirous of saving the great Hector who has offered up to him so many sacrifices, bethinks him of consulting the destinies, upon weighing the fates of Hector and Achilles in a balance. He finds that the Trojan must inevitably be killed by the Greek, and is not only unable to oppose it, but from that moment Apollo, the guardian genius of Hector, is compelled to abandon him. It is not to be denied that Homer is frequently extravagant, and even on this very occasion displays a contradictory flow of ideas, according to the privilege of antiquity; but yet he is the first in whom we meet with the notion of destiny. It may be concluded, then, that in his days it was a prevalent one.

The Pharisees, among the small nation of Jews, did not adopt the idea of a destiny till many ages after. For these Pharisees themselves, who were the most learned class among the Jews, were but of a very recent date. They mixed up, in Alexandria, a portion of the dogmas of the Stoics with their ancient Jewish ideas. St. Jerome goes so far as to state that their sect is but a little anterior to our vulgar era.

Philosophers would never have required the aid of Homer, or of the Pharisees, to be convinced that everything is performed according to immutable laws, that everything is ordained, that everything is, in fact, *necessary*. The manner in which they reason is as follows:

Either the world subsists by its own nature, by its own physical laws, or a Supreme Being has formed it according to His supreme laws: in both cases these laws are immovable; in both cases everything is necessary; heavy bodies tend towards the centre of the earth without having any power or tendency to rest in the air. Pear-trees cannot produce pine-apples. The instinct of a spaniel cannot be the instinct of an ostrich; everything is arranged, adjusted, and fixed.

Man can have only a certain number of teeth, hairs, and ideas; and a period arrives when he necessarily loses his teeth, hair, and ideas.

It is contradictory to say that yesterday should not have been; or that to-day does not exist; it is just as contradictory to assert that that which is to come will not inevitably be.

Could you derange the destiny of a single fly there would be no possible reason why you should not control the destiny of all other flies, of all other animals, of all men, of all nature. You would find, in fact, that you were more powerful than God.

Weak-minded persons say: 'My physician has brought my aunt safely through a mortal disease; he has added ten years to my aunt's life.' Others of more judgment say, the prudent man makes his own destiny.

> *Nullum numen abest, si sit Prudentia, sed te*
> *Nos facimus, Fortuna, deam cœloque locamus.*
> —JUVENAL, *Sat.* x. v. 365
> We call on Fortune, and her aid implore,
> While Prudence is the goddess to adore.

But frequently the prudent man succumbs under his destiny instead of making it; it is destiny which makes men prudent. Profound politicians assure us that if Cromwell, Ludlow, Ireton, and a dozen other parliamentary leaders, had been assassinated eight days before Charles I had his head cut off, that king would have continued alive and have died in his bed; they are right; and they may add, that if all England had been swallowed up in the sea, that king would not have perished on a scaffold before Whitehall. But things were so arranged that Charles was to have his head cut off.

Cardinal d'Ossat was unquestionably more clever than an idiot of the *petites maisons*; but is it not evident that the organs of the wise d'Ossat were differently formed from those of that idiot?—Just as the organs of a fox are different from those of a crane or a lark.

Your physician saved your aunt, but in so doing he certainly did not contradict the order of nature, but followed it. It is clear that your aunt could not prevent her birth in a certain place, that she could not help being affected by a certain malady, at a certain time; that the physician could be in no other place than where he was, that your aunt could not but apply to him, that he could not but prescribe medicines which cured her, or were thought to cure her, while nature was the sole physician.

A peasant thinks that it hailed upon his field by chance; but the philosopher knows that there was no chance, and that it was absolutely impossible, according to the constitution of the world, for it not to have hailed at that very time and place.

There are some who, being shocked by this truth, concede only half of it, like debtors who offer one moiety of their property to their creditors, and ask remission for the other. There are, they say, some events which are necessary, and others which are not so. It would be curious for one part of the world to be changed and the other not; that one part of what happens should happen inevitably, and another fortuitously. When we examine the question closely, we see that the doctrine opposed to that of destiny is absurd; but many men are destined to be bad reasoners, others not to reason at all, and others to persecute those who reason well or ill.

Some caution us by saying, 'Do not believe in fatalism, for, if you do, everything appearing to you unavoidable, you will exert yourself for nothing; you will sink down in indifference; you will regard neither wealth, nor honours, nor praise; you will be careless about acquiring anything whatever; you will consider yourself meritless and powerless; no talent will be cultivated, and all will be overwhelmed in apathy.'

Do not be afraid, gentlemen; we shall always have passions and prejudices, since it is our destiny to be subjected to prejudices and passions. We shall very well know that it no more depends upon us to have great merit or superior talents than to have a fine head of hair, or a beautiful hand; we shall be convinced that we ought to be vain of nothing, and yet vain we shall always be.

I have necessarily the passion for writing as I now do; and, as for you, you have the passion for censuring me; we are both equally fools, both equally the sport of destiny. Your nature is to do ill, mine is to love truth and publish it in spite of you.

The owl, while supping upon mice in his ruined tower, said to the nightingale, 'Stop your singing there in your beautiful arbour, and come to my hole that I may eat you.' The nightingale replied, 'I am born to sing where I am, and to laugh at you.'

You ask me what is to become of liberty: I do not understand you: I do not know what the liberty you speak of really is. You have been so long disputing about the nature of it that you do not understand it. If you are willing, or rather, if you are able to examine with me coolly what it is, turn to the letter L.

ENVY: We all know what the ancients said of this disgraceful passion and what the moderns have repeated. Hesiod is the first classic author who has spoken of it.

'The potter envies the potter, the artisan the artisan, the poor even the poor, the musician the musician—or, if anyone chooses to give a different meaning to the word *avidos*—the poet the poet.'

Long before Hesiod, Job had remarked, 'Envy destroys the little-minded.'

I believe Mandeville, the author of the 'Fable of the Bees,' is the first who has endeavoured to prove that envy is a good thing, a very useful passion. His first reason is that envy was as natural to man as hunger and thirst; that it may be observed in all children, as well as in horses and dogs. If you wish your children to hate one another, caress one more than the other; the prescription is infallible.

He asserts that the first thing two young women do when they meet together is to discover matter for ridicule, and the second to flatter each other.

He thinks that without envy the arts would be only moderately cultivated, and that Raphael would never have been a great painter if he had not been jealous of Michael Angelo.

Mandeville, perhaps, mistook emulation for envy; perhaps,

also, emulation is nothing but envy restricted within the bounds of decency.

Michael Angelo might say to Raphael, your envy has only induced you to study and execute still better than I do; you have not depreciated me, you have not caballed against me before the pope, you have not endeavoured to get me excommunicated for placing in my picture of the Last Judgment one-eyed and lame persons in paradise, and pampered cardinals with beautiful women perfectly naked in hell! No! your envy is a laudable feeling; you are brave as well as envious; let us be good friends.

But if the envious person is an unhappy being without talents, jealous of merit as the poor are of the rich; if under the pressure at once of indigence and baseness he writes 'News from Parnassus,' 'Letters from a Celebrated Countess,' or 'Literary Annals,' the creature displays an envy which is in fact absolutely good for nothing, and for which even Mandeville could make no apology.

Descartes said: 'Envy forces up the yellow bile from the lower part of the liver, and the black bile that comes from the spleen, which diffuses itself from the heart by the arteries.' But as no sort of bile is formed in the spleen, Descartes, when he spoke thus, deserved not to be envied for his physiology.

A person of the name of Poet or Poetius, a theological blackguard, who accused Descartes of atheism, was exceedingly affected by the black bile. But he knew still less than Descartes how his detestable bile circulated through his blood.

Madame Pernelle is perfectly right: *Les envieux mourront, mais non jamais l'envie.*—The envious will die, but envy never. (*Tartuffe*, Act V. Scene 3.)

That it is better to excite envy than pity is a good proverb. Let us, then, make men envy us as much as we are able.

EQUALITY: What does a dog owe to a dog and a horse to a horse? Nothing. No animal depends on his equal. But, man having received from God that which is called *reason*, what is the result? That almost everywhere on earth he is a slave.

If the earth were in fact what it might be supposed it should be—if men found upon it everywhere an easy and certain subsistence, and a climate congenial to their nature, it would be evidently impossible for one man to subjugate another. Let the globe be covered with wholesome fruits; let the air on which we depend for life convey to us no diseases and premature death; let man require no other lodging than the deer or roebuck, in that case the Genghis Khans and the Tamerlanes will have no other attendants than their own children, who will be very worthy persons, and assist them affectionately in their old age.

In that state of nature enjoyed by all undomesticated quadrupeds, and by birds and reptiles, men would be just as happy as they are. Domination would be a mere chimera—an absurdity which no one would think of, for why should servants be sought for when no service is required?

If it should enter the mind of any individual of a tyrannical disposition and nervous arm to subjugate his less powerful neighbour, his success would be impossible; the oppressed would be on the Danube before the oppressor had completed his preparations on the Volga.

All men, then, would necessarily have been equal had they been without wants; it is the misery attached to our species which places one man in subjection to another; inequality is not the real grievance, but dependence. It is of little consequence for one man to be called his highness and another his holiness, but it is hard for me to be the servant of another.

A numerous family has cultivated a good soil, two small neighbouring families live on lands unproductive and barren. It will therefore be necessary for the two poor families to serve the rich one, or to destroy it. This is easily accomplished. One of the two indigent families goes and offers its services to the rich one in exchange for bread, the other makes an attack upon it and is conquered. The serving family is the origin of domestics and labourers, the one conquered is the origin of slaves.

It is impossible in our melancholy world to prevent men living in society from being divided into two classes, one of the rich who command, the other of the poor who obey, and these two are subdivided into various others, which have also their respective shades of difference.

All the poor are not unhappy. The greater number are born in that state, and constant labour prevents them from too sensibly feeling their situation; but when they do strongly feel it, then follow wars such as those of the popular party against the senate at Rome, and those of the peasantry in Germany, England, and France. All these wars ended sooner or later in the subjection of the people, because the great have money, and money in a State commands everything; I say in a State, for the case is different between nation and nation. That nation which makes the best use of iron will always subjugate another that has more gold but less courage.

Every man is born with an eager inclination for power, wealth, and pleasure, and also with a great taste for indolence. Every man, consequently, would wish to possess the fortunes and the wives or daughters of others, to be their master, to retain them in subjection to his caprices, and to do nothing, or at least nothing but what is perfectly agreeable. You clearly perceive that with such amiable dispositions, it is as impossible for men to be equal as for two preachers or divinity professors not to be jealous of each other.

The human race, constituted as it is, cannot exist unless there be an infinite number of useful individuals possessed of no property at all, for most certainly a man in easy circumstances will not leave his own land to come and cultivate yours; and if you want a pair of shoes you will not get a lawyer to make them for you. Equality, then, is at the same time the most natural and the most chimerical thing possible.

As men carry everything to excess if they have it in their power to do so, this inequality has been pushed too far; it has been maintained in many countries that no citizen has a right to quit that in which he was born. The meaning of such a law must evidently be: 'This country is so wretched and ill-governed we prohibit every man from quitting it, under an apprehension that otherwise all would leave it.' Do better; excite in all your subjects a desire to stay with you, and in foreigners a desire to come and settle among you.

Every man has a right to entertain a private opinion of his own equality to other men, but it follows not that a cardinal's cook should take it upon him to order his master to prepare his dinner. The cook, however, may say: 'I am a man as well as my master; I was born like him in tears, and shall like him die in anguish, attended by the same common ceremonies. We both perform the same animal functions. If the Turks get possession of Rome, and I then become a cardinal and my master a cook, I will take him into my service.' This language is perfectly reasonable and just, but, while waiting for the Grand Turk to get possession of Rome, the cook is bound to do his duty, or all human society is subverted.

With respect to a man who is neither a cardinal's cook nor invested with any office whatever in the State—with respect to an individual who has no connections, and is disgusted at being everywhere received with an air of protection or contempt, who sees quite clearly that many men of quality and title have not more knowledge, wit, or virtue than himself, and is wearied by being occasionally in their antechambers—what ought such a man to do? He ought to stay away.

LIBERTY:

A. A battery of cannon is discharged at our ears; have you the liberty to hear it, or not to hear it, as you please?

B. Undoubtedly I cannot hinder myself from hearing it.

A. Are you willing that these cannon shall take off your head and those of your wife and daughter who walk with you?

B. What a question! I cannot, at least while I am in my right senses, wish such a thing; it is impossible.

A. Good; you necessarily hear these cannon, and you necessarily wish not for the death of yourself and your family by a discharge from them. You have neither the power of not hearing it, nor the power of wishing to remain here.

B. That is clear.

A. You have, I perceive, advanced thirty paces to be out of the reach of the cannon; you have had the power of walking these few steps with me.

B. That is also very clear.

A. And if you had been paralytic, you could not have avoided being exposed to this battery; you would necessarily have heard, and received a wound from the cannon; and you would have as necessarily died.

B. Nothing is more true.

A. In what then consists your liberty, if not in the power that your body has acquired of performing that which from absolute necessity your will requires?

B. You embarrass me. Liberty then is nothing more than the power of doing what I wish?

A. Reflect; and see whether liberty can be understood otherwise.

B. In this case, my hunting dog is as free as myself; he has necessarily the will to run when he sees a hare; and the power of running, if there is nothing the matter with his legs. I have therefore nothing above my dog; you reduce me to the state of the beasts.

A. These are poor sophisms, and they are poor sophists who have instructed you. You are unwilling to be free like your dog. Do you not eat, sleep, and propagate like him, and nearly in the same attitudes? Would you smell otherwise than by your nose? Why would you possess liberty differently from your dog?

B. But I have a soul which reasons, and my dog scarcely reasons at all. He has nothing beyond simple ideas, while I have a thousand metaphysical ideas.

A. Well, you are a thousand times more free than he is; you have a thousand times more power of thinking than he has; but still you are not free in any other manner than your dog is free.

B. What! am I not free to will what I like?

A. What do you understand by that?

B. I understand what all the world understands. Is it not every day said that the will is free?

A. An adage is not a reason; explain yourself better.

B. I understand that I am free to will as I please.

A. With your permission, that is nonsense; see you not that it is ridiculous to say—I will will? Consequently, you necessarily will the ideas only which are presented to you. Will you be married, yes or no?

B. Suppose I answer that I will neither the one nor the other.

A. In that case you would answer like him who said: Some believe Cardinal Mazarin dead, others believe him living; I believe neither the one nor the other.

B. Well, I will marry!

A. Aye, that is an answer. Why will you marry?

B. Because I am in love with a young, beautiful, sweet, well-educated, rich girl, who sings very well, whose parents are very honest people, and I flatter myself that I am beloved by her and welcome to the family.

[234]

A. There is a reason. You see that you cannot will without a motive. I declare to you that you are free to marry, that is to say, that you have the power of signing the contract.

B. How! I cannot will without a motive? Then what will become of the other proverb—'*Sit pro ratione voluntas*'—my will is my reason—I will because I will?

A. It is an absurd one, my dear friend; you would then have an effect without a cause.

B. What! when I play at odd or even, have I a reason for choosing even rather than odd?

A. Undoubtedly.

B. And what is the reason, if you please?

A. It is, that the idea of even is presented to your mind rather than the opposite idea. It would be extraordinary if there were cases in which we will because there is a motive, and others in which we will without one. When you would marry, you evidently perceive the predominant reason for it; you perceive it not when you play at odd or even, and yet there must be one.

B. Therefore, once more, I am not free.

A. Your will is not free, but your actions are. You are free to act when you have the power of acting.

B. But all the books that I have read on the liberty of indifference—

A. Are nonsense: there is no liberty of indifference; it is a word devoid of sense, invented by men who never had any.

LOVE: '*Amor omnibus idem.*' It is the embroidery of imagination on the stuff of nature. If you wish to form an idea of love, look at the sparrows in your garden; behold your doves; contemplate the bull when introduced to the heifer; look at that powerful and spirited horse which two of your grooms are conducting to the mare that quietly awaits him, and is evidently pleased at his approach; observe the flashing of his eyes, notice the strength and loudness of his neighings, the boundings, the curvetings, the ears erect, the mouth opening with convulsive gaspings, the distended nostrils, the breath of fire, the raised and waving mane, and the impetuous movement with which he rushes towards the object which nature has destined for him; do not, however, be jealous of his happiness; but reflect on the advantages of the human species; they afford ample compensation in love for all those which nature has conferred on mere animals—strength, beauty, lightness, and rapidity.

There are some classes, however, even of animals totally unacquainted with sexual association. Fishes are destitute of this enjoyment. The female deposits her millions of eggs on the slime of the waters, and the male that meets them passes over them and communicates the vital principle, never consorting with, or perhaps even perceiving the female to whom they belong.

The greater part of those animals which copulate are sensible of the enjoyment only by a single sense; and when appetite is satisfied, the whole is over. No animal, besides man, is acquainted with embraces; his whole frame is susceptible; his lips particularly experience a delight which never wearies, and which is exclusively the portion of his species; finally, he can surrender himself at all seasons to the endearments of love, while mere animals possess only limited periods. If you reflect on these high pre-eminences, you will readily join in the Earl of Rochester's remark, that love would impel a whole nation of atheists to worship the divinity.

As men have been endowed with the talent of perfecting whatever nature has bestowed upon them, they have accordingly perfected the gift of love. Cleanliness, personal attention, and regard to health render the frame more sensitive, and consequently increase its capacity of gratification. All the other amiable and valuable sentiments enter afterwards into that of love, like the metals which amalgamate with gold; friendship and esteem readily fly to its support; and talents both of body and of mind are new and strengthening bonds.

Self-love, above all, draws closer all these various ties. Men pride themselves in the choice they have made; and the numberless illusions that crowd around constitute the ornament of the work, of which the foundation is so firmly laid by nature.

Such are the advantages possessed by man above the various tribes of animals. But, if he enjoys delights of which they are ignorant, how many vexations and disgusts, on the other hand, is he exposed to, from which they are free! The most dreadful of these is occasioned by nature's having poisoned the pleasures of love and sources of life over three-quarters of the world by a terrible disease, to which man alone is subject; nor is it with this pestilence as with various other maladies, which are the natural consequences of excess. It was not introduced into the world by debauchery. The Phrynes and Laises, the Floras and Messalinas, were never attacked by it. It originated in islands where mankind dwelt together in innocence, and has thence been spread throughout the Old World.

If nature could in any instance be accused of despising her own work, thwarting her own plan, and counteracting her own views, it would be in this detestable scourge. And can this, then, be the best of all possible worlds? What! if Cæsar and Antony and Octavius never had this disease, was it not possible to prevent Francis the First from dying of it? No, it is said; things were so ordered all for the best; I want to believe it; but it is difficult.

MAN (*Is Man Born Wicked?*): Is it not demonstrated that man is *not* born perverse and the child of the devil? If such was his nature, he would commit enormous crimes and barbarities as soon as he could walk; he would use the first knife he could find, to wound whoever displeased him. He would necessarily resemble little wolves and foxes, who bite as soon as they can.

On the contrary, throughout the world, he partakes of the nature of the lamb, while he is an infant. Why, therefore, and how is it that he so often becomes a wolf and fox? Is it not that, being born neither good nor wicked, education, example, the government into which he is thrown—in short, occasion of every kind—determines him to virtue or vice?

Perhaps human nature could not be otherwise. Man could not always have false thoughts, nor always true affections; be always sweet, or always cruel.

It is demonstrable that woman is elevated beyond men in the scale of goodness. We see a hundred brothers enemies to each other, to one Clytemnestra.

There are professions which necessarily render the soul pitiless —those of the soldier, the butcher, the officer of justice, and the jailer; and all trades which are founded on the annoyance of others.

Whoever has been able to descend to the subaltern detail of the bar; whoever has only heard lawyers reason familiarly among themselves, and applaud themselves for the miseries of their clients, must have a very poor opinion of human nature.

Women, incessantly occupied with the education of their children, are everywhere less barbarous than men.

Physics join with morals to prevent them from great crimes; their blood is milder; they are less addicted to strong liquors, which inspire ferocity. An evident proof is, that of a thousand victims of justice in a thousand executed assassins, we scarcely reckon four women. It is also proved elsewhere, I believe, that in Asia there are not two examples of women condemned to a public punishment. It appears, therefore, that our customs and habits have rendered the male species very wicked.

If this truth was general and without exceptions, the species would be more horrible than spiders, wolves, and polecats are to our eyes. But happily, professions which harden the heart and fill it with odious passions, are very rare. Observe, that in a nation of twenty millions, there are at most two hundred thousand soldiers. This is but one soldier to two hundred individuals.

The number of other trades which are dangerous to manners is but small. Labourers, artisans and artists are too much occupied often to deliver themselves up to crime. The earth will always bear detestable wretches, and books will always exaggerate the number, which, rather than being greater, is less than we say.

If mankind had been under the empire of the devil, there would be no longer any person upon earth. Let us console ourselves: we have seen, and we shall always see, fine minds from Pekin to La Rochelle; and whatever licentiates and bachelors may say, the Tituses, Trajans, Antoninuses, and Peter Bayles were very honest men.

MARRIAGE: I once met with a reasoner who said: 'Induce your subjects to marry as early as possible. Let them be exempt from taxes the first year; and let their portion be assessed on those who at the same age are in a state of celibacy.

'The more married men you have, the fewer crimes there will be. Examine the frightful columns of your criminal calendars; you will there find a hundred youths executed for one father of a family.

'Marriage renders men more virtuous and more wise. The father of a family is not willing to blush before his children; he is afraid to make shame their inheritance.

'Let your soldiers marry, and they will no longer desert.

Bound to their families, they will be bound to their country. An unmarried soldier is frequently nothing but a vagabond, to whom it matters not whether he serves the king of Naples or the king of Morocco.'

The Roman warriors were married: they fought for their wives and their children; and they made slaves of the wives and the children of other nations.

A great Italian politician, who was, besides, learned in the Eastern tongues, a thing rare among our politicians, said to me in my youth: 'Caro figlio, remember that the Jews never had but one good institution—that of abhorring virginity. If that little nation had not regarded marriage as the first of the human obligations—if there had been among them convents of nuns—they would have been inevitably lost.'

MATTER. (A Polite Dialogue between a Demoniac and a Philosopher.):

Demoniac: Yes, thou enemy of God and man, who believest that God is all-powerful, and is at liberty to confer the gift of thought on every being whom He shall vouchsafe to choose, I will go and denounce thee to the inquisitor; I will have thee burned. Beware, I warn thee for the last time.

Philosopher: Are these your arguments? Is it thus you teach mankind? I admire your mildness.

Demoniac: Come, I will be patient for a moment while the faggots are preparing. Answer me: What is spirit?

Philosopher: I know not.

Demoniac: What is matter?

Philosopher: I scarcely know. I believe it to have extent, solidity, resistance, gravity, divisibility, mobility. God may have given it a thousand other qualities of which I am ignorant.

Demoniac: A thousand other qualities, traitor! I see what thou wouldst be at; thou wouldst tell me that God can animate matter, that He has given instinct to animals, that He is the Master of all.

Philosopher: But it may very well be, that He has granted to this matter many properties which you cannot comprehend.

Demoniac: Which I cannot comprehend, villain!

Philosopher: Yes. His power goes much further than your understanding.

Demoniac: His power! His power! thou talkest like a true atheist.

Philosopher: However, I have the testimony of many holy fathers on my side.

Demoniac: Go to, go to: neither God nor they shall prevent us from burning thee alive—the death inflicted on parricides and on philosophers who are not of our opinion.

Philosopher: Was it the devil or yourself that invented this method of arguing?

Demoniac: Vile wretch! darest thou to couple my name with the devil's?

(Here the demoniac strikes the philosopher, who returns him the blow with interest.)

Philosopher: Help! philosophers!

Demoniac: Holy brotherhood! help!

(Here half a dozen philosophers arrive on one side and on the other rush in a hundred Dominicans, with a hundred Familiars of the Inquisition, and a hundred alguazils. The contest is too unequal.)

MIRACLES: A miracle, according to the true meaning of the word, is something admirable; and agreeable to this, all is miracle. The stupendous order of nature, the revolution of a hundred millions of worlds around a million of suns, the activity of light, the life of animals, all are grand and perpetual miracles.

According to common acceptation, we call a miracle the violation of these divine and eternal laws. A solar eclipse at the time of the full moon, or a dead man walking two leagues and carrying his head in his arms, we denominate a miracle.

Many natural philosophers maintain, that in this sense there are no miracles; and advance the following arguments:

A miracle is the violation of mathematical, divine, immutable, eternal laws. By the very exposition itself, a miracle is a contradiction in terms: a law cannot at the same time be immutable and violated. But they are asked, cannot a law, established by God Himself, be suspended by its author?

They have the hardihood to reply that it cannot; and that it is impossible a Being infinitely wise can have made laws to violate them. He could not, they say, derange the machine but with a view of making it work better; but it is evident that

God, all-wise and omnipotent, originally made this immense machine, the universe, as good and perfect as He was able; if He saw that some imperfections would arise from the nature of matter, He provided for that in the beginning; and, accordingly, He will never change anything in it. Moreover, God can do nothing without reason; but what reason could induce Him to disfigure for a time His own work?

It is done, they are told, in favour of mankind. They reply: We must presume, then, that it is in favour of all mankind; for it is impossible to conceive that the divine nature should occupy itself only about a few men in particular, and not for the whole human race; and even the whole human race itself is a very small concern; it is less than a small ant-hill, in comparison with all the beings inhabiting immensity. But is it not the most absurd of all extravagances to imagine that the Infinite Supreme should, in favour of three or four hundred emmets on this little heap of earth, derange the operation of the vast machinery that moves the universe?

But, admitting that God chose to distinguish a small number of men by particular favours, is there any necessity that, in order to accomplish this object, He should change what He established for all periods and for all places? He certainly can have no need of this inconstancy in order to bestow favours on any of His creatures: His favours consist in His laws themselves: He has foreseen all and arranged all, with a view to them. All invariably obey the force which He has impressed for ever on nature.

For what purpose would God perform a miracle? To accomplish some particular design upon living beings? He would then, in reality, be supposed to say: 'I have not been able to effect by my construction of the universe, by my divine decrees, by my eternal laws, a particular object; I am now going to change my eternal ideas and immutable laws, to endeavour to accomplish what I have not been able to do by means of them.' This would be an avowal of His weakness, not of His power; it would appear in such a Being an inconceivable contradiction. Accordingly, therefore, to dare to ascribe miracles to God is, if man can in reality insult God, actually offering Him that insult. It is saying to Him: 'You are a weak and inconsistent Being.' It is, therefore, absurd to believe in miracles; it is, in fact, dishonouring the divinity.

These philosophers, however, are not suffered thus to declaim without opposition. You may extol, it is replied, as much as you please, the immutability of the Supreme Being, the eternity of His laws and the regularity of His infinitude of worlds; but our little heap of earth has, notwithstanding all that you have advanced, been completely covered over with miracles in every part and time. Histories relate as many prodigies as natural events. The daughters of the high priest Anius changed whatever they pleased to corn, wine and oil; Athalide, the daughter of Mercury, revived again several times; Æsculapius resuscitated Hippolytus; Hercules rescued Alcestis from the hand of death; and Heres returned to the world after having passed fifteen days in hell. Romulus and Remus were the offspring of a god and a vestal. The Palladium descended from heaven on the city of Troy; the hair of Berenice was changed into a constellation; the cot of Baucis and Philemon was converted into a superb temple; the head of Orpheus delivered oracles after his death; the walls of Thebes spontaneously constructed themselves to the sound of a flute, in the presence of the Greeks; the cures effected in the temple of Æsculapius were absolutely innumerable and we have monuments still existing containing the very names of persons who were eye-witnesses of his miracles.

Mention to me a single nation in which the most incredible prodigies have not been performed, and especially in those periods in which the people scarcely knew how to write or read.

The philosophers make no answer to these objections, but by slightly raising their shoulders and by a smile; but the Christian philosophers say: 'We are believers in the miracles of our holy religion; we believe them by faith and not by our reason, which we are very cautious how we listen to; for when faith speaks, it is well known that reason ought to be silent. We have a firm and entire faith in the miracles of Jesus Christ and the apostles, but permit us to entertain some doubt about many others: permit us, for example, to suspend our judgment on what is related by a very simple man, although he has obtained the title of great. He assures us that a certain monk was so much in the habit of performing miracles that the prior at length forbade him to exercise his talent in that line. The monk obeyed; but seeing a poor tiler fall from the top of a house, he hesitated for a moment between the desire to save the unfortunate man's life, and the sacred duty of obedience to his superior. He merely ordered the tiler to stay in the air till he should receive further instructions, and ran as fast as his legs would carry him to communicate the urgency of the circumstances to the prior. The prior absolved him from the sin he had committed in beginning the miracle without permission, and gave him leave to finish it, provided he stopped with the same, and never again repeated his fault.' The philosophers may certainly be excused for entertaining a little doubt of this legend.

But how can you deny, they are asked, that St. Gervais and St. Protais appeared in a dream to St. Ambrose, and informed him of the spot in which were deposited their relics? that St. Ambrose had them disinterred? and that they restored sight to a man that was blind? St. Augustine was at Milan at the very time, and it is he who relates the miracle, using the expression, in the twenty-second book of his work called the 'City of God,' 'immenso populo teste' in the presence of an immense number of people. Here is one of the very best attested and established miracles. The philosophers, however, say that they do not believe one word about Gervais and Protais appearing to any person whatever; that it is a matter of very little consequence to mankind where the remains of their carcasses lie; that they have no more faith in this blind man than in Vespasian's; that it is a useless miracle, and that God does nothing that is useless; and they adhere to the principles they began with. My respect for St. Gervais and St. Protais prevents me from being of the same opinion as these philosophers: I merely state their incredulity. They lay great stress on the well-known passage of Lucian, to be found in the death of Peregrinus: 'When an expert juggler turns Christian, he is sure to make his fortune.' But as Lucian is a profane author, we ought surely to set him aside as of no authority.

These philosophers cannot even make up their minds to believe the miracles performed in the second century. Even eye-witnesses to the facts may write and attest till the day of doom, that after the bishop of Smyrna, St. Polycarp, was condemned to be burned, and actually in the midst of the flames, they heard a voice from heaven exclaiming: 'Courage, Polycarp! be strong, and show yourself a man'; that, at the very instant, the flames quitted his body, and formed a pavilion of fire above his head, and from the midst of the pile there flew out a dove; when, at length, Polycarp's enemies ended his life by cutting off his head. All these facts and attestations are in vain. For what good, say these unimpressible and incredulous men, for what good was this miracle? Why did the flames lose their nature, and the axe of the executioner retain all its power of destruction? Whence comes it that so many martyrs escaped unhurt out of boiling oil, but were unable to resist the edge of the sword? It is answered, such was the will of God. But the philosophers would wish to see all this themselves before they believe it.

TOLERANCE: What is tolerance?—it is the consequence of humanity. We are all formed of frailty and error; let us pardon reciprocally each other's folly—that is the first law of nature.

It is clear that the individual who persecutes a man, his brother, because he is not of the same opinion, is a monster. That admits of no difficulty. But the government! but the magistrates! but the princes! how do they treat those who have another worship than theirs?

Madmen, who have never been able to give worship to the God who made you! Miscreants, whom the example of the Noachides, the learned Chinese, the Parsees and all the sages, has never been able to lead! Monsters, who need superstitions as crows' gizzards need carrion! you have been told it already, and there is nothing else to tell you—if you have two religions in your countries, they will cut each other's throat; if you have thirty religions, they will dwell in peace. Look at the great Turk, he governs Guebres, Banians, Greek Christians, Nestorians, Romans. The first who tried to stir up tumult would be impaled; and everyone is tranquil.

Of all religions, the Christian is without doubt the one which should inspire tolerance most, although up to now the Christians have been the most intolerant of all men. The Christian Church was divided in its cradle, and was divided even in the persecutions which, under the first emperors, it sometimes endured. Often the martyr was regarded as an apostate by his brethren, and the Carpocratian Christian expired beneath the sword of the Roman executioner, excommunicated by the Ebionite Christian, the which Ebionite was anathema to the Sabellian.

This horrible discord, which has lasted for so many centuries, is a very striking lesson that we should pardon each other's errors; discord is the great ill of mankind; and tolerance is the only remedy for it.

There is nobody who is not in agreement with this truth, whether he meditates soberly in his study, or peaceably examines the truth with his friends. Why then do the same men who admit in private indulgence, kindness, justice, rise in public with so much fury against these virtues?

I possess a dignity and a power founded on ignorance and credulity; I walk on the heads of the men who lie prostrate at my feet; if they should rise and look me in the face, I am lost; I must bind them to the ground, therefore, with iron chains.

Thus have reasoned the men whom centuries of bigotry have made powerful. They have other powerful men beneath them, and these have still others, who all enrich themselves with the spoils of the poor, grow fat on their blood, and laugh at their stupidity. They all detest tolerance, as partisans, grown rich at the public expense, fear to render their accounts and as tyrants dread the word liberty. And then, to crown everything, they hire fanatics to cry at the top of their voices: 'Respect my master's absurdities, tremble, pay and keep your mouths shut.'

It is thus that a great part of the world was long treated; but to-day, when so many sects make a balance of power, what course to take with them? Every sect, as one knows, is a ground of error; there are no sects of geometers, algebraists, arithmeticians, because all the propositions of geometry, algebra and arithmetic are true. In every other science one may be deceived.

If it were permitted to reason consistently in religious matters, it is clear that we all ought to become Jews, because Jesus Christ our Saviour was born a Jew, lived a Jew, died a Jew, and that he said expressly that He was accomplishing, that He was fulfilling the Jewish religion. But it is clearer still that we ought to be tolerant of one another, because we are all weak, inconsistent, liable to fickleness and error. Shall a reed laid low in the mud by the wind say to a fellow reed fallen in the opposite direction: 'Crawl as I crawl, wretch, or I shall petition that you be torn up by the roots and burned'?

WORKS OF

VOLTAIRE

(1694–1778)

DENIS DIDEROT

DENIS DIDEROT

by EDOUARD HERRIOT

I

EARLY YEARS AND DEVELOPMENT

I REMEMBER HOW IN 1913 THE FRENCH SENATE WISHED TO celebrate the second centenary of Diderot's birth. I was then a member, the youngest, of that assembly. I said a few words which met with very little response. The Chamber did not support the suggestion that his remains should be moved to the Panthéon, and Maurice Barrès expressed his satisfaction at this in a careful essay which appeared in his book *Les Maîtres*. He did not consider Diderot to be a national figure; he saw him merely as a remarkable revolutionary genius, able as no one else to place charges of dynamite under all the principles and pillars on which society rests; a professor, as it were, of anarchy and an enemy of tradition.

Actually Diderot had a strange destiny. In seeking to define his rôle or to assess his influence, we have to remember that much of his work was not published till after his death, that is to say, after 1784. *The Sceptic takes a Walk* and *Letters to Mlle Volland* appeared in 1830; *The Nun* in 1796. *Rameau's Nephew* was known first in Goethe's translation of 1805 and not until 1891 in the original French; his *Essay on Painting* appeared in 1795; *Letter to Mlle Jodin* in 1821; *A Letter Concerning the History and Politics of the Book Trade* in 1861; *Conversation between d'Alembert and Diderot* and *d'Alembert's Dream* in 1830; *Supplement to the Travels of Bougainville* in 1796; *The Paradox of Acting* in 1830; *James the Fatalist and his Master* in 1796; *Refutation of Helvetius* in 1875; *Project for a University for the Government of Russia* from 1813 onwards; a play, *Is He Good, Is He Bad?* in 1834. The posthumous publications of *Les Salons* and *Letters to Falconet* must be added to this list. It might indeed be said that Diderot's work, apart from the *Encyclopædia*, was the discovery of the nineteenth century and that his contemporaries knew nothing of his principal writings.

We shall be helped in our understanding of the man and

[249]

his philosophy if we consider certain aspects of his early life. The accounts left us by his daughter, Madame de Vandeul, are useful in this connection. He was born at Langres and was the son of a cutler; he had a sister who never married and a brother who later became a priest. He laughed at the changeability of his fellow-citizens. 'The head of a man of Langres,' he used to say, 'twists about on his shoulders like the weathercock on a church steeple.' We can judge of the kindness of his heart by his affection for his family, even for the clerical brother 'whose boundless charity more than made up for his slight faults.' As for his mother, when he thought of her, as in the *Journey to Bourbon*, a lovely line came spontaneously from his pen, a line which no grateful son can fail to appreciate: 'Oh thou who didst warm my cold feet in thy hands.'

His father was respected by all. He was a man of excellent judgment, pious and charitable. We see him in his armchair, wrapped in a dressing-gown, a pillow at his back, indulging in moral lectures and conversations with his children. At the age of about eight, little Diderot was entrusted to the Jesuits. His parents had chosen an ecclesiastical career for him, hoping that he would obtain the canonry of one of his uncles. At twelve he received the tonsure. In spite of his faults, notably a certain violence, he gained many scholastic honours. It is clear that he had no taste for the trade of a cutler. His father took him to Paris and installed him at the College of Harcourt. He was a source of satisfaction to his masters except when his excessive good nature prompted him to write his comrades' Latin verses for them. This is probably the origin of a poem on the somewhat inept theme: 'Speech delivered by the serpent seeking to seduce Eve.' Diderot considered a humanist education to be essential. 'For several years running,' he writes in his *Project for a University*, 'I would read a passage of Homer every night before going to bed as regularly as a good priest says his office. I began early to suck the milk of Homer, Virgil, Horace, Terence, Anacreon, Plato, and Euripides, mixed with that of Moses and the Prophets.'

As a matter of fact he wanted to study everything and to know everything. As soon as he left college his true nature became apparent. Unable to settle down in an attorney's office, refusing to choose a definite profession, flitting from literature to science and from Italian to English, mixing with company of every description both good and bad, but more often the latter, composing sermons, if necessary, for a Portuguese missionary, tutoring the children of Randon d'Haunecourt, the financier, but throwing up his job in order to be free again, sometimes reduced even to hunger, he managed to gain through his very independence a wide experience and culture which made him a singularly intelligent and well-informed Bohemian. At one moment we see him dressed in a grey plush coat taking a summer stroll along the Allée des Soupirs in the Luxembourg Gardens, and, at the next, wandering through the streets of Paris with torn cuffs and black woollen stockings sewn together at the back with white thread.

At thirty he married. It started off as a pretty enough romance. Anne Toinette Champion was sixteen; she had just left her convent school and was helping her mother to run a linen business. Denis introduced himself as a customer who was preparing to enter a seminary and needed the usual outfit. More and more diligent in his attentions, he finally married her against his father's wishes. They had four children of whom only one, a girl, survived. What became of the young couple? It seems that they were very unhappy. As far as we can see, Anne Toinette lacked neither common sense nor good taste. At any rate, in spite of Rousseau, who called her 'a shrew and a fish-wife,' she had a good heart. The *Memoirs* of Madame de Vandeul give us a picture of her. Every day she provided her husband with six sous so that he could go and take tea at the Régence and watch the chess. While he was away from her, Diderot had a liaison with the wife of a barrister, Madame de Pusieux, whose claims upon him necessitated his working harder than before, and publishing.

Until then he had only translated the *Essay on Merit and Virtue* of Lord Shaftesbury, a friend of Bayle and an amateur philosopher who had not been without influence on Reid and Stewart. Now, to satisfy the needs of Madame de Pusieux, he wrote one after the other, *Philosophical Thoughts, A Letter on the Blind for the use of Those Who See* and *The Jewels of Indiscretion,* whilst he was also preparing the first volume of the *Encyclopædia.* Thus from 1746 to 1751, between the ages of thirty-three and thirty-nine, he produced the first really important part of his work, which was stormy and uneven to the point of incoherence.

According to Madame de Vandeul, Diderot sold the *Essay on Merit and Virtue* for fifty pounds, which he immediately took to Madame de Pusieux; the *Philosophical Thoughts* were composed for the same purpose between Good Friday and Easter. On 7th July 1746 the Parlement condemned the little volume to the flames. This made a great stir and led to much controversy. Diderot, a reader of Bayle, took up his position; he praised passion, pronounced against asceticism, opposed the reasoning of the metaphysicians with arguments founded on discoveries due to the microscope and the telescope, maintained that scepticism was the first step towards truth and discounted revelation and miracles. He expressed daring opinions: 'The Scriptures do not bear so clear a stamp of divinity that the authority of the sacred historians is absolutely independent of the testimony of profane authors. Where should we be, if it were necessary to recognize the finger of God in the form of our Bible? . . . If we were permitted to regard the history of the Israelites simply as a human production, Moses and his followers would have no more weight than Livy, Sallust, Cæsar, and Josephus, none of whom has ever been suspected of writing under inspiration.' (*Thoughts*, XLV.) He does not wish, however, to cut himself off from Catholicism: 'I was born into the Catholic Apostolic and Roman Church and I subscribe to her decisions with all my might. I wish to die in the religion of my fathers and I believe as far as is possible for someone who has never witnessed any miracle.' (*Thoughts*, LVIII.) Actually in this profession of faith the reservations are important. Diderot evidently did not believe in the miracles which the credulity of the public at about this date attributed to the tomb of the deacon Paris in the parish of Saint-Médard.

Before coming to the *Letter on the Blind,* an essential part of his work, it is interesting to glance at two tracts both written in 1747 and published much later, *The Sceptic Takes a Walk, or The Pathways,* and *Concerning the Sufficiency of Natural Religion.* These throw light on the passage of his thought from Catholicism to deism and from deism to materialism. At the end of an avenue of old trees, Cléobule lives in an unpretentious house surrounded by busts of Socrates, Plato, Atticus, and Cicero; this dwelling is not surrounded by geometrically laid-out gardens, but by a park which is allowed to run wild. Cléobule has a contempt for metaphysical teaching and listens only to that of

Nature: 'A flower suggests a passing thought to him or a delicate sentiment.' In the pathway under the chestnuts he explains to his friend Aristo the extravagances of religions: 'Self-interest has produced priests, priests have produced prejudices, prejudices have produced wars, and wars will continue as long as there are prejudices, prejudices as long as there are priests, and priests as long as self-interest calls them into being.' *The Sceptic Takes a Walk* can only be understood by means of the key which follows. The headband is the symbol of faith, the scales the emblem of the Pyrrhonians. The stick with a crook-handle represents the bishop's crosier, the code the two Testaments, the staff officers the clergy, the supreme governor God, the viceroy the pope. Here the language has become far more biting. There is a viceroy who, for fear of hurting the soles of his delicate feet, has himself drawn in a chariot or carried in a litter. He constantly proclaims that he is the humble servant of all the world, but he patiently allows his satellites to declare that all men are his slaves. . . . This is the style throughout.

The little treatise on *The Sufficiency of Natural Religion* sets out to prove the uselessness of revelation which has provided only five or six propositions 'which I find as incomprehensible,' he writes, 'as if they were written in ancient Carthaginian.' Natural religion makes it possible for God to judge all men by the same law; therefore it alone is sufficient and universal, and Christianity is merely 'an added burden,' a dogma—beginning in history which has stained 'all lands with blood.' Diderot considers all the religions in the world as mere developments of natural religion.

At about the same time Diderot wrote *The Jewels of Indiscretion* to amuse Madame de Pusieux. The younger Crébillon, another ex-pupil of the Jesuits, though remarkably unfaithful to his early influences, specialized in licentious novels and was a frequenter of boudoirs and salons, though a royal proctor and, for the matter of that, respectable enough. In 1745 he published *Le Sopha,* which caused his exile from Paris. Already in 1734 the two volumes of *Tanzaï and Néardarné,* addressed to the Duchesse de Maine, had cost him a life sentence on account of allusions to Cardinal de Rohan's bull, *Unigenitus.* In 1746 the Amours of *Zeokinisul, King of the Kofirans*, recounted the adventures of Louis XV under cover of pseudonyms. *The Jewels of Indiscretion* (1748), inspired by an old ballad, belong to the same series. The author here embellishes a vulgar story with the most licentious embroideries which would be tedious did he not intersperse them with certain digressions attacking metaphysics or discussing the nature of the soul, 'which was originally situated in the feet.'

The *Letter on the Blind for the Use of Those Who See* (1749), defines Diderot's position, which was indeed a dangerous one. It is addressed once again to Madame de Pusieux. Diderot describes and defends the atheism of Saunderson, a man born blind, brilliant in mathematical science and literature, a professor of physics, famous for his lectures on light and colour. Condillac, with whom Diderot had much in common, had just published his first work, *Essay on the Origin of Human Knowledge*, in which, following in the footsteps of Locke, he expounded his ideas on sense perception as the origin of thought and on the laws of language. Such problems preoccupied and tormented men's minds at this period. Diderot had read Condillac and Berkeley. It seems as though he had made his own the words of the dying Saunderson: 'Should we consider a phenomenon to be beyond the comprehension of man? We hasten to explain it as the work of a divinity, otherwise our vanity is wounded. Could we not put a little less pride and a little more philosophy into our discussions? If nature presents us with a knot which is difficult to untie, let us recognize it for what it is, and do not let us seek to cut it with the hand of a being who will then become another knot for us to unravel, still more baffling than the first.'

The *Letter on the Blind* shows also the first traces of the theory of transformism, 'You can imagine if you choose that the order of things which confronts you has always existed, but let me believe that this is not the case and that if we went back to the origin of things and of seasons and could experience the movement of matter and the development of order from chaos, for every few well-defined entities, we should meet with innumerable formless ones.' The end of this work is frankly sceptical: 'When we have weighed human knowledge in the balance of Montaigne, we are not far from adopting his conclusions, for what certainty have we of anything? Can we explain matter? Not in the least. Or the nature of mind and thought? Still less. Do we know what movement is, or space, or duration? No, of all this we know nothing whatever.'

II

THE ENCYCLOPÆDIA

DIDEROT WAS NOW THIRTY-SIX. WE HAVE TRACED HIS passage from the Christianity of his Jesuit masters to deism, and thence to materialism. It is very surprising that until now the authorities had let him alone. On 24th July 1749, however, he was arrested and imprisoned at Vincennes. According to the Marquis d'Argenson he was punished for writing 'in favour of deism and against morality.' In the *Bibliothèque Nationale* an order has been found signed by the Lieutenant-General of Police 'for the detention at Vincennes of Diderot, author of the *Livre de L'Aveuglé*,' and 'a letter to the same Diderot protesting that he must have let the *Pensées (Philosophiques)*, the *Bijoux* and *La Lettre sur les Aveugles* escape from his pen in moments of intellectual intoxication.'[1] This imprisonment lasted until 3rd September 1749.

It is well known that at this time Diderot used to associate with Rousseau; Jean-Jacques, Condillac and he were in the habit of meeting every week in the Palais Royal where they dined together at the Hôtel du Panier Fleuri. It was while visiting him in the Donjon de Vincennes that Rousseau was given the idea of writing his famous *Discours sur les Sciences et les Arts*.

A wider scheme was now taking shape in the vast mind of Diderot. An English man of letters, Ephraim Chambers (who has been honoured with burial in Westminster Abbey) had devoted his life to compiling that much admired work: *Cyclopædia or An Universal Dictionary of Arts and Sciences* (London, 1728, 2 Vol. in fol.). The bookseller, Le Breton, wished to publish a French translation; after meeting with various difficulties he persuaded Diderot to undertake the task. The final result was an immense new work whose first volume (1751) bears the title: '*Encyclopédie ou Dictionnaire Raisonné des Sciences, des Arts et des Métiers*, par une Société de gens de lettres, mis en ordre et publié par M. Diderot de l'Académie royale des Sciences et des Belles Lettres de Prusse et, quant à la partie mathematique, par

---

[1] 'Des intemperances de l'esprit qui lui sont échappées.'

M. d'Alembert de l'Académie royale des Sciences de Paris, de celle de Prusse et de la Société Royale de Londres.'[1]

Jean le Rond d'Alembert, natural son of Mme de Tencin and of the Chevalier Destouches, was four years younger than Diderot. At twenty-three he had been elected a member of the Academy of Science, whilst a thesis on winds had led to his reception with acclamation by the Academy of Berlin. Finally, his *Discours Préliminaire de l'Encyclopédie* (Address introducing the Encyclopædia) was soon to gain him an entry into the Académie Française.

Diderot had drawn up the *Prospectus* and the *System of Human Knowledge*, and had already been working for several years on what was to be his great life's work when his imprisonment at Vincennes came as an interruption. For Science and Art the programme is simple. 'What an advantage it would have been for our fathers and for us if the achievements of ancient peoples, the Egyptians, the Chaldeans, the Greeks, and the Romans, etc., had been handed down in an Encyclopædia which at the same time would have set forth the true principles on which their languages were based. Let us, then, do for future generations what we regret that those of the past failed to do for us.' Practically nothing had yet been written on the mechanical and technical arts. Diderot consulted the artisans themselves, visited their workshops and watched them at their tasks. 'I found it necessary,' he writes, 'to exercise for them the function in which Socrates took such pride, the delicate and painful function of bringing ideas to birth.'

This is certainly the most daring and original part of his enterprise—it is something quite new. Here he is definitely in advance of his contemporaries; he is keenly interested in machinery, in the production and transformation of raw materials, in the use of tools, in the various departments of skilled labour. The text is illustrated with plates and diagrams. Diderot had grasped the important rôle of technical science in modern times and in the social conditions of the future.

In his *Discours Préliminaire*, d'Alembert sets forth the same

[1] 'Encyclopædia, or Systematic Dictionary of Arts, Sciences and Crafts by a Society of Men of Letters, set in order and published by M. Diderot of the Royal Academy of Science and Literature of Prussia, and in the mathematical part by M. d'Alembert, of the Royal Academies of Science of Paris and of Prussia and of the Royal Society of London.'

idea: 'The disdain with which the mechanical arts have always been regarded seems to have been extended in some measure to the very inventors themselves. The names of these benefactors of the human race are nearly all forgotten, whilst the story of its destroyers, that is to say, of the great conquerors, is familiar to everybody. Yet it is perhaps among the artisans that we shall find the most striking proofs of the wisdom, the patience, and the infinite resources of the human spirit. . . . Why should not those to whom we are indebted for the perfected production of a repeater watch be esteemed as highly as those who worked successively towards the perfection of algebra?' d'Alembert pays homage to Buffon, to Voltaire and Montesquieu. On the other hand he notes that the idea of progress, which is the foundation of the whole Encyclopædia, conflicts with the thesis recently printed by Rousseau concerning arts and science. He insists that the credit for the greater part of the work is due to Diderot, who has filled all the gaps and has gathered the necessary information on numerous special subjects such as the manufacture of stockings, velvet, brocaded materials, and the working of slate quarries, forges, iron foundries, wire-drawing mills, etc.

The section which Diderot drew up under the heading of 'Art' gives a very good idea of his opinions. He protests against those who hold that devotion to the technical arts involves 'loss of dignity over matters of which the study is laborious, the consideration ignoble, the exposition difficult, the traffic degrading, the number inexhaustible and the value trifling (minutielle).' He bases his position upon the authority of Bacon and Colbert. He even seems to have already had some notion of 'Taylorism.' When a manufacture is on a large scale, each operation is performed by a different man. One workman does one thing for the whole of his life, another something else, from which it comes about that each detail is carried out with efficiency and promptitude and that the best executed work is the cheapest.

The first volume of the *Encyclopædia* made a great impression in spite of the attacks of the Jesuits of the *Journal de Trévoux*. After the publication of the second volume an incident, due to the Abbé Jean Martin de Prades, led to the suppression of the *Encyclopædia*. De Prades, who was a friend of the 'philosophes,' had written some articles for the great work; his thesis for the doctor's degree, in which Diderot was suspected of having a hand, was declared to be heretical and condemned by the Archbishop of Paris. De Prades was obliged to leave for Holland, where he published his *Apology* and whence he proceeded to Prussia on 7th February 1752. The Conseil du Roi suppressed the two first volumes of the *Encyclopædia* without forbidding its continuation. The list of subscribers increased steadily. The work was dedicated to the Count of Argenson to whom Voltaire was indebted for much of the material he used in his *Siècle de Louis XIV*. The minister had the prohibition cancelled and the publication was recontinued in 1753. 'The government,' wrote Grimm, 'was obliged, not without a certain embarrassment, to approach M. Diderot and M. d'Alembert requesting them to go on with a work wantonly attacked by people who for a long time have occupied the lowest place in the world of letters.'

The storm which broke in 1758 was more violent and more serious; it was occasioned by the seventh volume. Under the designation of 'cacouacs' (quacks) the encyclopædists were attacked by the bishops and at the same time abandoned by Rousseau, who, anarchist as he was, had just published his *Discourse on the Origin and Causes of Inequality among Men* and who after having given the stage *The Village Soothsayer* and the *Comedy of Narcissus*, responded to the article entitled 'Geneva' in the *Encyclopædia* by a *Letter to d'Alembert concerning theatrical representation* in which he declared himself against all such performances, condemning in particular the plays of Voltaire. Other factors combined to alarm the authorities. Baron Holbach (the Wolmar of Rousseau's *Nouvelle Héloïse*) received all those on the philosophical side at his house and, twice a week, gave dinner parties where ideas were exchanged 'fit to bring down a thousand thunderbolts on the heads of his guests,' if Marmontel is to be believed. D'Holbach, whose pen was sometimes held by Diderot, and who wrote for the *Encyclopædia*, made violent attacks upon all religious and political institutions. An avowed atheist, he published in 1756 '*Le Christianisme Dévoilé*' (Christianity Unmasked)! Meanwhile the opulent Helvétius shocked everyone by producing in 1758 his book *De l'esprit* (On Intelligence), a treatise on sensualistic philosophy which the Parlement of Paris was to condemn to the flames. These polemical writers were not isolated examples. Mme du Deffand said of Helvétius: 'He is a man who has revealed everybody's secret.' The philosophers themselves gave signs of uneasiness, Voltaire with a joke, Rousseau with irritation. Turgot, notwithstanding that he was separated from the Church and preached universal toleration, did not dare to follow these violent rationalists.

On 23rd January 1759 the *parlement* (a legal body) sat to consider these cases. Joly de Fleury, in his address for the prosecution, denounced the materialistic programme of the philosophers and their hostility towards religion. *De l'esprit* was to be burnt and the *Encyclopædia* with its seven volumes already printed to be submitted for judgment by nine examiners. The Licence to Print was cancelled by the Council of State. 'Any advantages which may be drawn from a work of this kind,' ran the decree, 'in the furtherance of science and the arts, can never balance the irreparable harm which it must inevitably cause in matters of religion and morality.' Subscribers were to have their money returned by the booksellers.

Already, on 28th January 1758, d'Alembert had told Voltaire that it no longer seemed possible to him for the enterprise to continue; 'We collect the sticks at the seventh volume only to throw ourselves on to the fire at the eighth.' There was no more hope of moderate censors, in spite of the goodwill of M. de Malesherbes who, according to Voltaire, went 'almost half-way with the English.' d'Alembert concluded that the *Encyclopædia* must be abandoned. The question of money was added to the other preoccupations.

Diderot alone, in spite of his depression, held out, encouraging the booksellers, leaning on the support of M. de Sartine and of the Duc de Choiseul, helped also by Mme Geoffrin. Palissot, after having attacked Rousseau in his comedy *Le Cercle*, which so much annoyed King Stanislas, and after writing his *Petites Lettres* in 1757 against Diderot, was to get his play *Les Philosophes* acted at the Théâtre Français in 1760. Voltaire got round him; Diderot made headway. In 1765 he published simultaneously the ten last volumes of the text and the first five volumes of plates. The publication was only tolerated, not officially authorized, and it was necessary to hurry. The last volumes of plates could not be ready before 1772. In the *Avertissement* (notice) at the beginning of the eighth volume, Diderot could say with truth that over a period of twenty consecutive years he had scarcely had a moment's rest. How many times had he not dreamed of going abroad? But it was at the critical moment when the *Encyclopædia* was most threatened that they received the most courageous help. Diderot has special thanks for the Chevalier de Jaucourt, the friend of Condillac and Montesquieu. This Calvinist had studied mathematics at Cambridge and medicine at Leyden under Boerhaave. He supplied the *Encyclopædia* with articles on philosophy, chemistry, and botany, and superintended the whole of the production with his reliability and honesty. 'Thanks to the work we have done,' wrote Diderot, 'those who come after us can go further.' 'It will be a happy day when the world's rulers come to understand that their security depends upon the good education of those who serve them. Assassinations and crime are due always to blind fanaticism. How can we dare to complain of our difficulties or regret our years of labour, if we have the satisfaction of knowing that we have weakened the spirit of wild exaltation so contrary to social peace, if we can flatter ourselves that we have been able to lead our fellows in the direction of material kindness and tolerance, and to persuade them of the superiority of universal morality over all those individual codes which inspire hatred and confusion and destroy or weaken the common bond. This has been our constant aim.' In the construction of this work so vast and still so unjustly neglected even to-day, Diderot was, to use a simple word which he himself would have appreciated, the best of workmen.

PLAYS AND NOVELS

IDEROT'S ACTIVITIES WERE NOT CONFINED TO THE *Encyclo-pædia*. In 1751, between the first and second volumes, he wrote the *Letter on the Deaf and Dumb for the use of Those Who Hear and Speak*. The *Thoughts on the Interpretation of Nature* (1754) are inspired by the same principles as the *Encyclopædia* and give a summary of them. These letters draw the attention of the rising generation to the future awaiting natural science: 'We are approaching the moment of a great revolution in science,' affirms the author. Diderot as usual shows himself to be in favour of experiment rather than abstraction; in the course of his argument he returns to his theory of transformism; in his conclusion he throws out questions concerning the difference between inorganic and living matter, suggesting that the latter may be merely matter capable of movement. Auguste Comte held that this was one of Diderot's most important works. The *Essay on the History and the Secret of Painting in Wax* (1755) might serve as an example of the care with which Diderot studied those technical processes, whose importance is proclaimed throughout his entire work.

But the years which followed the storm over the *Encyclo-pædia* were employed in works of a new order. In a short introduction, Diderot tells us about the meeting and the incident which caused him to write, in 1757, *The Natural Son, or The Trials of Virtue*. This 'virtue,' personified yet remaining more or less of an abstraction, provides the essential character of his drama. The subject is not complicated. Old Lysimond has had a natural son, Dorval, and a daughter Rosalie. Dorval has for friends Clairville and his sister Constance. The characters in the play cry a great deal. From among their tears we learn that Clairville loves Rosalie who no longer returns his affection because she has fallen in love with Dorval. The latter, the moral hero of the drama, decides to sacrifice his love for his friendship. When the time came for the performance of this sermon in dialogue, weighty with lengthy commentaries, it was played only once and we can hardly be surprised. Diderot complains of the material conditions prevailing in the theatre of his day when the stage was still encumbered with spectators. 'Have you seen the hall at Lyons?' he writes, 'Give me but a building like that in the capital and I will blossom into a wealth of poems and produce perhaps some new styles.' (*Dorval et Moi*, second conversation.)

The Father of a Family (written in 1758 and acted in 1761) has more life and movement than *The Natural Son*. The author is accused of imitating Goldoni too closely, but the play is quite in the Diderot pattern. The *Mémoires Secrets* tell us that 'As many handkerchiefs were to be seen as there were spectators.' The plot, which is woven round M. d'Orbesson, the Father of the Family, his daughter Cecile and his son Saint Albin, is merely a pretext for moral dissertations. It drags in the same way as the plays of La Chaussée which preceded the dramatic work of Diderot, and without excessive irreverence we can apply to *The Father of a Family* the lines which Voltaire wrote in his *Pauvre Diable* with reference to 'L'École des Mères,'

> This tragic bourgeois often makes me yawn,
> Amphibious author whose attempts forlorn
> Disfigure and affront (the arrant dunce)
> Melpomene and Thalia both at once.[1]

Diderot's example finds imitators in Sedaine with his *Philosophe sans le Savoir*, in Mercier with *Le Déserteur*, in Baculard d'Arnaud with the *Comte de Comminges*, in Beaumarchais with '*La Mère Coupable*' and '*Eugénie*,' in Voltaire with his *Nanine* and *L'Enfant Prodigue*. He inspired Lessing, and the German stage was likewise inundated with tears. He gave birth to melodrama.

In 1760 Diderot wrote an imitation of Edward Moore's *Gamester*, but this adaptation did not come to light until 1819.

In *The Father of a Family* d'Orbesson is indignant at the thought that his daughter might enter a convent: 'I respect the religious vocation,' says he, 'but it is not for thee . . . thou hast not heard the groans of those unhappy creatures to whose number thou wouldst be added. Their cries pierce the silence of

---

[1] Souvent je baille au tragique bourgeois
Aux vains efforts d'un auteur amphibie
Qui défigure et qui brave à la fois,
Dans son jargon, Melpomène et Thalie.

their prisons in the night. Then it is, my child, that bitter, un-witnessed tears flow to water their lonely beds.' Actually this passage was cut out at the performance of the play.

This same argument which Diderot often upheld was to be the central idea of his celebrated novel, *The Nun*, written in about 1760 and published only in 1796. A sentence at the begin-ning sets the tone: 'For every hundred nuns who die before fifty there are exactly a hundred damned, without counting those who become mad, stupefied or raging in the meantime.' Diderot protests against the fact that a child should be allowed to pledge her liberty when she has not a penny of her own. According to him, in a well-governed state it should be difficult to enter religion and easy to come out. Christ did not appoint monks and nuns, He does not need so many mad virgins. A prayer is of less value than an act of mercy. The life of the cloister is contrary to the laws of nature.

This long protestation is interpolated with very expressive pictures, such as the portrait of the superior of the convent of Arpajon, a particularly agitated lady, or indeed, the description of the very cloister itself which was disturbed by such strange passions. The company of young nuns grouped round their handsome superior, embroidering or spinning with a little wheel, is an exquisite page in the style of Fragonard. It explains the disillusioned words of the young Benedictine to Sister Saint-Simon: 'In the midst of our penances we damn ourselves almost as surely as worldly people among their pleasures.' The various episodes which he imagines always bring the author back to the same conclusion: Convents must be abolished. *The Nun* protests against her confinement not because it impedes her worldly passions, but because of her love of liberty; this is where the novel is of a piece with all the work of Diderot. It matters little that it was called into being by a jest of Grimm; from whatever point of view we consider it, and whatever our attitude, it is infinitely superior to the disreputably obscene piece of mischief the *Bijoux Indiscrets*.

This superiority may be due to the influence of Samuel Richardson, of whom Diderot published a *Eulogy* at the same time as his *Reflexions on Terence* in a literary revue known as the *Journal Étranger*. In London at this same moment the cele-brated novelist, author of *Pamela*, of *Clarissa* and of the *History of Sir Charles Grandison,* lay dying. The likeness between the two authors is obvious; they had the same love of virtue, the same fondness for tears. 'Oh Richardson, Richardson,' writes Diderot, 'unique in my estimation, you shall ever be my study! If I am pressed by urgent needs, if my friend is starving and I am without the necessary means to educate and care for my children, I may be forced to sell my books, but you shall remain with me, you shall stay upon the same shelf with Moses, Homer, Euripides, and Sophocles, and I shall read you all in turn.' The influence upon Diderot of Richardson and his novel with a moral teaching was considerable. It explains many things about him. But this is also the period when he wrote *Rameau's Nephew,* which may well be considered as his masterpiece.

The story of this other novel is typical of the disorder in which Diderot's production has reached us. Schiller obtained a manuscript copy of it, which it appears Grimm passed on to him at some German Court. Goethe translated the text which was published in French by two young men, Viscomte de Saur and M. de Saint-Genies. The copy given by the author to his daughter appeared in 1823. In 1891 M. Monval found the original manuscript.

Schiller has summed up *Rameau's Nephew* very well in a few sentences: 'It is an imaginary conversation between the nephew of the musician Rameau and Diderot. This nephew is the perfect vagrant parasite but he is a hero among people of this kind and, while giving us a portrait of himself, he satirizes polite society and the world in which he lives.' Diderot has made use of this opportunity for piercing the enemies of the *Encyclopædia* through and through, specially Palissot, and for wreaking vengeance on behalf of all good writers of the time on the noisy rabble of conventional critics who attacked them. According to Goethe this novel is Diderot's best answer to those who accused him of 'knowing how to write fine pages without being able to write a fine book.'

The type whom Diderot puts on his stage had been introduced by Mercier; he lived in cafés and reduced all the actions of life, even of genius, to material for mastication. Behold us at the Café de la Régence where our author passes the time watching chess players. His interlocutor appears as he has described: he has a large forehead marked with wrinkles, keen eyes, a prominent nose, a well-shaped mouth with full lips, a square jaw. The conversation starts, sparkling with fantasy, abounding in paradoxes, bubbling over with contrasts. As for mental ability, the Nephew declares himself to be 'an ignoramus, a simpleton, a fool, impertinent, lazy, a truant, a knave and a glutton.' That is supposed to be all, but as we go on this simpleton shows himself capable of letting fly the most pointed and apt shafts upon the detractors of the philosophers, above all upon Palissot and Fréron. He accompanies his speech with lively gestures. He tells of all the tricks he practises in order to gain a living, for 'the voices of conscience and honour sound very faintly when the stomach is clamouring.' The work is a satire against the rich and their vices, against the organization of society. 'They praise virtue but they hate it; they fly from it; they leave it to perish with cold; and, in this world, the feet must be kept warm.' Once again, as in all his work, Diderot contrasts the standards of his age with the theory of well-being founded in virtue.

The Nephew is the type of a cheeky cynic, boasting of vice. He prides himself upon being sublime in knavery because society condemns the pickpocket but admires the important swindler. With the same eager animation he discourses also about music, and Diderot is surprised that, blind as he is in moral questions, he should be so sensitive in all that concerns art. The conclusion of the whole dialogue is that 'the beggars' antics are the great pivot of the world,' and support the whole social structure. But what no analysis can reproduce is the spirit of the work, the movement, the form, often so stark that many editors have thought it necessary to soften it down, and the life infusing this invention which remains one of the most original of Diderot's creations.

IV

THE MANY-SIDEDNESS OF DIDEROT'S GENIUS

SOMETHING VERY REMARKABLE DOMINATED THE LAST PART OF our author's life—his relationship with Catherine II. Strange, yet blissful period, when the most absolute of monarchs could take under her protection the most advanced of philosophers, guarantee the preservation of his library, appoint him as her special attendant and insist upon his presence at her Court. Diderot spent seven months in Russia during the year 1773 and, while there, saw none but the great Catherine herself. Nick-named by Voltaire *Catherin* he was singularly free and lacking in decorum during his stay, through sheer over-exuberance. His ideas amused his patroness and she was entertained by his advice without following it. 'Your Diderot,' she wrote to Mme Geoffrin, 'is a very extraordinary man; I always emerge from our discussions with my thighs bruised black and blue; I have been compelled to put a table between us in order to protect myself and my limbs from his gesticulations.'

During this last period of his life, Diderot wrote some major works, most of which were not published till after his death. To name only the principal ones we have:

1. *La Lettre Historique et Politique sur le Commerce de la Libraire* (*Letter on the History and Politics of the Book Trade*) written in 1767, found in 1861. The central idea is that 'the author is master of his own work or nobody in our social system is master of his own goods.'

2. *L'Entretien entre d'Alembert et Diderot* (*Conversation between d'Alembert and Diderot*), written in 1769, published in 1830, followed by the *Rêve de d'Alembert*—*d'Alembert's Dream*. Borden, the doctor, author of *Recherches sur le Pouls* (*Research on the Pulse*) is here introduced and also Mlle de Lespinasse. He maintains that the world is a huge mass of molecules which change places. There is little difference, according to him, between a man and a statue, between marble and flesh. 'There is only one substance in the universe, in man, or animal . . . the world is ceaselessly starting and finishing, it is at each moment at its

beginning and its end; there has never been any other world and never will be . . . organs are the cause of functions and reciprocally these functions produce organs.' Some of Lamarck's ideas are already in *Le Rêve de d'Alembert*. 'The substance of all beings circulates from one into another, consequently all the species are merged . . . everything is in a perpetual flux . . . every animal is more or less man, every mineral is more or less plant, every plant is more or less animal. . . . *There is only one great individual, and that individual is the whole.*' . . . 'What is a being? The sum of a certain number of tendencies. . . . And species? Species are merely tendencies limited to a certain degree which is peculiar to each one. *And life?* Life is a series of actions and reactions.' This definition marks the centre of the theory set forth in the *Rêve de d'Alembert*. Life is an action of the molecules moving in a mass; death a series of reactions by these same molecules. 'To be born, to live and pass on is to change form—form not essence.' In the *Suite de l'Entretien* (*Sequel to the Entretien*) Borden proves that 'nothing which exists can be either against nature or outside nature.' He thus attacks the very foundations of traditional morality, the whole work is tending in the direction of materialistic monism.

3. *Les Deux Amis de Bourbonne* (*The Two Friends of Bourbonne*). This time we have a work which Diderot published himself in 1773. He had been with Grimm to Bourbonne-les-Bains, near Langres, and there met Mme de Meaux and Mme de Prunevaux, her daughter. The story is a reply to something written by Saint-Lambert; according to Goethe it made a lively impression among the students of Strasbourg. The moral of this little story links it up with the main body of Diderot's work: 'As a general rule there can only be complete and lasting friendship between men who possess nothing. Then a man's only treasure is in his heart and he places and finds it in his friend.'

4. *The Supplement to Bougainville's Travels, or Dialogue between A. and B. touching the Difficulty of connecting Moral Ideas with certain Physical Actions which do not accord with them* (composed in 1772, published in 1796). During the years 1766 and 1769 Bougainville had accomplished the first journey round the world to be performed by a Frenchman. The story of this journey appeared in 1771. Diderot comments on it, denouncing, in passing, the methods of the Jesuits, 'those black-coated Spartans,'

in their treatment of the Indians, and philosophizing on his own account. 'All war springs from conflicting claims to the same property. The tiger's claim to possess the forests conflicts with that of man and is the more ancient; one man's claim conflicts with another's about a field of which each occupies a side.' Diderot is enthusiastic about the simple unsophisticated manners of the Tahitians. He makes Bougainville's journey a pretext for the defence of nature's laws and the moral code which they imply. This central idea leads him to some very bold conclusions about our social order, and such subjects as marriage or the possession of property.

5. The year 1772 is also the date of *Regrets for My Old Dressing-gown, or Advice to those who have more taste than Fortune*. Mme Geoffrin, to whom Diderot had been of service, thought she would refurbish his wardrobe, turn out his ragged clothes, embellish his philosophic retreat and put more comfortable furniture there. This transformation inspired him to write a charming little pamphlet, printed in Switzerland, and an indisputable masterpiece.

6. *Le Paradoxe sur le Comedien* (*Paradox concerning the Actor*), revised in 1778, published in 1830. Diderot considered that the great actor should have 'great subtlety but no sensibility'; his performance should spring '*not from the soul*' but '*from conscious thought.*' Sensibility is the cause of the mediocrity of most actors, 'it is extreme sensibility which makes actors limited; it is the lack of sensibility which makes actors sublime.' A great dramatic artist should have infinite experience and keep his head cool. 'But,' it is said, 'an orator has more power when he becomes heated, when he gets into a rage.' Diderot denies this, insisting that it is when he simulates rage. Actors move their audience not when they are furious but when they give a good imitation of fury. In tribunals, in public meetings, in every place where a man wishes to sway the minds of his fellows he feigns at one time anger, at another fear, then pity, so as to raise them to these pure emotions. What passion in itself cannot bring about is effected by its perfect counterfeit.'

7. *James the Fatalist and His Master* (written in 1773, published in 1796). This time Diderot takes the stage himself in the person of a man who, as he rides beside his master, promises to recount his love affairs, does not actually do so, but beguiles the journey

with a whole series of imaginary anecdotes and dissertations. The novel is an imitation of Sterne in *Tristram Shandy* or in *The Sentimental Journey*. It became known in Germany before it was known in France, thanks to Schiller and a translation of Mylius. Prince Henry of Prussia offered a manuscript of it to the *Institut National*. Goethe considered it to be a masterpiece, of which the best remembered parts are the *story of Mme de Pommeraye* and the *Chevalier des Arcis*. It is a masterpiece full of devilry in any case, written with remarkable vivacity in a dialogue which is at times luminous, interspersed with quaint and picturesque reflections. James—'If in this world one says scarcely anything which is understood in the sense in which it is spoken, yet there is something much worse, namely, that one does scarcely anything which is judged in the spirit in which it was performed!' The Master—'Maybe there is no other head under heaven which contains so many paradoxes as yours.' James—'And what harm is there in that? A paradox is not always a falsehood.' The central idea of the work is that all human destinies are written in advance 'on a great scroll.' Hence the title—*James the Fatalist*.

8. *Conversation of a Father with his Children, or The Danger of placing oneself above the Law* (published in 1773). Diderot, his father, his sister, and his brother have a discussion as they sit round the fire one winter's evening. The philosopher maintains that the sage should be beyond the law. 'I should not upset myself,' the old cutler replies to him, 'if there were two or three citizens like you in town, but I should not live here if they all thought this way.'

9. *Logical Refutation of Helvétius' Work, entitled 'On Man'* (written from 1773 to 1774, published in 1875). A single example will be enough to show the audacity of the work: 'Whatever the government may be,' writes Diderot, 'nature has set a limit to the sufferings of the people. Beyond this there must be death, flight or revolt. It is essential that a proportion of the wealth obtained from the soil should be returned to it; it is essential that the labourer and the farmer should live. This order of things is eternal; the most inept and cruel despot cannot violate it.'

10. *Plan for a University for the Government of Russia, or Public Education in all Sciences* (written from 1775 to 1776, published in part 1813–1814, completed in 1875). Diderot here criticizes the teaching of ancient languages, stresses the need for

technical training as well as for compulsory education free to all, and asks even that the children should be fed at school. He maintains that the best and most rational institutions for the instruction of the young are to be found in Protestant countries; Montesquieu and Voltaire were the disciples of the English philosophers. 'The study of words has held too large and important a place in the schools'; to-day its place must be taken by the study of things, including the mechanical arts. The encyclopædist is to be recognized in these ideas. He prefers the teaching of mathematics to that of logic and metaphysics. The university should be open to all the children of the nation *without distinction*; it would be as cruel as it would be absurd to condemn the lower classes of society to ignorance. This is the principle on which he founds his plan which is worked out and described down to the minutest detail. In general he reduces the study of the classics and of theology in order to increase the part played by science.

11. *Conversation of a Philosopher with the Marshal de Broglie* (composed in 1776). A very sharp criticism of religious ideas.

12. *Essay on the Reigns of Claudius and Nero and on the Life and Writings of Seneca* (composed in 1778 and rearranged in 1782). This work was written at the request of d'Holbach. Diderot introduces it into a justification of his own methods. 'The book,' he declares, 'is like my walks. Should I come upon a good view I should stop and enjoy it. I hasten or dawdle according to the luxuriance or sterility of the situation; wandering freely where my musings lead me, my only care is to prevent the approach of weariness.' In the course of these wanderings Diderot attacks Jean-Jacques Rousseau. Some of his ideas are worth recording; this one, for example (No. XXXVI): 'The people's man is the most mischievous and the stupidest of mortals; to become unpopular is one and the same thing as to improve. The voice of the philosopher contradicting that of the populace is the voice of reason.'

13. The four-act prose play, *Est-il Bon; Est-il Méchant?* (*Is He Good; Is He Bad?*) (published in 1834). Baudelaire was enthusiastic about this play and wanted to have it acted; he did not succeed. We can only hope that the wish of so good a judge may one day be realized. At any rate this play, written in 1781, proves that at the end of his life Diderot had not lost

any of his faculty for invention and expression—quite the reverse. As Eugène Laugier wrote when he was entrusted by Arsène Houssaye with the task of criticizing this comedy, 'It is a very lively picture of manners. Apart from the fact that Diderot himself bears a part on the stage, the style is stamped with the inimitable personality of the celebrated philosopher. It is in the finished language of the eighteenth century of which we have lost the secret.'

THE SALONS AND CORRESPONDENCE

THIS ALL TOO RAPID ENUMERATION SHOWS THE FECUNDITY and versatility of our universal essayist's genius—we must still add to it, besides such shorter works as *Ceci n'est pas un Conte* (*This is not a Tale*), two very important series.

1. *The Salons,* written between 1759 and 1775. Diderot was always interested in the technical side of art. At Grimm's request, he gave an account of exhibitions of paintings in his *Literary Correspondence*. In these studies he created art criticism, not as we know it to-day, when it is based upon a knowledge of craftsmanship, but from a purely intellectual point of view, interspersed with innumerable digressions, considering the *subject* more than the *treatment*. He understood Chardin: 'Oh, Chardin! It is not white, red, black which you spread on your palette, it is the very substance of things; it is air and light which you take on the tip of your brush and fasten to the canvas.' Diderot does not seem to have felt the charm of Watteau. He recognized talent in Boucher, but he objected to the depravity of his morals, his lack of taste, his ignorance of the reality of nature, his affectation, the rowdiness of his composition; his angels are licentious little satyrs. According to Diderot, Nattier has no good quality. He is fairer to La Tour who had made such a life-like portrait of d'Alembert's intelligent face; he is unjustly scornful of Péronneau; unduly hard on Parrocel, he extols Joseph Vernet, of whom he has a *Tempest* in his study. But the painter whom he prefers above all others on account of his moral pictures is Greuze; Greuze the friend of the Encyclopædists, habitual guest of Mme Geoffrin and Mademoiselle de Lespinasse; Greuze who revolts against the love scenes of Boucher or Fragonard, who defends the idea of the family but abandons his own children to the care of a distant nurse; Greuze, the emotional painter, with his declamations and tears. In discussing sculpture, it is surprising that his opinion of Houdon's bust of Voltaire should be so tepid. Diderot's *Essay on Painting* proves, however, that we must not exaggerate his lack of technical knowledge; he has written some

fine passages on drawing, on colour, on light and shade, on architecture. Faguet said: 'He treated the theatre as painting and painting as literature.' Such judgments seem to us to-day to need revision.

As might be expected with Diderot, that is to say, with a man whose interests were so widely scattered, his activities are supplemented by a continuous stream of correspondence. First there is his general correspondence. He tries to make up the quarrel with Jean-Jacques Rousseau and to dispel his anger: 'I am made so that I love you and cause you sorrow. . . . It is certain that you have other friends left besides me; but it is certain that I am left to you also. I have said it openly to all who would listen and this is the way I explain it: our friendship is like a mistress of whom I know all the faults but from whom my heart cannot separate itself.' To Grimm he pours out the most unrestrained confidences and precisely about 'this mad fury of a Jean-Jacques'; to Voltaire he explains himself on the subject of the *Encyclopædia,* commenting on *Tancrède* and praising the man who lives beside the lake of Geneva 'armed with a big whip'; another day he calls him his 'sublime, honest and dearly-beloved antichrist.' In some letters he announces the coming political storms; 'the principles of liberty and independence formerly hidden in the heart of a few thinkers are now becoming firmly established and are openly recognized' (written to Princess Dashkoff, 3rd April 1771). These letters show above everything else the kindness, simplicity, and generosity of his heart. 'I give everything I have to the needy folk of all descriptions who come to me. They have my money, my time, my ideas, but I am so poor in comparison to the great mass of poverty that after having given all I have overnight, I am left with nothing next day but the pain of my inadequacy.' (Letter to Mme Necker.)

Diderot's letters to Falconet, the Jean-Jacques of scuplture, are for the most part a gossip on the idea of posterity. When the artist visits Russia, his correspondent tells him what is going on in France. But it is the letters to Mlle Volland which form the most precious part of this series. It seems that she was the daughter of an official in the Excise Office, she owned a château with a park near Vitry-le-François. We have very little information about her; we know that she 'had dry hands and wore glasses,' also that she was well-informed and witty (she had 'the soul of an eagle in a habitation of gauze,' said Fronchin, and she was passionately interested in philosophy). The correspondence began in May 1759. From the Château d'Isle, which he visits in her absence, dreaming beneath its poplars on the banks of the Marne, or from his house at Grandval, near Boissy Saint-Léger in the *département* of Seine et Oise, he sends her impassioned letters; 'Oh my dearest, do not let us ever do any evil; let us love each other so that we may become better; let us go on being faithful tutors and critics of each other. Make me worthy of you; inspire me with the candour, sincerity, and gentleness which are natural to you. If I deceived you once I might deceive you a thousand times; but I will never deceive you.'

This correspondence is a joy. Diderot tells Sophie all about his conversations, his walks, his troubles and trials as an author. There is a fête at Chevrette. Young peasants all in their best rub shoulders with great ladies, their faces made up with rouge and patches, straw hats on their heads and reed canes in their hands. Grimm is having his portrait painted; Saint-Lambert is reading a pamphlet; Diderot is playing chess with Mme d'Houdetot. A harpsichord is gently murmuring the notes of Scarlatti. The delightful eighteenth-century society at the height of its summer comes to life in these letters dominated by the expression of a love which even from a distance is almost more than can be borne. Diderot's passion is unbounded. 'When one goes so far as to love a woman one must do so wildly, one must give oneself utterly as I do to you, my dearest.' Madame Geoffrin moves across the stage in a dress of severe hue, with wide sleeves and touches of fine linen. But Diderot, tormented by love, prefers to dwell less upon the conversations which he reports for the entertainment of his Sophie, than upon the violence of wind and rain and the continuous bass accompaniment of the storm. Here is romanticism already. Sophie has actually a slightly caustic nature; a certain angularity which distinguishes her in a society which tends to be monotonous. It even comes about that Diderot reproaches her, but always good-humouredly; she is the mirror in which all his actions, all his sufferings, are reflected.

In reading these letters we become aware of Diderot himself, of the amazing variety of his intelligence and the perpetual improvization which expresses the rhythm of his mind. He thinks while speaking or writing. Diderot might be said to typify the

average Frenchman. Emile Faguet used to say that we all have
a cousin who is like him. His originality lies primarily in his
vast culture and in his scientific knowledge, so far in advance
of that of his contemporaries. He had already reached an idea
of transformism, the doctrine of evolution. A materialist, in
favour of morality for sentimental and practical reasons, not from
philosophic conviction, laudably hard-working, curious about
everything, often confused, even incoherent but generous, cordial,
with a shade of coarseness, becoming intoxicated with ideas, as
others do with wine, vulgar at times and disordered as he was
said to be, his outstanding quality was life.

The extracts which follow could have been presented in two
different ways. They could have appeared in a form suitable for
school use, with all unorthodox passages deleted. This would
have been to mutilate Diderot and make him unrecognizable.
The other way was to omit only the more licentious passages
and to give a résumé of his work with all its daring paradoxes
and challenging heresies in chronological order. The second
course seemed the more honest. We have chosen it. It is not
essential to know Diderot but we have no right to distort him.

PHILOSOPHICAL THOUGHTS
(Written in 1746)

I

PEOPLE ARE FOR EVER DECLAIMING AGAINST THE PASSIONS;
they attribute to them all the pains that man endures, and
forget that they are also the source of all his pleasures. It
is an ingredient in man's constitution which cannot sufficiently
be blessed and banned. It is considered as an affront to reason
if one ventures to say a word in favour of its rivals; yet it is
passions alone, and strong passions, that can elevate the soul to
great things. Without them, there is no sublime, either in morality
or in achievement; the fine arts return to puerility, and virtue
becomes a pettifogging thing.

II

Sober passions make men commonplace. If I hang back before
the enemy, when my country's safety is at stake, I am but a
poor citizen. My friendship is but self-regarding if my friend's
peril leaves me considering my own danger. If life is dearer to
me than my mistress, I am a poor lover.

III

Deadened passions degrade men of extraordinary quality.
Constraint annihilates the grandeur and energy of nature. Look
at that tree; it is to the luxury of its branches that you owe
the coolness and breadth of its shade, which you may enjoy
until winter despoils it of its leafy honours. There is no more
excellence in poetry, in painting, and in music when superstition has wrought upon the human temperament the effect of
old age.

IV

It would be fortunate, people will say to me, for a man to
have strong passions. Certainly, if they are all in harmony.

Establish a just harmony among them, and you need fear no convulsions and disorders. If hope be balanced by fear, the point of honour by love of life, the taste for pleasure by consideration for health, there will be no libertines, nor rufflers, nor poltroons.

V

It is the very height of madness to propose the ruin of the passions. A fine design, truly, in your devotee, to torment himself like a convict in order to desire nothing, love nothing, and feel nothing. He would end by becoming a monster, if he were to succeed.

VI

Can what is the object of my respect in one man be the object of my scorn in another? Certainly not. Truth, independently of my caprices, should be the rule of my judgments, and I shall not call that quality a crime in one man which I admire as a virtue in another. Am I to think that the practice of self-improvement is to be restricted to some few, when nature and religion inculcate it on all alike? Whence comes this monopoly? If Pachomius did well in separating himself from the human race and burying himself in a wilderness, I may follow his example, and in imitating him I shall be equally virtuous; and I see no reason why a hundred others may not have the same right. Yet it would be a strange sight to see an entire province, dismayed at the dangers of society, dispersed in forests, the inhabitants living like wild beasts to sanctify themselves, and a thousand pillars rising above the ruins of all social affections; a new race of Stylites stripping themselves from religious motives of all natural feelings, ceasing to be men and becoming statues in order to be true Christians.

VII

What voices, what cries, what groans! Who has shut up in dungeons all these piteous wretches? What crimes have all these creatures committed? Some beat their breasts with stones, others lacerate their body with iron nails, all express in their eyes regret, pain, and death. Who condemns them to such torments? The God whom they have offended. Who then is this God? A God full of goodness. But would a God full of goodness take pleasure in bathing himself in tears? Are not these fears an insult to his kindness? If criminals had to appease the fury of a tyrant, what more could they do?

VIII

These are people of whom we ought not to say that they fear God, but that they are mortally afraid of him.

IX

Judging from the picture they paint of the Supreme Being, from his tendency to wrath, from the rigour of his vengeance, from certain comparisons of the ratio between those he abandons to perish and those to whom he deigns to stretch out a hand, the most upright soul would be tempted to wish that such a being did not exist. We would be happy enough in this world, if we were assured we had nothing to fear in another. The thought that a God did not exist has never terrified humanity, but the idea that a god such as is represented exists.

X

God must be imagined as neither too kind nor too cruel. Justice is the mean between clemency and cruelty, just as finite penalties are the mean between impunity and eternal punishment.

XI

I am aware that the sombre ideas of superstition are more generally approved of than accepted; that there are pietists who do not think it necessary to hate themselves in order to love God, or to live as desperate wretches, in order to be religious; their devotion is a smiling one, their wisdom very human; but whence comes this difference in sentiment between people who prostrate themselves before the same altars? Can piety thus be subject to the law of temperament? Alas! it must be so. Its influence is only too apparent in the same devotee: he sees in accordance with its variations a jealous or a merciful God, and hell or heaven opening before him; he trembles with fear or burns with love; it is a fever with its hot and cold fits.

XII

Yes, I maintain that superstition is more of an insult to God than atheism. 'I would rather,' said Plutarch, 'that people thought that a Plutarch never existed, than that they thought of Plutarch as unjust, choleric, inconstant, jealous, and revengeful, and such as he would be sorry to be.'

XIII

Only the deist can oppose the atheist. The superstitious man is not so strong an opponent. His God is only a creature of the imagination. Besides difficulties of a material nature, he is exposed to those which result from the falsity of his notions. A C— and a S— would have been a thousand times more embarrassing to a Vanini than all the Nicoles and Pascals in the world.[1]

XIV

Pascal was an upright man, but he was timid and inclined to credulity. An elegant writer and a profound reasoner, he would doubtless have enlightened the world, if Providence had not abandoned him to people who sacrificed his talents to their own antipathies. How much it is to be regretted that he did not leave to the theologians of his day the task of settling their own disputes; that he did not give himself up to the search for truth without reserve and without fear of offending God, by using all the intellect God had given him! How regrettable that he took for his masters men who were not worthy to be his disciples! One could say of him, as La Mothe said of La Fontaine that he was foolish enough to think Arnauld, de Sacy, and Nicole better men than himself.

XV

'I tell you that there is no God; that Creation is a fiction; that the eternity of the universe is no more of a difficulty than the eternity of spirit; that because I do not see how motion

---

[1] (Vanini, 1585–1619, was executed at Toulouse in 1619, on the charge of atheism. The initials C and S stand for the two English deists, Cudworth and Shaftesbury.)

could have caused this universe (though it keeps it going), it is ridiculous to solve the difficulty by supposing the existence of a being of whom I can have no real conception; that if the wonders of the physical universe show some intelligence, the confusions in the moral order are the negations of a Providence. I tell you if everything is the work of a God, everything should be the best possible: for if everything is not the best possible, it is impotence or malevolence on the part of God. Therefore it is fortunate that I am not better informed as to his existence. If it were proved satisfactorily (and it is by no means proved) that all evil is the source of good, that it was for the best that Britannicus, the best of princes, perished, and that Nero, the worst of men, should reign, how is it possible to prove that it was impossible to attain the same ends without using such means? To allow vice in order to throw virtue into relief is a poor advantage in comparison with its real disadvantage.'

That, says the atheist, is my case; what have you to say to it? 'That I am a miserable wretch, and that if I had nothing to fear from God, I should not be disputing his existence.' Let us leave such an answer to orators; it may be untrue; politeness forbids it and it has no savour of charity about it. Because a man is mistaken in his denial of God, should we insult him? People only take refuge in invective when they run short of proofs. Of two engaged in argument, it is a hundred to one that the man in the wrong will become angry. 'You thunder instead of answering,' says Menippus to Jupiter; 'are you then in the wrong?'

XVI

One day somebody asked a man if real atheists existed. Do you think, he responded, that real Christians exist?'

XVII

None of the vain speculations of metaphysics have the cogency of an argument *ad hominem*. In order to convince, it is sometimes only necessary to rouse the physical or moral instinct. The Pyrrhonist was convinced by a stick that he was wrong in doubting his own existence. Cartouche, pistol in hand, might have taught Hobbes a similar lesson: 'Your money or your life;

we are alone, I am the stronger, and between us there is no question of justice.'

XVIII

It is not from the metaphysician that atheism has received its most vital attack. The sublime meditations of Malebranche and Descartes were less calculated to shake materialism than a single observation of Malpighi's. If this dangerous hypothesis is tottering at the present day, it is to experimental physics that the result is due. It is only in the works of Newton, of Muschenbroek, of Hartzoeker, and of Nieuwentit, that satisfactory proofs have been found of the existence of a reign of sovereign intelligence. Thanks to the works of these great men, the world is no longer a God; it is a machine with its wheels, its cords, its pulleys, its springs, and its weights.

XIX

The subtilties of ontology have at best made sceptics, and it was reserved for the knowledge of nature to make true deists. The discovery of germs alone has destroyed one of the most powerful arguments of atheism. Whether motion be essential or accidental to matter, I am now convinced that its effects are limited to developments; all experiments agree in proving to me that putrefaction alone never produced any organism. I can allow that the mechanism of the vilest insect is not less marvellous than that of man; and I am not afraid of the inference that as an intestinal agitation of molecules is able to produce the one, it is probable that it has produced the other. If an atheist had maintained, two hundred years ago, that some day perhaps people would see men spring full-formed from the bowels of the earth just as we see a mass of insects swarm in putrefying flesh, I would like to know what a metaphysician would have had to say to him?[1]

XX

It was in vain that I made use of scholastic subtilties against the atheist; he found among his feeble reasons one argument of

[1] Diderot here alludes to Redi's experiments about the generation of insects, and in the preceding Thought he alludes to the discoveries due to the telescope and microscope.

[281]

some validity. 'A multitude of useless verities are proved to me without any doubt,' he said, 'and the existence of God, the reality of moral good and moral evil, and the immortality of the soul are still problems for me. What! Is it less important for me to be informed on these subjects than to be sure that the three angles of a triangle are together equal to two right angles?' While like a skilful orator he made me taste the full bitterness of this reflection, I joined battle with him again with a question which must have appeared singular to a man flushed with his first success. 'Are you a thinking being?' I asked. 'Can you doubt it?' he answered with a pleased air. 'Why not? What have I seen to prove it? Sounds and movements? But the philosopher sees the same in an animal to whom he denies the faculty of thought; why should I allow you what Descartes refuses the ant? Externally, your actions are designed to give me that impression; I should be tempted to maintain that you do think, but reason suspends my judgment. Between external actions and thought my reason tells me there is no essential connection; it is possible that your antagonist thinks no more than his watch; must one take for a thinking being the first animal taught to speak? Who has informed you that all men are not so many well-trained parrots?' 'That is very ingenious,' he returned, ' but it is not by motion or sounds but by the continuity of ideas, the connection between propositions, and the links of the argument that one must judge if a creature thinks. If there was a parrot which could answer every question, I should say at once that it was a thinking being. But what has this to do with the existence of a God? If you were to prove to me that the most intelligent man were perhaps but an automaton, should I be the more disposed to recognize an intelligent Being in nature?' 'That is my affair,' said I 'but admit that it would be madness not to credit your brother men with the faculty of thought?' 'Of course, but what follows?' 'It follows that if the universe—but why drag in the universe?—if a butterfly's wing shows me proofs of an intelligence a thousand times stronger than the proof you have that your fellow-man thinks, it would be a thousand times more foolish to deny that God exists than to deny that your fellow-man thinks. I appeal to your knowledge, to your conscience! Have you ever observed in any man more intelligence, order, wisdom, and reasonableness than in the mechanism of an insect? Is not the Deity as clearly apparent in the eye of a flesh-worm as in the works of the great Newton? What, does the formation of the world afford less proof of intelligence than its explanation? What a position!' 'But,' you reply, 'I admit the faculty of thought in another the more readily as I myself think.' That is an analogy I admit I cannot use, but against this must be set the superiority of my proofs to yours. Is not the intelligence of a first cause more conclusively proved in nature by his works than the faculty of reasoning in a philosopher by his writings? Remember, I only adduced a butterfly's wing, a flesh-worm's eye, when I could crush you with the weight of the entire universe. I am greatly deceived if this proof is not well worth the best that has ever issued from the schools. It is by this argument, and others equally simple, that I am convinced of the existence of a God, and not by those tissues of dry and metaphysical ideas which are better calculated to give to truth an air of falsity than to unveil it.

From *Diderot's Early Philosophical Works*.

Translated by Margaret Jourdain, 1915.

ON THE SUFFICIENCY OF NATURAL RELIGION
1747

XVIII

Everything which had a beginning will have an end, and anything which had no beginning will have no end. Now Christianity had a beginning, Judaism had a beginning, and there is not one single religion on earth whose date of origin is not known except natural religion; all others therefore will pass away and natural religion alone will not end.

XIX

Of two religions, that which is more evidently from God and less obviously of man's creation is to be preferred. Now natural law comes obviously from God and it is infinitely more clear that it does so than that any other religion comes from any source but man, since there is no argument about its divine origin, and it requires no proof, whereas there have been thousands of arguments about the divinity of the others and they require a multitude of proofs before they are accepted.

XX

That religion is most preferable which is most closely similar to the nature of God; natural religion is the most closely allied to the nature of God. A part of God's nature is to be incorruptible and incorruptibility is more in evidence in natural religion than in any other, for the precepts of all others are written in books and are subject to all human accidents such as destruction, misinterpretation, and obscurity. But natural religion is inscribed in men's hearts where it is sheltered from these vicissitudes; if there is fear of its being mutilated by prejudices and passions, other religions have this same liability in addition to the other sources of change peculiar to themselves.

XXI

Either natural religion is good or it is bad. If it is good, it is enough for me; I do not ask for anything better. If it is bad, then *your* religion is at fault in its very foundation.

XXII

If there were any reason for preferring Christianity above natural religion it would be because the former could offer some enlightenment, missing in the latter, on the nature of God and the nature of man. This is not the case, however; instead of enlightening us, Christianity gives rise to innumerable obscurities and difficulties. If you ask the Naturalist why man suffers in this world, he will reply, 'I have no idea.' Ask a Christian the same question and he will answer you in riddles or absurdities. Which of the two is better, ignorance or mystery? And, in point of fact, are not the two answers the same? Why does man suffer in this world? 'It is a mystery,' says the Christian. 'It is a mystery,' says the Naturalist. Because, mark you, that is what the Christian answer comes to in the end. He may say that man suffers because his forefathers sinned, but if you persist and ask him why the

[284]

descendent should suffer for the sins of his fathers, he will answer, 'It is a mystery.' Ha! I would reply to the Christian, why didn't you say at first, as I did, that the fact that man suffers on earth without apparently deserving it, is a mystery? Don't you see that you are explaining this question in the same way as the Chinese explain the suspension of the world in space? Chinaman, what holds up the world? A great elephant. And what holds up the elephant? A tortoise. And the tortoise? I've no idea. My friend, forget the elephant and the tortoise and admit your ignorance to start with.

XXIII

A religion to be preferred above all others is one which can only do good and can never do harm. Such is the natural religion engraved in the hearts of men. All men find in themselves the inclination to adopt it but other religions founded on principles foreign to mankind and most of them therefore necessarily obscure, can never fail to arouse dissension. Moreover, we must admit what experience confirms. Experience shows that the so-called revealed religions have caused untold misery, set men in arms against each other and stained the whole world with blood. Natural religion has not cost the world a single tear.

XXIV

A system which raises doubts about a universally benevolent providence or about the impartiality of God must be rejected. A system which rejects natural religion as insufficient auto-matically throws doubt on the benevolence of providence and the impartiality of God. It causes me no longer to see Him as anything but a being of limited affections and changing designs, reserving his goodwill for a minority of his creatures and altering in one age the commandments given in another; for if mankind is only to be saved by the Christian religion it makes of God a hard father to those to whom he has not vouchsafed it, as hard as a mother who would refuse her milk to some of her children. If, on the other hand, natural religion is enough, everything falls into place and I am bound to form the most sublime conception of the benevolence and impartiality of God.

XXV

Would it not be fair to say that all the religions of the world are no more than sects of natural religion; that Jews, Christians, Mussulmans, and even pagans are but heretical or schismatic Naturalists?

XXVI

Could one not therefore advance the theory that natural religion is the only one with any real existence? Take an adherent of any religion you like and ask him a few questions. Very soon you will see that among the dogmas of his religion there are some in which he believes rather less than in others or even denies altogether, quite apart from all those which he either does not understand or interprets to suit his own convenience. Try the same process on one of his co-religionists and you will find him in the same state with this sole difference that what he accepts and has no doubts about is exactly what the first man denied or considered suspect, what he cannot understand is what the former thinks he understands perfectly, what troubles him presents no difficulties to the other, and they do not even agree upon what does or does not require interpretation. All these men, however, flock to the same altar; you would think they agreed on all matters, but in fact they agree on practically none. So much is this the case that if they agreed to abandon all the points on which they differ they would find themselves to be Naturalists and would leave their churches for those of the Deist.

XXVII

The truth of natural religion bears to that of other religions the same relation as what I see for myself bears to what I learn at second hand; as what I hear for myself bears to what I am told about; as what I know to be written in my being by the hand of God bears to what vain, superstitious, and lying men have written on paper or carved in stone; as what I carry in my heart and recognize unchanged everywhere I go bears to something changeable outside me; as what has never been, is not, and never will be seriously denied bears to what, far from being accepted now or ever, has either never been known, or has been forgotten, is not now known or has even been declared false; as what neither time nor man has abolished or ever will abolish bears to something which passes like a shadow; as what brings together civilized man and savage, Christian, infidel, and pagan, worshippers of Jehovah, Jupiter, and God, philosopher and peasant, scholar and dunce, old and young, wise men and idiot bears to what separates father from son, arms man against his fellows, exposes scientist and sage to the hate and persecution of the ignorant and fanatical and from time to time sprinkles the world with the blood of them all; as what is held holy, venerable, and sacred by all nations of the world bears to what is cursed by all nations except one; as what has raised hymns and canticles of praise from every corner of the earth bears to what has given birth to anathema, impiety, execration, and blasphemy; as what pictures the universe to me as one unique and immense family, with God as the father of us all, bears to what represents mankind as divided into small sections and possessed by a host of wild malignant spirits who put daggers in their right hand and torches in their left and incite them to murder, pillage, and destruction. The centuries to come will continue to beautify the one picture with their most glowing colours while the other is more and more obscured by the darkest shadows. While human cults continue to disgrace themselves in the eyes of all people by their extravagances and crimes, natural religion will be crowned with even greater glory and it will perhaps be recognized everywhere and compel universal allegiance. Then men will form one community from which they will banish those strange laws which seem to have been conceived with the sole purpose of burdening us with sin and guilt, then they will listen only to the voice of nature and they will become simple and virtuous. O man, how have you managed to make of yourself the unhappy being that you are? How I pity you and how I love you! I have been carried away, I know, by compassion and tenderness and I have promised you a happiness which you have already forsworn and which has escaped you for ever.

LETTER ON THE BLIND
(Published in 1749)

As to me it has always been very clear, that the state of our organs and our senses has a great influence on our metaphysics and our morality; and that our most intellectual ideas, in a great measure, depend on the conformation and texture of our bodies, I put some questions to the blind man concerning the vices and virtues. I immediately perceived that he had a violent aversion to theft; possibly for two reasons, it being an easy matter to steal from him without his perceiving it; and still more, perhaps, that he could be immediately seen, were he to go about filching. Not that he is at any loss to secure himself against that sense which he knows we have above him, or that he is but awkward at hiding what he might steal. Modesty he makes no great account of. He would scarce understand the use of apparel, were it not for the weather; and he frankly owns, he cannot think why one part of the body is covered more than another, still less, how, among these parts, the preference is given to some, which, from their use, and the indispositions to which they are subject, ought rather to be kept free. Though living in an age when philosophy has rid us of a great number of prejudices, I don't think we shall ever go such a length as to set aside the prerogatives of modesty so absolutely as this blind man. Diogenes would have been no philosopher on his account.

As of all the external signs which raise our pity and ideas of pain, the blind are affected only by complaint, I have, in general, no high thoughts of their sympathy and tenderness. What difference is there to a blind man between him who is making water, and him whose blood is gushing out, but makes no complaint? And we ourselves; where is our compassion, when distance, or the smallness of objects, render them the same to us, as the want of sight does to the blind? So near akin are our virtues to our manner of sensation, and the degree in which external things affect us! Nay, I make no doubt but that, setting the law aside, many a one could sooner kill a man at such a distance as to seem no bigger than a swallow, than cut an ox's throat with his own hands. We pity a horse in pain, and we make nothing of crushing an ant; and still is it not by the same principle that we are moved? Ah, Madam, how different is the morality of the blind from ours? How different would that of a deaf man likewise be from his? And how deficient, to say nothing more, would our morality appear to one with a sense more than we have?

Our metaphysics and theirs agree no better. How many of their principles are mere absurdities to us, and vice versa? Concerning this, I might enter into a detail, which I am pretty certain would entertain you, but which a set of exceptious men exclaim against, as profaneness and infidelity, as if it was in my power to make the blind perceive things otherwise than they do. I shall therefore only observe one thing and that, I believe, everyone must allow; it is, that the mighty argument drawn from the wonders of nature, is a very weak one to the blind. The facility with which we, as it were, create fresh objects, by means of a small glass, is something more incomprehensible to them than constellations, from the sight of which they are totally excluded. That lucid globe, moving from east to west, astonishes them less than a small fire, which they are able to make greater and less: seeing matter in a much more abstract manner than we, they are less indisposed to believe that it thinks.

A man who has seen but a day or two must, among a blind people, either be silent, or be looked upon as brain-sick. He would be every day acquainting them with some new mystery, which would be such only to them, and thus free-thinkers would oppose it tooth and nail. Might not the champions of religion greatly avail themselves of such a stubborn infidelity, which, however just in some respects, is yet so very ill-grounded? Be pleased only to dwell a little upon this supposition. It will bring to your mind, under a borrowed imagery, the history and persecution of those whose misfortune it has been to find out truth in an age of darkness, and who imprudently made it their business to spread it among their blind contemporaries; and their most envenomed were those, who, from their class and education, one would have thought least remote from such opinions.

Translation published about 1750.

Printed for J. Barker, Drury Lane.

FROM A LETTER ON THE DEAF AND DUMB
(Published 1750)

IN FRENCH WE SAY THINGS IN THE ORDER IN WHICH THE MIND is obliged to consider them whatever the language employed. For example Cicero followed the laws of French syntax in his thought before obeying those of Latin in his speech.

From which it appears to me that French is of all languages the best organized, the most exact, and the most excellent, for it retains less than any other language what I may call the lispings of childhood; in other words, by avoiding inversions we have gained in clearness and precision, and these are essential qualities in writing. On the other hand, we have lost in warmth, in eloquence, and in energy. The orderly and didactic march of our language makes it peculiarly suitable for science, but those languages which permit inversions, such as Greek, Latin, Italian, and English are more suited to express the subtleties of literature. Common sense will choose French for its utterances, but the imagination and the passions will prefer the ancient tongues and those of our neighbours to ours. French is the language of society and of the schools of philosophy, but let us have Greek or Latin or English in our schools of literature, and our theatres. If truth returns to this earth, I believe French will be the language of her choice, while Greek and Latin and the other tongues will be used for fables and falsehoods. French is the language for teaching, enlightening, and convincing; Greek, Latin, Italian, and English are fit for persuading, for rousing emotions, for deceiving. Talk Greek or Latin or Italian to common folk, but talk French to the wise.

Another drawback to the languages using inversions is that the attention of the hearer is more severely taxed. In a long Latin or Greek phrase how many cases of nouns and adjectives and how many tenses there are to bear in mind, till one reaches the end of the sentence; while in French we are spared that fatigue and can understand as we go along. Ideas are presented in our speech in the order followed by the mind whether it employ the syntax of Greek or Latin. La Bruyère would tire you less in the long run than Livy; yet the one is a profound

[290]

moralist and the other a straightforward historian, but this historian wraps up his sentences so well that the mind, constantly busy unpacking them and arranging them in a logical and clear order, becomes weary, as would the strongest of arms constantly obliged to carry even a light weight. Thus, all things considered, our pedestrian language has the advantage over the others of being both useful and pleasant.

> Taken in great part from the translation of Beatrix Tollemache in *Diderot's thoughts on Art and Style*.

THE ENCYCLOPÆDIA
(Published 1751–1765)

Diderot the forerunner of technical teaching

ART S.M. (ENCYCLOPÆDIC ORDER. UNDERSTANDING. MEMORY. Natural Science. Applied Science. Art) Abstract metaphysical term. Originally observations were made of the nature, purpose, uses, and qualities of beings and their symbols; later the term art or science was applied to the centre or point of junction to which observations are related in order to form a system of principles, methods, and rules tending towards co-ordination. That, in general terms, is what an art is. *Example:* People pondered the use of words and then invented the word *grammar*. Grammar is the name given to the system of principles and methods applied to a certain subject; the subject in this case is articulate sound. The same applies to other arts and sciences.

ORIGIN OF ARTS AND SCIENCES: Arts and sciences derive from man's industry being applied to natural phenomena, whether for his needs, his comfort, his amusement, or just his curiosity. Our specialized observations and reflections on any subject are called either an art or a science according to the nature of what logicians would call their formal object. If it involves doing, the body of principles and observations relating to it constitutes an art: if, on the contrary, the object is one which involves examination and thought about its various aspects, the body of principles and observations is called a science. Metaphysics is thus a science while ethics is an art. The same distinction applies to theology and pyrotechnology.

THEORY AND PRACTICE OF ARTS: It follows from the foregoing that all arts must have both a theoretical and a practical side. The theory of an art consists merely of unapplied knowledge whereas the practice of it involves the habitual and instinctive application of the same knowledge. It is difficult, almost impossible, to progress very far in the practice of an art without any theory, and conversely it is hard to have a real grasp of the theory without some practical experience. In every art there are a great many things connected with material, instruments, and technique which are only learnt by use. Practice provides the physical phenomena and shows up the practical difficulties and it is the task of theory to explain the phenomena and solve the difficulties. It follows from this that in order to speak intelligently about his art, an artist must be able to bring his reason to bear on it.

DISTINCTION BETWEEN MECHANICAL AND LIBERAL ARTS: If one examines the products of various forms of art it is clear that some of them owe more to the mind of the artist than to his manual efforts while with others it is the opposite. This difference gives rise to two things: the fact that some arts are conceded a higher place in the scale of values than others, and the division into liberal arts and mechanical arts. Although this division is basically sound it has had the unfortunate effect of causing certain highly estimable and very useful people to be despised and of encouraging in us a very natural laziness which has already led us too easily to believe that a close application in studies of material things, particular experiments and the like is in some way a derogation of human dignity and further that to practise, or even to study, the *mechanical* arts is to lower oneself to subjects in which research is laborious, thought undignified, and exposition difficult. Occupation with them is considered to impart a slur and is moreover wearisome for their number is incalculable, and their value infinitesimal. *Minui majestatem mentis humanæ, si in experimentis et rebus particularibus. . . .* (Bacon—*Novum Organum*). This prejudice has tended to fill cities with intellectual snobs and useless contemplatives and the countryside with petty tyrants who are ignorant, idle, and haughty. It was not subscribed to by Bacon, one of the first geniuses of England, nor by Colbert, one of France's greatest ministers, nor by men of intelligence and wisdom in any age. Bacon regarded the history of the *mechanical arts* as the most important branch of true philosophy and was therefore not the man to disdain the practice of them. Colbert regarded the establishment of industries and factories as the surest source of wealth for a country. In the opinion of modern thinkers with sound ideas on the values of things, the man who gave France all her engravers, painters, sculptors, and artists of all sorts, who beat the English at the knitting-machine, the Genoese at making velvet, and the Venetians at glass-blowing, certainly did no less for the State than those who fought and

[293]

vanquished her enemies. In the eyes of the philosopher there is perhaps more merit in having produced the Le Bruns, the Le Sueurs, and the Audrans, in having painted and engraved the battle of Alexandria and woven the victories of our generals into tapestries than in having actually won the victories. If we put the real benefits derived from the highest science and most widely honoured arts on the one side of the scales, and on the other side those derived from the mechanical arts, we shall find that the relative esteem in which the two sides are held will in no way correspond with their true usefulness, and that far more praise is given to those who spend their time in making us think that we are happy than to those who exert themselves in seeing that we are so in fact. A strange set of standards which requires men to be usefully employed yet disdains one who is useful!

OBJECTS OF ART IN GENERAL: Man is only the minister or interpreter of nature: he is limited to what he knows, either from experience or as a result of reflection, about his surroundings. His arm, however strong and supple it may be, can achieve but little unaided: to achieve greater things man requires tools and knowledge. Tools are additional muscles to his arm, and knowledge is new energy for his mind. The object of all *art* in general, or of any system of laws tending towards a special end, is to superimpose on a basis provided by nature certain determinate forms. This natural basis can be either matter or thought, some emanation of the human brain or some manifestation of nature itself. In the *mechanical arts,* which I emphasize all the more here because others have neglected them, *men's capabilities are limited to bringing together or separating natural objects. Whether he can achieve all things or nothing, depending upon whether the bringing together or separating is or is not possible.* (See Bacon's *Novum Organum.*)

NOTES FOR A GENERAL TREATISE ON THE MECHANICAL ARTS: Very often little is known of the origin of mechanical arts and not much more of their history. This is the natural outcome of the contempt felt in all ages and by all nations, whether scholarly or warlike, for those who engage in them. Accordingly one has to fall back on philosophic speculation and, starting from some likely hypothesis or some fortuitous event, work one's way up to the present time. I will explain this by an example which I prefer to take from the *mechanical arts,* which are less known than from the *liberal arts* which have received much wider fame under a variety of forms. Supposing nothing were known of the origin of glass-making or paper-making, what would a philosopher do if he proposed to write a history of these arts? He might imagine a scrap of linen fallen by chance into a vessel of water and remaining there until it was dissolved, so that instead of a piece of cloth in the bottom of the vessel when it was emptied there was nothing to be seen but a sort of sediment and perhaps a few threads to indicate that the raw material of the sediment had once been in the form of linen. As for glass-making, he might imagine that man's earliest habitations were made of baked earth or brick: now it is impossible to bake bricks at any great heat without some of the material becoming vitrified; that, therefore, might be the form in which glass first became known. But what a difference between that dirty, greenish scale and the clear transparency of plate-glass! Nevertheless that is the sort of chance circumstance from which the philosopher will start in order to arrive at the point reached to-day in the art of glass-making.

ADVANTAGES OF THIS METHOD: Starting off like this, the progress of an art would be presented more clearly and more instructively than it would be by the actual history if it were known. The obstacles which had to be surmounted in order to perfect the art would appear in an entirely natural order, and the synthetic explanation of the successive steps in its development would make the process intelligible to even the most ordinary brains and would set artists on the right road in their search for perfection.

ORDER TO BE FOLLOWED IN SUCH A TREATISE: With regard to the order in which such a treatise should be presented, I think the best thing would be to relate the arts to natural phenomena. A comprehensive list of the latter would give rise to many unknown *arts.* Many more would arise from a circumstantial examination of the different aspects of the same phenomena. The first of these requires an extensive knowledge of natural history, and the second demands a considerable ability in dialectic. A treatise on the *arts,* therefore, is not, as I see it, the task for an ordinary man. Don't let it be imagined that the ideas I have put forward are profitless and that I am promising mankind merely imaginary discoveries. After remarking in company with a philosopher whom I never tire of praising, what I am never tired of saying, that natural science is incomplete without the arts, after having called upon the naturalists to crown their work in the animal, vegetable, and mineral kingdoms with some experience of the mechanical arts, I make bold to follow his example and add: *Ergo rem quam ago, non opinionem, sed opus esse; eamque non sectae alicujus, aut placiti, sed utilitatis esse et amplitudinis immensae fundamenta.* This is no mere system; these are no mere human fancies: they are the finding of experience and the foundations of a vast edifice. Anyone who thinks differently is only trying to narrow the scope of our studies and inhibit the human brain. Many of our fields of study we owe to chance: chance has opened up some of the most important ones without our ever having sought them; can we therefore assume that we shall find nothing new when we add our efforts to its caprice and bring some order and method into our researches. If we now possess secrets hitherto undreamed-of, and if history may serve as a guide, why should the future not hold for us secrets of which at present we have no inkling? If one had said a few centuries ago to the sort of people who measure possibilities by the restricted standards of their own genius and who cannot imagine anything they do not know, that there existed a powder which could split rocks and knock down even the thickest walls at fantastic distances, of which a small quantity buried in the earth could shake the ground, forcing its way to the surface and leaving a crater large enough to swallow a town, all they would have done would have been to compare these effects with those obtainable by wheels, pulleys, levers, counterweights and the other mechanical devices they knew, and pronounce the powder a myth or else say that only lightning or the force which produces earthquakes, and which cannot be imitated by man, would be capable of performing such terrifying prodigies. That is how the great philosopher put it to his own age and to all ages that followed. Still following his example, let us go on to ask how much false reasoning would have been caused by the projected machine to raise water by the use of fire, as it was first attempted in London, particularly if the inventor had had the modesty to admit to being ignorant of mechanics? If such were the only judges of inventions in the

[296]

world, nothing great or small would ever be achieved. Let those then who hasten to pronounce upon new inventions which have no implicit contradiction, and which are very often no more than slight modifications of existing machines bespeaking no more ability than that of a skilled worker; let those, I say, who are so limited as to classify such inventions as impossibilities, understand that they themselves do not know enough to be able to guess at the truth—As Lord Chancellor Bacon would say to them: *Qui sumpta*, or less pardonable still, *qui neglecta ex his quae praesto sunt conjectura, ea aut impossibilia, aut minus verisimilia, putet; eum scire debere se non satis doctum, ne ad optandum quidem commode et apposite esse.*

ANOTHER REASON FOR RESEARCH: A thought which should encourage us even more in our researches and determine us to study our surroundings closely is that centuries have passed by without men's having seen things which were, so to speak, under their noses. Printing and engraving are examples. How strange a thing is the human mind! When it is a question of research, it mistrusts its own powers and surrounds itself with difficulties of its own creation so that its quest appears impossible, but when things come to light by chance, it cannot understand why for so long it has not even been looking for them, and then it is sorry.

REMARKABLE DIFFERENCE BETWEEN MACHINES: Having put forward my ideas about a philosophical treatise on art in general, I shall pass on to some particular observations on the method of dealing with certain mechanical arts. One sometimes uses an extremely complicated machine in order to produce an apparently simple result; in other cases a really very simple machine is used for quite complicated performances. In the first case, the effect it is required to produce being easily understood and the knowledge of it not cluttering the brain or overtaxing the memory, we will start by naming the result and then proceed to describe the machine which achieves it. In the second case, on the other hand, it will be more to the point to start with the machine and then study the effect. The effect of a clock is to divide time into equal portions by the use of a hand which travels slowly and at a uniform speed in accordance with a fixed plan. If therefore I were showing a clock to someone who had not seen one before I should first of all teach him what it did and only after that come to the mechanism. I should be very careful not to follow the same course with someone who asked me what knitting was, or cloth, drugget, velvet, or satin. I should start here with the process involved in these manufactures. Once that is understood, the product of the machine becomes discernible in a flash, which would not be the case without the preliminary explanations. To convince oneself of the soundness of these observations one has only to try to give an exact definition of *gauze*, assuming one has no notion of gauze-making machinery.

GEOMETRY OF THE ARTS: It will be freely admitted that there are but few artists who do not need to know the elements of mathematics, but a paradox not so readily seen is that in many cases such knowledge would be harmful to them if their wide practical familiarity with physical things were not there as a corrective to theory—knowledge of places, positions, irregular figures, substances, and their characteristics, elasticity, rigidity, friction, consistency, durability, effects of air, water, cold, heat, dryness, etc. It is clear that academical mathematics consist only of the simpler and less involved elements of the mathematics of workshops. There is no such lever in real life as Varignon imagines in his propositions; there is no natural lever of which all the conditions can be brought to calculation. Among these conditions there are many of great practical importance which, though they are appreciable, cannot be measured by even the most precise mathematical computation. From this it follows that one whose knowledge of science is purely theoretical is usually a pretty clumsy fellow, while an artist whose knowledge of science is only practical is but a very limited craftsman. But, it seems to me, experience shows that an artist can more easily dispense with theory than any man, no matter what he be, can do without a certain measure of practical knowledge. The whole question of friction, for example, has remained, in spite of calculations, a matter of experience and experiment. How far would theory take us on its own? How many bad machines are designed every day by people who imagine that levers and wheels and pulleys and ropes work in a machine as they do on paper and who, having no practical experience, know nothing of the difference between an actual machine and its sectional drawing. Another observation which we shall make here, since it fits the occasion, is that there are machines which work perfectly well on a small scale but will not work on a large scale and, conversely, some which work all right on a large scale but will not function on a small scale. Among the latter must be classified, I think, all those of which the effect is mainly dependent on a considerable weight in the component parts, or on the force of reaction of a fluid, or on some considerable quantity of elastic material to which the machines are to be applied: in miniature the weight of the parts is reduced, the reaction of the fluid becomes hardly noticeable, the forces counted upon disappear, and the machine is ineffective. But as in the size of a machine there is a point, if one may so express it, beyond which it will be without effect, so there is another point beyond which, or short of which, it will not produce the greatest effect of which its mechanism is capable. Every machine has, in mathematical parlance, a dimension of maximum efficiency just as, in the construction of it, each part considered in relation to its most nearly perfect functioning is of a size determined by the other parts; all things are of a size determined, with a view to their most nearly perfect functioning, by the machine of which they are part, by the use to which they are to be put, and by a host of other factors. But, it will be asked, what is this point in the size of a machine above or below which it is either too large or too small? What is the true and absolute size of a really good watch, or a perfect mill, or the best possible ship? It is for the experimental science of centuries, assisted by the most accurate theoretical work, to provide an approximate answer to these questions, and I am convinced that a satisfactory answer is impossible to obtain from either of the branches of science working separately and very difficult when they are united.

THE LANGUAGE OF ART: I find the language of art very imperfect in two respects, the lack of accurate terms and the multiplicity of synonyms. There are some tools which have a number of names, while others have nothing but the generic term, *engine, machine,* etc., with no specific qualification; sometimes the smallest difference is enough to make the artist abandon the generic term and invent a special name, at others some instrument, peculiar both in form and in use, has no name or else shares a name with some other instrument with which it has nothing in common. It is desirable that more attention should be paid to the analogy between shapes and uses. Geometricians use more figures than names, but in the language of the arts, hammers, pliers, buckets, spades, etc., have almost as many names as there are crafts. The language changes very largely from one to another. I am convinced, however, that the most obscure processes and the most complicated machines could be explained in a few ordinary, familiar words, if one made up one's mind not to employ technical terms except where they represent particular ideas. One ought surely to be convinced of the truth of my contention when one considers that complicated machines are no more than a combination of simple machines, that the number of simple machines is limited, and that, in the explanation of any process, every movement of it can be reduced, without any great inaccuracy, to either a linear movement or a rotary movement. What is needed, then, is that a sound logician, familiar with the arts, should take their grammar in hand. The first thing he would have to do would be to fix the relative values of big, large, medium, narrow, thick, thin, small, light, etc. In order to do that he would have to try to find a constant in nature, or fix the mean values of height, size, and strength of man and relate to them all the existing vague expressions of quantity, or at least prepare a comparative table and invite artists to make their various languages conform to it. The second step would be to consider the differences and resemblances between one instrument and another, or between one process and another, and decide whether they should retain a common name or be given different ones. I have no doubt that whoever undertakes this task will find fewer new words to be introduced than synonyms to be got rid of, and more difficulty in defining common terms, such as *grace* in painting, a *knot* in lace-making, or a *groove* in a number of arts, than in explaining the most complicated machinery. It is the lack of exact definitions and their multiplicity rather than the variety of motions in the processes that makes clear speaking about the arts so difficult. The second difficulty can be remedied only by familiarizing oneself with the subjects; they are well worth it both from the practical advantage gained and on account of the honour they do to the human mind. In what physical or metaphysical system will one find more intelligence, more wisdom, more system than in a machine for spinning gold thread, or making stockings, or lace, or gauze, or in clothworking or the manufacture of silk. What mathematical exposition is more complicated than the mechanism of some clocks or the processes through which hemp passes or the silkworm's cocoon before either gives a workable thread. What more beautiful, more delicate, more singular projection is there than that of a pattern held by the cords of a simple[1] and passing from them on to the threads of the warp. What has anyone ever conceived in any field whatsoever more subtle than the shading of velvet. I should never be done if I undertook the task of citing all the marvels that manufacturing processes have to show to those whose eyes are neither too familiar nor too dull to see.

With the English philosopher I will stop at the three inventions, unknown to the ancients, whose inventors, to the shame of modern history and poetry are scarcely known: I mean the art of printing, the discovery of gunpowder, and of the properties of a magnetized needle. What a complete revolution these three discoveries made in the field of letters, in the art of war and in that of navigation! The magnetized needle guided our vessels into hitherto unknown parts of the globe; printing made possible the exchange of ideas between scientists all over the world and for all time to come; gunpowder has given birth to all those masterpieces of architecture which guard our frontiers and those of our enemies; these three arts have, one might almost say, changed the face of the earth.

Let us at last give the artists their due. The liberal arts have adequately sung their own praises; they might now use what voice they have left to celebrate the mechanical arts. It is for the liberal arts to lift the mechanical arts from the contempt in which prejudice has kept them so long, and it is for the patronage of kings to protect them from the poverty in which they still languish. Artisans have believed themselves contemptible because people have looked down on them; let us teach them to have a better opinion of themselves; that is the only way to obtain more nearly perfect results from them. We need a man to rise up in the academies and go down to the workshops and gather material about the arts to be set out in a book which will persuade artists to read, philosophers to think on useful lines, and the great to make at last some worthwhile use of their authority and their wealth.

[1] Set of cords in a draw loom holding the pattern. Edgar & Burnet Dictionary.

A suggestion which we make bold to advance to scientists is to practise what they themselves preach to us and not to judge things too hurriedly nor to condemn an invention as useless because it has not in its early stages all the advantages one might ask of it. Would not Montaigne, an extremely philosophic man be it said, blush if he were amongst us now at having written that firearms were of so little effect, apart from the shock to the ears, which people already scarcely noticed, that he hoped the use of them would soon be abandoned? Would he not have shown greater wisdom had he encouraged men of his day to find as a substitute for the slow-match and the wheel-lock some device which more nearly corresponded with the swift action of powder, or if he had predicted that such a device would one day be invented? Put Bacon in the place of Montaigne and you will see him examine the material philosophically and prophesy, I make bold to say, grenades, mines, guns, bombs, and the whole gamut of military explosives. But Montaigne is by no means the only philosopher to have pronounced hasty judgments on the possibility or impossibility of machines. Did not Descartes, that extraordinary genius whose fate it was to mislead as well as to lead, and others as worthy as the author of the *Essais*, pronounce the mirror of Archimedes to be a mere fable? Yet that very mirror is on view to all scientists in the *Jardin du Roi*, and the effects it produces in the hands of M. de Buffon, who discovered it, leave one in no doubt about its effects on the walls of Syracuse when it was in the hands of Archimedes. Such notable examples are surely enough to make us wary.

We invite artists for their part to consult with scientists and not to allow their discoveries to die with them. They must realize that it is a theft from society to keep useful knowledge secret and that to put individual before public interests in such cases is no less blameworthy than in a thousand others where they would not hesitate to speak out. If they are forthcoming they will rid themselves of a number of delusions, particularly the one under which they almost all labour, that their art has reached the highest peak of perfection. Their lack of knowledge often leads them to blame their material for what is in fact a limitation in themselves. Obstacles appear insurmountable to them as soon as they experience difficulty in seeing a way over them. Let us experiment: let every one join in the experiments, the artist offering his manual skill, the academician his knowledge and advice, and the rich man the cost of time and materials. Then, very shortly, our arts and manufactures will have all the superiority we wish over those of other countries.

THE SUPERIORITY OF ONE INDUSTRY OVER ANOTHER: What will give, however, one industry superiority over another is first and foremost the quality of the materials used. To this must be added speed and perfection in execution. The quality of the materials is a matter of careful choice. Speed and perfection in execution depend entirely on the number of workers employed. Where they are numerous, each process is the job of a different man. One man performs and always will perform one operation and one only; another will always perform some other operation; this results in each operation being done well and swiftly and in the best article still being the cheapest. Besides, taste and workmanship will necessarily improve where there is a large number of workers, because it is unlikely that among them there will be none capable of thinking and arranging things and finally discovering the one way by which they can surpass their fellows, be it a way to save material or time or to improve the industry by means of a new machine or a more convenient movement. If foreign manufacturers cannot beat those of Lyons it is not because they do not know how we work: everyone has the same methods, the same silks, and much the same way of doing things, but it is only at Lyons that you will find thirty thousand workers all engaged in the same manufacture.

We could carry this article even further, but what we have just said will be enough for those who are capable of thinking, while for the others we should never be able to say enough. Some rather heavy metaphysical passages will be found in it, but that could not be avoided. We had to speak about art in general and our propositions therefore had to be general. It is only common sense that the more general a proposition is the more abstract it must be, abstraction being the extension of a truth by removing from it the details which limit it to the particular. If we had been able to spare the reader these thorny passages we should also have saved ourselves a great deal of work.

(*Oeuvres Completes*, 13th Vol.)

NECESSITY FOR AN ENCYCLOPÆDIA AND
METHOD OF COMPILING ONE

W HEN WE COME TO CONSIDER THE VAST AMOUNT OF material in an encyclopædia, one thing emerges very clearly: it cannot be the work of a single man. How could one man in the short span of his life succeed in knowing and expounding the whole system of nature and the arts, when the 'de la Crusca' academicians, a numerous and learned body, spent forty years producing their vocabulary, and our own academicians spent sixty on their dictionary before they even produced a first edition? And yet, when you think of it, what is an etymological dictionary, what is the most perfectly achieved vocabulary, but a very accurate list of the headings to be filled in by a descriptive encyclopædia?

A single man, you will say, is master of everything that exists; he has at his disposal all the riches that other men have already amassed. I cannot subscribe to this idea: I do not believe that it is given to one man to know all that can be known, to use everything that can be used, to see everything there is to see, and to understand everything there is to understand. Were a descriptive encyclopædia to be no more than a methodical arrangement of the mere elements of these things, I would ask again, 'Who is to provide these elements? Are they to be the first attempts of a student or the *chef d'œuvre* of a master?'

But as a final proof of the difficulty of one man's producing an encyclopædia of general knowledge it is only necessary to emphasize the difficulties of producing a mere dictionary.

A universal dictionary is a work purporting to fix the meanings of the words of a language by defining those that can be defined, and giving a short, exact, clear, and precise enumeration of the qualities or ideas associated with them. The only good definitions are those which muster all the essential attributes of the object denoted by the word. But is it given to everyone to know and understand these attributes? Is the art of definition a common one? Are we not all to some extent in precisely the same case as children who, with the greatest precision, apply names to large numbers of things without in the least being able to substitute for the words an accurate list of the qualities or ideas which they represent? So it comes about that we are met by a host of unforeseen difficulties when we try to define even the commonest expressions. We discover at every turn that those we understand least are the very ones we use most! What is the reason for this curious phenomenon? It is just that we are always calling something such-and-such but are hardly ever required to say just exactly what such-and-such is. Mostly we deal with concrete objects where common usage is a sufficient guide and we are only repeating what we have heard and said all our lives. But it is quite a different matter when it comes to formulating general conceptions which embrace without exception a certain number of particular cases. Only the deepest thought and an astonishingly wide knowledge can be a sure guide then. I will make this clear with an example. Without any danger of being misunderstood, we apply to a vast number of all sorts of things the description *de luxe*. But what is this *luxe* we so gaily attribute to so many different objects? That is a question to which no satisfactory answer is forthcoming except after considerable discussion, and this the people who use the expression *de luxe* with the greatest sureness of touch have not undertaken and are perhaps not even competent to undertake.

Every term has to be defined, except radicals: that is, except terms designating simple sensations and the most general abstractions. If anything is left out, the dictionary is incomplete. If they are all included who is to define the adjective *conjugate* but a geometrician, or the verb *conjugate* but a grammarian? Who is to define *azimuth* but an astronomer, *epic* but a man of letters, *exchange* but a financier, *vice* but a moralist, *hypostasis* but a theologian, *metaphysics* but a philosopher, *chisel* but an artisan? From this I conclude that if the *Académie Française* did not assemble at its meetings men of every variety of knowledge and skill, it would be impossible for it to avoid either leaving out numbers of expressions which would be sought in vain in its dictionary, or including some wrong, incomplete, absurd and even ridiculous definitions.

I am well aware that my feelings on this subject are not shared by those who converse about everything and know nothing. They are not in our Academies and they never will be, because they are not fit to be, but they have a say in the

L* [305]

allocation of vacancies nevertheless, and, presuming to set bounds to the aims of the *Académie Française*, they were almost outraged at the election of the Mairans, the Maupertuis, and the d'Alemberts. Nor do they know that the first time one of these men spoke it was with the object of rectifying the definition of the word '*midi.*' To listen to them one would think they were trying to limit the knowledge of the language and the scope of the *Dictionnaire de l'Académie* to an insignificant number of words familiar to themselves. Moreover, if they looked carefully they would find, even among these words, plenty such as tree, animal, plant, flower, vice, virtue, truth, force, and law, for the definition of which they would be obliged to appeal for help to a philosopher, a lawyer, an historian, or a naturalist, to wit, a man who knew what are the concrete and abstract qualities which make something what it is and put it in a class with others of its kind or segregate it as unique.

We can conclude then that a good dictionary will never be achieved without the help of a great variety of talent, because the definitions of the names of things are no different from the definitions of the things themselves, and these things can only be properly defined or accurately described by those who have made a long study of them. If this is the case with a dictionary, then how much more will be required for the production of a work which, far from limiting itself to mere definitions, is to explain in detail everything connected with each item.

A universal encyclopædia of science and art cannot therefore be the work of one man. I will go further and say that it cannot be the work of one of the existing literary or learned societies, nor even of all of them together.

The *Académie Française* could only supply the Encyclopædia with material relating to language and its use: the *Académie des Inscriptions et Belles-Lettres* could only offer its knowledge of ancient and modern secular history, chronology, geography, and literature; the Sorbonne could provide only information on theology and the history of religion and superstition; the *Académie des Sciences* could only speak of mathematics, natural history, physics, chemistry, medicine, anatomy, etc.; the *Académie de Chirurgie* would be confined to surgery; that of painting to material on painting, engraving, sculpture, drawing, architecture, etc.: the *Université* could only answer for what are called the humanities—scholastic philosophy, jurisprudence, typography, etc.

Run through the other bodies which I may have omitted and you will see that while each of them concerns itself with one particular subject, which is no doubt within the scope of an encyclopædia, they ignore a large number of others which should also be included, and you will not find a single one to supply you with the overall knowledge which you require. Go one better and extract a contribution from all of them; you will soon see how much is missing and you will be forced to call upon large numbers of men of all classes. Valuable men, these, but the doors of the academies are none the less closed against them on account of their status. There are too many members of these learned bodies for just one branch of knowledge; but there are not enough learned bodies to cover the whole field.

Undoubtedly what one would get from each body individually would be very useful and the sum total of their contributions would set the Encyclopædia well on its way to completion. That is actually a task which would direct their activities towards the achievement of this work and which ought to be required of them. I distinguish two methods of scientific study: the first increases the sum of knowledge by research, and those who are engaged in it merit the title of inventor: the second assembles all discoveries and relates them to each other so that they are more widely available to the public who, according to their capacity, can thus partake of the enlightenment of the age—those who are engaged in this branch are the academic authors, and their task is not without its difficulties. I contend that if all the learned societies scattered over Europe were to busy themselves with assembling and relating modern and ancient knowledge and publishing complete methodical treatises as a result, things could not help being better. Compare the weighty quarto volumes of the *Académie des Sciences*, compiled in the prevailing tradition of our best-known academies, with eight or ten volumes produced according to my idea, and see which you would choose. The latter would contain a vast amount of excellent material gathered from widely scattered sources where it would otherwise remain useless, just as scattered coals will never make a fire, and of these ten volumes not more than one or two would suffice to contain all the information collected from the old academic books. Take a look at the *Mémoires* of the *Académie des Inscriptions* and work out how much of it you would extract for a scientific treatise. What shall I say about the *Transactions Philosophiques* or the *Actes des Curieux de la Nature*? All these top-heavy collections are beginning to totter, and the first abridger with taste and ability could bring them tumbling down. And that ought to be the end of them.

After serious consideration I think that the special aim of the academician might be to perfect the branch of science which he had adopted and to win immortality for himself by publishing non-academic work—i.e. not forming part of the Academy's collected publications—in his own name. Then the task of the Academy would be to gather together and digest, clarify, and co-ordinate all the published works on each subject and from them to publish a series of treatises in which each subject would be given the space it merited and no more. How many of the reports which swell our collections would be represented by even one line in such a series?

An Encyclopædia should help in the achievement of such a project, embracing not only the various subjects dealt with by our academies but all branches of human knowledge. It is a work which can only be done by an association of men of letters and artists, working separately, each one in his own sphere, and linked only by their common concern for the human race and by mutual goodwill.

I say 'an association of men of letters and artists' so as to include all kinds of talents. But I want all its members to work separately, because there is no society in existence which can provide all the necessary information and because the most certain way to ensure that a work is always in progress and never completed is to establish a society to do it. Societies hold meetings; there are intervals between meetings and they only last a matter of hours; a part of these few hours is wasted in discussion, and so the simplest matters take months to resolve. To quote a member of the *Academie* whose ordinary conversation contains more good sense than most authors manage to cram into their treatises, by working independently we can finish the twelve volumes of the Encyclopædia while the *Académie* is still at letter 'A' of its Dictionary; whereas if the authors of the Encyclopædia were to hold encyclopædic sessions as the *Académie* holds academic sessions, the Dictionary would be finished while the Encyclopædia was still at the letter 'A.' And he was right.

I add 'linked by their common concern for the human race and by mutual goodwill' because, being the purest motives, they are the most enduring. We feel a deep contentment with our task, we become enthusiastic and undertake for our colleagues or friends that which nothing would normally induce us to do, and I make bold to say from my own experience that success is more likely to crown our efforts. The Encyclopædia material has been gathered together in a comparatively short time. It was no base interest which united and sped its authors on their way; they saw their efforts backed by the majority of men of letters, from whom they could expect help, and only obstructed by those who had not the necessary ability to contribute one decent page.

If the Government interferes in a work of this sort it will bring failure. It should use its influence to encourage the enterprise and no more. A sovereign can with one word cause a palace to grow where before there was only grass, but a group of men of letters can not be treated in the same way as a gang of labourers. An Encyclopædia cannot be made to order. It is the sort of work that needs dogged persistence rather than an enthusiastic start. At Court, enterprises of this kind are mooted incidentally in the course of conversation and there is never enough real interest to prevent their being forgotten in the general confusion of a mass of other more or less important matters. Literary projects conceived in high places are like the leaves of the forest, which are born in spring, dry up in the autumn, and in the winter fall one on top of the other in the seclusion of the forest, having achieved nothing but the nourishment of a few sterile plants. From an infinity of examples known to me I will cite only one. Some experiments on the hardness of different kinds of wood were planned. The idea was to strip the trees of their bark and to allow them to die standing. The trees were stripped and duly died, and then were apparently cut down; that is to say, everything was done except the experiments on the hardness of wood. How could it have been otherwise. Six years had to elapse between the first order given and the last one to be carried out. If an individual to whom a sovereign confides a task happens to die or fall from favour, work ceases and is not resumed, because ordinarily ministers do not carry on the projects of their predecessors although this might give them if not greater glory than initiating their own projects at least a much rarer kind of glory. Individuals are always in a hurry to see a return for their outlay, but governments are subject to no such economic urgency. I wonder what evil genius it is that makes men deal less honestly with princes than with private individuals. They undertake the simplest tasks and demand the highest compensation for them. Uncertainty as to whether what they are doing will ever be of any real use is responsible for the unbelievable idleness in the workers and, to make matters as bad as possible, kings do not sponsor projects because of their usefulness but solely for personal glorification. This means that the undertakings are on a vast scale, difficulties multiply, and more men, skill and time are proportionately necessary to surmount them, till at last almost inevitably, a revolution follows which points the moral of the fable of the schoolmaster. If the useful life of an ordinary man is no more than twenty years, that of a minister is no more than ten. In literary enterprises backed by the Government, interruptions are not only more common than they are in private enterprises but they are also more fatal. An individual at least picks up the pieces of a shattered project and stores them away against a happier day: he looks to get some return for his outlay. Governments disdain such prudence: men die and the fruits of their labour are lost beyond recovery.

But the thing which should give the greatest weight to the foregoing considerations is that an encyclopædia must be begun and completed within a reasonable time, whereas with Government projects there are always people who for sordid motives keep them going as long as possible. If the long years which the wide range of subjects would seem to necessitate were spent in the compilation of a universal encyclopædia, changes, which are by no means less swift in the sciences and particularly in the arts than in language, would render the finished project a century out of date when it appeared, just as a dictionary compiled at leisure would be of the language of another reign. Opinions grow old and die just as words do: interest in inventions grows daily weaker and finally disappears. If the work is spread over a long period the authors will have wasted their energies on passing things which will be forgotten by the time the work is finished. This is a drawback which we ourselves have encountered already, although not much time has elapsed between the appearance of our work and the time of writing. One can see a disproportion, most disconcerting in a work purporting to present all things in their true perspective, between important items which have been crowded into a small space and over-elaborated items of little real importance. In a word, the work changes its features while still in the hands of its makers, the mere lapse of time mars it more than time spent on it can improve it, and it becomes poorer by what has to be shortened, deleted, corrected or replaced rather than richer by any positive additions.

Every day new variety is added to the language of the arts, to the speech of mechanicians and workers. Suppose a man spent a part of his life in describing the arts and then, bored with such tiring work, let himself be carried away by more amusing but less profitable occupations, leaving his papers locked away in his desk. In less than twenty years instead of novelties and curiosities, eye-catching in their newness and interesting on account of their usefulness, the prevailing taste of the day and an ephemeral importance, he would find only a set of false notions, out-of-date processes, and machines long since improved or abandoned. In all his many volumes there would not be one page which would not need correction and of all the plates hardly one but would need redrawing. They would be pictures whose originals had ceased to exist. Luxury, the father of all the arts, like Saturn in the fable, amuses himself by destroying his children.

Change may be less complete and less obvious in the sciences and the liberal arts than in the mechanical arts, but change there is. Look at the encyclopædias of the last century and you will find under *aberration* no mention of its astronomical meaning, and under *electricity*, that universal boon, you will find no more than a few lines of misinformation and old-fashioned prejudice. How many terms relating to mineralogy and natural history would be in the same case! If our own encyclopædia had appeared earlier than it did we should have repeated the errors of past centuries on wheat-blight and other diseases of grain because the discoveries of M. Tillet and the work of M. Herbert are of recent date.

When dealing with natural phenomena, what can one do but scrupulously assemble all that is known about them at the time of writing? But observations and experiments are constantly acquainting us with new phenomena and new facts while reason and philosophy, comparing and combining, widen or narrow the scope of our knowledge, thus varying the accepted meanings of words, making old definitions inexact, false or incomplete, and even necessitating entirely new ones.

What will, however, make the work appear out of date and cause it to lose its appeal more than anything else, is the change in men's hearts and in national character. Now that philosophy is making such great strides, dominating everything within its province, now that its voice is heard above all others and the yoke of authority and precept is shaken off to give way to the laws of pure reason, there is hardly one fundamental, dogmatic book which remains entirely satisfactory. We realize that such books are based on man-made rules rather than on the truths of nature. People now dare to doubt Aristotle and Plato, and the time has come when works which still enjoy the highest reputation will soon lose part of it or fall entirely into oblivion. Some types of literature not modelled on real life and customs will be neglected; for they have no permanent appeal, others, kept alive by their intrinsic worth, will take on quite a new form. Such is the effect of the progress of reason, a progress which will destroy a number of existing monuments and re-erect some which have been neglected in the past—those of that rare body of men who were ahead of their times. We had, if I may so express it, contemporaries of our own in the reign of Louis XIV.

The times which have dulled our taste for criticism and controversy have also deprived part of Bayle's *Dictionnaire* of its interest. There is no author who has lost so much in some ways and gained so much in others. But if such has been his fate, imagine what would have happened to the Encyclopædia of his day! If one excepts Perrault and certain others whom the poetaster Boileau was incapable of appreciating—La Mothe, Terrasson, Boindin, and Fontenelle—under whom reason and philosophic doubt made such great strides, there was probably not a man who could have contributed a single page which we should deign to read to-day. For, let there be no mistake about it, there is a world of difference between giving birth by mere force of genius to a work which captures a nation, despite its tastes, ideas, and contemporary prejudices, and writing poetic criticism based on a genuine and considered knowledge of the heart of man, of the nature of things, and of true reason, all of which are unchanging. Genius knows no laws, but its successes do not stray far from them. Philosophy knows only laws based on the immutable and external nature of things. It is for the past century to supply examples if it is for the present one to formulate the rules.

(*Oeuvres Completes*, 19th vol.)

THE FATHER OF A FAMILY
(Written in 1758)

SCENE VI

THE FATHER, SAINT-ALBIN

SAINT-ALBIN (*entering and speaking eagerly*). Father!

(*The Father walks up and down in silence.*)

SAINT-ALBIN (*following his father and entreating him*). Father.

THE FATHER (*stopping and speaking in a grave voice*). My son, if you have not taken counsel with yourself, if reason has not brought you back to your senses, don't start adding to your offences and to my distress.

SAINT-ALBIN. My own distress consumes me. I come to you trembling. . . . I will be calm and sensible . . . yes, indeed I will. . . . I have promised it to myself.

(*The father goes on walking—*SAINT-ALBIN, *going timidly up to him, says in a low faltering voice*). You have seen her?

THE FATHER. Yes, I have seen her: she is beautiful and I imagine virtuous. But what do you want with her? To amuse yourself? I would not sanction that. If you want to make her your wife, I can only say, she is not suitable for you.

SAINT-ALBIN (*controlling himself*). She is beautiful, she is virtuous and she is not suitable for me! What sort of a wife is suitable for me then?

THE FATHER. One who by education, birth, and the size of her fortune can ensure your happiness and fulfil my expectations.

SAINT-ALBIN. And so my marriage is to be an affair of self-interest and ambition! Father, you only have one son: do not sacrifice him to such ideas, which fill the world with unhappy marriages. I need a modest and tender partner capable of teaching me to endure life's hardships, not a rich, titled wife who would add to them. Indeed, I would rather die than marry a woman such as some I have seen.

THE FATHER. I do not suggest anyone for you; but I will never allow you to be united to the one you have been mad enough to choose. I could assert my authority and say to you:

[314]

Saint-Albin, this displeases me, this shall not take place, think no more about it. But I have never asked anything of you without giving you my reasons; I have always sought your willing obedience and I still condescend to require your approval. Control yourself, then, and listen to me.

It will soon be twenty years since the first time I shed tears over you. My heart swelled with emotion for I saw in you a friend given me by nature. I gathered you into my arms from your mother's bosom, and, raising you up towards heaven, my voice mingling with your cries, I prayed thus: 'Oh God, who hast granted me this child, if I fail in the charge you have this day laid upon me, or if he does not respond to my care, have no regard for his mother's joy at his birth, but take him back.'

That is the vow which I made concerning you and me. I have never forgotten it. I did not leave you to the care of a hireling: I myself taught you to speak, to think, to feel. As you grew up I studied your propensities, I planned your education in accordance with them, and I have devoted myself tirelessly to it. What trouble I have taken to spare you any! I have arranged for your future so that it should harmonize with your talents and your tastes. I have left nothing undone which could help you to acquit yourself with distinction, and when I am about to see the fruits of my solicitude, at the very moment when I am congratulating myself on having a son whose birth promises him great advantages and whose personal qualities fit him for the most distinguished career, a crazy infatuation, a passing fancy, destroys everything; and I have to see his best years wasted, his opportunities missed, and all my expectations come to nothing. That is what I am to accept, is it? . . . You have promised yourself that?

SAINT-ALBIN. I am so miserable!

THE FATHER. You have a rich uncle who is fond of you and intends to make you his heir; a father who has devoted his life to you and who ever strives to show you his loving affection; a name, a family, good prospects for a delightful future; and you are miserable! What more do you want?

SAINT-ALBIN. Sophie; Sophie's heart and my father's consent.

THE FATHER. How dare you suggest such a thing? That I should share your folly and the shame which it would incur? What an example for other fathers and children! You expect

[315]

me to authorize, by my disgraceful weakness, social irregularities, confusion of rank and blood and the degradation of families.

SAINT-ALBIN. How miserable I am! If I do not have my loved one now I shall be forced some day to have one I do not love; for I shall never love any but Sophie. I shall constantly be comparing anyone else with her; the other will be miserable; I should be too; you will see it all and you will pine away with remorse.

THE FATHER. I shall have done my duty, and woe betide you if you fail in yours.

SAINT-ALBIN. Father, don't take Sophie away from me.

THE FATHER. Stop making this request.

SAINT-ALBIN. You have told me a hundred times that a virtuous woman is the greatest treasure heaven can bestow. I have found one and you want to deprive me of her! Father, don't take her from me. Now she knows who I am, what must she not be expecting of me? Shall Saint-Albin be less generous than Sergi? Don't take her from me; it is she who has restored virtue to my heart; she alone can keep it there.

THE FATHER. Which means that her example will succeed where mine has failed.

SAINT-ALBIN. You are my father and you are in command: when she becomes my wife there will be a new empire.

THE FATHER. What a difference there is between a lover and a husband! Inexperienced as you are you don't know that.

SAINT-ALBIN. I hope I never shall.

THE FATHER. Does any lover ever see his mistress with other eyes or differently?

SAINT-ALBIN. You have seen Sophie! . . . If I leave her for the sake of rank, position, expectations or prejudices, I shall not deserve to know her. How could you insult your son so much as to believe it of him, Father?

THE FATHER. She has not disgraced herself by yielding to your passion: imitate her yourself.

SAINT-ALBIN. Should I disgrace myself by becoming her husband?

THE FATHER. Ask the world that.

SAINT-ALBIN. In things of no importance, I am content to take the world as it is; but when the happiness of my life is at stake, when it is a question of choosing a companion . . .

[316]

THE FATHER. You will never change its ideas, so you must conform.

SAINT-ALBIN. When people upset everything, spoil everything and subordinate everything to their miserable conventions, am I to agree to it?

THE FATHER: If not they will despise you.

SAINT-ALBIN. I will flee from them . . .

THE FATHER. Their scorn will follow you, and the wife whom you will have led away will be as much to be pitied as you . . . you love her?

SAINT-ALBIN. I should think I do!

THE FATHER. Listen, then, and tremble at the fate you are preparing for her. You will find you are alone together, without position, without money, without anyone's respect. You will be seized with boredom and vexation. You will hate her, you will hurl reproaches at her, her patience and gentleness will end by embittering you, you will hate her still more, you will hate the children she has borne you and you will cause her to die of sorrow!

SAINT-ALBIN. Me!

THE FATHER. You!

SAINT-ALBIN. Never, never!

THE FATHER. Passion imagines everything is eternal; but our human nature requires that there should always be an ending.

SAINT-ALBIN. The very idea that I could stop loving Sophie! If I were capable of such a thing, I think I should begin to doubt whether I loved you.

THE FATHER. Do you want to be sure you do and to prove it? Do what I ask you.

SAINT-ALBIN. It would be useless to try, I can't. I am carried away, Father, I can't do it.

THE FATHER. You fool, you want to be a father yourself. Do you know a father's duties? If you know them, would you allow your son to do what you expect me to allow.

SAINT-ALBIN. Oh, if only I dared to reply.

THE FATHER. Answer me.

SAINT-ALBIN. You will really let me?

THE FATHER. I order you to do so.

SAINT-ALBIN. When you wanted my mother, when all the family rose up against you, when my grandfather called you an

[317]

ungrateful child and you from the bottom of your heart called him a cruel father; which of you two was in the right? My mother was virtuous and beautiful like Sophie; you loved her as I love Sophie; did you allow them to snatch her away from you, Father, and have not I a heart too?

THE FATHER. I had something to live on and your mother was well born.

SAINT-ALBIN. And it may turn out that Sophie is too.

THE FATHER. Rubbish.

SAINT-ALBIN. Something to live on! Love and poverty will satisfy me.

THE FATHER. Beware of the troubles which are in store for you.

SAINT-ALBIN. Not to have her is the only one I am afraid of.

THE FATHER. Beware of losing my affection.

SAINT-ALBIN. I should get it back.

THE FATHER. Who told you that?

SAINT-ALBIN. You would see Sophie's tears; I should clasp your knees; my children would hold their innocent arms out to you and you would never drive them away.

THE FATHER (aside). He knows me too well . . . (After a short pause, he assumes a more severe manner and tone, and says): My son, I perceive that I am wasting my breath on you, that you are no longer accessible to reason and that the method which I always feared to adopt is the only one left to me; since you drive me to it, I have no alternative. Give up this idea; I wish it and I order it with all my paternal authority.

SAINT-ALBIN. Authority! Authority! That is the only word in their vocabulary!

THE FATHER. Kindly respect it!

SAINT-ALBIN (walking to and fro). That is what they are all like. That is the way they love us. If they were our enemies what more could they do?

THE FATHER. What is that? What are you muttering to yourself?

SAINT-ALBIN (as before). They think themselves wise because they have different passions from ours.

THE FATHER. Will you be quiet.

SAINT-ALBIN. They have only given us life so that they can use it for their own purposes.

THE FATHER. Be quiet!

SAINT-ALBIN. They fill it with bitterness; and when we are unhappy what do they care? They have grown accustomed to seeing us like that.

THE FATHER. You forget who I am and to whom you are speaking. Please be quiet or beware of drawing down upon yourself the most terrible judgment of those who incur the wrath of fathers.

SAINT-ALBIN. Fathers! Fathers, indeed! There are no such things, there are only tyrants.

THE FATHER. Gracious heaven!

SAINT-ALBIN. Yes, tyrants.

THE FATHER. Leave my sight, ungrateful and unnatural child. I give you my curse: go far from me. (*The son is about to go, but he has scarcely started when his father runs after him and says*): Where are you going, unhappy child?

SAINT-ALBIN. Father.

THE FATHER (*flinging himself into an armchair, while his son takes up his position at his knees*). Am I indeed your father? Are you my son? I am nothing to you any more; I have never been anything to you. You poison my life, you long for my death. Eh! why is it so long in coming? Why am I not laid beside your mother? She has departed this life and my days of wretchedness still go on!

SAINT-ALBIN. Father!

THE FATHER. Be off! Don't let me see your tears; you rend my heart and yet I am quite unable to banish you from it.

THE NUN
(Written in 1760)

IT WAS MONSIEUR L'ABBÉ BLIN, A DOCTOR OF THE SORBONNE, who exhorted me, and Monsieur the Bishop of Alep who gave me the dress. This ceremony was not gay of itself; the day on which it was performed was one of the most sorrowful. Though the nuns thronged round to support me, twenty times I felt my knees shake, and was like to fall upon the steps of the altar. I heard nothing, I saw nothing. I was stupid; they carried me, and I went; they interrogated me, and they answered the questions for me. At length this cruel ceremony was concluded; all the strangers withdrew, and I remained among the flock to which I had just been united. My companions came round me; they embraced me and said; 'But look at my sister, how handsome she is! How this black veil relieves the paleness of her complexion! How well this bandeau becomes her! How it rounds her face! How it extends her cheeks! How this habit displays her waist and her arms. . . .' I listened to them with pain, I was distressed; at the time I found it necessary to agree with them; when I was alone in my cell I remembered their flatteries, and could not refrain from putting them to the test in my little mirror, and I thought them not altogether false. There were some honours attached to this day; they increased them on my account. I paid little attention to them; but they affected to think and say the contrary, though it was clear they had no reason. At night, on coming out from prayers, the Superior repaired to my cell. 'Troth,' said she after a little consideration, 'I know not why you expressed so much reluctance to assume this dress; it makes you a wonder, you are quite charming; Sister Susan is a very pretty nun; we shall love you the better for that. Here, let us see you walk. . . . You don't keep yourself upright enough, it is not necessary that you stoop. . . .' She set right my head, feet, hands, waist, and arms; it was almost as good as a lesson of Marcel upon the monastic graces, for every condition has its own. She then sat down and said to me: 'It is very well; but let us now talk a little seriously. Before the lapse of two years, your parents may have altered their resolution;

[320]

and even you yourself may wish to remain here when they wish to take you away; this is not impossible.'—'Madam, don't believe it.'—'You have been a long time amongst us, but you are still unacquainted with our mode of life; it certainly has its pains, but it also has its pleasures. . . .' You can imagine everything she said of the world and of the cloister, it is written everywhere, and always in the same way; for I thank God! they made me read all the monks have said of their state, which they know well, and which they detest; and of the world, which they love, against which they rail, but with which they are unacquainted.

I shall not enter into a long detail respecting my noviciate: if it were a fair specimen of the austerity of the convent, one could not have so much objection to it, but it is the most pleasant period of the monastic life. A mother of novices is the most indulgent sister that they can find. She makes it her study to divest the condition of everything that is unpleasant: it is a course of the most artful and refined seduction. She thickens the surrounding darkness, she lulls you into tranquillity, she decoys you into her snares, she fascinates you. Ours was particularly attached to me. I do not believe that any young soul without experience could be proof against this fatal art. The world has its precipices, but I don't imagine that the descent to them is so easy. If I had a cold, my presence was dispensed with at service, at penance, and at prayers; I went early to bed, I rose late, I was exempted from discipline. Conceive, sir, that there were some days in which I would have sighed for the moment of sacrificing myself. There are no distressing occurrences which pass in the world of which they do not speak to you; they arrange facts, they fabricate stories, and then it is praises without end, and the operation of the grace of God, which prevents you from incurring these humiliating disgraces. In the meanwhile, the period drew near which I had sometimes hastened by my wishes. Then I awakened from my dream; I felt my reluctance return with increased strength. I went to inform the superior, or the mother of our novices. These women take ample vengeance for the trouble you occasion them; for it is not to be thought that they have any amusement in the hypocritical part which they act, as from the foolish things which they are under the necessity of so often repeating to you, the task becomes in the end stale and disgusting to them; but they undertake it for the sake of bringing a thousand crowns into their house. This is the important object for which they lead a life of deceit, and prepare forty or fifty years of despair, and perhaps eternal misery for young innocents; for it is certain, that of every hundred nuns who die before they reach the age of fifty, there are fifty damned, exclusive of those who become foolish, stupid, or mad in the prospect.

One day, a nun of the last description happened to escape from the cell in which she was confined. I saw her. This, sir, is the moment in which my good or bad fortune must be irrevocably fixed, according as you act by me. I never saw anything so frightful. Her hair was dishevelled, and her body almost naked; she dragged iron chains; her eyes were wild, she tore her hair, she beat her breast with her fists; she ran, she roared; she imprecated upon herself and others the most dreadful curses; she wanted to throw herself out at a window. Terror seized me, I trembled at every joint, I saw my fate in that of this unfortunate wretch, and I immediately resolved in my mind to die a thousand times rather than to encounter it. They perceived the effect which this incident would have upon my spirits, and they endeavoured to prevent it. They told me I know not how many absurd and contradictory stories about this nun; that her intellects were deranged before she came to the house; that she had had a terrible fright at a critical time; that she had become subject to visions; that she thought she held intercourse with angels; that some preachers of an extravagant morality had so terrified her about the judgments of God, that her disordered brain had been turned by the description; that she saw nothing but demons, hell, and gulphs of fire; that they had been very unlucky; that it was a thing quite unheard of before in their house; and I know not what. This made no impression upon me. Every moment the mad nun recurred to my mind, and I renewed the oath of never taking a vow.

The period arrived at which it became necessary for me to show whether I could keep my word. One morning after service the superior entered my cell. She held a letter in her hand. Her looks were sorrowful and dejected. Her arms sunk; it seemed as if she had not power to lift up the letter; she looked at me; tears stood in her eyes; we were both silent; she waited till I should speak; I was tempted to begin first, but I contained myself. She asked me how I did; she observed that service had been very long to-day; that I had a little cough; that I appeared to be indisposed. To all this I answered—No, my dear mother. She still kept the letter in her hand, which was hanging down; while she was putting these questions, she put it upon her knee, and her hand in part concealed it; at last, after having put some questions respecting my father and mother, finding that I did not ask what this paper was, she said, Here is a letter. . . . When she uttered this word, I felt my heart quake, and I added in a trembling voice: Is it from my mother?—It is; take and read it. . . . —I recovered myself a little; I took the letter; I read it at first with tolerable firmness; but as I advanced, terror, indignation, resentment, contempt, succeeding one another in my breast, I displayed different tones, different voices, and different motions. Sometimes I scarcely held the paper, at other times I held it as if I meant to tear it, and at other times I grasped it with violence as if I had been tempted to twist it in my hand and throw it away.—Alas! my child, what answer shall we make to this?—Madam, you know best.—No, I do not know. The times are unfortunate, your family has sustained some losses; your sister's affairs are embarrassed; they both have a number of children; your parents impoverished themselves by marrying them, they are ruining themselves in order to support them. It is impossible that they can make any permanent settlement upon you; you have assumed the habit, they have been at some expense; by taking this step you have made them conceive some hopes; they have announced to their acquaintances that you are immediately about to commence the profession. At all events, you may depend upon every assistance which I can give you. I have never enticed any person into a convent; it is a state into which we are conducted by the voice of God, and it is extremely dangerous to blend our voice with His. I shall never attempt to speak to your heart, if grace is silent; hitherto I never have had to reproach myself with the misfortunes of any person, and I should not wish to begin with you, my child, you who are so dear to me. I have not forgotten that it was at my persuasion that you took the first steps, and I will not suffer them to take advantage of this to bring you into engagements contrary to your inclination. Let us consider then together, let us concert.

[323]

Do you wish to make profession—No, Madam.—You have no relish for the religious state?—No, Madam.—You will not obey your parents?—No, Madam.—What do you wish to be, then?—Anything but a nun. I do not wish to be one, I will not be one.—Well, you shall not be one. Let us deliberate and draw up an answer to your mother. . . . We agreed in some ideas. She wrote, and showed me the answer, which seemed to be very proper. In the meantime; they sent the director of the house to me; they sent me the doctor who had pronounced the discourse in my praise when I assumed the habit; they recommended me to the mother of the novices; I saw M. the Bishop of Alep; I had to enter the lists with some pious women whom I did not know, but who took an interest in my affairs; I had continual conferences with monks and priests; my father came, my sister wrote to me; at last my mother appeared: I resisted them all. In the meanwhile, the day was fixed for my profession: they omitted nothing to obtain my consent; but when they saw that all their solicitations were to no purpose, they resolved to proceed without it.

They shut me up in my cell, they imposed silence upon me; I was separated from all the world, abandoned to myself; and I saw that they were determined to dispose of me without consulting me any further. I did not wish to take the vows, it was a settled point with me; and all the false or real terrors which they inflicted upon me, did not shake my purpose. In the meantime I was in a most deplorable state, I did not know how long it might last; and if it ceased, I knew still less what was to become of me. Amid these uncertainties, I adopted a plan of conduct of which you will form whatever judgment, sir, you please. I saw no person, neither the superior, nor the mother of the novices, nor my companions. I sent notice to the first, pretending to be reconciled to the will of my parents; but my design was to put an end to this persecution, by rendering it notorious, and publicly to protest against the violent measures which they had in contemplation. I said that she was mistress of my fortune, that she might dispose of it according to her wishes, that she might require of me to take the vows, and I should do it. Conceive the joy which was diffused through the whole house, the caresses renewed with every species of flattery and seduction. 'God had spoken to my heart, there was no person fitter than I for the state of perfection. It was impossible for this not to happen, they had always expected it. Those did not discharge their duty with so much profit and constancy who were not really called. The mother of the novices had never seen, in any of her pupils, a call so truly characteristic; she was quite surprised at the cross fit that I had taken, but she had always told our mother superior to persevere, and that it would pass over; that the best nuns had moments of a similar kind, that they proceeded from suggestions of the evil spirit, who always redoubled his efforts when he was on the point of losing his prey; that I was about to make my escape from him; that my path henceforth would be strewed with roses; that the restraints of the religious life would appear to me to be the more supportable, because I had greatly exaggerated them; that this sudden pressure of the yoke was a favour of heaven, for the purpose of afterwards lightening it. . . .' It appeared to me rather singular that the same things should proceed from God and the Devil, according as they might think proper to view it. There are many circumstances similar to this which occur in the convent; and I have often been told, by way of consolation by some, that my thoughts were the instigations of Satan, and by others, that they were the inspirations of God. The same evil proceeds from God by whom we are tried, and from the Devil by whom we are tempted.

I conducted myself with prudence. I thought I could answer for myself. I saw my father, he spoke to me coldly; I saw my mother, she embraced me; I received letters of congratulation from my sisters, and a great many others. I knew that it would be a M. Sornen, Vicar of Saint-Roch, who would preach the sermon, and M. Thierry, Chancellor of the University, who would receive my vows. Everything went on well till the evening before the important day; only after being informed that the ceremony would be private, that there would be few people there, and that the church door would be open only to my parents, I invited, by means of the maid of the turning-box, every person in the neighbourhood, my male and female friends; I had permission to write to some of my acquaintances. All this company, whom they did not expect, presented themselves; it was necessary to permit them to come in, and the assembly was almost as numerous as my plan required. Oh, sir! what a dreadful night the preceding was to me! I did not lie down. I sat upon my bed, I raised my hands to heaven, and called God to witness the violence which they were going to offer me. I represented to myself the part which I was to act at the foot of the altar— a young girl loudly protesting against an action to which she seemed to have consented; the scandal of the bystanders, the distress of the nuns, the fury of my parents. O God! what is to become of me? . . . While I was pronouncing these words I was seized with a general faintness, I fell in a swoon upon my bolster; a general coldness, in which my knees shook, and my teeth chattered, succeeded the swoon, and this coldness was followed by a burning heat. My mind was troubled. I do not remember undressing myself nor going out of my cell; but I was found naked in my shift, stretched upon the ground at the door of my superior, motionless, and almost dead. I have learned these things since. In the morning I found myself in my cell with the superior, the mother of the novices, and some of those whom they call assistants, round my bed. I was very much distressed. They put some questions to me; they saw from my answers that I had no knowledge of what had passed, and they did not tell me of it. They asked me how I did, if I persisted in my holy resolution, and if I found myself in a condition to support the fatigue of the day. I answered in the affirmative, and, contrary to their expectation, no derangement of the plan took place.

Everything had been arranged on the preceding evening. They rang the bells to let the world know that they were about to add another to the list of the unfortunate. They came to dress me; it was a toilette day. Now, when I recollect all these ceremonies, there seems to be in them something solemn and affecting for a young innocent, whose inclination is not averse to them. They conducted me to the church, they performed high mass. The good vicar, who gave me credit for a resignation which I did not possess, preached a long sermon, which was every word inapplicable to me: there was something very ridiculous in what he said of my happiness, my grace, my courage, my zeal, my fervour, and all those fine sentiments which he supposed that I felt. In the meanwhile, the contrast between this eulogium and the step which I was about to take, troubled me; I was staggered for a few moments, but my uncertainty did not last long. It only taught me better than I had learnt before, that I was deficient in those qualities which are necessary to constitute a good nun. At last the dreadful moment arrived. When it was necessary for me to enter the place, where I was to take my vows, I could not walk; two of my companions took me by the arms, and, with my head leaning upon one of them, they dragged me along. I knew not what passed in the hearts of the bystanders; but at the sight of a young victim carried dying to the altar, on all sides sighs and sobbings burst forth, among which, I am sure, those of my father and mother were not heard. The assembly rose up: there were some young persons mounted upon the chairs, and hanging by the bars of the railing; a profound silence was observed, and the priest who presided at my profession said to me: Maria-Susannah Simonin, do you promise to tell the truth?—I promise.—Do you come here of your own accord, with good will? I answered, No; but those who accompanied me answered, Yes.—Maria-Susannah Simonin, do you promise to God, chastity, poverty, and obedience?—I hesitated a moment, the priest waited, and I replied, No, sir.—He repeated: Maria-Susannah Simonin, do you promise to God, chastity, poverty, and obedience? I replied in a firmer tone: No, sir, no.—He stopped, and said to me: Recollect yourself, my child, and listen to me.—Sir, said I to him, you ask me if I promise to God, chastity, poverty, and obedience? I understood you perfectly, and I answered you no. . . . And turning round to the bystanders, among whom considerable murmuring had arisen, I made a sign that I wished to speak; the murmurs ceased, and I said: 'Sirs, and you in particular, my father and mother, I take you all to witness . . .' When I uttered these words, one of the sisters let fall the veil over the railing, and I saw that it was to no purpose to speak. The nuns surrounded me, and loaded me with reproaches; I heard them without saying a word. They conducted me to my cell, where they locked me in.

Being left alone to my reflections, I began to take courage and to consider my conduct, of which I did not repent. I saw that, after the notoriety which I had occasioned, it was impossible I could long remain here, and that perhaps they would not dare to take me back into the convent. I did not know what they intended to do with me, but I was sensible there was nothing worse than for one to become a nun contrary to inclination. I lived in confinement without hearing a single word from any person. Those who brought me my victuals, came in, put my dinner down upon the floor, and went away without speaking. In about a month they brought me a secular habit, when I put off that of the house; the superior came, and told me to follow her. I followed her to the door of the convent, where I went into a carriage; I there found my mother alone, waiting for me; I sat down before her, and the carriage set off. We continued opposite one another for some time, without saying a word: I kept my eyes downward, and did not presume to look her in the face. I know not what passed in my mind, but all on a sudden I threw myself at her feet, and leaned my head upon her knees; I said nothing, but sobbed till I was almost stifled. She repelled me harshly without speaking. I did not rise; the blood sprang from my nose; I seized one of her hands in spite of her, and bathing it with a stream of blood and tears, putting my mouth upon her hand, I kissed it, and said to her: You are still my mother, I am still your child. . . . She answered me, pushing me from her with greater violence, and tearing her hand from between mine at the same time: Rise, wretch, rise. I obeyed her, I rose up, and drew my hood over my face. She had assumed such an air of authority and sternness, that I dared not look at her. My tears, and the blood which flowed from my nose mingling together, ran down my arms till I was all besmeared before I was aware of it. From some words that she dropped, I conceived that her robe and linen were stained with it, and that this offended her. We arrived at the house, where I was conducted to a small room which was prepared for me. I threw myself down upon my knees on the staircase: I held by her clothes; but all that I could obtain from her was a contemptuous cast of the head, with an expression of indignation from her mouth and eyes, which you can conceive better than I can describe.

I entered my new prison, where I passed six months, soliciting in vain the favour of speaking to her, of seeing my father, or of writing to them. I was served with provisions and attended: a domestic accompanied me to mass on holy days, and locked me up. I read, I worked, I wept, I sung, and in this manner did I pass my days. A secret sentiment supported me, and it was the consciousness that I was free, and that my lot, cruel as it was, might change. But it was decided that I was to be a nun, and I was one.

Extract from Vol. I. Diderot: *The Nun.*

(*The parents, still bent on getting rid of their daughter by forcing her into a convent, sent her to another one, of which the following passage is a description.*)

In the afternoon I repaired to the superior's apartment, when I found a pretty numerous company of nuns, the youngest and handsomest in the house. The rest had paid their visits and returned. I assure you, sir, who are yourself a judge of painting, that the assemblage presented a very agreeable picture. Conceive to yourself a group of between ten and twelve persons, the youngest of which might be about fifteen, and the eldest not twenty-three; a superior bordering upon forty, fair, ruddy, plump, half raised up in her bed, with a double chin, which became her extremely; arms round as if they had been turned; fingers taper and interspersed with dimples; two black eyes, large, lively and tender, seldom quite open, half shut, as if she to whom they belonged had felt some difficulty in opening them; lips that displayed the vermilion of the rose; teeth white as milk; the most beautiful cheeks; a very pleasing head, sunk in a pillow of down; her arms extended carelessly by her sides, and little cushions to support her elbows. I was seated on the edge of the bed, doing nothing; another in an armchair, with a small embroidery frame upon her knee. Others, near the windows, were employed in working lace. Some were seated on the ground, upon the cushions they had taken from the chairs, sewing embroidery or spinning on small wheels. Some were fair, others brown; no one resembled another, though all were beautiful. Their characters were as various as their physiognomies. Some were serene, some sprightly, others serious, sad or melancholy. They were all engaged upon some kind of work, as I have mentioned, except myself. It was not difficult to discover who were friends, who indifferent, and who enemies. The friends were placed beside or opposite to each other. As they worked, they talked, they consulted, they looked by stealth at each other, and pressed each others fingers on pretence of lending a needle, a pin, or the scissors. The superior surveyed them all; she blamed one for assiduity, another for idleness; this for her indifference, that for her sadness; she made them bring her their work; she praised or blamed; she adjusted the head-dress of one. . . . That veil comes too much forward . . . that cap encroaches too much upon the face, it does not display enough of your cheeks . . . these folds have a bad effect. . . . And upon all she bestowed either slight reproof or endearments.

Extract from Vol. II. Diderot: *The Nun.*
Translation of 1797.

RAMEAU'S NEPHEW

(Written in 1762)

AIN OR SHINE, IT IS MY CUSTOM TOWARDS FIVE O'CLOCK in the afternoon to walk in the Palais Royal. There I may be observed, always alone, musing on the bench by the Hotel d'Argenson. I am my own interlocutor, and discuss politics, love, taste, and philosophy. I give my mind full fling: I let it follow the first notion that presents itself, be it wise or foolish, even as our wild young rakes in Foy's Alley pursue some courtesan of unchaste mien and welcoming face, of answering eye and tilted nose, and then quit her for another; touching all and cleaving to none. My thoughts are my wantons.

If the weather be too cold or too rainy I seek shelter in the Café de la Régence. There I amuse myself watching the chess-players. Paris is the corner of the world, and the Café de la Régence the corner of Paris where the best chess is played: here, at Rey's, the profound Légal, the subtle Philidor, the solid Mayot do battle with each other; here may one witness the most astonishing strokes, and hear the most foolish conversation, for if, like Légal, one may be a man of parts and a great chess-player, one may equally be a great chess-player and an ass, like Foubert or Mayot. I was there one evening after dinner, observing everything, keeping my own counsel, and listening as little as possible, when I was accosted by one of the oddest personages this country affords, where God has not been sparing of them. He is a fellow made up of insolence and cringing, of folly and good sense: notions of good and bad conduct must needs be strangely mixed up in his head, for he shows the good qualities of his nature without ostentation, and the bad ones without shame. For the rest, he is endowed with a strong build of body, a singularly vivid imagination, and a pulmonary vigour such as is seldom met with. Should you meet him one day and fail to be arrested by his original turn, either you will stop your ears with your fingers, or you will flee from him. Ye gods, what terrible lungs! No one can change so utterly. Sometimes wasted and haggard like a sick man in the last stage of consumption, his teeth show through his cheeks, and he looks as though he

[331]

had not eaten for days, or were newly come from La Trappe. A month later, and he is fat and full fed as though he has dined throughout the period at a financier's table, or has spent the time in a Benedictine convent. To-day, in dirty linen and ragged breeches, rags on his back and almost shoeless, he hangs his head and skulks in by-ways, and seems to call for charity. To-morrow, powdered and curled, well clothed and shod, he carries his head high, shows himself everywhere, and you might almost take him for a man of position. He lives from day to day, brisk or downcast, according to circumstances. His first business of a morning, once he is up, is to find out where he may dine, and after dinner, where he may sup. Night also brings its anxieties: perhaps his feet will take him to the little attic of his habitation, unless his landlady, weary of waiting for her rent, has reclaimed the key; or he will fall back on some tavern in the suburbs, and sit and wait for day over a crust of bread and a pot of beer.

When he has not a penny in his pocket, which is often enough, he appeals either to some friendly hackney-coachman, or to the coach-driver of some great man, to give him a shake-down on the straw among the horses, and the next morning the remains of his mattress show in his hair. If the weather is mild he will pace the Cours-la-Reine or the Champs-Elysées all night. Dawn sees him once more in town, dressed from over-night for the next day, and perhaps from next day for the rest of the week. I do not care for these eccentric people: some there are who know them freely, and even make friends of them. They interest me once in a twelvemonth, when I come across them, because their character cuts across that of other men, breaking the fastidious uniformity which our education, social conventions, and niceties of usage, have brought about. A man of this sort joining a party is a grain of yeast, a ferment, which wakes in each something of his natural self. He stirs up and agitates, calls for blame or approval; he brings out the truth, reveals people's good qualities, unmasks the scoundrel; and your man of understanding listens, and sorts out his acquaintance.

I had known this particular man for a long time. He was a frequent visitor at a house where he was welcomed for his brains. There was an only daughter. He swore both to the father and to the mother that he would marry their daughter. They shrugged their shoulders, laughed in his face, told him he was mad; I was there at the time it happened. He borrowed a few crowns which I let him have. He had gained an introduction, I do not know how, to some respectable houses, where he had his place at table on the understanding that he was not to talk without permission. He held his tongue and bottled up his rage. It was good to see him under such constraint. Did he feel the need to break his contract and open his mouth, at the first word all the guests would exclaim, 'Oh, Rameau!' whereupon his fury would blaze from his eyes, and he would return to his plate more enraged than ever. You were curious to know the man's name, and now you have it. He is the nephew of that celebrated musician who has delivered us from Lulli's plain-chant that we have droned out for more than a hundred years, he who has put forward so many incomprehensible points of view and obscure truths about the theory of music, about which neither he nor anyone else understood anything, and who has given us a certain number of operas wherein may be found harmony, scraps of song, disconnected ideas, noise, thefts, triumphs, lances, glories,[1] murmurs, and victories without end, dance tunes that will live for ever, and who, after having buried the Florentine, will in turn himself be buried by the Italian virtuosi, a fact of which he had no presentiment which tended to make him gloomy, sad, and morose, for no one is so cross—not even a pretty woman when she awakes in the morning with a pimple on her nose—as an author in danger of outliving his reputation, witness Marivaux, and the younger Crébillon.

He accosts me: 'Haha! There you are, my Philosopher; and what are you doing here among this crowd of idlers? Are you also wasting time wood pushing? . . .' (It is thus that chess and draughts are disdainfully referred to.)

I. No, but when I have nothing better to do, it amuses me to look on at those who push well.

HE. At that rate you cannot often be amused; for with the exception of Légal and Philidor, not one of them knows anything about it.

I. And what about Monsieur de Bissy, then?

HE. As a chess-player, he is what Mademoiselle Clairon is as an actress: they both know all there is to know about these games.

---

[1] Allusion to lyrical phrases much abused in old Opera.

1. You are difficult to please. I perceive you have no patience with anything but the best.

HE. Yes. In insipid things like chess, draughts, poetry, eloquence, and music. What good is mediocrity in these things?

1. Very little good, I grant. But there must be a great number of men working at these things so as to bring forth the man of genius. He is one in a multitude. But enough of that. It is an eternity since I saw you. I never think of you when I do not see you, but I am always delighted to meet you again. What have you been doing?

HE. What you, I, and everybody else does; some good, some evil, and nothing. And then I have been hungry, and I have eaten when occasion presented itself; after eating, I have been thirsty, and have drunk occasionally. And then my beard grew, and when it came, I shaved it.

1. You were wrong there: it is the only thing you lack to be a wise man.

HE. Maybe! My forehead is high and wrinkled, my eyes are keen; I have a prominent nose, large cheeks, black, thick eyebrows, a big slit of a mouth, full lips, and a square face. If this large chin were covered with a long beard, do you know it would look very well in bronze or marble?

1. Beside Cæsar, Marcus Aurelius, and Socrates.

HE. No. I should be better between Diogenes and Phryne. I am as impudent as the one, and I consort very willingly with the other.

1. Have you been quite well, as usual?

HE. Yes, on the whole, but not remarkably so to-day.

1. What! There you sit with the belly of a Silenus and a face . . .

HE. A face you might take for his antagonist. The temper that dries up my dear uncle apparently fattens his dear nephew.

1. Talking of that uncle, do you ever see him now?

HE. Yes, I sometimes pass him in the street.

1. Does he do nothing for you?

HE. If he does anything for anyone he is quite unconscious of it. He is a philosopher in his way; he thinks only of himself, and he does not care a fig for the rest of the world. His wife and daughter may die when they please, but so long as the parish bells which toll for them continue to sound their twelfths and seventeenths, all will be well. It is lucky for him, and it is what I particularly value in people of genius. They are only good for one thing, and for nothing else: they do not know what it is to be citizens, fathers, mothers, brothers, relations, or friends. Between ourselves, we should do well to resemble them in all points, but it is hardly desirable that the seed should be raised everywhere. Men we must have; but men of genius, no. No, in faith, we want none. They are the people who change the face of the globe; and, even in the smallest particulars, folly is so common, and has such force, that there is no reforming it without disturbance and fuss. A part of their imaginings gains a footing, the rest remains where it was—hence two gospels, like a harlequin's coat. The wisdom of Rabelais's monk is the true wisdom, both for his own peace and for the peace of others. Do your duty more or less, always speak well of the Prior, and let the world wag. It works well, for the multitude is content with it. If I knew any history I would show you that all trouble here below has always come through some fellow of genius, but I do not know history, by reason that I know nothing. Devil take me if I have ever learnt anything, or if I am any the worse off for it. I was once at the table of one of the King's Ministers of State, a man who had wit enough for four; well, he demonstrated to us, as clearly as that one and one make two, that nothing was so beneficial to the people at large as a lie, and that nothing was so mischievous as the truth. I cannot remember all his reasoning, but it followed plainly enough that people of genius were detestable, and that if a new-born child bore the mark of this dangerous gift of Nature, it should be smothered, or thrown out into the sewers.

I. And yet these very people, so hostile to genius, all pretend to it.

HE. I think so too, in their innermost thoughts, but I do not think that they would dare avow it.

I. That is their modesty. You were seized, then, with a terrible hatred of genius?

HE. Thenceforward and for ever.

I. Yet I remember a time when you were in despair at being but an ordinary man. You will never be happy if opposite points of view can give you equal distress: you must make your choice, and stick to it. While agreeing with you that men of genius are commonly eccentric, or, as the proverb puts it, 'Great wits are sure to madness near allied,' there is no getting over it —periods which cannot produce them will be despised. They become an honour to the people among whom they arise, and sooner or later statues are raised to them, and they are regarded as benefactors of the human race. With all respect to His Sublimity, the Minister whom you have cited, I think that if a lie may serve for the moment, it is necessarily mischievous in the long run, and that, on the contrary, truth necessarily serves best in the end, though it may be a hindrance at the moment. Whence I am tempted to conclude that a man of genius who denounces a widespread terror, or establishes a great truth, must always be worthy of our veneration. It may happen that he falls a victim to prejudice and the law; but law is of two sorts, for there are equitable laws, general and absolute, and others which are incongruous and only owe their sanction to short-sightedness or expediency. The latter cast but a passing stigma on the law-breaker, an ignominy reversed by lapse of time, to fall on judges and peoples, there to remain for ever. Consider Socrates, and the judge who made him drink the hemlock—which of them is honoured to-day?

HE. Much good it has done him! Was he any the less condemned? Was he any the less put to death? Was he any the less a turbulent citizen? Because he held a bad law in contempt, did he any the less encourage madmen to despise good laws? Does it absolve him from his bold and outstanding eccentricity? Just now you were not far from reflecting unfavourably on men of genius.

I. Listen, my dear man. Society should not frame bad laws, and if it had but good ones, it would never be put to persecuting a man of genius. I never told you that genius was inseparably attached to ill-doing, nor ill-doing to genius. The wicked man will be a fool more often than the man of genius. Were a man of genius commonly hard in his dealings, difficult, thorny, even insupportable, even were he a wicked man, what would you conclude about him?

HE. That he ought to be drowned.

I. Gently, my dear man. We will not take your uncle for an example. He is a hard man, and a brutal; without humanity, avaricious, a bad father, a bad husband, a bad uncle; but it is

not so certain that he is a man of genius, that he has extended
the range of his art, or that his works will be talked of in ten
years' time. But Racine? He, certainly, had genius, and did not
pass for so very good a man. And Voltaire? . . .

HE. No need to press me, I can draw a conclusion.

I. Which would you prefer? That he should be a good man,
tied to his desk, like Briasson, or to his yard-wand, like Barbier,
increasing his legitimate offspring year by year, good husband,
good father, good uncle, good neighbour, honest tradesman,
but no more than that; or that he should be a false rogue,
ambitious, envious, and wicked, but author of *Andromaque,
Britannicus, Iphigénie, Phèdre, Athalie*?

HE. Faith! For him, perhaps, it would be better that he were
the former.

I. That is, indeed, infinitely truer than you imagine.

HE. Oh, that is just like you, you and your kind! We, if we
say a good thing, it is by chance, the word of an inspired idiot.
It is only such as you who speak intelligibly; but, my Philosopher,
I understand what I say, and mean what I say, just as you do.

I. Well, well, but why should it be better for him?

HE. Because all these fine things he did were not worth twenty
thousand francs to him; whereas, had he been a worthy silk
merchant in the Rue Saint-Denis, or Rue Saint-Honoré, a
wholesale grocer, a successful apothecary he would have amassed
an immense fortune, and while making it would have enjoyed
every kind of pleasure. From time to time he would have flung
a pistole to a poor devil of a buffoon like me who had made
him laugh, and who could have got a girl for him on occasion
to relieve the monotony of his wife's caresses; we should have
had famous dinners under his roof, gamed high, drunk good
wine, liqueurs, coffee, gone for picnics; you see I know what
I mean well enough—you laugh—but allow me to say, it would
have been better for those around him.

I. There is no contradicting that. Provided that he did not
put honest wealth to dishonest use, that he had kept his door
shut to all your gamesters, your parasites, and easy-going companions, all idlers, and vicious good-for-noughts, and set his
'prentices with their staves to beat the life out of busybodies
who offer variety to husbands sick of the humdrum pleasures
of matrimony.

HE. Beat, sir? Beat? People are not beaten to death in a well-ordered city. And it is an honest calling: many persons, even titled persons, engage in it. And what the devil would you have him do with his money, if he did not keep a good table, and good company, good wine, and pretty women, seek pleasure under all colours, amusement of every kind. I would as soon be a beggar as have a great fortune without any of these enjoyments. But to return to Racine. The man was of no use except to people he never knew, living in times when he was no more.

I. Agreed; but weigh the good and the ill of it. A thousand years hence he will cause tears to flow; he will be the admiration of mankind in every country of the globe; he will evoke humanity, commiseration, kindness. It will be asked who he was, what his country; and France will be envied on account of him. He gave pain to a certain few who are now no more, persons in whom we now have little or no interest; we have nothing now to fear from his faults or from his vices. It would have been better, no doubt, had Nature given him the virtues of an easy man as well as the talents of a great man. He was as a tree which starved other trees in its vicinity, and stifled the undergrowth near it—but it has borne its head to the skies, and its branches are widely spread; it has lent its shade to all who came, to those who come to-day, to those who will come to rest near its majestic trunk; and it has borne fruit of exquiste savour, and bears incessantly. We would like Voltaire to have the suavity of a Duclos, the ingenuousness of an Abbé Trublet, the rectitude of an Abbé D'Olivet; but since this may not be, let us look at the matter from a more interesting point of view, forgetting for a moment the point we occupy in space and time, and extending our vision to centuries yet to come, to regions the most remote, and peoples not yet born. Let us think of the good of our kind; if we have not sufficient generosity, then let us forgive Nature in that she is wiser than we. If you throw cold water on the head of a Greuze, you are in danger of extinguishing his talent along with his vanity. If you made Voltaire less sensitive to criticism, he could no longer delve into the soul of Mérope, no longer touch you.

HE. But if Nature were as powerful as she is wise, why should she not have made these men as good as she made them great?

I. But do you not perceive that by such reasoning you reverse the order of Nature, and that if everything were excellent here below, nothing would be excellent?

HE. You are right: the important point is that you and I are, and that we are you and I; let the rest be as it may or can. The best order of things, to my mind, is the one I am in, and a fig for the best of worlds if I form no part of it. I would rather exist, even as an impertinent reasoner, than not exist at all.

I. People who think like you, and do not arraign the existing order of things, never see that they are threatening their own existence.

HE. True.

I. Let us then accept things as they are. Let us see what they cost us and how much they give us in return, and leave aside all that we do not know well enough either to praise or blame, and which is, perchance, neither good nor evil, though necessary, as many good folk imagine.

HE. All this flow of words does not mean much to me. Apparently it is philosophy; I warn you that is a thing that I never meddle with. All I do know is that I should very much like to be someone else, on the chance of being a genius, a great man. Yes; I must acknowledge it, something within me tells me so. I never in my life heard one of them praised, without being filled with rage by it. I am envious. When I hear something about the private life of such men that does them no credit, I listen with glee: it brings us nearer together, it helps me to bear my mediocrity more easily. I say to myself: True, you could never have written *Mahomet,* but then neither could you have written the eulogy on Maupeou. So I have always been, and always shall be, vexed at my own mediocrity. Yes, yes! I am mediocre and I am vexed. I have never listened to the overture to the *Indes Galantes* nor heard them sing the *Profonds abîmes du Ténare; Nuit, eternelle nuit,* without saying sorrowfully to myself: 'That is what thou wilt never do.' Consequently, I was jealous of my uncle; and if some beautiful pieces for the harpsichord had been found in his portfolio after his death, I should not have hesitated about which personality to adopt.

I. If that is your only cause for sorrow, it seems hardly worth it.

HE. 'Tis nothing. One has these moments. (He fell to singing the overture to the *Indes Galantes* and the air *Profonds abîmes,* and then added): Something within me, and that speaks to me, says: Rameau, you would like to have written those two pieces; had you done so, you would soon have done two others; and after a certain number, they would have been played and sung everywhere. You would have carried your head high, your conscience would have borne witness to yourself of your own merit, others would have pointed you out, saying: There is the man who has written such pretty gavottes (and he warbled the gavottes. Then, like a man much moved, with tears of joy in his eyes, he added, rubbing his hands together): You would have a fine house (he measured its size with his arms), a good bed (he stretched himself carelessly), excellent wine (smacking his tongue against his palate), a handsome carriage (he raised his foot as if to get in), pretty women (and his eyes feasted on them, his arms embraced them), a hundred lackeys would come and perfume you every day (and he fancied he saw them all around him: he saw Palissot, Poinsinet, the Frérons—father and son—La Porte; he heard them, he smirked with pride, approved them, smiled on them, disdained them, despised them, drove them away, recalled them; then continued): And so, getting up in the morning, you would be told you were a great man; you would read in *L'Histoire des Trois Siècles* that it was so, you would be convinced by evening that it was so, and the great man Rameau would fall asleep to a soft murmur of praise ringing in his ears even as he slept; he would smile complacently, his chest would dilate, would rise and fall in fullness of ease, and he would snore like a great man. (And so talking, he let himself sink slowly on a bench; he closed his eyes, and imitated the happy sleep he had imagined. After tasting this sweetness of repose for an instant, he awoke, stretched his arms, yawned, rubbed his eyes, and looked round for his fawning sycophants.)

I. You think, then, that sleep visits those favoured by fortune?

HE. Do I think so? I, poor outcast that I am, when at night I return to my garret and burrow into my pallet, I lie all curled up under my blanket, my chest contracted. I breathe with difficulty, with a sort of feeble whine, scarcely to be heard. Now a rich man snores loud enough to make the room ring, and amazes the whole street. But what troubles me to-day is not only the matter of snoring and sleeping wretchedly, like a pauper . . .

I. Yet that is bad enough.

HE. What has befallen me is far worse.

I. And what is it, then?

HE. You have always taken an interest in me because I am a good fellow, whom you inwardly despise, but who amuses you.

I. True.

HE. So I will tell you. (Before beginning, he heaved a profound sigh, and rested his head on his hands, then recovering his tranquillity, he said): You know that I am ignorant, foolish, mad, impertinent, idle . . . what in Burgundy is called a *fieffé truand,* an utter vagabond, a swindler, a glutton. . . .

I. What a panegyric!

HE. It is true, every word of it, there is nothing I can withdraw; we will not argue about that, I pray you. No one knows me better than I know myself, and I have not told all.

I. I do not want to annoy you, and I agree, therefore, with all you say.

HE. Well, I used to live with people who took a fancy to me precisely because I was gifted to a rare degree with all these qualities.

I. That is strange. Up to now I always thought that one either hid these things from oneself, or else pardoned them in oneself and despised them in others.

HE. Hide them from oneself! Is it possible? You may feel sure that when Palissot is alone, and contemplates himself, he tells himself a very different tale; rest assured that when alone with his colleagues they candidly admit that they are a pair of notorious rogues. Despise them in others! The people I speak of were more just in their views, and my character gained me a very great success among them: I was in clover; I was fêted, and I never left their company but I was regretted. I was their little Rameau, their dear Rameau, their mad, impertinent, ignorant, idle Rameau, their glutton, jester, old beast. None of these familiar epithets but was accompanied by its smile, caress, slap on the shoulder, kick or cuff; if at table, it meant a choice morsel on my plate; otherwhere, it was a liberty of no consequence, for I am of no consequence myself. People do what they please with me and with my person, and before my face, without affronting me. And then the shower of small perquisites that fell on me! And I have lost all, stupid hound that I am! I have lost all, for once, just for once, showing common *sense*. Ah! If ever it happens again!

I. What passed?

HE. 'Twas an incomparable folly—incomprehensible, unforgivable.

I. But what folly was it?

HE. Rameau, Rameau, did they really take you for that? The folly of showing a little taste, a little intelligence, a little reason! Rameau, my friend, learn for the future to be what God made you, what your patrons wish you to be. Then and there were you taken by the shoulders and shown the door, and were told, 'Be off, rapscallion, show yourself no more; the fellow pretends to sense, to reason; be off! We have those qualities without you!' You went away, biting your fingers: it was your accursed tongue you should have bitten first. For want of that forethought behold yourself, on the street, without a halfpenny, not knowing where to lay your head. You were spoon-fed to your heart's content—and you go back to your refuse; well lodged, and you may think yourself lucky if you can get hold of your garret again; soft-bedded, and now your straw is laid between M. de Soubise's coachman, and friend Robbé; instead of the warm and untroubled sleep you have enjoyed, you will hear in the one ear the neighing and stamping of horses, and in the other the thousand times worse noise of harsh and barbarous rhymes. Unhappy wretch and ill-advised, what million demons possessed you?

(From *Rameau's Nephew and Other Works,*
by Mrs. Wilfred Jackson, 1926.)

THE TWO FRIENDS OF BOURBON[1]

A MORAL TALE BY M. DIDEROT

(Translation published in 1797)

THERE WERE TWO MEN WHO MIGHT BE CALLED THE PYLADES and Orestes of Bourbon: the one was named Oliver, and the other Felix. They were born on the same day, in the same house, and of two sisters: they were nourish'd with the same milk, for one of the mothers dying in child-birth, the other took both the children. They were brought up together, and conversed with none but each other. Their mutual love was like existence, which admits of no doubt; they perceived it incessantly but, perhaps, had never spoken of it to each other. Oliver once saved the life of Felix, who piqued himself on being a great swimmer and was near being drowned. This action neither of them remember'd. Felix had a hundred times extricated Oliver from dangerous adventures, in which the impetuosity of his temper had involved him, yet he never thought of thanking the other; they return'd home without speaking, or talking of other matters.

When they drew for the militia, the lot fell on Felix; Oliver said—the other is for me. When they had served out their time they returned home; more dear to each other than before—that I can't affirm, for, my dear brother, though reciprocal benefits cement friendships form'd by reflection, perhaps they are nothing to those I freely call animal and domestic friendships. At a rencounter in the army, a stroke with a faulchion was aimed at the head of Oliver; Felix put himself mechanically in the way, and received the gash: they pretend he was proud of the scar, but, for my own part, I don't believe it. At Hastenbeck, Oliver drew Felix from amidst the heap of dead that was left on the field. When they were questioned, they related sometimes the assistance they had received from each other—never that they had given. Oliver talked of Felix, and Felix of Oliver—but neither of himself. After they had lived a considerable time in the country, they both, at the same time, became in love

[1] The town is really Bourbonne-les-Bains.

with the same girl; but there was no rivalry between them; he who first perceived the passion of his friend gave up his own pretensions. It was Felix, and Oliver married. Felix, disgusted with life, without knowing why, plunged into all kinds of hazardous enterprises; the last was to become a smuggler. You know, my dear brother, that there are four tribunals for trying smugglers; Caen, Rheims, Valence, and Toulouse, and that the most severe of the four is Rheims, where a man named Coleau[1] presides, who has a soul the most ferocious that nature ever produced. Felix was taken when arm'd, conducted before the terrible Coleau, and condemned to die, as five hundred had been before him. Oliver heard of the fate of Felix. One night he rose, without speaking to his wife, and went to Rheims. He waited on the judge Coleau, threw himself at his feet, and begged permission to see and embrace Felix. Coleau looked at him, remained silent for a moment, and then made a sign for him to sit down. Oliver sat down. About half an hour after, Coleau pulled out his watch, and said to Oliver—'If thou wouldst see and embrace thy friend alive, make haste; he is on the road; and, if my watch goes right, in less than ten minutes he will be hanged.' Oliver rose, transported with fury, and struck the judge a prodigious blow with a club on the back of his neck, that laid him almost dead on the floor, and then ran to the place. 'Down with the executioner!' he cry'd—'attack the officers!'—He roused the people, already fired with indignation against those shameful executions. The stones flew about, and Felix made his escape. Oliver endeavour'd to retreat; but a soldier of the band had wounded him in the side, without his perceiving it. He gain'd the gate of the city but could go no farther. Some charitable country people put him in a cart, and laid him down at the door of his cottage the minute before he expired: he had only time to say—'Wife, come near and let me embrace thee!—I die, but Felix is saved!'

One evening, as we were taking our usual walk, we saw at the door of the cottage a tall woman, surrounded by four small children. Her dejected yet resolute aspect attracted our attention, and our attention excited hers. After a minute's silence she said to us—'Behold these four infants; I am their mother, but I have now no husband!' This intrepid way of exciting commiseration

[1] In the translation from Gestner the name is Talbot.

was well adapted to affect us. We offer'd our contributions which she accepted with decency. It was on this occasion that we learn'd the history of her husband Oliver and his friend Felix. We have talk'd of her, and I trust that our recommendation has not been useless to her. You here see, my dear brother, that greatness of mind and noble endowments are common to all conditions and all countries; that some men die obscurely, not for want of ambition, but a proper theatre to display them; and that two friends may be found in a cottage, or among the Iroquois.

You desire, my dear brother, to know what is become of Felix. Your curiosity is so natural, and the motive of it is so laudable, that we were a little scandalized at not having made any enquiry ourselves. To repair that fault, we thought at first of Mr. Papin, doctor in theology and rector of St. Mary's at Bourbon; but our mother, upon reflection, gave the preference to the subdelegate Aubert, who is an honest, jolly fellow, and who has sent us the following account on the veracity of which you can rely:

'The man named Felix is still alive. When he escaped from the hands of justice at Rheims, he took refuge in the forests of the province, with all the intricacies of which he had become acquainted while he was a smuggler. He endeavoured to approach, by degrees, the dwelling of Oliver, of whose fate he was ignorant.

'In the centre of the wood, where you have sometimes walked, there was a collier, whose cottage served for an asylum to the smugglers; it was also the magazine where they deposited their merchandise and their arms. There Felix retreated, not without danger of falling into the hands of the officers, who followed him by his track. Some of his associates had carry'd thither the news of his being imprison'd at Rheims, so that the collier and his wife, when they saw him return, thought themselves in the hands of justice.

'I shall now relate what I had from this collier's wife, who died not long since.

'It was the children, who were rambling about the wood, that saw him first. While he stopped to caress the youngest, who was his god-child, the others ran to the cottage crying—"Felix! Felix!" The father and mother ran out, repeating the same cry of joy; but the wretch was so harass'd with fatigue and hunger, that he had not the power to reply, but fell into their arms, almost void of life.

'The honest collier and his wife gave him what assistance they could. They set before him bread, wine, and some vegetables. He ate, and laid down to rest.

'When he awoke, the first word he pronounced was "Oliver! Children, do you know nothing of Oliver?" "No," they reply'd. He then related what had happened at Rheims. He pass'd the next day and night with them. He sigh'd; he repeated the name of Oliver, whom he supposed to be in the prison of Rheims; he wou'd go thither and die with him; and it was not without difficulty they dissuaded him from that design.

'In the middle of the second night he took a musket, he put a sabre under his arm, and said to the collier in a low voice—"Collier!"

' "Felix!"

' "Take thy hatchet and away!"

' "Whither?"

' "What a question!—to Oliver!"

'They set off. But just as they got out of the forest, they were surrounded by a party of the militia.

'I relate what was told me by the collier, though it appears incredible. These two men, on foot, were able to defend themselves against twenty horsemen. Probably the latter were scatter'd and they wanted to take their prey alive. Be that as it may, the action was very hot. There were five horses maim'd, and seven of the riders cut down by the hatchet or sabre. The poor collier remain'd dead on the spot, by a shot in the head. Felix regain'd the forest and, as he is of an incredible agility, he retreated from one part to another, and, as he retreated he charged his musket—he fired and whistled. These firings and whistling, repeated at different intervals and in different places, made the horsemen think there was a large gang of smugglers, and they retired with precipitation.

'When Felix found they were dispersed, he returned to the field of battle. He took the body of the collier on his shoulders, and went back to the cottage where the woman and her children were still asleep. He stopped at the door, sat himself down with his back against a tree, his face turned towards the entrance of the hut, and the dead body at his feet.

'The wife awoke and found that her husband was gone from her side. She look'd round for Felix—he too was gone. She arose—she went forth—she saw—she cry'd out—she fell to the earth. The children ran out—they saw—they cry'd—they fell upon their father and their mother. The mother, recall'd to life by the tumultous distracted cries of her children, pluck'd out her hair by the roots, and tore her face with her nails. Felix remain'd immoveable at the foot of the tree, with his eyes closed, and his face turned away, and said in a faint voice—"Kill me." A moment's silence ensued; then again the cries of grief and distraction burst forth, and Felix said again—"Kill me, children; for pity's sake, kill me!"

'Three days and nights they passed in this state of desolation. On the fourth morning, Felix said—"Woman, take thy sack, put bread into it, and follow me." After a long circuit through the forest and over the mountains, they arrived at the cottage of Oliver, which is situate, as you remember, at the extremity of the town, where two roads meet, one of which goes to Franche Comté and the other to Lorraine.

'There Felix learnt the death of Oliver, and found himself between the widows of the two men both massacred for him. He enter'd and said hastily to the widow of Oliver—"Where is Oliver?" By her silence, by her dress, and her tears he found that Oliver was no more. A dejection seiz'd him; he fell senseless to the earth, and cut his head against a kneading trough. As the two widows raised him up, his blood ran over them, and while they were busied in stopping it with their aprons he said to them —"You are their widows and yet you succour me!" Then again his senses left him, and again they returned; then he sigh'd and cry'd out— "Why did he not leave me to my fate? Why did he come to Rheims? Why was he suffer'd to come thither?" Then his reason left him—he became furious—he roll'd on the earth, and tore his clothes. In one of these fits, he drew his sabre, and wou'd have kill'd himself; but the two women threw their arms around him, and call'd for help; the neighbours ran in, they bound him with cords, and bled him profusely. As his strength was exhausted his fury subsided, and he remain'd as dead for several days. At last his reason return'd. At first he look'd round him, as a man just waked from a sound sleep, and said—"Where am I? Women, who are you?" One of them said—"I am the collier's widow." "Ah!" he cry'd; "yes, you are his widow. And who are you?"—The widow of Oliver remain'd silent. Then he burst into tears. He turned himself toward the wall and said, with sobs—"I am in the house of Oliver! This is his bed—and that woman there was, alas! his wife."

'The two widows attended him with so much solicitude; they inspired him with so much commiseration; they entreated him so earnestly to live; they represented to him, in so affecting a manner, what wou'd be their wretched condition without him, that he suffered himself at last to be overcome.

'During all the time he remain'd in that house, he never went to rest. When the night came on, he issued forth—he wander'd about the fields—he roll'd upon the ground, and call'd on Oliver.—One of the women followed him and brought him back at break of day.

'Several persons knew that he was in Oliver's dwelling, and some among them had unfriendly intentions. The two widows informed him of his peril. One afternoon he was sitting on a bench, his sabre on his knees, his elbows resting on a table, and his hands before his eyes. He gave no answer to anything that was ask'd him. The widow of Oliver had a son, about eighteen years; the collier's widow a daughter of fifteen. On a sudden he said to the latter—"Go find thy daughter, and bring her hither." He had some mowed grass hard by, which he sold. The collier's widow returned with her daughter. The son of Oliver married her. Felix gave them the money he receiv'd for his grass, and ask'd their forgiveness with tears. They fix'd their habitation in the cottage where they now dwell, and where they serve as father and mother to the other children. The two widows lived together, and the children of Oliver had one father and two mothers.

'It is now a year and a half since the collier's widow died; and the widow of Oliver still daily laments her loss with tears.

'One evening, as they were watching Felix (for one or other of them was constantly with him) they observed him melt into tears. He turn'd his hands in silence toward the door that separated him from the women, and then went to making up his wallet. They said nothing to him, for they were sensible how necessary his departure was. They all sigh'd without speaking. In the night he rose. The women were unable to sleep. He advanc'd on tip-toe to the door; there he stopp'd, look'd toward the bed where the two widows lay, dry'd his eyes with his hands and went forth. The two women clasp'd each other in their arms, and pass'd all the rest of the night in tears. It was not known whither he had retired; but there was scarce a week that he did not send them some relief.

'The forest where the daughter of the collier lived with the son of Oliver, belongs to M. Leclerc de Rançonnières, a man of great wealth and lord of another village in those cantons, called Courcelles. One day as M. de Rançonnières, or de Courcelles, as you please, was hunting in the forest, he came to the hut of young Oliver; he went in and diverted himself with the children, who are pretty. The figure of the wife, which is not disagreeable, pleased him; the manly tone of the husband, that much resembles his father's, struck him. He learn'd the history of their parents. He promised to solicit a pardon for Felix. He sought it, and obtained it.

'Felix enter'd the service of M. de Rançonnières, who gave him the place of a keeper of the forest. After he had lived about two years in the castle of Rançonnières (during which time he sent the two widows a large part of his salary) an attachment to his master and the impetuosity of his own temper involved him in an affair which, though trifling at first, was followed by the most serious consequences.

'M. de Rançonnières had at Courcelles a neighbour named Fourmont, a judge in the principal court of judicature at Ch—— Their two houses were separated only by a boundary, which crowded the gateway of M. de Rançonnières and made it difficult for carriages. He therefore put it some feet nearer to M. Fourmont, who replaced it as much nearer M. de Rançonnières; from hence arose hatred, insults, and a law-suit between the two neighbours. The suit of the boundary produced two or three others more considerable. Matters were in this state, when one evening M. de Rançonnières, returning from the chase, attended by his keeper Felix, met in the highway Mr. Fourmont, the magistrate and his brother, an officer, who said— "Brother, suppose we were to cut the throat of that old scoundrel; what think you of it?" The proposal was not heard by M. de Rançonnières, but was, unfortunately, by Felix who, addressing himself boldly to the young man, said— "Captain, are you valiant enough only to try to do what you have said?" and, at the same instant, laid down his gun and put his hand upon his sabre, for he never went without it. The young officer drew his sword, and advanced on Felix. M. de Rançonnières ran to him and seized the butt of his sword; the officer then took up his gun and fired at Felix, but missed him; he return'd the fire with a stroke of his sabre, by which he cut down the officer's sword, and with it a part of his arm. From this a criminal process was added to three or four civil actions; Felix was confined in the jail, a horrible prosecution carry'd on, and, in consequence of this procedure, a magistrate was degraded from his rank and rendered almost infamous, and an officer excluded from his corps; M. de Rançonnières died of chagrin, and Felix was doom'd to perpetual imprisonment and exposed to all the resentment of the Fourmonts. His end must have been miserable if Love had not come to his aid. The jailer's daughter conceiv'd a passion for him, and contriv'd his escape. If this was not the fact, it is at least the common opinion. He fled into Prussia, where he now serves in the regiment of guards. He is said to be esteem'd by his comrades, and even noticed by the king. His military name is Le Triste. The widow of Oliver tells me that he still sends her assistance.

'This, madam, is all I have been able to collect of the history of Felix. I have enclosed in this account a letter from our rector, M. Papin. What it contains I know not; but I fear much that the poor priest, whose mind is rather contracted, and whose heart is none of the best, will be directed solely by prejudice in his account of Oliver and Felix. I must conjure you, madam, to attend to facts, on the veracity of which you may rely, and to the goodness of your own heart, which will advise you better than the first casuist of the Sorbonne, who is not M. Papin.'

The letter of M. Papin follows. It is most disapproving of the two friends and finally dissuades madame from giving any assistance to their families. It illustrates Diderot's delicate irony. He must have enjoyed writing it.

(This text is taken from a translation, published in 1797, of *New Idyls* by S. Gessner of Zurich which contains the following advertisement: 'The story of the Two friends of Bourbon was communicated to the author who thought proper to publish it with these Idyls, as a monument of friendship that the cultivation of letters alone has produced between two men whom distant countries have ever held apart.')

SUPPLEMENT TO BOUGAINVILLE'S VOYAGE

(Written in 1772)

COMMUNISM IN TAHITI

II

THE OLD MAN'S FAREWELL

HE WAS THE FATHER OF A LARGE FAMILY. WHEN THE Europeans arrived, he cast on them looks of disdain, but no look of astonishment, fear, or curiosity. They addressed him; he turned his back, and retired to his hut. His silence and his uneasiness showed his thoughts but too plainly; he groaned inwardly for that his country had seen its best days. When Bougainville sailed again, and the natives ran in crowds to the beach, and clung to his garments, and wept, and embraced his companions, the old man came forward with a stern air, and said:

'Weep! unhappy Tahitians! Weep! But let it be for the arrival, not for the departure of these wicked and ambitious men: one day you will know them better. One day they will come again, bearing in the one hand the piece of wood you see attached to this one's girdle, and in the other the iron which hangs at that one's side, to bind you, to cut your throats, or to subject you to their extravagances and vices; one day you will serve them, be as corrupt, as vile, as wretched as they. But I have my consolation: I draw near to the end of my career; and the calamity I foretell for you I shall not see. O Tahitians! O my friends! You have a means of escaping this dire future; but I would rather perish than point it out to you. Let them go, and let them live!'

Then addressing himself to Bougainville, he went on: 'And you, chief of the brigands who obey you, turn your bark promptly from our shore; we are innocent, we are happy; and you can but injure our well-being. We follow Nature's pure promptings, and you have tried to efface her character from our souls. Here all things are to all; and you have preached I know

[351]

not what of *thine* and *mine*. Our wives and daughters we hold in common: you have shared this our privilege; and you have lighted in them flames unknown before. They are maddened in your arms, and you are ferocious in theirs. They have begun to hate one another; you have cut one another's throats for them; and they have come back to us stained with your blood. We were free, and behold, you have planted in our soil the title-deeds of our future slavery. You are neither god nor demon; who are you, to make slaves? Orou! You, who understand the speech of these men, tell to us all, as thou hast told it me, what is written on that sheet of metal: *This country is ours.* This country is yours? Why? Because you have set foot in it? Did a Tahitian land one day on your shores and grave on one of your stones, or cut on one of your trees *This country belongs to the inhabitants of Tahiti,* what would you think? You are the stronger! And what has that to say to the matter? Did anyone take from you one of the despicable trifles which fill the hold of your ship, you it was who made outcry, who must have vengeance; and on the instant you are plotting in your heart the theft of a whole country. You are not a slave. You would rather die than be one; and now you would enslave us! Think you the Tahitian cannot defend his liberty, and die? The Tahitian, even he whom you would seize upon as though he were a brute, is your brother. You are both Nature's children; what right have you against him that he has not against you? You came; did we fling ourselves upon your person? Did we pillage your vessel? Did we seize upon you and expose you to our warriors' arrows? Did we make you work in the fields with our cattle? We respected our own likeness in you.

'Leave us our ways: they are wiser and more virtuous than yours; we have no wish to barter our ignorance, as you call it, for your useless instruction. What we hold good and necessary, that we have. Are we to be disdained because we have not known how to create superfluous wants for ourselves? When we are hungry we can feed ourselves; when we are cold we can clothe ourselves. You have entered our huts: what do you think they lack? Pursue to your liking what you call the comforts of life, but allow sensible beings to stop short, when, by continuity of laborious effort, there is but imaginary good to be attained. Were we persuaded to cross the narrow confines of our wants, where would our labours end? When should we enjoy life? We have reduced the sum total of our daily and year-long fatigues to the least possible, for to us nothing seems preferable to repose. Go busy yourself in your own country, torment yourself as you please; let us repose; cease to press your factitious needs upon us, and your idle virtues. Look on these men: how upright they stand, how healthy and robust. Look on these women: how upright, healthy, fresh and fair. Take this bow of mine, call on your comrades; one, two, three, and four, to aid thee; try to bend it. I bend it alone. I till the ground; I climb the mountains; I pierce the forest; I cover a league of level ground in less than an hour. Your young men have difficulty in following me; and I am ninety years and more. Woe to this isle! Woe to the Tahitians, woe to Tahitians to come, woe the day you came among us! . . .'

IV

The Dialogue Continued (between A and B)

A. I have great respect for this gentle Almoner.

B. I also, but yet more for the manners of Tahiti and the discursions of Orou.

A. Though perhaps somewhat on the European model.

B. No doubt of that.

Then the good almomer laments the shortness of his stay in Tahiti, and the difficulty of getting to know properly the ways of a people wise enough to have halted their progress of their own accord, and happy enough to live in a climate where fertility assured them long periods of torpor; active enough to avoid absolute want, and indolent enough to fear not for its innocence, peace, and happiness, from any too rapid progress of enlightenment. Nothing, in opinion or law, was held evil save what was evil in itself. Labour and harvest were shared in common. Property had a very restricted signification. The passion of love, reduced to physical appetite, set up none of our disorders. The whole island offered the picture of one numerous family, where each hut might be considered as the separate apartment of one of our big houses. He ends by protesting that the Tahitian will always dwell in his memory, and that he had been much tempted to cast his habit into the ship's hold, and to pass the rest of his days among them; and he much fears that he may regret not having done so. . . .

A. And now, after that eulogy, what useful conclusions are to be drawn from the strange customs and habits of an uncivilized people?

B. I perceive that as soon as man's intelligence is called into play by some physical cause, for example the necessity of conquering an ungrateful soil, its impetus carries him far beyond his immediate aim, and that the need having been met, he is transported into a boundless ocean of fantasies, from which he can never more emerge. If only the happy Tahitian could stop at the place he has now reached! I see that except in this distant corner of our planet there have never been any real manners and there never will be.

A. What do you mean by manners?

B. I mean a general submission to laws either good or bad and the behaviour which goes with it. If the laws are good the manners are good, if the laws are bad the manners are bad; if the laws good or bad are not observed, and that is the worst possible condition for any society, there are no manners. Now how do you suppose laws are to be observed when they contradict each other? Look through the history of centuries and nations, both ancient and modern, and you will find men subjugated to three codes, natural, civil, and religious, and obliged alternatively to infringe all three, for they have never agreed together; from which it follows that there has never been in any country as Orou guessed of ours either a man, a citizen, or a religious.

A. From which you conclude, no doubt, that when morality is founded upon the eternal relationships existing between one man and another, the laws of religion may perhaps become superfluous and that the civil law should be no more than the setting forth of the laws of nature.

B. Otherwise there is a risk of multiplying evil-doers instead of making people good.

A. Or, you hold that, if all three codes are to be preserved, the second two should be no more than rigorous copies of the first which we bear written in the depths of your hearts and which will always be the strongest.

B. That is not accurate. When we are born we have nothing but a constitution like other beings, the same needs, an attraction for the same pleasures, and a common aversion for the same pains: that is what man is made up of, what he is, and it should provide the basis for a moral system which is suitable for him.

A. That is not easy to find.

B. It is so difficult that I am ready to believe the most backward tribe on earth, the Tahitians who have kept scrupulously to the laws of nature are nearer to a good system of legislation than any civilized nation.

(From *A Supplement to Bougainville's Voyage, or A Dialogue between A and B on the expediency of attaching moral ideas to certain physical actions which have nothing to do with them.* Translated by Mrs. Wilfred Jackson, 1926.)

THIS IS NOT A FICTION

(Written about 1772. Published 1798)

IF THERE ARE WICKED WOMEN AND VERY GOOD MEN, THERE
are also very good women and very wicked men; and what
follows is no more a fiction than what precedes.

'I am sure of it.'

'M. d'Hérouville . . .'

'The one who is still alive? The Lieutenant-General of the
King's army? He who married that charming creature called
Lolotte?"

'The very same.'

'He is a man of honour, a patron of science.'

'And of learning. For a long time he has been preparing a
general history of war in all countries throughout the ages.'

'That is a vast project.'

'In order to carry it out, he gathered round him some young
men of distinction such as M. de Montuela, author of the History
of Mathematics.'

'Good gracious! Had he many of that calibre?'

'Among them all Gardeil, hero of the adventure I am going
to describe, yielded to no one in his own line. A common
passion for the study of Greek brought us together and in time,
through the interchange of advice, the taste we both had for
retirement and the ease with which we could see each other,
we became fairly intimate.'

'You were then living at the Estrapade.'

'Yes, and he in the Rue Sainte-Hyacinthe, while his friend,
Mlle de la Chaux, lived in the Place Saint-Michel. I give you
her name because the poor wretch is no longer alive, because
her story can bring her nothing but honour in the eyes of all
right-minded people, and because she deserves the admiration,
the pity and the tears of those whom nature has favoured or
punished with a fraction of her own tender-heartedness.'

'But your voice falters and I think you are crying.'

'It seems to me that I still see her great dark eyes, with their
melting lustre and that her voice still sounds in my ears and moves

my heart. Charming and unique creature! You are no more! It is nearly twenty years since you died and yet my heart is wrung even now at the thought of you!'

'Did you love her?'

'No. Oh, La Chaux! Oh Gardeil! You were both of you prodigies, the one of woman's tenderness, the other of man's ingratitude. Mlle de la Chaux came of a good family. She left her parents to throw herself into the arms of Gardeil. Gardeil had nothing. Mlle de la Chaux had a little money of her own, this was entirely sacrificed to the needs and fancies of Gardeil. She deplored neither the loss of her fortune nor her honour. Her lover made up for everything.'

'So this fellow, Gardeil, was very attractive, very charming?'

'Not in the least. A morose little man, taciturn and caustic; with a sour expression and a sallow complexion, altogether a mean and puny figure; ugly with the ugliness of his mind, if such a thing is possible.'

'And it was this which turned the head of a charming girl?'

'You are surprised at such a thing?'

'Of course.'

'*You?*'

'Yes, me.'

'But have you forgotten your adventure with La Deschamps and the deep despair into which you fell when the creature shut her door on you?'

'Let's leave that now; go on with your story, please.'

'I used to say to you: "So she is very beautiful?" and you replied sadly: "No" . . . "Then she is witty?" "She is very stupid" . . . "You are attracted by her talents then?" "She only has one." "And what can this rare, this sublime, this marvellous talent be?" "It is the power to make me happier in her arms than I have ever been in those of another woman." But Mlle de la Chaux, the virtuous and affectionate Mlle de la Chaux, without realizing it, was instinctively grasping at the happiness which you knew and which led you to say of your Deschamps: "If this infamous creature persists in driving me away, I will take a pistol and blow out my brains in her entrance hall." Did you say that or did you not?'

'Yes, I did say it; and even now I don't know why I did not carry out my intention.'

'Then you agree with what I have been saying.'

'I agree with anything you please.'

'My friend, the wisest among us is very lucky if he never meets the woman, be she beautiful or ugly, witty or stupid, who is capable of making him qualify for the asylum of the Petites-Maisons. We must greatly pity our fellows, we must not blame them too severely; we must look upon our past years as so many moments saved from the cruelty of fate; and let us tremble at the thought of the violence of certain natural attractions, above all where emotions are inflammable and imagination impressionable. A spark falling by accident on a barrel of gunpowder does not produce a more terrible effect. Perhaps the hand ready to drop such a fatal spark on you or me is already raised.'

'M. d'Hérouville, eager to hurry on his work, exhausted those who were co-operating with him. Gardeil's health was affected. In order to lighten his task Mlle de la Chaux learnt Hebrew, and while her friend was resting she sat up part of the night interpreting and transcribing fragments from Hebrew writers. The time came for ransacking the Greek authors; Mlle de la Chaux hastened to perfect herself in this language of which she already had a smattering; and, while Gardeil was sleeping, she was busy translating and copying passages from Xenophon and Thucydides. To her knowledge of Greek and Hebrew she added that of Italian and English. She was so proficient in English that she could put into French Hume's fine metaphysical essays where the difficulty of the subject adds considerably to that of the idiom. When she was worn out with study she amused herself by engraving music. When she feared that her lover might be getting bored she sang. I am not exaggerating anything; all this could be confirmed by M. Le Camus, the doctor of medicine who comforted her in her sufferings and came to the rescue in her dire need, who placed his services constantly at her disposal, who followed her to the garret whither poverty drove her and who closed her eyes when she died. But I am forgetting one of her first troubles, which was the persecution she had to endure from her family outraged by the publicity and scandal of her attachment. They used both fair means and foul to interfere with her liberty in the most infamous manner. Her parents and the priests followed her from one district to another and from house to house and obliged her for several years to live alone and in hiding. She spent her days working for Gardeil. We came to see her at night and at the sight of her lover all sorrows and worries faded away.'

'What! Young, faint-hearted and sensitive, in the midst of so great misfortunes she could be happy?'

'Happy! Yes indeed. She did not stop being so when Gardeil was ungrateful.'

'But it is impossible that such rare qualities, such tenderness, such sacrifices, of every description should have met with ingratitude.'

'You are mistaken, Gardeil was ungrateful. There came a day when Mlle de la Chaux was left alone in the world, without honour, fortune or support. But no, that is not quite true, because she still had me for some time, and she had Dr. Camus for always.'

'Oh, men, men!'

'Of whom are you speaking?'

'Of Gardeil.'

'You have your attention fixed on the wrong-doer and you don't notice the good close at hand. That day of despair she came running to me. It was in the morning. She was pale as death. She had only known her fate the evening before but she was the picture of long-drawn-out misery. She was not in tears, but it was obvious that she had been crying a great deal. She flung herself into an armchair; she stretched her arms towards me, at the same time calling out in her despair. "What is it," I asked, "Is he dead?" . . . "It is worse than that: he does not love me any longer; he is leaving me . . ."'

'Come, come, pull yourself together.'

'I can't help it; I see her, I hear her and my eyes fill with tears. "He does not love you any more?"—"No."—"He has abandoned you!" "Alas, yes! After all I have done for him! . . . Monsieur, I am bewildered; have pity on me; do not leave me; please do not leave me . . ." In saying these words she had seized my arm which she clung to as if someone had been standing there threatening to drag her away. "Don't be afraid, Mademoiselle."—"I am only afraid of myself." "What can I do for you?" "First save me from myself. . . . He no longer loves me! I tire him! I get on his nerves! I bore him! He hates me! He abandons me! He leaves me!" A deep silence followed this repetition, and after the silence came a burst of convulsive laughter a thousand times more terrifying than the moans of despair or the death-rattle of someone *in extremis*. Then came tears, cries, inarticulate words, eyes cast heavenwards, trembling lips, a torrent of distress which had to be allowed to take its course. I waited accordingly and did not begin to reason with her until I saw her spirit broken and inert. Then I started again. "He hates you! He is leaving you! And who told you that?" "He did." "Come, Mademoiselle, a little hope and courage. He is not a monster. . . ." "You don't know him; but you are going to. He is a monster such as you could find nowhere else, such as there never has been." "I can scarcely believe it." "You will see." "Is it because he loves someone else?" "No." "Have you ever given him any cause for suspicion or annoyance?" "None, absolutely none." "What is the matter then?" "My uselessness. All I had is gone. I am no good for anything. His ambition; he has always been ambitious. The loss of my health and my charm; I have suffered so much and been so tired. Boredom, disgust." "People may cease to be lovers, but they can remain friends." "I have become unendurable to him; my presence weighs upon him, the sight of me pains and wounds him. If you only knew what he said to me! Yes, sir, he told me that if he were condemned to spend twenty-four hours with me, he would throw himself out of the window." "But this aversion is not the work of a moment." "How can I tell? He is always so disdainful! So indifferent! So cold. It is so difficult to see to the bottom of such souls! And one is so unwilling to read one's death sentence! That is what he has pronounced on me and with what severity!" "I can't understand it at all." "I have a favour to ask you; that is why I have come; will you grant it to me." "Yes, whatever it may be." "Listen, he has a respect for you; you know how much he owes me. Perhaps he would blush to show himself to you in his true colours. No, I do not think he is brazen-faced or strong enough for that. I am only a woman, and you are a man. A kindly, upright and just man has an influence. You will influence him. Give me your arm and do not refuse to accompany me to his house. I want to talk to him in front of you. Who knows what my distress and your presence might not accomplish with him? You will come with me?" "Willingly." "Let us go then." '

'I am afraid that her distress and your presence made no difference. Disgust! Why, disgust in love is a terrible thing and especially when it is felt for a woman! . . .'

'I sent to fetch a carrying chair, for she was scarcely in a fit state for walking. We arrived at Gardeil's, that big new house, the only one there is on the right-hand side of the Rue Hyacinthe coming from the Place Saint-Michel. There the bearers stopped; they opened the door. I waited. She did not get out. I approached and saw her seized with a violent attack of shivering: her teeth were chattering as they do in cases of high fever, her knees were knocking against each other. "One moment, Monsieur; I beg your pardon; I really don't know. . . . What should I be doing here? I have interrupted your work for nothing; I am truly sorry; I beg your pardon. . . ." Nevertheless I held out my arm for her. She took it, she tried to get up; she was unable to do so. "One more moment, Monsieur." She said to me; "I make you grieve, you have pity for my condition. . . ." Finally she recovered her confidence a little, and getting out of her chair she whispered: "We must go in; we must see him. Who knows? Perhaps I shall die here. . . ." And there we were, having crossed the courtyard; there we were, at the door of the apartments; there we were, in Gardeil's study. He was at his desk wearing a dressing-gown and night cap. He greeted me with a sign of his hand and went on with something he had just started. When it was done he came up to me and said, "You must agree, Monsieur, that women are very troublesome. I offer a thousand apologies for Mademoiselle's extravagant behaviour." Then turning to the poor creature who was more dead than alive he said: "Mademoiselle, what do you still want of me? I should have thought that, after the clear and precise manner in which I explained myself, all would have been finished between us. I told you I did not love you any longer; I told it to you in private, when we were alone; apparently you want me to repeat it before Monsieur. Very well, Mademoiselle, I do not love you any more. The flame of love is extinguished in my heart; it burns neither for you nor, I might add, if that is any consolation, for any other woman." "But tell me why you no longer love me." "I am totally ignorant of the reason; all I can tell you is that I began without knowing why and I have stopped without knowing why and that I feel it to be impossible that the passion

N   [361]

should ever return to me; it is a malady I have thrown off and from which I congratulate myself that I have completely recovered." "What have I done wrong?" "Nothing." "Have you by chance some secret objection to anything in my conduct?" "Not the slightest; you have been the most constant, the most virtuous and the most loving woman a man could desire." "Have I omitted anything which it was in my power to do?" "Nothing." "Did I not sacrifice my parents for you?" "Yes, that is true." "My fortune?" "I am in despair about it." "My health?" "That is quite possible." "My honour, my reputation, my repose." "All you like to mention." "And I am odious to you!" "That is a hard thing to say, hard to hear, but since it is the truth we must admit it." "I am odious to him! I feel it, and I am the same in my own estimation! . . . Odious! Ye Gods! . . ." At these words a deathly pallor spread over her face, her lips lost their colour; drops of cold sweat formed on her cheeks and mingled with her tears; her eyes were shut, her head had fallen back into the chair, her teeth were clenched; all her limbs were trembling: this shivering was followed by a loss of consciousness which seemed to me to be the fulfilment of the desire she had expressed at the door of the house. The length of time she remained in this condition brought my fears to a climax: I removed her cloak, I loosened the strings of her dress, I untied those of her petticoats and I threw some drops of cold water on her face. Her eyes began to open, a stifled mumbling sound came from her throat; she wanted to say, "He thinks I am odious" and she could only articulate the last syllables of the word; then she gave a sharp cry, her eyelids closed and she fainted once more. Gardeil, remaining coldly seated in his armchair, his elbow resting on the table and his head on his hand, looked at her without emotion and left the care of her to me. I said to him several times, "But Monsieur, she is dying." He replied, shrugging his shoulders with a smile: "Women are tough: it takes more than that to kill them; it is nothing; it will pass off. You don't know them; they do whatever they like with their bodies." "She is dying, I tell you." And indeed her form was without strength or life; it was slipping off the chair, and she would have fallen to the ground on one side or the other if I had not held on to her. Gardeil, however, got up abruptly and walking up and down his room said with impatience and anger, "I could have gladly

[362]

dispensed with this unpleasant scene, but I sincerely hope it will be the last. What the devil does the creature want? I have been fond of her. If I should beat my head against a brick wall it would not make any difference. I don't love her any longer; she knows it now, or she never will. There is no more to be said. . . ." "On the contrary, Monsieur, there is a great deal more to be said. What! You think that an honest man has only to despoil a woman of all she has and then desert her." "What do you want me to do? I am as hard up as she is." "What I want you to do? Why, to share your poverty with that to which you have reduced her." "It's all very well for you to talk like this. She would be no better off and I should be much worse." "Would you treat a man friend thus if he had sacrificed everything for your sake?" "A friend, indeed! I have not much faith in friends, and this experience has taught me to have none in human passions. I am sorry I did not realize it sooner." "Is it fair that this unhappy woman should be the victim of your mistake?" "And what is to tell me that one day, in a month or so, I should not have suffered equally cruelly as the victim of hers." "What is to tell you? Why, everything that she has done for you and the state in which you now see her." "What she has done for me! . . . Well, upon my word, that has been amply repaid by the waste of my time." "Oh, Monsieur Gardeil, how can you compare your time with all those things beyond price which you have taken from her!" "I have done nothing as yet, I have no position and I am thirty; it is time now to think of myself if I am ever to do so and to see all this sentimental rubbish for what it is . . ."

'The poor young lady had come round a little by now. At these last words she began speaking with a certain amount of energy: "What did he say about the waste of his time? I learnt four languages to relieve him of his work; I read a thousand volumes; I wrote, translated, copied by day and by night; I have exhausted my strength, ruined my eyes, made myself feverish; I have contracted a troublesome illness from which I shall perhaps never be cured. As for the cause of his disgust, he does not dare to admit it, but you shall know what it is." At that moment she tore off her scarf, she slipped one of her arms out of her dress; she bared her shoulder, and showing me a patch of erysipelas, she said: "There you see the reason for the change in him, you have it there! This is the result of the nights I sat up. He used to arrive in the morning with his rolls of parchment. 'M. de Hérouville is in a great hurry to know what is in there,' he would say, 'the job must be finished by to-morrow'; and it always was. . . ." At this moment we heard the step of someone at the door; it was a servant coming to announce the arrival of M. d'Hérouville. Gardeil grew pale. I invited Mlle de la Chaux to arrange her toilet and to retire. . . . "No," said she, "no; I am going to stay. I want to unmask the scoundrel. I will wait for M. d'Hérouville, I will speak to him." "And what will be the use of that?" "It will be of no use," she replied; "you are quite right." "To-morrow you will be wretched about it. Leave him all his faults; it is a vengeance worthy of you." "But is it worthy of him? Do you not see that that man . . . Let us go, Monsieur, let us go quickly; for I cannot answer for what I should do or say. . . ." In an instant Mlle de la Chaux readjusted the clothes which had been disarranged in the course of this scene and darted out of Gardeil's study. I followed her and heard the door slam behind us. Later I learned that the porter had been given a description of her.

'I took her back to her home where we found Dr. Camus waiting for us. The passion which now filled him for this girl differed little from that she felt for Gardeil. I gave him an account of our visit which he punctuated with signs of rage, distress, and indignation.'

'It was not so very difficult to discover from his face that your lack of success did not displease him too much.'

'That is true.'

'There you have man all over. He is no better than that.'

'This quarrel was followed by a severe illness during which the good, the honest, the affectionate and tactful doctor tended her with more care than he could have bestowed on the greatest lady of France. He came three or four times a day. As long as she was in danger he slept in her room on a camp bed. An illness is a blessing in cases of great sorrow.'

'In turning our attention upon ourselves it keeps it off other people. Besides it is an excuse for giving way without indiscretion or constraint.'

'This remark, though true, cannot be applied to Mlle de la Chaux.'

During her convalescence, we arranged for the employment of her time. She had more intelligence, imagination, taste, knowledge than was necessary for admission to the Académie des Inscriptions. She had so often heard our metaphysical discussions that she was familiar with the most abstract subjects, and her first literary effort was the translation of the Essay concerning Human Understanding by Hume.[1] I revised it, and I can truly say that there was very little to correct. This translation was printed in Holland and well received by the public.

My letter on the Deaf and Dumb appeared almost at the same time. Some very discerning criticisms she suggested led me to add a supplement which I dedicated to her. This addition is not among the worst things I have done.

[1] Actually this is by Locke, but Diderot may be referring to Hume's Moral and Philosophical Essays, or his Treatise on Human Nature.

A LAMENT FOR MY OLD DRESSING-GOWN
(Written in 1772)

WHY NOT HAVE KEPT IT? IT SUITED ME, AND I JUST SUITED it. It followed the lines of my body without cramping me. I looked well and picturesque in that old dressing-gown, while the new one, so stiff and starched, makes me look like a lay-figure. My old friend, too, was always at hand to serve me in any emergency, for poverty is generally kindly. If a book were dusty, a corner of my gown was ready to wipe it. If the ink in my pen got thick and refused to flow, there were the skirts of my dressing-gown ready, and you could see the long black lines traced on them by the stubborn pen. These long lines were tokens that the owner was a writer, a man of letters, a man who toils; now I look like a well-to-do idle fellow, and no one can tell what I am.

Under its shelter I feared no mishaps, neither those of my valet, nor my own, neither sparks from the fire nor splashes of water. I was complete master of my old dressing-gown; I have now become the slave of the new.

The dragon watching the Golden Fleece was not more on the alert than I am now; I am surrounded by cares. An old man, overcome by passion, who has yielded himself up, bound hand and foot, to the caprices and follies of a young girl, regrets his old housekeeper and nurse at every hour of the day. 'What demon possessed me,' he cries, 'to drive her away in exchange for this girl?' and he sighs and weeps.

I neither weep nor sigh, but every minute I say 'Cursed be he who invented the scarlet dye which makes common stuff precious. Cursed be the costly garment which I must treat with respect. Where is the venerable, humble, and comfortable piece of chintz?'

Oh, my friends, cling to your old friends and fear the approach of riches. Let my example warn you. Poverty has its freedom, but riches bring restraints. Oh! Diogenes, if you saw your disciple dressed in the rich cloak of Aristippus, would you not laugh? Oh! Aristippus, you paid dearly for that sumptuous garment. What a difference between your soft, effeminate, cringing ways, and the free and vigorous life of the ragged cynic; I have left the tub where I reigned to become a tyrant's slave. That is not all. Listen, my friend, to the evil consequences of luxury, of luxury which tries to creep into your life.

My old dressing-gown was in harmony with the rest of my poor rubbish. A straw chair, a wooden table, Bergamo hangings, a deal board with a few books on it, some smoky prints unmounted, and just nailed at the four corners on the wall; between these prints were three or four plaster casts, all these, together with my old gown, produced a most harmonious effect of poverty.

Now everything is out of tune. Everything is discordant, there is no unity, no beauty. The scarlet intruder has produced as much trouble in my house as a new and stingy housekeeper causes in a rectory, or as when a widower receives a lady visitor, or a new minister succeeds another who has fallen from power; or as when a Molinist Bishop gets hold of the diocese of a Jansenist.

I am not disgusted at the sight of a peasant woman with a coarse piece of sacking on her head, her hair straggling down her cheeks, and her tattered clothes that hardly cover her. I don't mind her short skirts that only come to her knees, nor her bare feet soiled with mud; she is just a peasant in her working-dress whom I can respect, while I pity the misery and poverty inevitable to this state.

But what does offend my eyes in spite of the perfumed atmosphere around her, what I dislike and turn away from is a low woman in a lace cap and torn ruffles, with silk stockings, and down-trodden shoes, who brings before me her present misery mingled with traces of the ill-gained luxury of former days.

My house would have been like this ill-assorted dress if the imperious scarlet gown had not driven away all tokens of poverty. I saw the Bergamo hangings taken down from the wall, where they had lived so long, to give way to damask draperies. Two prints, not without some merit, Poussin's 'The Fall of Manna in the Desert,' and his 'Esther before Ahasuerus,' were driven away ignominiously; sad Esther gave place to 'An Old Man' by Rubens, while the 'Fall of Manna' has been exchanged for 'The Storm' by Vernet. The new leather armchair has in like manner sent the straw one off in disgrace to the ante-chamber.

No longer do Homer, Virgil, Horace, and Cicero bow down the hanging deal board by their weight; they are now enclosed in an inlaid cabinet, a refuge more suited to their importance than to me. A large mirror now occupies the place of honour over the chimney-piece, and the two pretty plaster casts, which were the gift of my friend Falconet, and which he himself had mended, have been turned out by a stooping Venus—modern clay trampled by antique bronze.

I thought my wooden table had escaped notice, for it was completely hidden under a mass of papers and pamphlets heaped upon it. These should have been a protection, but they were unable to save it from its fate, and one day, without my being consulted, all my papers and pamphlets were neatly arranged in a handsome bureau.

The tendency of fashion is, alas! destructive, it leads to ruinous expense and constant change; it alters, it builds up, it pulls down, it empties the father's purse, and prevents his giving a portion to his daughter or educating his son.

Oh, Fashion, it is you who produce so many beautiful things and such great evils, it is you who changed my wooden table for this costly and fatal bureau; it is you who destroy nations, and it is you who one day, perchance, may take all my goods to the St. Michel bridge,[1] where the auctioneer will shout out in his hoarse voice, 'A stooping Venus going for twenty louis.'

The blank space between the top of the bureau and 'The Storm,' by Vernet, was unpleasing to the eye, and this has been filled up by a clock—a clock worthy of the donor, where gilt and bronze make an artistic contrast.

There was an empty corner near my window; it seemed to be waiting for the writing-table which was sent to fill it.

There was another vacant space between the table and the fine head of Rubens, and here two pictures by La Grenée were placed. On one side hangs a Magdalene by the same artist, and on the other a sketch by de Vien or de Marchy, for I am fond of sketches.

It was in this manner that the sober retreat of the philosopher was changed into the shameful den of the publican, while I flaunt my luxury in the face of a nation's misery.

---

[1] The place where goods seized for debt are sold.

The only relic of my former simplicity is a list carpet. I feel that this shabby rug is out of harmony with my other luxuries; but I have solemnly sworn that I will keep this carpet, as the peasant who exchanged a cottage for his Sovereign's Palace kept his sabots; the foot of Denis the philosopher shall never tread the rich carpets of la Savonnerie. When I enter my study in the morning, clothed sumptuously in scarlet, I have but to look down, and the sight of my old list rug reminds me of my former state and checks all feelings of pride.

No, no, my friend, I am not yet spoilt by prosperity. My door still opens freely to those who are in need. I am ready to listen with kindly interest and to give my advice, my sympathy, and my help. My heart has not grown hard; I do not hold my head proudly aloof. My back is still as round as ever, and as ready to stoop as before. I am as frank and as pitiful as erst. My luxury is but recent, and the poison has not yet got into my veins. But who knows what may happen in time? What can you expect from a man when he forgets his wife and his daughter, when he ceases to be a good husband and father, when he gets into debt, and dissipates the money which he should be laying by for them?

Oh, holy prophet, lift up your hands in prayer to Heaven for a friend in peril, and say: 'O God, who readest the hearts of men, if Thou seeest that Denis is becoming corrupted by riches, do not spare the treasures which he worships; destroy them, and let him return to his former poverty.' And I on my part will also pray to Heaven, and say: 'O God, I resign myself to Thy will, and to the prayer of the holy prophet; I give up all my wealth to Thee, take all, yes, all—except the picture that Vernet painted. Oh, leave me my Vernet! It is Thy work, not the artist's. Spare this gift from friendship and from Thee. Behold this lighthouse, this ancient tower beside it, and this old tree torn by the gales. How beautiful is this composition! And below these dark masses are rocks with green vegetation springing from them; they are the work of Thy hand, Thy power made them, Thy bounty gave them their grace.

'Look at this broken ground which stretches from the foot of the rocks to the sea; it is an image of the gradual wearing away by time of what seems most enduring in this world, and it is by Thy permission that time exercises this power. See how the painter has imitated the sunshine. O God, if Thou destroyest

N*   [369]

this work of art, men will say Thou art a jealous God. Have pity on these poor shipwrecked folk; hast Thou not shown them the abysses of the deep? Hast Thou rescued them only that they may perish? Hear the prayer of him who now kneels to express his gratitude; help him who is there gathering up his scattered remnants of wealth. Close Thy ear to the curses of this fellow who rages against his lot. Alas! he had reckoned a prosperous voyage; this was to be his last, and then he would retire to enjoy ease and tranquillity. A hundred times during the voyage he had calculated what his capital would be, and how he would invest it, and now all his hopes are disappointed, and he has hardly enough left to clothe his naked limbs. Look kindly on the affection of this attached couple; see how the frightened mother lifts up her eyes to heaven with gratitude, while the young child, ignorant of the perils it has passed through with its parents, is busy fastening the collar of the dog who has been a faithful playmate. Have pity on the innocent child whose mother trembled for its life more than for her own in the hour of their common danger. See how she clasps the child to her breast and kisses it. Behold, O God, these waters which Thou hast made; behold them alike when they rage and when they sink to rest at Thy command. Behold these dark clouds which Thou didst gather and which are now dispersing in obedience to Thy will. The dark masses are breaking up and speeding away, and now the light of dawn begins to spread on the face of the waters, and the rosy horizon seems to foretell a calm day. How far the horizon seems, and how indefinite; it does not appear to touch the sea, no, that sky is over-arching the round earth beyond our sight.

'Let the blue sky everywhere appear, and let the sea regain her calm. Suffer these shipwrecked sailors to launch out their vessel again; strengthen them for their task, help them, but leave me my picture. Leave it to me, even as a rod to scourge my vanity, for it will not be my discourse which men will care to hear, nor is it me they will care to visit; it is Vernet who will be the object of their admiration, and the painter will supplant the philosopher.'

Oh, my friend, what a fine picture I possess; the subject is a shipwreck where no one has been drowned; the sea is still rough, the sky is dark with clouds, the sailors are busy about the wreck, while the peasants are flocking to the shore from the neighbouring hills. How cleverly the artist has managed with the aid of a few figures to bring all the incidents of the event before us. How realistic is the scene, and how vigorously yet delicately painted, and with what ease. I am resolved to keep this token of the painter's friendship, and my son-in-law shall leave it to his children and children's children.

If you could only see this work of art, and observe how every part is in harmony; there are no detached points, but one part leads to another with easy grace, and each has its own value in the whole. What an atmosphere is round the mountains, and how well the rocks and buildings stand out from the background. Here is a picturesque tree, and there a ledge of ground catching the light in a charming way. Look at these groups of figures, how well arranged, how natural, they seem to live and move before us and to claim our attention. How pure these outlines; what richness of colour and well-balanced contrasts. What a width of horizon beyond these moving waters; the sky and clouds and distance all seem to us real. The foreground is in light against a dark background, which is contrary to the usual disposition of light and shade. Come and see my Vernet, but spare my treasure. If time be granted me, my debts can be paid off; then remorse will vanish, and pure enjoyment be left. Do not fear that I shall be bitten by the mania of buying works of art; I keep my old friends, but do not add to their number. I have Laïs, but Laïs has no power over me; I am ready to give her up to one who could love her better, and who would appreciate her more than I do. And—to whisper a secret in your ear—Laïs, though dearly bought by others, has cost me nothing.

(Taken in great part from the translation of Beatrix Tollemache in *Diderot's Thoughts on Art and Style*.)

THE PARADOX OF ACTING

(Revised about 1778, published 1830)

THE FIRST SPEAKER. If the actor were full, really full, of feeling, how could he play the same part twice running with the same spirit and success? Full of fire at the first performance, he would be worn out and cold as marble at the third. But take it that he is an attentive mimic and thoughtful disciple of Nature, then the first time he comes on the stage as Augustus, Cinna, Orosmanes, Agamemnon, or Mahomet, faithful copying of himself and the effects he has arrived at, and constantly observing human nature, will so prevail that his acting, far from losing in force, will gather strength with the new observations he will make from time to time. He will increase or moderate his effects, and you will be more and more pleased with him. If he is himself while he is playing, how is he to stop being himself? If he wants to stop being himself, how is he to catch just the point where he is to stay his hand?

What confirms me in this view is the unequal acting of players who play from the heart. From them you must expect no unity. Their playing is alternately strong and feeble, fiery and cold, dull and sublime. To-morrow they will miss the point they have excelled in to-day; and to make up for it will excel in some passage where last time they failed. On the other hand, the actor who plays from thought, from study of human nature, from constant imitation of some ideal type, from imagination, from memory, will be one and the same at all performances, will be always at his best mark; he has considered, combined, learnt and arranged the whole thing in his head; his diction is neither monotonous nor dissonant. His passion has a definite course—it has bursts, and it has reactions; it has a beginning, a middle, and an end. The accents are the same, the positions are the same, the movements are the same; if there is any difference between two performances, the latter is generally the better. He will be invariable; a looking-glass, as it were, ready to reflect realities, and to reflect them ever with the same precision, the same strength, and the same truth. Like the poet he will dip for ever into the inexhaustible treasure-house of Nature, instead of coming very soon to an end of his own poor resources.

What acting was ever more perfect than Clairon's? Think over this, study it; and you will find that at the sixth performance of a given part she has every detail of her acting by heart, just as much as every word of her part. Doubtless she has imagined a type, and to conform to this type has been her first thought; doubtless she has chosen for her purpose the highest, the greatest, the most perfect type her imagination could compass. This type, however, which she has borrowed from history, or created as who should create some vast spectre in her own mind, is not herself. Were it indeed bounded by her own dimensions, how paltry, how feeble would be her playing! When, by dint of hard work, she has got as near as she can to this idea, the thing is done; to preserve the same nearness is a mere matter of memory and practice. If you were with her while she studied her part how many times you would cry out, *That is right!* and how many times she would answer, *You are wrong!*

Just so a friend of Le Quesnoy's once cried, catching him by the arm, 'Stop! you will make it worse by bettering it—you will spoil the whole thing!' 'What I have done,' replied the artist, panting with exertion, 'you have seen; what I have got hold of and what I mean to carry out to the very end you cannot see.'

I have no doubt that Clairon goes through just the same struggles as Le Quesnoy in her first attempts at a part; but once the struggle is over, once she has reached the height she has given to her spectre, she has herself well in hand, she repeats her efforts without emotion. As it will happen in dreams, her head touches the clouds, her hands stretch to grasp the horizon on both sides; she is the informing soul of a huge figure, which is her outward casing, and in which her efforts have enclosed her. As she lies careless and still on a sofa with folded arms and closed eyes she can, following her memory's dream, hear herself, see herself, judge herself, and judge also the effects she will produce. In such a vision she has a double personality; that of the little Clairon and of the great Agrippina.

THE SECOND. According to you the likest thing to an actor, whether on the boards or at his private studies, is a group of children who play at ghosts in a graveyard at dead of night, armed with a white sheet on the end of a broomstick, and sending forth from its shelter hollow groans to frighten wayfarers.

THE FIRST. Just so, indeed. Now with Dumesnil it is a different matter: she is not like Clairon. She comes on the stage without knowing what she is going to say; half the time she does not know what she is saying: but she has one sublime moment. And pray, why should the actor be different from the poet, the painter, the orator, the musician? It is not in the stress of the first burst that characteristic traits come out; it is in moments of stillness and self-command; in moments entirely unexpected. Who can tell whence these traits have their being? They are a sort of inspiration. They come when the man of genius is hovering between nature and his sketch of it, and keeping a watchful eye on both. The beauty of inspiration, the chance hits of which his work is full, and of which the sudden appearance startles himself, have an importance, a success, a sureness very different from that belonging to the first fling. Cool reflection must bring the fury of enthusiasm to its bearings.

The extravagant creature who loses his self-control has no hold on us; this is gained by the man who is self-controlled. The great poets, especially the great dramatic poets, keep a keen watch on what is going on, both in the physical and the moral world.

THE SECOND. The two are the same.

THE FIRST. They dart on everything which strikes their imagination; they make, as it were, a collection of such things. And from these collections, made all unconsciously, issue the grandest achievements of their work.

Your fiery, extravagant, sensitive fellow, is for ever on the boards; he acts the play, but he gets nothing out of it. It is in him that the man of genius finds his model. Great poets, great actors, and, I may add, all great copyists of Nature, in whatever art, beings gifted with fine imagination, with broad judgment, with exquisite tact, with a sure touch of taste, are the least sensitive of all creatures. They are too apt for too many things, too busy with observing, considering, and reproducing, to have their inmost hearts affected with any liveliness. To me such an one always has his portfolio spread before him and his pencil in his fingers.

It is we who feel; it is they who watch, study, and give us

the result. And then . . . well, why should I not say it? Sensibility is by no means the distinguishing mark of a great genius.
He will have, let us say, an abstract love of justice, but he will
not be moved to temper it with mercy. It is the head, not the
heart, which works in and for him. Let some unforeseen opportunity arise, the man of sensibility will lose it; he will never be
a great king, a great minister, a great commander, a great
advocate, a great physician. Fill the front of a theatre with
tearful creatures, but I will none of them on the boards. Think
of women again. They are miles beyond us in sensibility; there
is no sort of comparison between their passion and ours. But
as much as we are below them in action, so much are they
below us in imitation. If a man who is really manly drops a
tear, it touches us more nearly than a storm of weeping from
a woman. In the great play, the play of the world, the play
to which I am constantly recurring, the stage is held by the
fiery souls, and the pit is filled with men of genius. The actors
are in other words madmen; the spectators, whose business it
is to paint their madness, are sages. And it is they who discern
with a ready eye the absurdity of the motley crowd, who
reproduce it for you, and who make you laugh both at the
unhappy models who have bored you to death and at yourself.
It is they who watch you, and who give you the mirth-moving
picture of the tiresome wretch and of your own anguish in his
clutches.

You may prove this to demonstration, and a great actor will
decline to acknowledge it; it is his own secret. A middling actor
or a novice is sure to contradict you flatly; and of some it may
be said that they believe they feel, just as it has been said of some
pious people that they believe they believe; and that without
faith in the one case and without sensibility in the other there
is no salvation.

This is all very well, you may reply; but what of these
touching and sorrowful accents that are drawn from the very
depth of a mother's heart and that shake my whole being? Are
these not the result of true feeling? Are these not the very
inspiration of despair? Most certainly not. The proof is that they
are all planned; that they are part of a system of declamation;
that, raised or lowered by the twentieth part of a quarter of
a tone, would ring false; that they are in subjection to a

[375]

law of unity; that, as in harmony, they are arranged in chords and in discords; that laborious study is needed to give them completeness; that they are the elements necessary to the solving of a given problem; that, to hit the right mark once, they have been practised a hundred times; and that, despite all this practice, they are yet found wanting. Look you, before he cries '*Zaïre vous pleurez,*' or '*Vous y serez ma fille,*' the actor has listened over and over to his own voice. At the very moment when he touches your heart he is listening to his own voice; his talent depends not, as you think, upon feeling, but upon rendering so exactly the outward signs of feeling, that you fall into the trap. He has learnt before a mirror every particle of his despair. He knows exactly when he must produce his handkerchief and shed tears; and you will see him weep at the word, at the syllable he has chosen, not a second sooner or later. The broken voice, the half-uttered words, the stifled or prolonged notes of agony, the trembling limbs, the faintings, the bursts of fury—all this is pure mimicry, lessons carefully learned, the grimacing of sorrow, the magnificent aping which the actor remembers long after his first study of it, of which he was perfectly conscious when he first put it before the public, and which leaves him, luckily for the poet, the spectator, and himself, a full freedom of mind. Like other gymnastics, it taxes only his bodily strength. He puts off the sock or the buskin; his voice is gone; he is tired; he changes his dress, or he goes to bed, and he feels neither trouble, nor sorrow, nor depression, nor weariness of soul. All these emotions he has given to you. The actor is tired, you are unhappy; he has had exertion without feeling, you feeling without exertion. Were it otherwise, the player's lot would be the most wretched on earth: but he is not the person he represents; he plays it, and plays it so well that you think he is the person; the deception is all on your side; he knows well enough that he is not the person.

For diverse modes of feeling arranged in concert to obtain the greatest effect, scored orchestrally, played *piano* and played *forte,* harmonized to make an individual effect—all that to me is food for laughter. I hold to my point, and I tell you this: 'Extreme sensibility makes middling actors; middling sensibility makes the ruck of bad actors; in complete absence of sensibility is the possibility of a sublime actor.' The player's tears come from his brain, the sensitive being's from his heart; the sensitive being's soul gives unmeasured trouble to his brain; the player's brain gives sometimes a touch of trouble to his soul: he weeps as might weep an unbelieving priest preaching of the Passion; as a seducer might weep at the feet of a woman whom he does not love, but on whom he would impose; like a beggar in the street or at the door of a church—a beggar who substitutes insult for vain appeal; or like a courtesan who has no heart, and who abandons herself in your arms.

Have you ever thought on the difference between the tears raised by a tragedy of real life and those raised by a touching narrative? You hear a fine piece of recitation; by little and little your thoughts are involved, your heart is touched, and your tears flow. With the tragedy of real life the thing, the feeling and the effect, are all one; your heart is reached at once, you utter a cry, your head swims, and the tears flow. These tears come of a sudden, the others by degrees. And here is the superiority of a true effect of nature over a well-planned scene. It does at one stroke what the scene leads up to by degrees, but it is far more difficult to reproduce its effect; one incident ill given would shatter it. Accents are more easily mimicked than actions, but actions go straighter to the mark. This is the basis of a canon to which I believe there is no exception. If you would avoid coldness you must complete your effect by action and not by talk.

So, then, have you no objection to make? Ah! I see! You give a recitation in a drawing-room; your feelings are stirred; your voice fails you; you burst into tears. You have, as you say, felt, and felt deeply. Quite so; but had you made up your mind to that? Not at all. Yet you were carried away, you surprised and touched your hearers, you made a great hit. All this is true enough. But now transfer your easy tone, your simple expression, your everyday bearing, to the stage, and, I assure you, you will be paltry and weak. You may cry to your heart's content, and the audience will only laugh. It will be the tragedy outside a booth at a fair. Do you suppose that the dialogue of Corneille, of Racine, of Voltaire, or, let me add, of Shakespeare, can be given with your ordinary voice and with your fireside tone? No; not a bit more than you would tell a fireside story with the open-mouthed emphasis fit for the boards.

[377]

THE SECOND. Perhaps Racine and Corneille, great names as they are, did nothing of account.

THE FIRST. Oh, blasphemy! Who could dare to say it? Who to endorse it? The merest word Corneille wrote cannot be given in everyday tone.

But, to go back, it must have happened to you a hundred times that at the end of your recitation, in the very midst of the agitation and emotion you have caused in your drawing-room audience, a fresh guest has entered, and wanted to hear you again. You find it impossible, you are weary to the soul. Sensibility, fire, tears, all have left you. Why does not the actor feel the same exhaustion? Because there is a world of difference between the interests excited by a flattering tale and by your fellow-man's misfortune. Are you Cinna? Have you ever been Cleopatra, Mérope, Agrippina? Are these same personages on the stage ever historical personages? Not at all. They are the phantoms fashioned from this or that poet's special fantasy. They are well enough on the stage, these hippogriffs, so to call them, with their actions, their bearing, their intonations. They would make but a sorry figure in history; they would raise laughter in society. People would whisper to each other, 'Is this fellow mad? Where in the world does this Don Quixote come from? Who is the inventor of all this stuff? In what world do people talk like this?'

(Translated by W. H. Pollock. Published with an Introduction by H. Irving, 1883.)

JAMES THE FATALIST AND HIS MASTER

(Published in 1796)

HOW DID THEY MEET? BY CHANCE LIKE OTHER PEOPLE. WHAT were their names? What signifies it to you? From what part of the world did they come? From the place they left last. Whither were they going? Must people then always know where they go? For what sayings were they remarkable? The master said nothing particular; and James used to say that his captain was wont to repeat, that all the good and evil which befalls us here below was decreed on high.

MASTER. It is a grand apophthegm this.

JAMES. My captain would add that every ball that was fired from a musket had its billet.

MASTER. And he was right. . . .

JAMES (After a short pause). 'Devil take the inn-keeper and his inn!'

MASTER. Why send your neighbour to the devil? This is not like a Christian.

JAMES. Why? because while I got drunk with his bad wine I forgot to take our horses to water. My father observes it and turns angry. I shake my head; he takes a cudgel and rubs down my shoulders not with all the tenderness in the world. A regiment is passing by on its route to the camp at Fontenoy, and I enlist in disgust. We arrive and the engagement takes place.

MASTER. And you received a ball with your address.

JAMES. You have guessed it; a shot in the knee; and God knows the good and the bad adventures to which this shot has given rise. They are just as closely connected with each other as the links of a chain. Without this shot, for instance, I believe I should neither have been in love nor a cripple all my life.

MASTER. You have then been in love?

JAMES. What though I have?

MASTER. And in consequence of a shot?

JAMES. In consequence of a shot.

MASTER. You never told me a word of this.

JAMES. True, I never did.

[379]

MASTER. Why so?

JAMES. Why, because it could be told neither sooner nor later.

MASTER. And is the moment of communicating the history of these amours arrived?

JAMES. Who knows that it is?

MASTER. As all adventures begin. . . .

James began the history of his amours. It was after dinner. It was the drowsy time of day, and his master fell asleep. Night surprised them in the middle of the fields and they lost their way. Conceive the master then in a terrible passion and horse-whipping his valet without mercy, while the poor devil observed between every stroke, 'This one too it seems was decreed on high.' . . .

You see, reader, that I am in a fine way, and that I have it in my power to make you wait a year, two years, three years, for the story of James's amours, by separating him from his master and making each of them encounter all the dangers I please. What hinders me from marrying the master and making him a cuckold? from embarking James for the Isles? and conducting his master to the same place? from bringing them both to France in the same vessel? How easy it is to invent stories. But both of them will get off with spending a bad night, and you merely for this short delay.

Dawn appeared. Conceive them again mounted upon their horses and pursuing their journey—And where are they going? This is the second time you have asked me the question; and this is the second time that I answer, What is that to you? If I explain the object of their journey, farewell to my James's amours. . . .

They proceeded some time on their way in silence. When they had both a little recovered from their chagrin the master said to the valet: 'Well, then, James, how far had we got with your amours?'

JAMES. I believe we had got the length of the defeat of the enemy's army. They endeavoured to save themselves. They were pursued. Everyone consulted his own safety. I remained upon the field of battle, buried under the number of the dead and wounded, which was prodigious. Next day I was placed, along with a dozen others, upon a cart, in order to be conducted to one of our hospitals. Ah ! Sir, I do not believe that there is any wound more severe than one in the knee.

MASTER. Come, come, James, you are mistaken.

JAMES. No indeed, Sir, I am not mistaken: there are in that spot I know not how many bones, tendons, and other things, which are distinguished by I cannot tell what names. . . .

A country-looking man who followed them, with a girl whom he carried behind him, having listened to their conversation, took up the subject, saying: 'The gentleman is right' . . . It is not ascertained to whom this expression of 'the gentleman' was addressed; but it was not well received by James and by his master. James said to the person who interfered thus indiscreetly in the conversation, 'How come you to introduce your remarks upon this affair?' . . . 'I only obtrude upon a point of my profession; I am a surgeon at your service, and I am going to demonstrate to you that . . .' The woman whom he carried behind him, said to him, 'Good Mr. Doctor, let us pursue our way, and leave these gentlemen, who have no taste for demonstrations.' 'No,' replied the surgeon, 'I wish to demonstrate to them, and I will demonstrate . . .' and, in the act of turning himself round to demonstrate, he pushes against his companion, makes her lose her balance, and throws her to the ground, with one of her feet entangled in the skirts of her dress, and her petticoats turned over her head. James dismounts, extricates the foot of this poor creature, and puts down her petticoats. I don't know whether he began with smoothing her petticoats, or disentangling her foot; but if you could judge of this woman's situation by her cries, she certainly was grievously wounded. And James's master said to the surgeon, 'See what you have done by your eagerness to demonstrate'; and the surgeon returned, 'See what it is to have refused to attend to my demonstration.' . . . Meanwhile James addressed the woman in her fallen state, or after she had got up again, 'Comfort yourself, my good woman; it was neither your own fault, nor the fault of Mr. the Doctor. It is because it was decreed on high, that, upon this day, on this very road, at the present hour, Mr. the Doctor should choose to prattle, that my master and I should be a little cross, that you should get a contusion on the head, and that we should see your . . .'

What might not this adventure grow to in my hands, should I take a fancy to tease you? I might give a great deal of importance to the woman; I might make her the niece of the rector of the neighbouring village; I might set all the peasants in it by the ears; I might prepare stories of battles and of loves; for, in fact, this country girl, under her plain attire, was very pretty. James and his master did not fail to perceive it. Love does not always wait for so seducing an opportunity. Why should not James fall in love a second time? Why should he not a second time be the rival, and the successful rival too, of his master?—And how do you know that they had been in this situation already?—What! always at your questions: you have no inclination then that James should continue the story of his amours? Once for all, pray explain what you would have me do. Will this afford you pleasure, then, or will it not? If it will give you satisfaction, let us again mount the woman on the crupper behind her conductor; allow them to proceed on their journey, and return to our travellers. Upon this occasion it was James who first took up the conversation, and said to his master,

'Observe what is the way of the world. You who never were wounded in the whole course of your life, and who know nothing of what it is to receive a shot on the knee, will persist in maintaining to me, who have had my knee bruised to pieces, and have been a cripple these twenty years. . . .'

MASTER. You may be in the right. But it is owing to this impertinent surgeon that you are still upon the waggon with your comrades, yet far from the hospital, far from being cured, and far from falling in love.

JAMES. Whatever you may choose to think of the matter, the pain of my knee was excessive; it was sadly increased by the hardness of the carriage, by the ruggedness of the roads, and at every jolt I uttered most piercing cries.

MASTER. Because it was decreed on high that you should cry?

JAMES. Assuredly: I had bled to death, and all had been over with me, if our cart, the last of the line had not stopped at the door of the cottage. I requested to come down, and I was laid upon the ground. A young woman, who was standing at the door of the cottage, went in, and almost immediately returned with a glass and a bottle of wine. I drank one or two glasses in haste. The carts which preceded ours drove on. They were going to replace me among my companions, when, clinging to the clothes of this woman, and to everything around me, I protested that I would not mount again, and that, if I was to die,

I preferred meeting death where I was, rather than two leagues farther on. As I uttered these last words I fell in a swoon. When I recovered from this state, I found myself undressed, lying on a bed which occupied one of the corners of the cottage, and beside me a peasant, the owner of the place, his wife, the person who had given me assistance, and some little children. The woman had dipped the corner of her apron in vinegar, and was rubbing my nose and temples.

MASTER. Ah wretch! Ah, knave! . . . Villain, I see you coming.

JAMES. Master of mine, I believe you see nothing at all.

MASTER. Is not this the woman with whom you are about to fall in love?

JAMES. And though I were to fall in love with her, what is there to be said on the subject? Have people in their power to fall in love, or not to fall in love, as they please? And, if people are in love, are they at liberty to act as if they were not? Had this been decreed on high, whatever you have a mind to say to me, I too might have said to myself; I might have beat my breast, dashed my head against the wall, torn my hair, but things would neither have been better nor worse, and my benefactor had still been a cuckold.

MASTER. But, reasoning in your way, there is no crime which may not be perpetrated without remorse.

JAMES. More than once I have perplexed my brain with this objection; but notwithstanding this, in spite of all I can do, I always recur to the saying of my captain—'All the good and evil which befalls is decreed on high.' Are you, sir, acquainted with any means of erasing this decree. Can I help being myself? and, being myself can I act otherwise than I do? Can I be at once myself and a different person? And, since I came first into the world, has any single moment occurred in which this has not been true? preach as long as you please: your arguments, perhaps, may be very good; but if it is decreed within me, or on high, that I should think them bad, pray what would you have me to do?

(Translation of 1797)

LETTERS TO MADEMOISELLE VOLLAND

HOW BEAUTIFUL IT WAS ON ALL SAINTS DAY! DID YOU MAKE
the most of it? At eight in the morning were you up and
dressed? Had you put on your hat and taken your walking-
stick? I am sure not. You were still asleep, you lazybones, and I
was still asleep too, lazybones that I am. I heard someone
knocking at my door. It was the Scotsman. He came in, pulled
back my curtains and said, 'Come along! up you get; the sun
is lovely out in the hills. M. Marchais will be one of the party.'
This M. Marchais is a young sailor whom I have already mentioned to you. As we were going along I asked him his age. 'I
am thirty,' said he. 'Thirty,' I exclaimed with surprise. 'You
look at least forty-five. What has aged you so quickly?' 'The sea
and hard work.' Oh, my dear, you can't imagine what a picture
they gave me of life at sea! People's skin gets wrinkled and black
with exposure, their lips are parched, their muscles stand out
hard as bricks, in less than three or four journeys they look for
all the world like those Tritons in the Gobelins tapestries. They
eat nothing but dry bread and salted meat. Often they have to
go without water, and then there are storms that keep them
suspended between life and death for twenty-four hours at a
stretch. It is impossible for you to conceive what a ship looks
like after a storm. A propos of that the Scotsman said to us:
'You must imagine our sails torn, our masts broken, our sailors
exhausted, the ship without a rudder at the mercy of the waves,
the wind driving us with fury straight towards the rocks; twelve
others and myself were all sitting in the captain's cabin, silent,
our heads bowed, our arms crossed, our eyes shut awaiting
shipwreck and death at any minute. After passing an entire
day in such a state of terror one is old indeed. It was a drunken
sailor who saved us. There was an old sail all rotten and full of
holes at the bottom of the hold; he went to fetch it and put it up
as best he could. The new sails, which received the whole force
of the wind, had been torn like paper. This one, while checking
it, let some through and so withstood the blast and guided the
ship which skimmed past the foot of those terrible rocks without

touching them'—We never seem to learn by experience; why should we not have sails with holes in them for heavy weather.

While in the middle of this storm we had come to the top of the hill and found we were on a level with Chennevières, whither we took our way with the idea of kissing the little children, but they were still in their cots. We contented ourselves with turning back their coverlets and looking at them; always a touching sight. After having paid a few compliments to the nurse, whom Raphael might have taken for a model of the Blessed Virgin, according to what Marmontel said the first time he saw her, and consoling her a little for our teasing by our liberality, we crossed the plain of Champigny to Ormesson-d'Amboile, and regained Le Grandval, where we found Baron Dieskau, who had taken advantage of the beautiful day to fulfil the promise he had made to Mme d'Aine and the Baron to come and see them. There was a recognition between him and young Marchais. They had known each other at Quebec.

I think I have already told you of Baron Dieskau. If you read the gazette you will have found his name mentioned with praise. Four or five years ago he was in command of a handful of French and Canadians in the neighbourhood of Quebec and Montreal; he was attacked by a considerable force of English and Iroquois savages. The inequality of numbers did not alarm him, he held his ground; all his followers were cut to pieces; he himself was left, stretched on the battlefield, with numerous gashes and a broken leg. He would have got off all right with that, but, after the action, when they were stripping the dead, a French deserter who noticed some sign of life in him, instead of helping him, let off his musket into the lower part of his abdomen, and so his bladder was burst, his sexual organs damaged and he goes on living, if you can call it living, with one leg shorter than the other by four or five inches and an artificial tube contrived for him to pass his urine.

The enemy general had his ribs broken. What a charming profession! The two of them were carried to the same tent. The Englishman would never allow his wounds to be attended to till those of his enemy had been dressed. What occasions natural goodness and humanity choose for showing themselves! They flourish in the midst of blood and slaughter. I could give you a hundred examples.

We have just had this one from general to general, would you like one from soldier to soldier? Here it is just as Baron Dieskau told it to us. Two soldiers who were comrades found themselves side by side in a dangerous action. The younger, tortured with the presentiment that he would not come back, was marching along dejectedly; the other said to him: 'What is the matter with you, comrade? Why, upon my word, I believe you are shivering!' 'Yes,' replied his friend, 'I am afraid this is going to end badly and I am thinking of my poor wife and my poor children.' 'Cheer up!' replied the old corporal; 'why, if you are killed and I come back, I give you my word of honour that I will marry your wife, and that I will take care of your children.' And indeed, the young soldier was killed, and the other kept his word to him. It is an absolute fact, for the Baron does not tell lies.

But do you know what happened at the beginning of the engagement between M. de Castries and the young prince before the walls of Wesel just recently? This M. de Castries is a friend of Grimm, so I leave you to imagine how pleased the latter was about this success which is the most important the French have had in the whole war. M. de Ségur, who was in command of the left wing, was attacked in the darkness by the prince. The two forces were almost touching each other. M. de Ségur was going to be butchered. The young prince heard him mention his name, he flew to his rescue. M. de Ségur, who did not realize what was going on, saw him at his side, recognized him, and cried out to him: 'Hi! Prince, what are you doing there? My grenadiers who are only twenty paces away are going to fire.' 'Sir,' replied the young prince, 'I heard your name and I ran up to prevent these people from massacring you.' While they were speaking, the two forces on either side of them began to fire simultaneously. M. de Ségur got off with two sabre strokes and became the prisoner of the young prince, who nevertheless was obliged to retire and two days later to raise the siege of Wesel. Are you not surprised at the generosity of these two men, each thinking only of the other's danger and so forgetful of their own safety that it is a marvel that they were not both killed at the same moment? This story was told to Grimm who was inclined not to believe it, but Mme de Ségur herself confirmed it when he met her at Mme de Geoffrin's a few days ago; so there is no doubt whatever about it.

No, my dearest, we are not wicked by nature, it is bad education, bad example, bad laws which corrupt us. If this is an illusion, I am glad all the same to cherish it and I should be very sorry if experience or reflection ever undeceived me; what would become of me then? I should either have to live in complete solitude or to believe that I was constantly surrounded by rogues; neither the one nor the other would suit me at all.

The generous behaviour of the English general, of the two soldiers, of M. de Ségur and the young prince follow each other naturally. We are left wondering which of the two, M. de Ségur, or the prince, was the most to be admired. That would be a fine question for Urania and her sister to discuss!

Baron Dieskau, continuing his story, said that General Johnson and he had only just had their wounds dressed when the chiefs of the Iroquois savages entered their tent.

There was a very animated conversation between them and Johnson. Baron Dieskau, who did not speak Iroquois, could not understand what they were saying, but he saw by their gesticulations that it had to do with him and that the savages were asking the Englishman for something he refused them. The natives went off very sullenly and Baron Dieskau asked Johnson what they wanted. 'By God!' answered Johnson, 'what they want! why, to avenge on you the death of three or four of their chieftains who have been cut to pieces in the fighting; they want to cook you, smoke you and eat you. But have no fear, it will not take place. They are threatening to desert me, they can do worse; but either you shall live or they shall feast on both of us.'

While they were thus talking, the savages came back; the conversation started once more but with less heat; the savages calmed down little by little. Before departing they came up to the baron, shook hands and made peace. They were scarcely out of the tent when General Johnson said to the baron: 'My friend, you are very much mistaken if you think you are no longer in danger; in spite of your wounds you must be got away from here and carried to the town.' Meanwhile they interwove some branches of trees, laid him on the improvised stretcher and took him to the town under an escort of forty soldiers. Next day the savages, having heard about this escape, went to the town, made their way into the house where he was being looked after.

They had poignards hidden under their clothing; they fell upon him and would have quickly made an end of him if help had not been instantly forthcoming. He only had two or three wounds added to his others.

'Well,' you might say to me, 'where is this natural goodness? Who corrupted the Iroquois? Who inspired them with vengeance and treason?' The gods, my dear, the gods; vengeance is a religious virtue in the eyes of these wretches. They believe that the Great Spirit who lives behind a mountain not far from Quebec will be waiting for them after their death, that he will judge them, and that their merit will be measured by the number of scalps that they bring him. So, when you see an Iroquois strike his enemy down with a club, lean over him, pull out his knife, split open his forehead and tear the skin from his head with his teeth, you know it is to please his god. There is not a single country, there is not a single nation where the orders of some god have not hallowed some crime.

The Canadians say that the Scottish Highlanders are the savages of Europe—You see you must read all this as a conversation.

'True enough!' said Father Hoop, 'our Highlanders are naked, they are brave and vindictive; when a troop of them are eating together, towards the end of the meal as their brains grow heated by wine, and old quarrels are remembered, and high words begin to pass, do you know how they control themselves? They all draw their poignards and place them on the table beside their glasses. There is the answer ready for the first insult.'

The Pretender, on whose head the English have put a high price and whom for many months they hunted from mountain to mountain like a wild beast, found safety in the caverns of these miserable Highlanders who could have exchanged their dire poverty for opulence by giving him up and who never even thought of it for a moment. There is another proof of natural goodness.

It is not necessary to tell you that I am still continuing our conversation, you will see that for yourself. Father Hoop had a friend at the battle between the Scottish Highlanders commanded by the Pretender and the English. His friend was on the English side. He received a sword blow which cut off his hand. There was a diamond ring on one of the fingers. The Highlander saw something shining on the ground, he leant down, put the severed hand in his pocket, and went on fighting. These men knew the value of gold and silver, and if they do not betray the Pretender it is because they do not want money at such a price.

You see, my dear, that we do honour to our guests in this house. We have a soldier and we make him talk about war. We learnt things from him that we did not know before; we were polite; that was better than telling him things which we knew but which perhaps he did not.

Baron Dieskau served a long time under the Marshal of Saxony. He used to spend the autumn with him at Piple, a house near Grandval, which belongs to Mme de la Bourdonnaye. This woman spends all the year there, alone with her lover. You will be saying to yourself, 'What more can she want?'

He told us a great deal about the Marshal, of his occupations, his love-affairs, his companions, the dangerous battles in which he had been engaged, the countries he had visited, etc.

Oh, my dear! what a difference there is between reading history and listening to a man's account. Things take on a new interest. To what is it due? Does it come from the person who is telling or the one who is listening? Could it be that we are so flattered at being singled out by fortune to hear someone who has experienced so many extraordinary things, and at the advantage given us over other people by the certainty which we are gaining and which we shall be able to claim for our own version, when we repeat the story in our turn? We are very proud if we can add to anything we are recounting: 'I saw the man to whom that happened; he told me about it himself.' There is only one better boast than that; it is to be able to say; 'I saw that happen; I was there myself.' Still I am not sure that it is not sometimes better to be able to claim for our story the first-hand evidence of an important personality, than to rest it on our own experience. I do not know whether a man is not more likely to be believed when he says, 'I was told this by the Marshal of Turenne or the Marshal of Saxony,' than when he says, 'I saw it myself.' Although it would be just as easy for him to lie on either of these points it seems to me he would find us more ready to believe one false-hood than the other. In the first case there would have to be two liars, where only one is needed in the second; and one of these two liars would be a very important person. Again, anybody can have the book which I am reading, but they cannot speak with the hero. There is no vanity in having read a book, but there is vanity in having been in the company of a great man and having spoken with him.

Are we so mortified then when people don't believe what we say? Most certainly we are. Ask Mlle Boileau. First it means that they question the validity of our information, and often the chief reason for telling anything is to show how much one knows. Then they accuse us either of folly or fraud. If we are trying to persuade others of something we don't believe ourselves we are dishonest, if we are in good faith and really believe the absurdity we are announcing we must be fools. And after all, is it better to be a liar or an idiot? It is possible to cure oneself of lying, but not of imbecility. One hardly lies any more when one has given up trying to impress people. Oh, in what wonderful *marivaudage*[1] we are becoming involved! If I chose to pursue the line of thought to the end it would be possible to hop all the way round the earth on one foot before I had finished. However the circumference of the world measures about nine thousand leagues—and may nine thousand devils carry off Marivaux and all his insipid votaries such as I am!

Baron Dieskau has all the difficulty in the world to get up from his armchair and he would have found it easier ten years ago to visit the Equator or the North Pole than he does to-day to reach the end of one of our garden paths. We kept him company all day long. I played chess with him. He played at dice with the Baron. Yesterday he played doubles or quits with us.

We went to bed early. The sky promised that the next day would be fine; and then the wind got up, the stars disappeared, a deluge came down, the trees which shelter us in the west were blowing violently against each other, so that there was a terrible noise and we were obliged to shut ourselves indoors and crouch round the fire. We passed the Sunday as best we could.

Baron Dieskau left us at five o'clock. We had all put on our night-caps and dressing-gowns, with the permission of the ladies who had arranged that we should have a stand-up supper in the drawing-room for the benefit of our Baron who is indisposed, and while we were waiting, we went on with our gossiping. I thought that never in my life would I talk to you

---

[1] Analytical arguments like those used in the plays of Marivaux.

again about the Chinese, and here I am coming back to them; but it is really Father Hoop's fault; you must blame him if I bore you.

He told us that one of their sovereigns was waging a war with the Tartars north of China. The season was severe. The Chinese general wrote to the Emperor that his soldiers were suffering greatly from the cold. The sole reply of the Emperor was to send his pelisse with these words: 'Tell your brave soldiers from me that I wish I had one for each of them.'

Father Hoop remarked that the Chinese are the only people on earth who have had many more good kings and ministers than bad ones. 'Why, Father Hoop, how is that?' asked a voice from the far end of the room. 'It is because the Emperor's children are well brought up in that country and that it has scarcely ever come about that a bad prince should die in his bed.' 'What,' said I, 'the people are the judges whether a prince is good or bad?' 'Certainly they are, and they make as few mistakes as children do about their father or their tutor. In China, a good prince is one who keeps the laws; a bad prince breaks them. The Law is above the throne. The prince is under the Law and above his subjects. He himself is the first subject of the Law.'

Father Hoop told us how the mandarins said to the Emperor one day: 'Lord, the people are in great poverty; something must be done to help them.' 'Go,' replied the Emperor; 'you must hasten as you would in the case of a flood or a fire.'—'It will be necessary to give help which is in proportion to the need.' —'I agree to that, so long as the enquiry does not take too long and is not too scrupulous. Above all do not be afraid that your liberality may be in excess of my wishes.'

He said that another Emperor was besieging Nankin. This town has several million inhabitants. The inhabitants had defended themselves with the utmost valour; but nevertheless they were on the point of being carried by storm. The Emperor perceived from the heat and indignation of his officers and men that it would be beyond his power to prevent a frightful massacre. He was overcome with anxiety. The officers were urging him to lead them to the assault; he did not know what line to take; he pretended to be taken ill; he shut himself into his tent. He was much beloved; sadness spread through the camp. The operations of the siege were suspended. On all sides people were praying for the Emperor's recovery. They came to consult him. 'Friends,' he said to his generals, 'my health is in your hands; let us see if you really wish my life to be spared.' 'Indeed we do! Speak, Sire, tell us quickly what we are to do. We are all ready to die for you.' 'It is not a question of dying for me, but of swearing to perform something far easier for my sake.' 'We swear it.' 'Very well,' he went on, suddenly rising and drawing his scimitar. 'You see me quite recovered. Let us march against the rebels, let us scale their walls and enter their town, but, once the town is taken no single drop of blood is to be shed. That is what you have sworn to me and what I demand of you,' and so it was done.

Ly-Wang-Ti (it is still Father Hoop who is speaking) had the Great Wall built which separates China from Tartary. It extends for six hundred leagues, has three thousand towers, is thirty feet high and fifteen thick. Great rivers pass beneath it, it crosses an arm of the sea, it surmounts swamps several leagues wide. Ly-Wang-Ti had it constructed within five years. Moreover it was he who made the wisest laws the world has ever known, who delivered the nation from the tyranny of the royal princes by whom it had always been held in subjection—even reducing his own children to the rank of simple citizens. Well, this prince ordered the burning of all books, and no one, on pain of death, was to preserve any except those concerning agriculture, architecture, and medicine. If Rousseau had known this piece of history what a fine thing he would have made of it! To what advantage would he not have turned the reasoning of the Chinese Emperor!

Ly-Wang-Ti used to say that in a state where there were so-called people of talent the honest folk came second; that in every place where more glory was attached to mental than to manual occupations the number of so-called thinkers would always go on increasing and with them the number of idlers, proud folk, useless folk, do-nothings; that these jabberers tie the hands of the prince by perpetuating the old constitutions through their ridiculous eulogies, so that nothing can be innovated without the nation being up in arms, although there's not a law which is not completely out of date by the end of fifty years . . . ! He said that all the mind produces will be cold and tedious, unless genius is the instrument of the passions and that then it is dangerous. There's a beautiful text for you! You must love me madly.

What did the councillors of the Iron Safe, who were all literary people, say of Ly-Wang Ti's logic? That he argued like a barbarian.

I will not weary you with all the considerations which these historical facts suggested to us; they and many others will certainly occur to you too.

The Baron, who is ill in spite of having given himself up completely to medicine, thought it very wrong that Ly-Wang-Ti should have spared the medical books. He said that nothing is known about the human body or about the functioning of its different parts, that nothing is known either about the nature of the substances given as remedies, that we know nothing at all and that he cannot understand how a science can have been made out of so many unexplored and unknown things.

I replied to him after the style of Abbé Galiani. Some Spaniards landed one day in the New World where the natives were so backward that they did not yet know the use of fire. It was winter. They told the inhabitants that with some wood and other things they were going to imitate the sun and produce a flame on earth like that which shone upon them from the sky. 'So you know what wood is,' said the inhabitants of this country to the Spaniards—'No.' 'You must at least know how the fire burns the wood?' 'No.' 'And when you have lit the fire you doubtless know how to put it out?' 'Yes.' 'What with?' 'With water.' 'So you know what water is?' 'No.' 'And you know then how fire is put out by water?' 'No.' The natives began to laugh and turned their backs on the Spaniards who lit a fire they didn't know with wood they didn't know without knowing how the fire burnt the wood, and then with water they didn't know put out the fire they didn't know without knowing how the water put out the fire.

At the end of our conversation, when we were on the point of retiring, I asked the Baron if he was going to Paris during the week. He answered that he was not. 'In that case,' I said to him, 'may I avail myself of the place in Mme d'Aine's coach which is taking these gentlemen back to-morrow?' He gave his consent and here I am in Paris once more, on the Quai des

Miramionnes, trying to stop your letters from going to Grandval when they are there already!

In the evening Damilaville and I had the pleasure of meeting each other and it was delightful. That was on Monday. On Tuesday morning Grimm and I had the pleasure of meeting each other and it was very delightful. We dined together. I asked him for news of the health of Mme d'Epinay.

As to Pouf, Thisbé, and Taupin, a new and important personage of whom you have not heard before, I could tell you some good stories if I had time. Taupin is the miller's dog. Ah, my dearest, you must please have a great respect for Taupin. I used to think I knew how to love, but Taupin has shown me how little I understood it and I am greatly humiliated. Perhaps you believe yourself to be loved; if you had seen Taupin you would begin to have some doubts about it. He has taken a liking for Thisbé. Well now, just imagine, in the weather we have been having he would come to the door every day and stretch himself out on the wet gravel with his nose resting on his paws, his eyes gazing fixedly at our windows, faithfully keeping his uncomfortable watch in spite of the rain which was coming down in buckets and the wind which was blowing his ears about, oblivious of food, drink, his home, his master, his mistress, groaning and sighing for Thisbé from morning till night. I suspect, it is true, that there is a little sensuality in the fact of Taupin's devotion, but Mme d'Aine maintains that it is impossible to analyse the most delicate of sentiments without finding a little coarseness. Ah! my dearest, what strange names we give to our tender feelings! I couldn't repeat them to you. If Nature heard them she would heighten them all considerably.

Mme de Holbach will have it that Saurin and the lady of La Chevrette are playing us a trick and that they are lying to us by telling us the truth.

I can well imagine how much you are enjoying Racine. He is perhaps the greatest poet who has ever lived. Take care not to attack the character of Iphegenia. A lofty enthusiasm of several hours inspired her renunciation. The character is poetic, and throughout, a little above nature: if the poet has shown her to us in an epic, where the episode lasted several days, you would have seen her agitated by all the emotions you demand; she undoubtedly experienced some of them but always tempered

by gentleness, deference, submission, obedience; all your objections come down to this: 'I cannot identify myself with Iphegenia.'
Her character was easy to paint, those of Achilles and of Ulysses
were easy too, that of Clytemnestra still easier; but that of
Agamemnon, whom you do not mention, how can you fail to
think about that? A father immolates his daughter because of
his ambition and yet we must not dismiss him as odious. What
a problem to solve! See all the poet has done for this! Agamemnon
had called his daughter to Aulis; that was his only fault and he
committed it before the play began. He was filled with remorse;
he got up during the night; he tried to prevent her from coming
to Aulis; he did not succeed in this, he was in despair about
her arrival, the gods themselves deceived him. Who came to
him pleading the cause of his daughter? An infuriated lover,
who ruined this very cause by his threats; an enraged mother,
who tried to subjugate her husband. In the middle of all this,
when the father was thoroughly irritated, he was abandoned to
the influence of the cleverest scoundrel in all Greece. He was,
however, on the point of saving his daughter from the sword,
when Eriphilia denounced him to the Greeks and to Calchas who
called for him with angry shouts; besides, the Greeks had been
ten years outside Troy. There wasn't a leader in the army who
had not lost a father, a son, a brother, a friend for the injury
done to the Atrides. Was the blood of the Atrides the only
blood of value in Greece? Leaving all questions of ambition on
one side, had Agamemnon nothing to settle with the gods, did
he owe nothing to the Greeks? What an accumulation of circumstances to palliate the error of a moment! The secret out
of that box has escaped you.

Here, my dear, is the ticket for the funeral of the Jesuits. I
have cut it down as small as I can so as to disguise it in the post,
but I have numbered all the pages. So now I am delivered from
a great many powerful enemies. Who could have guessed that
this was going to happen eighteen months ago? They had so
much time to prepare for the blow that either they must have had
very little credit or else the King had determined to ruin them.
The latter solution seems the more probable. The Portuguese affair
must have taught him something about the situation in France,
showing the Jesuits to him in an odious light. He must have been

waiting for an opportunity to rid himself of people who had struck at him, and whom he always imagined with their hand raised to attack him; Father Valette's scandalous bankruptcy seemed to offer him a good one; they have mixed themselves up in too many matters. During the two hundred years or so that they have been in existence scarcely one has passed without some striking dispute. They embroiled the Church and the State; subject to the most extreme despotism in their own houses they went about abjectly praising the rule of despots everywhere, they preached to the people blind submission to kings and the infallibility of the Pope, so that, by becoming the masters of one they might be the masters of all. They recognized no authority but that of their General: he was for them the Old Man of the Mountain. Their rule is nothing but Machiavelism set out in precepts. With all that, a single man such as Bourdatone might have saved them, but they had not got one. What is amusing is the way the Jansenists are triumphing over their enemies. They don't see the oblivion in to which they will themselves fall. It is the fable of the two arched rafters propped up and quarrelling with the house top. The master, out of patience with their folly, cut down one and the other fell of itself. The Bishops who realize better what is happening are not so pleased. This Jesuit shop contained all kinds of commodities, good and bad; but it was well stocked, those who kept it were great wheedlers, they gathered a crowd of people round them and the Ship of Saint Peter rode the waves. These events are very diverting for the philosophers. Well, to continue, these good Fathers had kept up their hopes to the very end, to judge by the surprise and consternation which they showed when told of their arrest. Several appeared just like condemned criminals. A man I know placed among them by force of circumstances, not caring much about them, could not endure the sight of their despair and went off; to-day people are already pitying them; to-morrow they will make up songs about them; the day after to-morrow they will think no more about them; such is the charming character of the people of France.

They spent all yesterday morning, Wednesday, in saying masses in their three churches and in asking God to deliver them, but their prayer was not granted. Between eleven and twelve o'clock there was a flock of pious women, wringing their hands, tearing at their veils and howling like mad things. You can imagine the commotion it all made here. Everybody is expecting a third decree of the Parlement to be published in a few days, though I don't know what it is to be about, and immediately afterwards a decree from the King confirming the decrees of Parlement.

I can just imagine how Voltaire is feeling and picture him in my mind's eye; he raises his eyes and hands to heaven, he says: '*Nunc dimittis servum tuum, Domine, quia viderunt oculi mei salutare tuum.*' This incomprehensible man wrote a paper which he calls an Eulogy of Crébillon. You will see what a comical eulogy it is; it is the truth, but the truth is offensive when it issues from an envious mouth. I can't forgive so great a man for such pettiness. He attacks all pedestals. He is working at an edition of Corneille. I will take on a bet with anyone that the notes with which it will be stuffed will contain as many little satires. He can do what he will and belittle whom he pleases, I see a dozen men in the nation who, without standing on their toes, are still taller than he is by a head. This man is no more than second rate in any branch of literature.

Before taking up my journal again, I should like to be able to give you an account of a conversation which started about the word instinct, a word we use constantly, applying it either to taste or conduct, yet never defining it. I maintained that it was the result in us of an infinite number of little experiences which started at the moment we first opened our eyes to the light and continued until the time when, secretly guided by attempts of which we have no memory, we pronounced something to be good or bad, beautiful or ugly, right or wrong, without having any explicit reason for our favourable or unfavourable judgment.

Michael Angelo considered what shape he should give the dome of Saint Peter's in Rome, it is one of the most beautiful forms which could possibly have been chosen. Everyone is impressed and enchanted by its elegance. The width was given, the first question was to decide upon the height. I can see the architect feeling his way, adding a little or taking away from this height, until at last he found what he wanted and could exclaim, 'That is it!' When he had discovered the height, the next thing was to sketch the curve, using the determined height and width. How many new experiments! How many times he would rub out his line to try another shape, rounder, flatter, more bulging, until at last he found the one he used for his building! Where had he learnt just when to stop? What reason had he for choosing as he did from so many successive shapes which he sketched on his paper? Trying to solve these difficulties I remembered about M. de la Hire, a great mathematician of the Academy of Science. When, in the course of a journey in Italy, he reached Rome, he was moved like everybody else at the beauty of the dome of Saint Peter's. His admiration, however, was not without fruit; he wanted to have the curve formed by this dome; he had a sketch made of it and examined its properties from the geometrical point of view. What was his surprise when he found it to be the curve of greatest resistance! Michael Angelo, in aiming at giving his dome the most beautiful and elegant shape possible, after much careful groping had happened upon the very form which he would have given it if he had been aiming at the greatest possible solidity and strength. How is it that the curve of greatest resistance for a dome or vault should also be the curve of elegance and beauty? It is not a question of conscious thought you will say, but of instinct. And what is instinct? Oh, that is understandable enough! I suggest that Michael Angelo, a young urchin at school playing and wrestling with his companions and pushing with his shoulder, soon found what angle he must give to his body to offer the greatest resistance to his antagonist; that it is impossible that hundreds of times in his life he did not have to prop up things that wanted steadying so that he had to find the slant that gave the best support; that he had sometimes heaped books one on top of another and when they all began to topple down he had to find a way of counter-balancing them without upsetting the whole pile; I suggest that he learnt in this way how to construct the dome of St. Peter's on the curve of greatest resistance. A wall is about to fall down; send for a carpenter. When the carpenter has done his work, send for d'Alembert or Clairaut, and, the slant of the wall being given, ask one or other of these mathematicians to find the slant at which the prop would be most effective. You will find that the angles of the carpenter and the mathematician are identical. You may have noticed that the arms of a windmill are slanting and make an angle with the axle to which they are fixed, otherwise they would not go round: the size of the angle is what causes the arms to revolve easily. How is it that when mathematicians examined the angle fixed upon by habit and use, they found it was precisely the same as the one which the most advanced geometry would have led them to select. It is a matter of calculation on the one hand and of experience on the other. Well now, it is impossible for the one if it is well done not to agree with the other.

Actually, how is it that what is strong in the natural order should also be judged beautiful in art or imitation? It is because our approval is always won by strength, or more generally goodness. This goodness can be inherent in a work without showing, then the work is good but it is not beautiful. It can show on the surface without being inherent, then the work has only an apparent beauty. But if the goodness is really there and shows itself then the work is truly beautiful and good.

Only in an imaginary world where all the laws of nature were reversed could it come about that something which was both intrinsically and outwardly good lacked beauty. But in order to make up to you a little for what you have found dry and abstract in all this, I am going to finish the rest of the conversation in a few words. I said: 'What is more hidden, what is more inexplicable than the beautiful oval of a dome? Yet here it is authorized by a law of nature.' Someone added: 'But where can we find in nature a means of justifying or contradicting the various judgments we make, particularly about women's faces? They seem very arbitrary.' 'Not in the least,' I replied, 'however great the variety of our taste in this matter it is explicable. We can discern and prove what is true and what is false; we can trace our judgments back to questions of health, animal instincts and passions, and you will always find your reasons. This woman is beautiful, her eyebrows follow the orbit of her eyes; raise these eyebrows a little in the middle and you have an indication of pride, and pride is unpleasing. Leave these brows placed the way they are but make them very bushy so that they overshadow the eye; then the eye will become hard, and hardness is repellent. Do not touch the eyebrow but push the lips a little forward and there you have a pout and bad temper. Pinch the corners of the mouth and there you have an affected or supercilious woman. Let the eyelids fall and she is of a sad temperament, swell out certain muscles of the cheek a little and there she is, in a rage. Fix the pupil and she is stupid. Give some fire to this fixed pupil and she is impudent. There you have reasons for all our tastes. If nature has given a face outward characteristics which denote a virtue or a vice the face will please or displease us accordingly; add health which is the basis of everything else, and add also the greatest facility for carrying out the functions proper to our nature. A fine labourer is not necessarily a fine man, nor is a fine dancer or a fine old grey-beard, or a fine blacksmith. A fine man is one whom nature has formed to fulfil as adequately as possible the two great functions, the preservation of the individual, which covers a great many activities, and the propagation of the species, which covers only one. If by custom or habit we have developed certain faculties at the expense of others we have no longer the beauty of the natural man but the beauty of some order of society. A back grown bent, shoulders broadened, arms shortened and sinewy, legs thickened and bowed and hips enormously enlarged from carrying heavy burdens, these qualities will make a good porter. The natural man did nothing but live and produce children and nature made him beautiful, so he has remained. It seems as though artists had wanted to show us the two extremes in their greatest works of sculpture; the Apollo of antiquity is the idle man, the Hercules of the Farneze is the labourer; everything is exaggerated in the latter; nothing is extreme in the former, there is no evidence of any particular effort; he has done nothing as yet, but he appears apt for anything: do you want him to wrestle, he will wrestle, to run, he will run, to caress a woman, he will caress her. To paint well it is necessary to study the natural man first, after that the man of each profession. But let us leave living beings and pass on to works of art such as architecture for example.

A piece of architecture is beautiful when it has solidity and when this is obvious; when it is suitable for its purpose and when it is noticeable. In this department solidity corresponds with health in the animal world; suitability to its purpose with the functions and special callings of living beings. But here you must notice the amazing influence of manners and customs; it seems as though they are at the root of everything. You go to Constantinople, and there you find walls that are high and thick, low archways, small doors, high barred windows, apparently the more a building resembles a prison the more beautiful it is; as a matter of fact the houses are prisons in which one-half of the human race confines the other. Go to Europe, on the other hand, and you find the doors and windows are large, everything is open, it is because there are no slaves: and it is a question whether the climate has anything to do with it. In this case, before judging of artistic taste it is necessary to determine which customs are the better, whether women can be left to their good faith, or whether they must be shut up; whether it is better to live under the fiery rays of the torrid zone or in the glacial atmosphere of the tropic (arctic?) or whether a temperate zone will not give man a better chance of health and long life. A young libertine is walking in the Palais Royal when he sees a little snub nose, laughing lips, wide-awake eyes, a free way of walking, and he exclaims, 'Oh! how charming she is!' As for me I turn my back with disdain and I rest my gaze on a face where I can read innocence and candour, simplicity, nobility, a dignity and decorum. Do you think it would be very difficult to decide which of us is wrong, the young man or I? His taste can be reduced to this: 'I love vice,' and mine to this: 'I love virtue.' It is thus with nearly all judgments; in the end they can all be summed up in one or other of these phrases.

There you have the greater part of our conversation. The details would furnish matter for an excellent work on taste and a vindication of mine for you, my dear sisters. . . .

I am worn out, but it is less from fatigue than from irritation. During the night I heard the most doleful groaning; I got up; I went to see what it was and it was nothing.

They were not asleep; they remembered that they had omitted to wind up my watch; they rang the bell; they obliged a poor servant girl who was asleep to get up; she was tired out; they sent her to my room at two o'clock in the morning to wind up this watch. There are a thousand attentions of this kind which can not be excused on the plea of ill-health. Invalids have their foibles, that is recognized, their mind is hard at work, they sometimes can only be satisfied by things which have no common sense about them; the more they are opposed by those around them, the more do they exaggerate the importance of their crazy ideas. They have to be humoured for fear of adding some disease of the mind to that of the body, but what can it matter whether a watch is wound up or not?

While we are on this subject, have you ever noticed that there are circumstances in our life which tend to make us more or less superstitious? As we do not always see the real reasons for effects we sometimes imagine the strangest causes will bring about what we desire: and then we try out experiments which would qualify us for a mad-house.

A girl in the fields takes some thistles in flower; she blows on them to see if she is fondly loved or not. Another seeks to know her fortune from cards; I have seen some who pulled to pieces all the full-blown flowers that they found in the meadow and who said at each petal they tore off: 'He loves me—a little— a great deal—not at all,' until they reached the last petal which was prophetic. When they were happy they laughed at the prophecy, when sad they put rather more faith in it, they said: 'The petal is quite right.'

I myself once told my fortune under Platonic guidance. I had been shut up in the tower of Vincennes for thirty days; I remembered all the ideas of the ancients about Chance. I had a small volume of Plato in my pocket and opened it at random. I sought to discover the length of my imprisonment from the first sentence which presented itself to my eyes. At the top of the page where it opened I read: 'This affair should by its nature be soon over.' I smiled, and a quarter of an hour afterwards I heard the keys turning in the door of my cell; it was the lieutenant of police Berryer, who was coming to tell me I should be set at liberty next day.

If in the course of your life you happened to have two or three presentiments which came true, and that on important occasions, I wonder what impression it would make upon your mind! Wouldn't you be tempted to believe a little in inspiration, especially if you had come up against some very extraordinary results, far removed from what might have seemed probable?

I no longer know where to take up my journal again; I only remember that when the adventure of President Montesquieu and Lord Chesterfield was being discussed, someone told the story of another one which happened to M. Montesquieu. He was in the country with some ladies, one of whom was English. He addressed a few words to her in her own language but so

mutilated by his abominable pronunciation that she could not
help laughing; upon which the President said: 'This is not the
first time in my life I have been so mortified. I was going to
see the famous Marlborough at Blenheim. Before paying my
visit I recalled all the agreeable sentences that I had ever known
in English and as we passed through the apartments of his mansion
I said them to him. I must have been talking English to him
for nearly an hour when he said: 'Sir, I beg you to speak to me
in English, for I can't understand French.'

Suard, to whom the same President said one day in the course
of a conversation about religion: 'You must admit, Monsieur
Suard, that Confession is a good thing,' replied 'Agreed, Monsieur
le President, but you must also admit that Absolution is a bad
one.'

Someone told a fact about the King of Prussia which shows
a great deal of penetration and a strong sense of justice. He was
going from Wesel, I think, to a neighbouring town, he was
travelling along the high road when, without any apparent
reason, his coachman left the road and took him across a newly
sown field. He made him stop. The owner of the field was
there; he called him and asked whether by chance he had not
had some dispute with his coachman. The man replied that a
law-suit was actually going on between them. The King,
without asking him who was wrong or right in this law-suit,
paid for the damage done and dismissed his coachman.

We started for Marly on Monday morning in the rain, and
we were rewarded for our courage by the most beautiful day.
Oh, my dearest, what an abode! I think I have told you about
it once already. First, whoever planted this garden conceived of
the great and beautiful schemes of decoration which he had
achieved as of something which should remain hidden until the
time when it could be seen as a whole. There are yews without
number and clipped in a hundred different shapes which border
a flower garden of the greatest simplicity and which lead up
towards leafy bowers whose lightness and elegance cannot be
described. These bowers still going upwards lead the eye on till
it rests on the edge of a forest of which only the branches of the
trees immediately above the bowers have been trimmed up.
Otherwise the trunks have been left in their natural state, rustic,
bushy, and wild; you ought to see the effect which this makes.

If they had cut the upper branches of the trees as well as the lower ones, all the garden would become uniform, small, and in bad taste. But this gradual passing from nature to art, and from art to nature creates a pure enchantment. Leave this flower-garden when the hand of man and his intelligence are displayed in so exquisite a manner and wander on the heights above; there you will find solitude, silence, the wilderness, the awe of the Thebaïd. How sublime! What a mind must have conceived of these gardens! Oh the great spaces, to the right and left, at the highest part the octagonal reservoirs are to be found. Each of these sides is a hundred and fifty paces long, and they are consequently twelve hundred paces all round. They are approached by dark, lonely paths, and are invisible, these immense expanses of water, except from the banks. The dark, deserted pathways are decorated with sad and solemn bronzes; one represents Laocoön and his two children encircled and devoured by the serpents of Diana, I think. The father in such grievous pain, the dying child, the other one who forgets his own peril as he watches his father's suffering, all that throws you into the deepest melancholy; and how marvellously such melancholy fits in with the character and influence of the place! We saw the apartments too. They are contained in the principal building which faces into the gardens, and which represents the Palace of the Sun. Twelve separate pavilions, half hidden by the forest surrounding the garden, represent the twelve signs of the zodiac. The proportions are so perfect in all parts that the central pavilion seems to be of quite ordinary dimensions, and when you come to measure it, you find that it stretches over a surface of four thousand nine hundred paces. If you open one of the doors, it is then that you are surprised by the height and length. One of the most beautiful drawing-rooms it is possible to imagine forms the centre of the building. I went into it and when I was in the middle I reflected that that was the place where the King came once a year to reverse the fortunes of two or three noblemen of his court with a card.

As I stood there in the garden, my mind full of admiration for Le Nôtre whose work and indeed masterpiece it is, I called up before me the shades of Henry IV and Louis XIV. The latter showed the superb edifice to the former, who said to him: 'You are right, my son, this is certainly magnificent; but I would

very much like to see the houses of my peasants of Gonesse.'
What would he have thought when he found, just beyond the
immense buildings of this sumptuous palace, when he found, I
say, the peasants lying on straw without a roof and without
bread.

Why is it that the fuller our life is, the less we are attached
to it? If that is true it must be because a busy life is also an
innocent one; it must be because we think less about death and
therefore fear it less; it must be because unconsciously we become
resigned to the common fate of all those beings that we see
dying and being born around us; it must be because having
fulfilled for a certain number of years tasks which nature brings
us regularly with the returning seasons, we become detached
and grow weary of them; strength begins to fail, we are en-
feebled, we long for the end of life, as after hard work we long
for the end of the day. It is because, living close to nature, we
do not rebel against orders which we see carried out so necessarily
and so universally; it is because, having dug the ground so many
times, we can view the prospect of descending into it with less
repugnance, it is because, having slept so many times on the
surface of the earth, we are readier to sleep underneath; it is
because, to come back to a previous point, there is no one
among us who, after having laboured hard, is not ready for his
bed, and does not see the time for rest drawing near with extreme
pleasure; it is because, for certain people, life is nothing but a
long day of toil and death a long sleep, the coffin only a bed of
repose and the earth nothing but a pillow where in the end
it is sweet to lay one's head for ever. I own to you that death,
considered in this way, after the long misfortunes I have had to
endure seems all that is most agreeable. I want to accustom
myself more and more to think thus about it.

As I do not know when my invalids will have recovered,
and as my occupations continue to fill the mornings and as the
greater part of my evenings is taken up by friends, by amusements, by walks, by the education of Angélique of whom, by
the way, I shall never make anything, because they smother in
an instant all that I have taken a month to implant, I am going
to send your letter to Mme Gendre by the post.

I do not know whether my letters take a long time to arrive;

but I can assure you that I have made it a regular duty to write to you every Thursday and Sunday, and that not one of my duties is carried out with more exactitude and more pleasure.

Gentleness and violence fit marvellously into the same character; I compare such children to milk which is so sweet and which heat causes suddenly to swell up and overflow; take the saucepan away from the fire, blow on the liquid, throw an ivy leaf into it or a drop of water and it will go down at once.

Mademoiselle, you will await safe opportunities for dispatching your letters: I shall be ten days without receiving one, if need be. I will resign myself to this; but on one condition, it is that I shall no longer expect them on certain special days, but I shall take them when they come. I suffer too much when I am disappointed! I am no longer good for anything, neither for society, nor for my duties; my temper is affected, I grumble at nothing; I am bored by everything and everywhere; I am sullen and I do myself no end of harm. This must not be allowed to put you to inconvenience; but all the same you must not make me worse than I am, so that because a letter that I was expecting from my friend has not arrived I enrage all around me.

God be praised! Twenty-five have now arrived; there are still three to go to you, without counting this one.

I have just seen the Baron off from Paris. He is leaving his wife, his children, and his friends for two months. I am writing to you from Damilaville's. He is going off to Geneva to-morrow. I am very much afraid that he will end by paying with his life for some vague and ill-chosen pleasures. It is a very high price to give. Yesterday was a very difficult day for a man who has lost his legs and who was obliged to go to the four corners of Paris. I had promised the Baron to dine with him on the eve of his departure and had forgotten that Damilaville had chosen the same day for saying good-bye to his friends. The latter had reserved the Swiss's room at the Luxembourg and ordered everything, so willy nilly I was obliged to fail the Baron. The meeting-place for the guests was in the Allée des Carmes. Three or four of us were sitting on a bench quite near the gate of the same name when we heard some cries coming from the monks' entrance court. It was a woman who had fallen in a swoon on her way out of the church. One of us ran to help and knocked at the door of the convent; the porter opened: 'Father, quick, a drop of your cordial (eau de mélisse); it is for a woman there, who is dying.' The monk answers coldly, 'We haven't any,' and shuts the door. After that, my dearest, I leave you to muse at your leisure upon the great effect of the spirit of religion. A monk of a different order was among our party. 'Well,' he exclaimed sorrowfully, 'see how a hard and brutal porter dishonours the whole house.' 'Sir,' I replied, 'you need have no fear, the action which we have just witnessed is so atrocious that if any one of us had a mind to recount it he would pass for a slanderer.'

This other friar was a good fellow, quite broad-minded and not at all monkish. We talked about fatherly affection. I told him that it was one of the strongest attachments proper to man. 'A father's heart,' said I. 'No, only those who have been parents can realize what it is; it is a secret happily unknown even to the children.' Then, continuing, I added: 'During the first years that I spent in Paris my life was very disordered; my behaviour was quite enough to anger my father without there being any need to exaggerate it; however, slander played its part. They told him —what didn't they tell him? I started off full of confidence in his goodness, I thought that he would see me, that I should throw myself into his arms, that we should weep on each other's necks and that all would be forgotten. I thought rightly.' There I stopped and I asked my religious if he knew how far it was from here to my home. 'It was sixty leagues, Father, and if it had been a hundred do you think I should have found my father less indulgent and less tender? On the contrary. And if it had been a thousand? Oh how could anyone be hard on a child who came back from such a distance? And if it had been in the moon or in Jupiter, or Saturn?' In saying these words I had my eyes turned heavenwards, and my monk, with his cast down, meditated upon my apologue.

We dined together merrily. We dared to criticize political evils and celibacy without our monk taking offence; he did not defend the defects of his state too hotly: he only proposed that we should spare those bachelors who followed a religious calling until we had exterminated from the republic all those who remained so out of a spirit of debauchery and self-indulgence. We observed that the latter took no vows and that we should be indulgent for the others if they would renounce theirs; that there was an appreciable difference between a bad citizen and a man who swore at the foot of the altar to be one. All that went off very well.

You may or may not know that in a petition presented to the King and published in print, the Benedictines have asked to be secularised; but you would never guess that the ministry has had the stupidity not to take them at their word. Yet it is a fact. In allowing each of these monks to lead a reasonable existence, large endowments would have been available to pay off some of the debts of the State. Their example would have encouraged the Carmelites and the Augustinians to ask to be unfrocked, and without any violence in less than twenty years France would have been rid of vermin who are gnawing at her and will continue gnawing until she is destroyed. Our monk remarked judiciously that there was nothing more indecent than to say, as the Benedictines had done in their petition, that they asked to be stripped of a dishonoured habit; that nothing but evil conduct could bring dishonour and that they had thus owned themselves to be guilty of it.

After dinner, we went for a walk. On the way my monk asked me why a man seems to forget his self-love when he hears the story of a good action, and what is the cause of the involuntary and secret joy which he feels at it. I answered that it is because he immediately identifies himself with the author or the recipient of the kindness; that every time we do not feel we are capable of a great deed, we determine to show that we appreciate it to the full and that, unable to be great, it only remains for us to be just. I added that it is not true that the story of a fine deed is always agreeable to us. Supposing you are placed between a hard-hearted opulent man and his needy friend; tell some anecdote about a friendship marked by helpful generosity and look at their faces. We do not enjoy a lesson upon which we have not the courage to act.

At six o'clock in the evening the guests dispersed. I was left alone with Damilaville and as we were discussing the Praises of Descartes set forth in the Académie, I made two remarks about eloquence which pleased him very much: one was that we must not try to stir the passions before we have convinced the reason, and that pathos is ineffective if the ground is not prepared by argument; the other was that after an orator has touched us deeply I cannot bear him to disturb the calm surface of my soul by something startling; that pathos should be followed by something mild and vague which calls for no kind of debate on my part; that after a violent appeal the exhausted orator should need a rest and so do I. This chat, in which I include you as a third, brought us to eight o'clock when we separated, he to go and do his packing and I to salute the Baron. I looked worried. It seemed to me that I should have been less so if my sight and my arms had been long enough to reach him, warn him, help him in the remote parts of England. Fate threatens us wherever we are, but nevertheless we seem to fear it less in the place where it has never done us any harm; we do not know what it is preparing for us elsewhere.

If I could see you from here; if I only had a magic mirror which showed me my friend at every instant; if she walked about under my eyes in the glass as in those places she inhabits, I think I should be more at rest. I should never leave that glass; how many times I should get up during the night to go and watch you sleeping: how many times I should call out to you: 'Dearest, take care, you will tire yourself too much; go in this direction it is more beautiful; the sun will be too much for you; you sit up too late; you read too long; don't eat that; what is the matter? you seem sad.' You would not hear me, but when your good sense led you the way I should have chosen for you, I should be as pleased as though you were obeying me. It is quite uncertain whether my glass would not cause me more pain than pleasure. It is not at all certain that one fine day I should not break it in vexation; it is quite certain though that having broken it I should collect all the pieces. If I happened to see someone kissing your hand; if I saw you smile; if I thought that you were forgetting me too much and for too long a time! No, no, none of this magic glass, I don't want it; my imagination is better for both of us.

It was past midnight when I left the Baron. I went all the same to Grimm's to fetch my dear one's ninth letter. A little German count who took a fancy to me accompanied us and left me at my door at one in the morning. I read you before going to bed. How could I have slept with a letter from my dearest still stuck under my pillow? To-day I went to see d'Alembert,

who has had himself moved from his own place to M. Vatelet's.
I found him alone: our interview was very affectionate. From
there, to dinner with the charming sister accompanied by La Rue.
We were supposed to be going together to see the pictures at
the Luxembourg; but pressure of work at the studio did not
permit of it.

Our conversations are still delightful; we talk constantly
about the mother, the children, the grandchildren, of all that
is most dear to us in the world; do not fail to tell them so. The
dear sister has had a great adventure; I shall know about it
to-morrow; but, chut! Good-bye, my dearest. Good-bye.

I promised to let you follow the Baron's impressions of
England and I have nothing better to do. It is a distraction for
me, and it instructs and amuses you. You needn't think that only
in France is wealth unequally divided. There are two hundred
English lords who each of them have an income of six, seven,
eight, nine, up to eighteen thousand pounds; clergy who are
numerous and possess like ours a quarter of the wealth of the
State but who contribute proportionately to public expenses,
which ours do not do; merchants of exorbitant opulence; you
can judge for yourself what remains for the other citizens.
The monarch appears to have his hands free for what is good and
tied for what is evil; but he is as much the master of everything
as any other sovereign, in fact more so. Elsewhere the court
commands and makes itself obeyed. There, it corrupts and does
what it pleases and the corruption of subjects is perhaps worse
than tyranny in the long run. There is no public education.
The colleges, sumptuous mansions, palaces comparable to our
Château des Tuileries, are occupied by rich idlers who sleep
and get drunk for part of the day, using the remainder of it
for rudely fashioning a few loutish apprentice ministers. The gold
which flows into the capital both from the provinces and all
over the world makes labour exorbitantly expensive, encourages
smuggling and causes manufactures to fall. As a result either of
the climate, or of the use of beer and strong liquor, of heavy
diet, continual fogs and coal smoke in which they are ceaselessly
enveloped they are a sad and melancholy people. Their gardens
are intersected by narrow, tortuous paths; everywhere one is
aware of an inhabitant who escapes and likes to be alone. There

you find a Gothic temple, in another place a grotto, a Chinese
summer-house, ruins, obelisks, caves, tombs. One opulent individual had a large expanse planted with cypress trees; among
these trees he had scattered busts of philosophers, sepulchral
urns, antique marbles, on which one read *Diis Manibus*: To the
Shades. This spot which the Baron called a Roman cemetery
had been named Elysium by its owner. But it is their manner of
living in the immense and sumptuous mansions which they have
erected for their pleasure, which completes the picture of natural
melancholy. You could hear the running of a mouse. A hundred
women, stately and silent, move round an orchestra set up in
the centre, where the most delicious music is being played.
The Baron compares their progress to the seven processions of
the Egyptians round the mausoleum of Osiris. They have public
gardens which are little frequented; on the other hand the people
are not more crowded in the streets than at Westminster, the
celebrated Abbey, adorned with the monuments of all the
illustrious dead of the nation. A delightful saying of my friend
Garrick is that London pleases the English, but that Paris pleases
everybody. When the Baron paid a visit to this celebrated
actor, he led him by an underground passage to the edge of an
island watered by the Thames. There he found a cupola raised
on black marble pillars and under this cupola the statue of Shakespeare in white marble. 'There,' said he, 'is the tribute of gratitude
which I owe to the man who has made my fame, my fortune
and my talent.'

The Englishman is a gambler; he gambles with terrifying
sums. He plays without speaking, he loses without complaining;
he uses up all he has to live on in an instant; nothing is more
common than to find there a young man of thirty who has
become oblivious of riches, food, women, study, even kindness.
Despair seizes them in the midst of their exaltation and leads them
to the Thames, unless they prefer to take the end of a pistol
between their teeth. In a lonely part of St. James's Park there is
a pond which is exclusively reserved for women: it is there that
they go and drown themselves. Listen to this story which must
surely fill any sensitive soul with sorrow. The Baron was taken
to the house of a charming man, full of gentleness and consideration, polite, agreeable, well informed, rich and honoured; this
seemed to be a man after his own heart; the closest friendship

grew up between them; they lived together and separated from each other with sorrow. The Baron came back to France; his first thought was to thank the Englishman for the welcome he had received from him and to renew the expression of the affection and esteem which he had vowed to him. His letter was half written when he was told that two days after his departure from London this man had blown out his brains with a pistol. But what is strange is that this weariness of life which drives them from country to country never leaves them, and that an Englishman who travels is often merely someone who leaves his country to go and kill himself elsewhere. Wasn't there one just lately who threw himself into the Seine? He was fished up alive; he was taken to the Grand-Châtelet, and the Ambassador had to use all his authority to get him off his punishment. M. Hume told us a few days ago that no political negotiation had intrigued him so much as this affair and that he had been obliged to go twenty times to the first president before he could make him understand that in none of the treaties between France and England was there an article which stipulated that an Englishman was forbidden to drown himself in the Seine on pain of being hanged; and he added that if his fellow-countrymen had unhappily been entered in the gaol book, he would have risked losing his life ignominiously for drowning, or failing to drown himself. If the English are crazy you must agree that the French are ridiculous.

The English, like us, have a mania for converting people. Their missionaries go off into the depths of the forests to take the catechism to the savages. There was a native chief who said to one of our missionaries: 'Brother, look at my head; my hair is quite grey: seriously, do you think you can make a man of my age believe all these stories? But I have three children. Don't address yourself to the eldest, you will make him laugh; get hold of the little one, you can persuade him of anything you like.' Another missionary was preaching our holy religion to some different savages. After listening for some time they asked for a question to be put to the missionary about what they would get out of it all. The missionary said to the interpreter: 'Tell them that they will be the servants of God.' 'Not that, please,' answered the interpreter to the missionary; 'they don't want to be anyone's servants.' 'Well,' said the missionary, 'tell them that they will be the children of God.' 'That will do very well,' said the interpreter. And indeed, the answer pleased the savages very much.

While I am on this subject here is another story which I have from M. Hume and which will show you what to think of these imagined conversions among the cannibals or the Hurons. A minister thought he had achieved a little masterpiece in this line; he had the vanity to show off his proselyte; he took him to London. They questioned the little Huron; he replied marvellously. He was taken to the chapel; he was admitted to the Lord's Supper or Communion which, as you know, is given in both kinds; after the service the minister said to him: 'Well, my child, don't you feel yourself more animated with the love of God? Is the grace of the Sacrament not at work within you? Is not your soul warmed?' 'Yes,' replied the little Huron, 'the wine does very well; but if you had given me brandy, I think it would have had even more effect.' The Christian religion has nearly died out in England. Deists are innumerable; there are scarcely any atheists, those there are hide themselves. An atheist and a scoundrel are practically synonymous over there. The first time that M. Hume found himself at the table of M. de —— he was seated next him. I do not know what led the English philosopher to say that he did not believe in atheists, that he had never seen one. M. de —— said to him: 'Count how many we are here.' We were eighteen. M. de —— added: 'It is not difficult to be able to count you fifteen straight off: the three others don't know what to think about it.'

A nation which thinks that it is belief in God and not good laws which makes people honest does not seem to me very advanced. I treat the existence of God, in relation to a people, as I do marriage. The one is a state, the other a notion, excellent for one or two well-constituted minds, but disastrous for the majority. The indissoluble marriage vow makes, and will always make, nearly as many unhappy people as it does husbands and wives. Faith in God makes, and will always make, nearly as many fanatics as it does believers. Wherever people acknowledge a God, there is a cult; wherever there is a cult the natural order of moral duties is upset and morality corrupted. Sooner or later there comes a moment when the idea which prevented the theft of half-a-crown leads to the massacre of a hundred thousand men.

A fine compensation! Such has been, such is, such will for all time and among all nations be the effect of a doctrine upon which it is impossible to agree and to which people attach more importance than they do to their lives. An Englishman decided to publish a work against the immortality of the soul; a very cruel answer was given him in the public papers. It was a letter of thanks couched in these terms: 'We all, libertines, harlots, cheats, highwaymen, assassins, tax-gatherers, ministers, and sovereigns, offer our most humble thanks to the author of the Treatise against the immortality of the Soul, for having taught us that, if we have been clever enough to escape punishment in this world, we shall have nothing to fear in the next.'

But this is quite enough about our Englishmen; I have a fancy to tell you something about the Spaniards now. I have it from Baron Gleichen who was Danish Ambassador at Madrid and is now Danish Ambassador in France. A little while ago he gave one of those elegant dinners of which I have sometimes spoken to you. After this dinner, at which the service was so superb, the meats so delicate, and the conversation so charming, we had the most delightful music; a reading of the three first cantos of a poem in the style of Ariosto followed the music; after the reading came more music, then conversation and walking. While we were on the subject of Spanish literature, the Baron helped us to form some idea of it by giving an analysis of one of their best religious comedies which he had seen performed. The theatre showed the interior of a church where Exposition of the Blessed Sacrament was in progress and all the people were at prayer. The scene changed and it showed a fair with shops among which were three special ones, the shop of Death, the shop of Sin, and between them the shop of Christ. Each one had its sign; each one invited customers; Sin had plenty; so had Death, but our poor Saviour waited in vain; tired of selling nothing, He grew angry, the scene changed, and He was seen armed with a whip, the Blessed Virgin at His side armed with another, rebuking and driving before them Death, Sin, and all their customers.

The present Papal Nuncio thought that shows of this sort discredited religion and he asked the authorities to put an end to them. The only answer he received was to be sent to the auditorium of the theatre for the first performance of the play

I have just been describing. As a matter of fact, added the Baron Gleichen, the words of the people prostrate before the Blessed Sacrament were most moving and eloquent, and the audience, dissolving into tears and filled with penitence, beat their breasts with great blows of the fist; it is because what makes you laugh to-day, formerly made you cry, and what makes the Spaniard weep now, will make him laugh one day.

Whoever would think that all this is the letter of a tender and passionate admirer to the woman he loves? No one. The thing is true none the less.

I thought we had finished with England and the English. I am bringing you back to them, however, to show you how one traveller differs from another. Helvetius came back from London completely mad about the English. The Baron has come back thoroughly disillusioned. The former wrote to the latter: 'My dear friend, if, as I have no doubt, you have rented a house in England, write to me as quickly as you can so that I can pack off my wife and children and come and join you.' The other replied: 'Poor Helvetius, all he saw in England was the persecution which his book had brought upon him in France.'

We have dined twice at the dear sister's with M. de Neufond. The first time he was in excellent spirits, he drank, he laughed, he joked, he talked, he played, he won, he was gay; the second time he was sad. I can't tell you how sad he was. He was silent at dinner, on rising from table he did not speak; he took up his position in a corner with his back to the company, his head erect, his eyes fixed towards the door, his face red and furious looking. Do you understand what it was all about? Can you guess what was the matter with him? Mlle Boileau always maintains that he is jealous; the dear sister was even worried about it; she thinks that he was saddened by my good humour.

There is midnight striking; good night my dearest, good night. When shall I be with you again at this time to say it in person?

I am very tired of sleeping so far away from you all. If this letter goes to-morrow, you might very likely receive four of them at once.

I am very much on edge. It is high time that Grimm arrived so that I could put his working apron on him again and let him run his own show. I am weary of this job and you must agree that it is the flattest occupation in the world reading all the common-place work which comes out. I would not go on with it if I were offered my weight in gold, and I am not the lightest of mortals. You can rejoice that I have at last quite got rid of that edition of the Encyclopædia, thanks to the impertinence of one of the patrons, M. Panckoucke, puffed up with the arrogance of a recent parvenu, and thinking he could treat me as he apparently treats some poor devils to whom he gives bread which costs them dear if they are obliged to stomach all his nonsense with it, was ill-advised enough to give his tongue free rein at my place. I let him go on to his heart's content, then, getting up abruptly, I took his hand; I said to him: 'Monsieur Panckoucke, wherever we may be in the whole world, whether in the street, in church, or in some place of ill fame, it always behoves us to speak civilly; but this is still more important when addressing a man who has as little patience as I have and in his own house at that. Go to the devil—you and your book; I don't want to work at it. If you were to give me twenty thousand sovereigns for something which I could accomplish in a flash, I would do nothing about it. Have the kindness to go away and leave me in peace.' So there I think we have an anxiety, brought to an end.

The *Père de Famille* has continued to be the greatest success. There is always a full house in spite of the emptiness of Paris. The last performance will be the day after to-morrow; they don't want it to get stale; they are reserving it for next winter; and besides, Molé cannot go on with it any longer.

A week ago I found myself at the orchestra between M. Perronet and Mme de la Ruette. I invited myself to go and see the work he was carrying out at Neuilly on condition that we should be only four including himself. Very well; the day came; we were to meet at my home; it was not M. Perronet who came to fetch me but M. de Senneville; we started off and found that we were fourteen or fifteen at table, without counting the master of the house who did not put in an appearance. It all went off very well: M. de Senneville was as gay and affable as possible; we spoke a little of Mme de Gendre; he owned that his heart had been slightly smitten. We came back together in M. Perronet's carriage; it put me down at the Pont-Tournant and we separated quite pleased with each other.

I live a great deal in my dressing-gown; I read, I write fairly good things about very bad ones that I read. I see nobody, because there is nobody left in Paris. M. Bouchard paid me a visit, and I was very glad to see him come from the Rue des Vieux-Augustins to the Rue Taranne and climb to the fourth floor; that is the performance of a man in good health.

When there are no new books for me to review, I do extracts from books which do not yet exist while waiting for them to appear. When this fairly fruitful occupation fails me, I have another which is to write short things. I have done a *Dialogue between d'Alembert and myself*; we were talking gaily enough, and even fairly clearly in spite of the dryness and obscurity of the subject. This Dialogue is followed by a second, much wider in its range, which serves as an explanation of the first; this one is called *The Dream of d'Alembert*. Those taking part in it are: d'Alembert who is dreaming, Mlle de l'Espinasse the friend of d'Alembert, and Doctor Bordeu. If I had been willing to sacrifice deeper values to heroic style, Democritus, Hippocrates, and Leucippus would have been my characters; but the law of probability would have imprisoned me within the narrow confines of ancient philosophy and the whole point would have been lost. It is a combination of the wildest extravagance and the deepest philosophy; it is rather clever to have put my ideas into the mouth of a man who is dreaming: often wisdom has to be disguised as madness in order to gain a hearing; I prefer people to say: 'But that isn't so foolish as one might have expected' rather than: 'Listen, here is something very learned.'

My talks with the little maid-servant still take their course. In the last I set myself to make her understand that there is no virtue which does not have two rewards: the pleasure of doing right and that of gaining the goodwill of other people; no vice which does not have two punishments: one in the depths of our heart and another in the aversion with which we always inspire our fellows. The text was not barren; we went through most of the virtues; next I shall picture to her the envious man, his hollow eyes and the paleness of his thin face; the glutton with his ruined digestion and his gouty legs; the libertine with his asthmatic chest and the remains of numerous diseases which are either incurable or only to be cured at the expense of the rest of the constitution. This is all for the best. We shall eventually have hardly any prejudices; but we shall have discretion, manners, and principles common to all nations for all the centuries. This last thought came from her.

Yesterday I was at a very odd dinner party: I passed nearly all day at a friend's house in company with two monks, also friends of his, who were nothing short of hypocrites. One of them read the first exercise book full of a treatise he had written on atheism, very fresh and very vigorous, full of daringly new ideas; I was edified to learn that this was the doctrine current in their corridors. For the rest, these monks were people of importance in their monastery; they had wit, gaiety, courtesy, knowledge. Whatever our opinions may be, those who spend three-quarters of their time in study are always people of culture and I wager that these atheistical monks are the most exemplary of their convent. I was very much amused by the efforts of our apostles of materialism to find a sanction for our laws in the eternal order of nature; but what will amuse you far more is the simplicity with which this apostle claimed that his system which attacked everything the world holds sacred, was innocent and could not have any awkward consequences for him; when there wasn't a sentence in it which would not have added a fagot to his burning.

The only reply I send my fond one is a letter of M. Dubucq, received almost at the same moment as her own.

I salute you all three, and I kiss you with all the affection of my heart. There come, put your cheeks near, my fond one; Mamma, give me your hand; you, Mademoiselle Volland, whatever you please.

ESSAY ON EDUCATION IN RUSSIA

IF WE CONSIDER THE DEVELOPMENT OF THE HUMAN MIND SINCE the invention of printing brought to a close the long centuries of its darkness, the first thing we notice is that after the revival of literature in Italy, good culture and the best schools were established in Protestant countries rather than in those which kept to the religion of Rome, and that up to the present day it is in them that advancement is more rapid. Without attempting to prove this assertion I will content myself with remarking that the spirit of the Catholic clergy who have always assumed the responsibility of public instruction is entirely opposed to the progress of reason and enlightenment which everything in Protestant countries encourages, and that it is not a question here of examining whether many very great men have existed in Catholic countries since the revival of literature, but whether the majority, the body of the nation, has become better instructed and more intelligent: for it is the privilege of a small number of great minds to be in advance of their times and no general law can be deduced from their achievements. Well now, we see that since the time of the Reformation all the Protestant countries have made rapid strides towards a better police system, that absurdities and prejudices have decreased perceptibly and that if we keep in mind their respective advantages and possibilities there is not one of these countries which is not more flourishing than its Catholic counterpart. One can even add that Catholic countries have profited by the reflected light from Protestant ones; that once a prejudice was overcome by the power of reason in those countries where an ambitious clergy no longer had either the interest or the influence to uphold it, that same prejudice would be discredited and finally destroyed in the neighbouring country, much to the annoyance of the priests. It is plain for all who have eyes to see that, without the English, reason and philosophy would still be in their infancy in France, and that their true founders among us, Montesquieu and Voltaire, had been the pupils and disciples of the philosophers and great men of England. It is then in Protestant countries that the best and soundest institutions for the instruction of youth must be sought.

It is a great question whether the exclusive study of ancient languages is worth the time given to it and whether the most valuable period of youth could not perhaps be used for more important occupations. Either from reason or prejudice I find it difficult to believe that we could do without a knowledge of the Ancients. Their literature has a stability, an attraction, a force which will always fascinate great minds. But I think that the study of ancient languages could be considerably shortened, and combined with many useful branches of knowledge. Generally in fixing school time-tables too much importance and space has been given to the study of words. To-day we should substitute the study of things for it. I think that in our schools we should give an idea of all the branches of knowledge necessary to a citizen, from legislation to the mechanical arts which have contributed so much to the convenience and advancement of society; and in these mechanical arts I include the profession of the lowest class of our citizens. The spectacle of human industry is in itself great and satisfying: it is a good thing to know the different ways in which each one contributes to the well-being of the community. Such instruction has a natural attraction for children whose chief characteristic is curiosity. Besides even in the most ordinary of mechanical arts there is so exact, so complicated, and at the same time so clear, a method that we cannot adequately admire the depth of man's reason and genius, whilst so many more high-flown branches of learning serve only to prove the absurdity of the human mind.

I was forgetting to say that in these schools there is a great deal of music and that it is taught particularly to a certain number of poor scholars, who, by a special foundation are fed, housed and sometimes clothed after individual inspection by a prefect, and who do all their lessons with the others. Foundations of this kind can have advantages in that the child of an artisan, a man so poor that he has absolutely no means at his disposal, may be born with such promising tendencies that these could be nothing better than to come to its aid and help it to develop its natural gifts. More than one great man has owed the beginning of his education to scholarships of this kind. In France we call them *bourses*.

INDEX

INDEX